Improving Educational Outcomes for Children with Disabilities
Principles for Assessment, Program Planning, and Evaluation

This book is printed on recycled paper. ✹

IMPROVING EDUCATIONAL OUTCOMES FOR CHILDREN WITH DISABILITIES
PRINCIPLES FOR ASSESSMENT, PROGRAM PLANNING, AND EVALUATION

by

Martin A. Kozloff, Ph.D.

Professor
Department of Sociology
Boston University

·PAUL·H·
BROOKES
PUBLISHING Co.

Baltimore • London • Toronto • Sydney

Paul H. Brookes Publishing Co.
P.O. Box 10624
Baltimore, Maryland 21285-0624

Typeset by Brushwood Graphics, Inc., Baltimore, Maryland.
Manufactured in the United States of America by
BookCrafters, Falls Church, Virginia.

**Improving Educational Outcomes for Children with Disabilities:
Guidelines and Protocols for Practice** by Martin A. Kozloff, Ph.D.,
is also available from Paul H. Brookes Publishing Co. To order,
write to the address above or call 1-800-638-3775.

Library of Congress Cataloging-in-Publication Data

Kozloff, Martin A.
Improving educational outcomes for children with disabilities :
    principles for assessment, program planning, and evaluation / Martin
    A. Kozloff.
        p.   cm.
    Includes bibliographical references and index.
    ISBN 1-55766-132-4
    1. Developmentally disabled children—Education—United States.
2. Developmentally disabled children—Education—Social aspects—
United States. 3. Learning, Psychology of. 4. Developmental
disabilities—United States—Diagnosis. 5. Home and school—United
States. 6. Child psychology—United States. I. Title.
LC4031.K694   1994
371.91—dc20   93-30853
                                                                        CIP

British Cataloguing-in-Publication data are available from the British Library.

CONTENTS

ABOUT THE AUTHOR

Martin A. Kozloff, Ph.D., Department of Sociology, Boston University, 96 Cummington Street, Boston, Massachusetts 02215

Martin Kozloff is Professor of Sociology at Boston University. He completed his undergraduate work in Psychology and his master's degree and doctorate in Sociology at Washington University in St. Louis, Missouri. From 1967 to 1971, Dr. Kozloff was a teacher and later Director of the Autism Program at Washington University, where a number of innovative instructional methods and classroom curricula were developed for children with autism and other disabilities. Since 1972, Dr. Kozloff has continued to develop, test, and disseminate educational programs for children with disabilities and training and support programs for families and professionals. His work has been funded by grants from the National Institute of Mental Health ("Delivery Systems for Training Subprofessionals," 1972–1975, and "Community-Based Training Programs," 1976–1982) and from the National Institute for Handicapped Research ("Rehabilitation and Family Adjustment for Handicapped Children," 1983-1985).

Dr. Kozloff has written five other books—*The Humanization Processes* (co-authored, 1971); *Reaching the Autistic Child* (1973); *Educating Children with Learning and Behavior Problems* (1974); *A Program for Families of Children with Learning and Behavior Problems* (1979); and *Productive Interaction with Students, Children, and Clients* (1988). He has published numerous book chapters and journal articles and has presented at local, national, and international conferences.

PREFACE

Education can be of great benefit to children with disabilities and their families. It can bring children into the social world, help them acquire needed skills, and enable them to enjoy the richness of experience that is taken for granted by persons without disabilities. If well-designed, education programs can also assist families to make essential and significant contributions to their children's development.

Too often, the promise of education is *unfulfilled*. Many children do not learn functional skills. In addition, children develop challenging behaviors that become more frequent and durable, disrupt family and school life, strain caregivers' resources, and consign children to restrictive environments. Finally, despite the necessity and benefits of family involvement in all phases of education, few families receive adequate information, training, in-home assistance, and opportunities for contribution.

In large part, unsatisfactory outcomes such as the above stem from common *practices*. For example, the typical assessment gives scores on tests and behavior checklists, but does not provide detailed information on children's competencies and difficulties in natural environments (e.g., family and community). Thus, assessment information is not adequate to plan educational programs that are both congruent with children's needs and strengths and relevant to children's natural environments. Moreover, plans usually focus on the early phase of learning—skill acquisition—but ignore fluency, generalization, adaptation, and maintenance. Thus, the skills children learn in school either fail to generalize or quickly weaken in outside environments.

Instruction inherits the inadequacies of assessment and program planning. Specifically, instruction is often fragmented; for example, oversimplified aspects of communication, adaptive skills, and social skills are taught by different people at different places and times. Moreover, instruction rarely coordinates opportunities for learning and participation among school, home, and community.

Finally, program evaluation is seldom done in a way that reveals how instruction (e.g., tasks, scheduling, prompting methods, child–caregiver interaction) could be altered to facilitate progress. Thus, children's programs may be unchanged for years or may change in a haphazard way.

In trying to improve educational practices (and children's prospects), many professional educators and families attend workshops, read current articles and books, and hire consultants. Unfortunately, these laudatory efforts rarely have a lasting or substantial effect, for they do not remove the deeper obstacles to progress. One obstacle is the flawed model of psychosocial development that encourages educators to divide human conduct into artificial domains (e.g., language, play, social skills) that are then addressed separately in assessment, planning, and instruction. A second obstacle is the organization of school programs. Common features—such as the overspecialization of jobs, the segregation of school and family activities, and the lack of leadership—invite fragmentation, inhibit innovation, and contribute to the burnout of staff and families.

In the author's opinion, the promise of education can be *fulfilled* only when practices are derived from a more adequate model of psychosocial development and when the social organization of schools encourages innovation and integrates teachers, therapists, and families in a larger common endeavor—seeing children with disabilities as members of the social world, teaching children functional skills, and providing children with opportunities to play more valued roles.

The aim of this volume and its companion is to help teachers, therapists, families, physicians, and administrators to foster children's psychosocial development. Chapters 1 and 2 of this volume examine education for children with disabilities. The focus is on outcomes, flaws in the currently used model of psychosocial development, shortcomings in practices, and how school organization stifles innovation. Chapters 3–6 offer a more adequate model of psychosocial development and suggest specific improvements in assessment, program planning, instruction, and program evaluation.

Chapter 7 identifies challenges confronted by many families and the resources that may help families to better foster their children's development. Chapter 8 focuses on the organization of schools. It suggests ways to empower caregivers, increase resources to a program, and facilitate caregivers' sharing of complementary skills. It also provides guidelines for organizational development. Chapters 9 and 10 discuss qualitative and quantitative methods for collecting and analyzing information needed for assessment, planning, and program evaluation. Chapter 11 summarizes the main points made in earlier chapters.

The companion to this volume, *Improving Educational Outcomes for Children with Disabilities: Guidelines and Protocols for Practice* (Kozloff, 1994), begins where this volume ends. It offers detailed guidelines, methods, and instruments for: 1) planning comprehensive assessments; 2) assessing children's competencies, capacities, social participation, and learning needs in relation to features of children's environments, such as patterns of child–caregiver interaction, caregivers' teaching skills, and the tasks and activities in a child's round of daily life; 3) planning programs to increase children's competence and social participation and to prevent or reduce challenging behaviors; 4) identifying caregivers' strengths, resources, and needs; 5) planning assistance to caregivers; and 6) evaluating and revising programs.

REFERENCE

Kozloff, M.A. (1994). *Improving educational outcomes for children with disabilities: Guidelines and protocols for practice.* Baltimore: Paul H. Brookes Publishing Co.

ACKNOWLEDGMENTS

Many persons made important contributions to this volume and its companion, *Improving Educational Outcomes for Children with Disabilities: Guidelines and Protocols for Practice*. Barbara Cutler, David Helm, Darleen Douglas-Steele, and Alice Wells—my co-workers in recent training programs with families and schools—were a source of inspiration and good advice. As program developers, advocates for children, family and school consultants, and researchers, they are the best.

The high priority given to assessing and improving child–caregiver interaction (exchanges) stems from the research and thinking of Robert L. Hamblin, former Director of the Social Exchange Laboratory at Washington University in St. Louis, Missouri. Dr. Hamblin was among the first to apply social exchange theory to the education of children with disabilities.

I am grateful to the administration of Boston University for the space to conduct projects and for a sabbatical leave during which the first draft was written.

A special debt is owed to Mark Wolery, currently at the Allegheny-Singer Research Institute in Pittsburgh, Pennsylvania. Dr. Wolery's critique of early drafts was immensely helpful and revealed a breadth of expertise, intellectual honesty, and generosity that are unmatched.

Words are insufficient to express my thanks to the Paul H. Brookes Publishing Company, and to six persons in particular. Melissa A. Behm, Vice President, gave me the opportunity to prepare the volumes for review. Sarah B. Cheney, Editorial Director, provided enormous help—reading and re-reading drafts, offering wonderful suggestions on content and organization, and gently but persistently prompting me to improve each section and chapter. Roslyn Udris, Production Manager, scheduled and oversaw the entire production process. Sue Vaupel and Ken Foye, Production Coordinators, orchestrated the movement of the manuscripts and proofs. Tania M. Bourdon copyedited both volumes, which, before delivery into her capable hands, were endlessly detailed and mercilessly complex. Ms. Bourdon's skill, dedication to excellence, and artistic sense of organization and expression are without peer.

The love and encouragement from Karen L. Gardner, my wife, are gifts that will be hard to repay.

FOR THE READER

This volume, *Improving Educational Outcomes for Children with Disabilities: Principles for Assessment, Program Planning, and Evaluation,* has a companion volume entitled *Improving Educational Outcomes for Children with Disabilities: Guidelines and Protocols for Practice. Guidelines and Protocols for Practice* builds upon the theoretical principles discussed here. It contains 17 instruments that can be photocopied and used for collecting qualitative and quantitative information through interviews, questionnaires, and direct observations; summarizing information; selecting competencies to teach and problem behaviors to replace; and formatting planning programs.

The case studies that appear in this book are synthesized composites based on the author's actual experiences. The names of individuals and places used in these cases are fictitious.

To Julian

* *. . . at thy birth, dear boy,*
Nature and Fortune join'd to make thee great;
Of Nature's gifts thou mayst with lilies boast,
And with the half-blown rose.

—Shakespeare, *King John*

Improving Educational Outcomes for Children with Disabilities

Principles for Assessment, Program Planning, and Evaluation

Innovative Practices Have Not Become Common Practices

Observations by this writer and his colleagues in programs in more than half the United States reveal that innovations are found mainly in model classrooms and school systems guided by creative applied researchers. Innovative practices are also evident in rare programs where administrators, teachers, and families work together to improve curricula (Hundert & Hopkins, 1992). When innovative practices are used, inclusionary aims are achieved—persons with developmental disabilities become more valued and competent participants in the everyday world (Donnellan & Neel, 1986; Evans, Salisbury, Palombaro, Berryman, & Hollowood, 1992; Osborne, Schulte, & McKinney, 1991; Walker et al., 1988; Wilcox & Bellamy, 1982).

The common program in special education, however, is quite different. Despite the inclusionary aims and strenuous efforts of teachers, therapists, administrators, and families, common programs in special education are characterized by outmoded practices and chronic concern with problem behavior. In addition, there is little evidence that instruction yields substantial improvement in a child's place in the social world. There is also conflict between families and educators, and a high rate of teacher and family burnout. In other words, in thousands of classrooms and schools across the country, educators regard innovative practices as a good idea, but do not use them (Williams, Fox, Thousand, & Fox, 1990). The following sections examine the gap between innovative and actual practices.

Outmoded Instruction   In many programs, teaching and therapy are still done in one-to-one sessions or in "groups" that are really one-to-one teaching with children sitting near each other. Instruction often uses massed practice, contrived reinforcement contingencies, and the same tasks and materials month after month. Instead of teaching families and teachers how to do different therapies, specialists take children to separate rooms for 30 minutes a few times a week. Often, guidelines based on research on "normal" development are used to select curriculum tasks, although the research may not apply to many children with developmental disabilities. Children receive too much or too little prompting, simpler behaviors are seldom built into more complex chains (i.e., children learn small pieces of tasks), and there is little concern for generalization. (Chap. 2, this volume, describes common instructional practices in detail.)

Still "Controlling" Problem Behaviors   Despite the existence of methods for replacing problem behaviors (Belfiore, Browder, & Lin, 1993; Evans & Meyer, 1985; O'Neill, Horner, Albin, Storey, & Sprague, 1990), professionals and families continue to search for ways to reduce noncompliant, self-injurious, disruptive, and aggressive behavior. At educational planning meetings and arbitration sessions, one hears the same story now as in the early 1970s. Caregivers overwhelmed by problem behaviors are offered minor variations of outmoded prescriptions, such as ignoring, time out, and punishment.

Quantitative Instead of Qualitative Change   Quantitative change in a child's competence does not necessarily amount to qualitative change in a child's place in the world. Observations of this writer and his colleagues indicate the following:

1. Students with moderate to severe disabilities often begin their educations by working on "good sitting," "compliance," puzzles, stringing beads, and pointing to pictures; many are still working on the same sorts of nonfunctional, age-inappropriate tasks when they are adolescents.
2. Little attention is given to the generalization of behavior. For example, one rarely finds that "language skills" worked on between 9:00 A.M. and 9:30 A.M. at a table in the corner are also being worked on (or even occasionally reinforced) at other important times and places. Understandably, improvements in "language skills" between 9:00 A.M. and 9:30 A.M. at the table are not apparent elsewhere.
3. Many students show more improvement on their year-end evaluations (e.g., make more eye contact or say more words), but are not much different in their participation in daily life; that

is, they are still seen as largely incompetent and troublesome, and as playing disvalued roles of adversary, object of pity, or burden.

Conflict with Parents   Most school systems are engaged in costly and wasteful conflict with families, usually over placement and the amount of services the child or family should receive. Conflicts start with phone calls and letters, escalate to meetings and special evaluations, and end with both sides bringing lawyers and experts. If parents get some of what they want (perhaps an extra hour per week of speech therapy) and are temporarily placated, the services may be too late and will nevertheless have little effect on their child's future. If parents do not get what they want, their resentment increases, setting the stage for more conflict.

"Fresh Faces" Become "Old Hands"   Many teachers and therapists learn that curricula found in textbooks and journal articles (where most innovations abide) are neither usable nor effective in their environments. This is because teachers are usually alone except for an untrained aide or an occasional visit from a speech or physical therapist. Moreover, they get little additional training, feel unsupported by administrators and others on the educational staff, and have little flexibility in scheduling activities (Williams et al., 1990). Thus, several weeks into the school year, as students become inattentive, uncooperative, and disruptive, and when improvements in desirable behaviors are found difficult to sustain, the teacher increasingly resembles a circus performer trying to keep a dozen plates spinning. At this point, the worthy aim of bringing children into society seems to have been wishful thinking.

The continued use of outmoded teaching methods, persistence of students' problem behaviors, small and tenuous changes in skills that are usually nonfunctional anyway, frequent conflict with families, frustration and burnout of families and staff, all suggest serious flaws in the whole range of practices that constitute special education (described in chap. 2, this volume). It is tempting to offer quick solutions to narrow the gap between innovations and common practices. However, one ought to be cautious, as suggested below.

Errors To Avoid

If, as Snell (1988) asserts, the gap between excellent programs that are possible (but rare) and programs that are far too common is to be narrowed, perfectionism, dependence on experts, and a narrow view of the problem must be avoided.

Perfectionism   There never will be a best way to provide education to children with disabilities. Future research, changes in the understanding of behavior development (see chap. 6, this volume), and changes in values will render today's innovations obsolete (Peters & Heron, 1993). Thus, there will always be a gap between current practices and innovations. The task is not to close the gap, but to make it easier for caregivers in ordinary environments to adopt the better innovations. (Chap. 8, this volume, which discusses facilitating coordination, addresses this issue in more detail.)

Dependence on Experts   As long as educators in ordinary (as opposed to special research) environments wait for experts to provide new methods, there will be a large gap between current and improved practices. Reliance on experts fosters dependency, lethargy, and needless stoicism. For example, "I'm not trained (or supported) enough to improve my methods. I'll make do until a better way is invented." In the opinion of this author, special educators in ordinary environments would benefit by adopting the self-empowering experimental stance of applied researchers; that is, noticing what works and what does not, developing and testing alternative remedies, keeping records on results, and writing up and distributing descriptions of new methods to colleagues (including families). One aim of this book and its companion, *Guidelines and Protocols for Practice,* is to provide the reader with tools for doing that.

Narrow View   The shortage of effective practices has hampered the quality of programs. Yet, improved practices alone cannot substantially improve programs. There are three reasons why. First, as described in Chapter 2, this volume, outmoded practices are sustained by a flawed view of psychosocial development. For instance, as long as educators believe it is reasonable to dissect communication into separate "areas" of audition, speech (articulation), and language (i.e., rule-governed production), they will continue to use separate assessments, goals, therapies, and instructional activities for each contrived area, which in the end will inhibit children's ability to learn to communicate (Fitzgerald & Fischer, 1987).

Second, innovative practices are made sterile and outmoded practices are sustained by the way special education programs are organized. For example, a teacher's new knowledge of how to foster generalization reaps little reward when classroom, family, and therapy activities are segregated. Therefore, to incorporate innovative practices, educators have to change both the way they understand psychosocial development (the subject of chaps. 3–6, this volume) and the organization of special education programs (the subject of chaps. 2 and 8, this volume).

Third, education programs are (mis)shaped and beneficial innovations are hindered by cultural perceptions of persons with developmental disabilities and by the functions of special education for society. The next section introduces three children—Jerry, Indra, and Juan—whose lives show that something bigger than practices must be examined and changed if excellent programs are to become the norm.

LONG-TERM EFFECTS OF SOCIAL DISTANCE

Social distance refers to socially created perceived differences between people. Social distance is one outcome of societal practices by which members define who is more "normal" in appearance and competence, who is more valuable, and therefore who is entitled to full membership in society or even humanity. Social distance characterizes the relationship between children (and families and teachers of children) with developmental disabilities and the rest of society (Goode, 1984). Many people who consider themselves "normal" feel anxiety or disgust when around children such as Jerry, Indra, and Juan. These people often feel awkward interacting with them and are more comfortable knowing the children are somewhere else. Furthermore, many have a hard time imagining that Jerry, Indra, and Juan experience the same kind of pain and pleasure as other children, and they seriously question if the time and money spent on them could not be better spent on other (i.e., more worthy, cost-effective) projects and people. In sum, students with disabilities are perceived to be in a class of people who are not as valuable, understandable, and human as others, which affects the kind of education they receive. Despite educators' and families' aims and efforts, common methods of assessment, program planning, and instruction do not markedly lessen social distance. Indeed, certain practices sustain it.

Social distance does not produce children's initial disabilities. Rather, social distance hinders the creation of programs that could bring children with developmental disabilities into the social world, as shown by the following case studies.

Jerry

Jerry, who is 6 years old, is diagnosed with autism and mental retardation. He can feed himself, put on a few items of clothing, dry his hands and face with a towel, and perform several other routine tasks. He enjoys watching some television programs, including Sesame Street and Alf; he loves to take long rides in the car; and he is wild about pistachio ice cream.

Jerry understands some speech, such as "Do you want ice cream?", but he rarely speaks himself, except to say "Eat" or "Go out." He shows little interest in what is going on, seldom cooperates with requests, and frequently disrupts family and school activities. Jerry occupies himself with television, spinning objects, and water play in the sink. When frustrated, he bites his hands, yells, breaks things, and throws tantrums.

Feeling challenged by his disruptive behavior, and believing that children must learn a number of developmental readiness skills before they can work on more functional skills,

Jerry's teachers expend much time and effort keeping him in his seat doing simple motor tasks, such as puzzles and bead-stringing. Jerry no longer goes to the gym, cafeteria, or art class with other students. Furthermore, his family rarely takes him into public places anymore.

Given his limited participation in everyday tasks and activities, and his worsening "problem" behaviors, Jerry's family and teachers see him as more of a stranger than a member in their social worlds. Without noticing it, keeping Jerry quiet and occupied is now the main objective. In other words, Jerry's role at home and school has become an outsider and an adversary, whereas the complementary role played by his parents, siblings, and teachers has become an attendant or a guard.

Part of the vicious circle is that much of Jerry's "problem" behavior results from the restrictive and (as he experiences it) "boring sameness" of his curriculum, as well as from the reinforcement he gets when people try to control him: "Hands down! I said, hands down!" When he is a teenager, where do you think Jerry will be living?

Indra

Ten-year-old Indra has cerebral palsy. She understands just about everything said to her, uses speech to communicate her understandings and wants, is interested in what people are doing, and enjoys taking part in people's activities. However, her neuromuscular difficulties make it hard to perform the actions needed for many tasks. Often, the odd movements that she makes with her head, arms, and mouth when she speaks or when she reacts to the speech of others lead many people to assume she is "mentally retarded."

Although people enjoy being with her, Indra is treated as though she has fewer competencies and capacities than she really has. For instance, placed in a classroom with other children with severe physical disabilities, many of whom require much physical management, Indra spends most of the time in a special chair watching what is going on. Her occasional plaintive vocalizing is considered the result of pain from tight muscles rather than boredom and frustration, and she is not given much chance to read or talk about things of interest to a preteenage girl, such as clothes, movies, boys, and current events.

In other words, the role Indra plays is "lovable onlooker"; that is, people spend more time hugging and speaking nicely to her than teaching her to interact with her environment. The complementary role played by others is "kindly caregiver." Does it seem that Indra's school experiences will do as much as possible to help her achieve a valuable place in the social world and enjoy the richness of experience of which she is capable?

Juan

Juan is 12 years old. He wants to learn to play sports, participate in intimate social relationships, prepare meals, make his bed, read, and do a host of other normal, age-appropriate tasks. In addition, the fact that he carefully adjusts his Detroit Tigers baseball cap and lifts a portable tape player onto his shoulder before leaving his building for a walk suggests that Juan is attuned to what is considered "normal" in the culture and is skilled at presenting himself as a style-conscious teenager.

Juan was born with physical disabilities. The lower part of his face is small, which causes his teeth to crowd and form ragged and twisted rows. The upper part of his face is broad and his eyes appear to be far apart and to protrude. His arms and legs and his fingers and toes are short and crooked. Many people, unable to see past Juan's disabilities, do not experience him as a person with intelligence and common human feelings. Instead, his body evokes fear and pity. At birth, experts believed (erroneously) that Juan had so little capacity to learn that he would need constant care. Juan's parents put him in "Pinebrook," a state institution for persons with mental retardation.

Juan does not have anything to do at the institution except walk around, watch television, thumb through magazines, listen to his tapes, and pretend that he is a member of society. During the day he attends a "substantially separate" class for students with multiple disabilities in a nearby public school. Because his physical deformities have always led people to assume that he has mental retardation, and because his years at Pinebrook have left him incompetent at most everyday tasks and social relationships, Juan's education consists of learning to sort nuts and bolts, stuff envelopes, follow pictured instructions, and count money.

The teachers work hard with Juan and are proud (justifiably so) that they are helping him to learn what it takes to make it in sheltered employment. The irony is that if Juan is ever adopted by a family or enters a community residence, it will not take him much more than a year to learn the competencies he did not learn in school.

How Social Distance Is Created and Sustained

Social distance is created and sustained in three ways: use of special language, societal apparatus for excluding "deviant" persons, and special education practices.

Special Language One way social distance is created and sustained is through the use of special words for describing disabilities. Although the terms help practitioners communicate with one another, they can become filters. What is seen may not be common "humanness," but "differentness"—what is called out by labels, what is relevant to "mental retardation," "autism," "cerebral palsy," and "craniofacial deformity." This is especially likely when assessment, program planning, teaching, and evaluation are specialized and routinized in schools and clinics; that is, when interpersonal relationships have become formal and time-limited, or when interaction with children, students, or clients is strained. Under such conditions many practitioners really do not want to know, or do not think they need to know, much more about children than the labels tell them to look for.

Labels also suggest qualitative differences. People may view a person with a disvalued "ailment" as being outside the circle of members in good standing. The person with a label may be seen as an object to be studied, managed, and changed; an entity whose feelings, thoughts, potentials, and needs are a mystery. For example, "This kid is so ('weird,' disabled, 'retarded,' or different)! What makes her tick? What does she need?"

Societal Apparatus for Excluding "Deviant" Persons Special terms alone do not produce social distance. Children's "deviance"—rocking back and forth, physical abnormalities, slow development—produces fear, disgust, and vulnerability (Goffman, 1963; Goode, 1984) in many onlookers. Some people handle vulnerability by avoiding or even rejecting children with disabilities. Yet, avoidance and rejection are not merely reactions of uninformed, insensitive individuals. Avoidance and rejection have long been orchestrated into a societal apparatus for identifying, officially labeling, isolating, and "treating" persons considered too different, threatening, disruptive, costly, or strange to be allowed to "be themselves" or to be in the mainstream (Tomlinson, 1982; Wolfensberger, 1981).

An apparatus for excluding "deviant" persons exists at the community and societal levels and it thwarts the efforts of families and special educators to bring children into the social world. This is evident in several ways: 1) the separate, special places (not created by teachers or families) where people with developmental disabilities are to live and/or be taught (Braginsky & Braginsky, 1971; Morris, 1969); 2) the medical-sounding labels (not invented by teachers or families) used for conduct that disrupts social order (e.g., attention deficit hyperactivity disorder, conduct disorder) (Bart, 1984); 3) the commonplace exclusion of children with developmental disabilities by regular education teachers who either do not allow them in their classrooms ("They would be too much of a distraction.") or send them back to segregated classrooms with little provocation ("She kept making funny noises."); and 4) the experience of rejection (e.g., stares, insults, ignoring) when families and teachers take children to public places (Darling, 1979).

Special Education Practices Ironically, social distance is embedded in common practices (see chap. 2, this volume). For instance, assessment typically documents how identified children deviate from the cultural image of the typical or standard child (Martin, 1988). The child being assessed is often seen as outside the circle of those considered "normal," those whose place in society is taken for granted. After all, one use of assessment is to decide where to put the child.

In addition, program plans, derived from assessments, specify how to change children so that they approximate the image (the standard) of normality, or become easier to live with. Rarely, however, do plans indicate how school, family, and community environments could be improved to satisfy children's learning needs.

Lastly, instruction frequently resembles a factory. Children work at tasks not of their choosing for reinforcers they cannot get unless they do what they are told. If children resist (engage in "off-task" behavior), they may be given aversive consequences and/or more sessions on the very same tasks. If children make little progress under these conditions, it is often considered evidence of even more difficulties (e.g., oppositional, not developmentally ready), rather than something wrong with the curriculum.

This is not meant to imply that children with developmental disabilities have no areas of difficulty, can take care of themselves, and ought to be seen and treated as absolutely equal with respect to decision making. Rather, what is asserted is that certain features of existing practices make more equal, more inclusionary, less contrived, and less aversive relationships with children nearly impossible.

Implications of Social Distance

At the heart of social distance is exclusion—exclusion from the category of "those who are full members," and exclusion from things to do as well as valued self-images in the social order. Indeed, social distance is a denial of common humanity. In this author's opinion, the worthy aim of educators and families to bring children into the social world can be achieved only when common human needs are identified and understood, and only when all special education practices—assessment, program planning, instruction, and program evaluation—are, without compromise, guided by that understanding (Schwartz, 1992).

THREE COMMON HUMAN NEEDS

Persons with disabilities have the same overriding needs as other human beings. Human needs fall into three categories: membership and personhood, competence, and family involvement.

Membership and Personhood

The quality of human life is largely a function of participation in the social world, from which experiences of personhood are derived. What is our place in the social world? Are we pulled in or pushed out? How are we regarded? What roles do we play—member-in-good-standing, friend, incompetent, clown, object of pity, fool, alien, or adversary?

> It is **not** the case that individual personality and human nature exist on their own, apart from our participation in the social world. Nor do we choose to interact with others because it helps pass the time or makes life easier. We **have** to interact with others of our kind. Social interaction is the **CONTEXT** in which our behavior becomes organized and develops, and it is only through social interaction that our human potentials—language, mind, self-consciousness, kindness, evil—are achieved. (Kozloff, 1988, p. 45)

The "Personalization" Process   When members of society regard a child as another member of society, a member of the species, culture, and group who shares human needs, feelings, capabilities, understandings, and destiny, they offer the child a place in the social order where he or she can play valuable roles, make contributions, and experience intimacy (Henry, 1966). Furthermore, when others see a child as a person—a unique being who acts out of intention, is capable of profound feeling, and lives in terms of a conception of a world that includes him- or herself—not merely as a body and behavior, then they are likely to provide caring and respectful assistance (e.g., "Here, let me help you wipe your nose."); protection from vulnerabilities (e.g., "Don't be afraid. Daddy's here."); and access to resources or reinforcers (e.g., "Hey, look at you! You dressed yourself!").

What appears mundane may have profound effects. When people act toward a child in ways that superficially can be called giving nurturance, protection, reinforcement, and opportunities to participate, the child may experience these actions as powerfully significant. Others seem to be communicating that they see the child as one of them, as valuable, and as worthy. Indeed, their actions bestow personhood and membership on the child. When, for instance, a teacher gently guides a child's arms through a hard task, while softly praising the child, the teacher undoubtedly experiences an essential ingredient of the event as communication with the person inside the child's skin, and not merely moving limbs. Simultaneously, the child may experience the event as meaning, "She must care enough about me to be so gentle. She must assume that there is a self inside that is trying to move these arms."

Seldom protecting, reinforcing, or giving a child much chance to contribute to social life, however, denies or takes away personhood and membership. Such actions communicate and may be interpreted by the child as meaning, "I am not valuable. There is nothing in me that they see as a self. I am in a group of those who are 'weird,' sick, threatening, and not worth better treatment."

Most adults can remember being insulted (e.g., "That's four incorrect responses," which implies, "You dummy!"); nagged (e.g., "How many times do I have to tell you?"); rejected (e.g., "Get back to your seat!"); unprotected (e.g., "Stop crying. It doesn't hurt!"); or ignored after finishing a hard job. Imagine the cumulative effects on a child's feelings, self-image, view of the world, and participation if the child is seen as the type of person for whom such treatment is not given a second thought.

Competence

A second category of needs includes psychosocial development and, to the extent that a valuable place and self have been denied, "psychosocial repair."[1] Both must be met if a child is to participate more competently and enjoyably in society. In other words, humans need to develop competence at tasks that are biologically important and socially expected of "persons" and "members in good standing" in the culture; that is, functional tasks.

The congruence between so-called "normal" children and their environments is such that the instructional repertoires of their caregivers are usually sufficient to foster competent turn-taking, communicating, dressing, locomotion, and other tasks. The nature of moderate developmental disabilities implies that a different sort of teaching and membership-bestowing repertoire is required of caregivers, one that involves: 1) accurately assessing children's learning and performance in a variety of environments; 2) creating and sustaining productive interaction (exchange) between children and significant others as a social context for bonding and skill learning; 3) artfully engineering the environment and using instructional cues, prompts, and feedback to strengthen competent performances; and 4) systematically building and generalizing behavior within educational sequences guided by considerations of bio-psychosocial development (i.e., teaching children what they can learn) and functionality (i.e., ensuring that what they do learn is useful in the everyday world).

Family Involvement

A final human need is the involvement of family in major life projects. This need is connected to the first two because much of the process by which membership is bestowed, personhood is achieved, competence is acquired, and roles are played occurs in the family. Indeed, family involvement greatly improves the quality of children's educational programs and benefits the fam-

---

[1] I am indebted to my long-time friend and colleague, Dr. Barbara C. Cutler, for the idea of psychosocial repair.

ily as well (Bailey & Simeonsson, 1988; Bricker & Casuso, 1979). This was acknowledged and codified by the passage of PL 99-457 in 1986, which amends the Education for All Handicapped Children Act of 1975 (PL 94-142). PL 99-457 aims to increase family involvement in prevention, identification, assessment, and service delivery. It also requires that individualized family service plans (IFSPs) be prepared for families of infants and toddlers receiving services.

When families are involved, the benefits are likely to include the following:

1. The assessment of children's needs and strengths and the ongoing evaluation of progress are more accurate when families collect and provide information (Gitler & Gordon, 1979; Wolfensberger & Kurtz, 1971). This is because family members have rich information on children's competencies, capacities, difficulties, and learning needs (e.g., what events are the strongest reinforcers). Moreover, family members can observe a child in a variety of everyday environments.
2. Parents who receive training in teaching and advocacy (see chap. 8, this volume) experience greater empowerment, judge themselves to be more competent and their children as improved, participate more in educational decision making, have higher expectations, have more knowledge of learning principles, and display greater skill at teaching (Baker, Landen, & Kashima, 1991; Brinkerhoff & Vincent, 1986; Jennings, 1990; Kozloff et al., 1988).
3. Counterproductive parent–child exchanges (e.g., parents accidentally reinforcing problem behaviors) are replaced by productive exchanges (e.g., reinforcing desirable behaviors) (Kozloff, 1983).
4. Beneficial changes in families and in family–child interaction increase children's desirable behaviors and decrease problem behaviors (Kaufman, 1976; Kirkham, 1993; Seifer, Clark, & Sameroff, 1991; Tannock, Girolametto, & Siegel, 1992).

SUMMARY

This chapter argues that despite the aims and efforts of educators and families, many education programs for children with disabilities do not satisfy children's common human needs to be seen and treated as persons and members in society, to become competent at personally and socially important (functional) tasks, and to have family intimately involved in all phases of education. In part, this is because special education programs are influenced by a societal apparatus for finding, excluding, and treating people judged deviant. A better understanding of that apparatus may help educators and families remove themselves from it. In addition, although there have been many innovations in assessment and instruction (e.g., functional analysis, prompting, generalization, and chaining), there is a wide gap between best practices and common practices.

To improve practices, and, therefore, outcomes of education, the main shortcomings need to be identified. The next chapter examines special education in detail. It identifies weaknesses in practices, and traces these weaknesses to a flawed understanding of how behavior is organized and psychosocial development proceeds, and to the social organization of programs themselves. The remaining chapters suggest how to improve the guiding model of psychosocial development, practices, and the organization of programs so that best practices can become common practices.

REFERENCES

Bailey, D., & Simeonsson, R.J. (1988). Home-based early intervention. In S.L. Odom & M.B. Karnes (Eds.), *Early intervention for infants and children with handicaps: An empirical base* (pp. 199–215). Baltimore: Paul H. Brookes Publishing Co.

Baker, B.L., Landen, S.J., & Kashima, K.J. (1991). Effects of parent training on families of children with mental retardation: Increased burden or generalized benefit? *American Journal on Mental Retardation, 96*(2), 127–136.

Bart, D.S. (1984). The differential diagnosis of special education: Managing social pathology as individual disability. In L. Barton & S. Tomlinson (Eds.), *Special education and social interests* (pp. 81–121). New York: Nichols Publishing Company.

Belfiore, P.J., Browder, D.M., & Lin, C. (1993). Using descriptive and experimental analyses for the treament of self-injurious behavior. *Education and Training in Mental Retardation 28*(1), 57–65.

Braginsky, D.D., & Braginsky, B.M. (1971). *Hansels and Gretels: Studies of children in institutions for the mentally retarded.* New York: Holt, Rinehart & Winston.

Bricker, D., & Casuso, V. (1979). Family involvement: A critical component of early intervention. *Exceptional Children, 46,* 108–116.

Brinkerhoff, J.L., & Vincent, L.J. (1986). Increasing parental decision making in the individualized educational program meeting. *Journal of the Division for Early Childhood, 11*(1), 46–58.

Bristol, M. (1985). Designing programs for young developmentally disabled children: A family systems approach to intervention. *Remedial and Special Education, 6*(4), 46–53.

Cutler, B.C. (1986). The community-based respite residence: Finding a place in the system. In C.L. Salisbury & J. Intagliata (Eds.), *Respite care: Support for persons with developmental disabilities and their families* (pp. 167–193). Baltimore: Paul H. Brookes Publishing Co.

Cutler, B.C., & Kozloff, M.A. (1987). Living with autism: Effects on families and family needs. In D.J. Cohen, A. Donnellan, & R. Paul (Eds.), *Handbook of autism and pervasive developmental disorders* (pp. 513–527). New York: John Wiley & Sons.

Darling, R.B. (1979). *Families against society: A study of reactions to children with birth defects.* Beverly Hills: Sage Publications.

Donnellan, A.M., & Neel, R.J. (1986). New directions in educating students with autism. In R.H. Horner, L.H. Meyer, & H.D.B. Fredericks (Eds.), *Education of learners with severe handicaps: Exemplary service strategies* (pp. 99–126). Baltimore: Paul H. Brookes Publishing Co.

Dunst, C.J., Trivette, C.M., & Deal, A.G. (1988). *Enabling and empowering families.* Cambridge, MA: Brookline Books.

Evans, I.M., & Meyer, L.H. (1985). *An educative approach to behavior problems: A practical decision model for interventions with severely handicapped learners.* Baltimore: Paul H. Brookes Publishing Co.

Evans, I.M., Salisbury, C.L., Palombaro, M.M., Berryman, J., & Hollowood, T.M. (1992). Peer interactions and social acceptance of elementary-age children with severe disabilities in an inclusive school. *Journal of The Association for Persons with Severe Handicaps, 17*(4), 205–212.

Fitzgerald, M.T., & Fischer, R.M. (1987). A family involvement model for hearing-impaired infants. *Topics in Language Disorders, 7*(3), 1–18.

Fitzgerald, M.T., & Karnes, D.E. (1987). A parent-implemented language model for at-risk and developmentally delayed preschool children. *Topics in Language Disorders, 7*(3), 31–46.

Gitler, D., & Gordon, R. (1979). Observing and recording young handicapped children's behavior: A comparison among observational methodologies. *Exceptional Children, 46,* 134–135.

Goffman, E. (1963). *Stigma: Notes on the management of spoiled identity.* New York: Simon & Schuster.

Goode, D.A. (1984). Socially produced identities, intimacy and the problem of competence among the retarded. In L. Barton & S. Tomlinson (Eds.), *Special education and social interests* (pp. 228–249). New York: Nichols Publishing Company.

Henry, J. (1966). Personality and aging—with special reference to hospitals for the aged poor. In J.C. McKinney & F.T. DeVyver (Eds.), *Aging and social policy* (pp. 281–301). New York: Meredith.

Hundert, J., & Hopkins, B. (1992). Training supervisors in a collaborative team approach to promote peer interaction of children with disabilities in integrated preschools. *Journal of Applied Behavior Analysis, 25*(2), 385–400.

Jennings, S.E. (1990). *Understanding differences in families with developmentally disabled children: A stress and coping approach.* Unpublished doctoral dissertation, Boston University.

Kaufman, K.F. (1976). Teaching parents to teach their children: The behavior modification approach. In B. Feingold & C. Bank (Eds.), *Developmental disabilities of early childhood* (pp. 92–120). Springfield, IL: Charles C Thomas.

Kirkham, M.A. (1993). Two-year follow-up of skills training with mothers of children with disabilities. *American Journal on Mental Retardation, 97*(5), 509–520.

Kozloff, M.A. (1983). *Reaching the autistic child.* Cambridge, MA: Brookline Books. (Originally published by Research Press, 1973.)

Kozloff, M.A. (1988). *Productive interaction with students, children, and clients.* Springfield, IL: Charles C Thomas.

Kozloff, M.A. (1994). *Improving educational outcomes for children with disabilities: Guidelines and protocols for practice.* Baltimore: Paul H. Brookes Publishing Co.

Kozloff, M.A., Helm, D.T., Cutler, B.C., Douglas-Steele, D., Wells, A., & Scampini, L. (1988). Training programs for families of children with autism or other handicaps. In R.DeV. Peters & R.J. McMahon (Eds.), *Social learning and systems approaches to marriage and the family* (pp. 217–250). New York: Brunner/Mazel.

Martin A. (1988). Screening, early intervention, and remediation: Obscuring children's potential. *Harvard Educational Review, 58*(4), 488–501.

McDade, H.L., & Varnedoe, D.R. (1987). Training parents to be language facilitators. *Topics in Language Disorders, 7*(3), 19–30.

Morris, P. (1969). *Put away: A sociological study of institutions for the mentally retarded.* London: Routledge & Kegan Paul.

Muir, K.A., Milan, M.A., Branston-McLean, M.E., & Berger, M. (1982). Advocacy training for parents of handicapped children: A staff responsibility. *Young Children, 37,* 41–46.

O'Neill, R.E., Horner, R.H., Albin, R.W., Storey, K., & Sprague, J.R. (1990). *A functional analysis of problem behavior: A practical assessment guide.* Sycamore, IL: Sycamore Publishing.

Osborne, S.S., Schulte, A.C., & McKinney, J.D. (1991). A longitudinal study of students with learning disabilities in mainstream and resource programs. *Exceptionality, 2,* 81–95.

Peters, T., & Heron, T.E. (1993). When best is not good enough: An examination of best practice. *Journal of Special Education, 26*(4), 371–385.

PL 94-142, Education for All Handicapped Children Act of 1975. (23 August 1977). 20 U.S.C. 1401 et seq: *Federal Register, 42*(163), 42474–42518.

PL 99-457, Education of the Handicapped Act Amendments of 1986. (22 September 1986). *Congressional Record, 132*(125), H 7893–7912.

Schwartz, D.B. (1992). *Crossing the river: Creating a conceptual revolution in community and disability.* Cambridge, MA: Brookline Books.

Seifer, R., Clark, G.N., & Sameroff, A.J. (1991). Positive effects of interaction coaching on infants with developmental disabilities and their mothers. *American Journal on Mental Retardation, 96*(1), 1–11.

Snell, M. (1988, December). Curriculum and methodology for individuals with severe disabilities. *Education and Training in Mental Retardation, 23*(4), 302–314.

Tannock, R., Girolametto, L., & Siegel, L.S. (1992). Language intervention with children who have developmental delays: Effects of an interactive approach. *American Journal on Mental Retardation, 97*(2), 145–160.

Timm, M. (1985, November). *RIP: A parent-implemented treatment model for families with behaviorally disordered and/or developmentally delayed young children.* Paper presented at the National Strategy Conference, President's Committee on Mental Retardation, Washington, DC.

Tomlinson, S. (1982). *A sociology of special education.* London: Routledge & Kegan Paul.

Walker, D.K., Singer, J.D., Palfrey, J.S., Orza, M., Wenger, M., & Butler, J.A. (1988). Who leaves and who stays in special education: A 2-year follow-up study. *Exceptional Children, 54*, 393–402.

Wilcox, B., & Bellamy, G.T. (1982). *Design of high school programs for severely handicapped students.* Baltimore: Paul H. Brookes Publishing Co.

Williams, W., Fox, T.J., Thousand, J., & Fox, W. (1990). Level of acceptance and implementation of best practices in the education of students with severe handicaps in Vermont. *Education and Training in Mental Retardation, 25*(2), 120–131.

Wolfensberger, W. (1981). The extermination of handicapped people in World War II Germany. *Mental Retardation, 19*(1), 1–7.

Wolfensberger, W., & Kurtz, R.A. (1971). Measurement of parents' perception of their children's development. *Genetic Psychology Monographs, 83*, 3–92.

CHAPTER 2

THE COMMON PROGRAM IN EDUCATION

GUIDING IDEAS, PRACTICES, AND WORKING CONDITIONS

CHAPTER 1 OF THIS VOLUME ACKNOWLEDGES IMPORTANT INNOVATIONS IN ASSESSMENT, PLANNING, instruction, and program evaluation. Despite their hopes and efforts, however, educators and families cannot do much more to foster children's psychosocial development until programs satisfy children's human needs to be seen and treated as persons and members of the culture, and until functional skills are taught and families become intimately involved in all practices.

This chapter describes the typical education program for children with moderate to severe developmental disabilities. It identifies shortcomings in practices with respect to the three human needs described in Chapter 1. It then traces inadequate practices to a flawed model of psychosocial development and working conditions in schools.

OVERVIEW OF EDUCATION PROGRAMS

A common way of conducting special education has emerged since the 1970s in response to federal and state requirements that communities provide services to all children regardless of their disabilities, as well as in response to the development of effective practices, the efforts of educators and families, and regular education and preschools as models for special education.

Figure 2.1 illustrates how this common approach is organized. It shows that many educators' *ideas* about psychosocial development lead them to assess and teach certain behaviors and to follow what they consider "normal" developmental sequences. In addition, practices are affected by the *social organization* of schools. Specialization among teachers and therapists, for instance, divides instruction into separate times and places, whereas the isolation of teachers and the lack of leadership inhibit coordination. Moreover, because practices follow a sequence, shortcomings in one (e.g., assessment) are passed along to the others. Finally, as practices become routine, educators develop explanations and legitimations (e.g., "Everyone knows you must follow normal maturational sequences."), which makes it hard to recognize shortcomings and incorporate innovations.

This author wishes to make clear that few programs have all the difficulties identified in this chapter. The reader might use this chapter not as criticism of his or her program, and certainly not of the whole field, but as a source of guidelines, which are more formally presented in Chapter 8, this volume, and Chapters 1–4 of *Guidelines and Protocols for Practice,* for evaluating and improving programs.

MODEL OF THE STANDARD BEHAVIORAL REPERTOIRE

Special education often resembles an assembly line with different people working on different competencies. The outcome often is *not* children who are more competent and valued members of

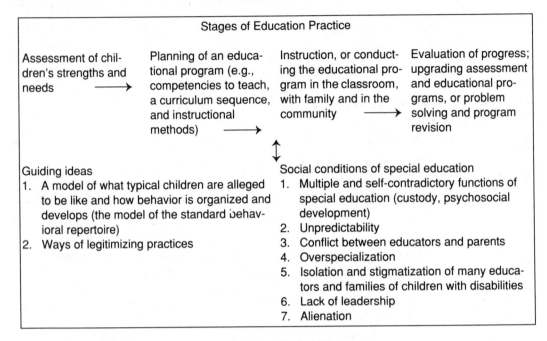

Figure 2.1.   The organization of education for children with disabilities.

the culture. The assembly line nature of programs is fostered by educators' understanding or model of behavior organization and development—a model this author calls the *standard behavioral repertoire*.

Standard Behavioral Repertoire

The model of the standard behavioral repertoire is educators' way of understanding children's behavior and their own practices. Educators' conversations, protocols, instruments, findings, plans, schedules, and teaching methods suggest that they see the human repertoire as a number of *areas* or *domains,* such as language and social skills. Each domain is defined by performances that appear as items on assessment instruments and target behaviors on program plans. For instance, the language domain contains naming, asking questions, and using plurals. Educators also depict change in children's repertoires as a series of stages or periods defined by the emergence of new behaviors, sometimes called *milestones.* Overall, the stages, domains, and behavioral items constitute a model of the "normal" or standard child in this culture.

Particular teachers and therapists use different versions of the model of the standard child. For instance, some models include job skills. However, the overall model has the same sources; one is Piaget's formulation of development proceeding through several stages. Between 0 and 24 months, the *sensorimotor* stage, children switch gaze from one visual stimulus to another and use tools to obtain objects. Between 2 and 7 years, the *preoperational* stage, children begin using symbolic language and imitation. During the stage of *concrete operations,* 7–11 years, children begin to understand and use new concepts and organize objects into series, such as increasing height. Finally, during the stage of *formal operations,* 11 years and older, children begin to engage in mental hypothesis testing, for instance, about the likely effects of different actions (Flavell, 1963).

A related source is the scheme proposed by Gesell and his colleagues that portrays change between 1 and 72 months across four areas: motor (e.g., walking, throwing); adaptive (e.g., stacking cubes, coloring forms); language; and personal-social (e.g., feeding, playing) (Ames, Gillespie, Haines, & Illg, 1980; Gesell & Amatruda, 1969).

A third source for the model of the standard child is the standard preschool and primary school curriculum for typical children, which, drawing on Piaget (Kamii & DeVries, 1974; Schwebel & Ralph, 1973), Gesell, and others, divides the day into sessions when specific behaviors from different domains that are relevant to various stages of development are worked on. For example, a child is taught to find hidden objects, which demonstrates an understanding of object permanence developed during the sensorimotor stage. In circular fashion, the common preschool and elementary curriculum defines "normal" competence and psychosocial development and uses it as the standard against which children with developmental disabilities are judged. The next few sections examine what is wrong with this commonly used model of behavior.

Flaws in the Standard Behavioral Repertoire Model

Models can be judged by their accuracy and usefulness. The model of the standard behavioral repertoire falls short on both counts. The five flaws of this model are: oversimplification, treating words as if they are objects, treating domains as separate entities, decontextualization, and oversimplified notions about psychosocial development. Each of these flaws is discussed below.

Oversimplification   The human behavioral repertoire is complex. Movements are assembled into actions that are organized into tasks, and tasks are organized into activities that in turn are combined into roles and identities. Moreover, the developing repertoire is an ongoing accomplishment that results from the constant adjustment of action to its settings (this is discussed further in chaps. 3–6, this volume). However, educators typically segment children's repertoires into a small number of stages, domains, and their respective behavior items. Most assessment instruments and curriculum plans contain fewer than 200 behaviors in all domains. The first flaw, then, is that educators oversimplify and see too little of what children do. Thus, assessments, plans, and curricula include too little to accurately describe or improve competence and participation.

Treating Words as If They Are Objects   Categories are words that direct attention and stop the stream of behavior so that it can be analyzed. Many educators unwittingly treat categories (e.g., stages of development, domains) as object-like things. The following examples reveal a failure to separate behavior from the words used to talk about it (Baker & Hacker, 1984; Phillips, 1991).

Treating the Idea of Stage as a Thing

Ms. Blake: You teach Jerry to put objects into containers, but not to dump them out. Why?
Ms. Tyler: Well, Jerry is in sensorimotor stage 4—coordination of secondary circular reactions. Dumping objects is in a later part of the sensorimotor period—stage 5, or tertiary circular reactions. I don't want him to get ahead of himself.

Ms. Tyler sees Jerry's repertoire as a thing with definite characteristics and boundaries. Because Jerry "has" a sensorimotor stage 4 repertoire, he is not considered capable of behavior in a sensorimotor stage 5 repertoire. Perhaps Ms. Tyler also regards a series of stages as an object similar to an escalator. Therefore, just as Jerry cannot be two places at once, he cannot be in two stages at once.

Nevertheless, Ms. Tyler treats words, such as *repertoire* and *stage*, as more than labels for an ongoing relationship between Jerry's actions and environments. Her static model—a child *has* one or another type of repertoire, or is *in* one or another stage—results in not giving Jerry more advanced tasks, thus slowing his development.

Treating the Idea of Domain as a Thing

Ms. Blake: During the cooking lesson, Juan had few chances to use words he had worked on during the earlier language lesson. Won't he forget those words?
Mr. Carson: No. The words are part of his receptive language. You know, he has a lot of receptive language.

Mr. Carson sees language as an object that a person possesses, and not simply a name for certain performances. According to Mr. Carson, just as children acquire toys, they learn words, store them, and use them when needed. Whether Juan learns to identify cooking utensils outside the language lesson is not problematic for Mr. Carson because, as he sees it, Juan carries language knowledge with him. Ironically, because Mr. Carson creates few chances for talk outside of language lessons, Juan rarely talks outside of them.

Treating the Name of a Problem Behavior as a Thing

Ms. Blake:　　Sam squirms in his seat and roams around a lot. I wonder why.

Ms. Gonzales:　He has attention deficit hyperactivity disorder. It makes him unable to control his impulses. I think he should be on medication.

Ms. Gonzales treats a diagnosis (label) for Sam's behavior as an object-like condition that Sam "has" and that causes him to run around. Because the "attention deficit hyperactivity disorder" (cause) is seen as a part of Sam's person, it does not occur to Ms. Gonzales to conduct descriptive or functional analyses to find out if Sam gets as much reinforcement for paying attention as he does for running (see chap. 10, this volume).

In sum, many educators and their collaborators treat abstract ideas and names for disorders, stages, domains, competencies, and responses as if they were objects. Although this enables them to communicate with one another and routinize education, it obscures seeing a behavioral repertoire as an ongoing accomplishment developing in interaction with environments.

Treating Domains as Separate Entities　Many educators regard domains as if they are distinct. Imitation, for instance, is treated only as a skill and not also as a form of social interaction. Similarly, waving "hello" is seen as a social skill, but not also as a way to express feelings and flag down cabs. One result of placing a behavior in only one category is that perception becomes narrow and rigid. When assessing social skills, for instance, a teacher's observations are limited by a list of items defining social skills (e.g., standing in line, greeting people). Items in other domains that are social in nature (e.g., imitation) may not be included in the assessment of social skills. Thus, assessment underestimates competence in the social skills domain.

The narrow perception of behavior constrains teaching. The few items defining "social skills" may be taught at one time or place, whereas motor imitation, language, and hygiene are taught at others. Teaching, therefore, resembles an assembly line.

Decontextualization　Decontextualization means that behavior is understood on the basis of form (i.e., movements involved), rather than function (i.e., connections to environments) (Neel & Billingsley, 1989; White & Haring, 1976). The result is that educators focus too much on *what* children are doing and too little on *how* environments facilitate or hinder learning and development.

One example of decontextualization is not seeing the multiple functions of behavior. During language assessment we observe the following interchanges:

Ms. Adams:　(Holds up a picture of a potato.) And this one?

Indra:　　　You eat it.

Ms. Adams:　No. It's a potato. Let's try another. (Holds up a picture of a duck.) What is this?

Indra:　　　Swimming.

Ms. Adams:　No. It's a duck. Say, "duck."

Indra:　　　Duck.

Ms. Adams:　Very good. (Still showing picture of a duck.) Now, what is this?

Indra:　　　Swimming!

There are many competent ways to respond to "What is this?". Indra said what potatoes are for and what the duck was doing. Ms. Adams scores Indra's answers incorrect because the test Ms. Adams is using narrowly defines as correct those answers with an object-naming function. Thus,

Ms. Adams underestimates the size of Indra's object-naming repertoire and does not notice the other functions of Indra's vocabulary. One also wonders why Indra and Ms. Adams are examining drawings rather than the objects themselves, or, in the case of swimming ducks, a videotape of animals in natural habitats.

Similarly, when Indra flaps her hands and moans in Mr. Hawkins' class, he judges the behavior by how it looks—its form ("weird" in his opinion). He does not see that Indra performs the behavior only when she is having trouble with tasks. The communicative intent of flapping hands and moaning, in other words, is to request help (Sasso et al., 1992; Sigafoos & Dempsey, 1992). Instead of teaching her socially acceptable ways to request help, Mr. Hawkins ignores the flapping. Recently, Indra has stopped flapping and started yelling.

In sum, when teachers define and respond to behaviors on the basis of form (i.e., viewing them as incorrect or "weird"), not function, children appear less competent and/or more pathological. Moreover, by ignoring or punishing children because they judge the forms incorrect or "weird," teachers weaken the desirable functions children are trying to have served, for example, to answer questions, describe things, or get help.

Oversimplified Notions About Psychosocial Development   How do educators decide what to assess and teach throughout a child's education? The answer is they either follow guidelines in published curricula or make them up as they go.

Educators have the tough job of continually selecting target behaviors and instructional materials for children with a variety of changing needs. Most published curricula represent one of two main perspectives on development: developmental-maturational or functional-ecological. Being pressed for time and receiving little help, the typical educator uses only part of a published curriculum. What emerges is often narrow.

Developmental-Maturational Perspective   The developmental-maturational perspective is based on the assumption that, through a combination of maturation and interaction with the environment, there are changes in a person's sensitivities, purposes, actions and/or competencies, and knowledge. Changes accumulate to the point that children have a qualitatively different way of understanding and participating in the world, which is called a stage or period. Psychosocial development, therefore, is thought to proceed in a series of stages: cognitive and sensorimotor (Piaget, 1952, 1954), communicational (Brown, 1973), psychosexual (Freud, 1964), and even existential (Erickson, 1959).

Proponents of the developmental-maturational perspective often use assessments to determine how children with disabilities "stack up" to their model of the standard child. Important assessment instruments in this perspective include The McCarthy Scales of Children's Abilities (McCarthy, 1972), Uzgiris and Hunt Scales (Dunst, 1980; Uzgiris & Hunt, 1975), and Bayley Scales of Infant Development (Bayley, 1969).

Many using this perspective also believe it is easier for children with developmental disabilities to progress if "normal" sequences are followed. Thus, curricula consist of levels or stages, each with specific tasks, some of which are "readiness" criteria for deciding when a child can be moved to a higher level. For instance, some curricula based on surveys of children without disabilities stress that those with disabilities should learn behaviors considered developmental "milestones" (Bluma, Shearer, Froham, & Hillard, 1976; Furano et al., 1979). The developers may believe "children's capabilities emerge in an invariant, sequential manner that is directly linked with neurophysiological factors" (Neisworth & Bagnato, 1987, p. 66). Other curriculum developers stress that there is a network of ways by which behaviors facilitate and/or serve as alternatives to one another. Their curricula stress progressive behavior change through interaction with environments, tend to be more flexible, and focus on skills relevant to a child's natural environment (Dunst, 1981).

Examples of developmental-maturational curricula that many teachers adopt include Bricker (1986); the *Carolina Curriculum for Infants and Toddlers with Special Needs* (2nd ed.) (Johnson-Martin, Jens, Attermeier, & Hacker, 1991); Schopler and Reichler (1978, 1982); the *Broward*

County Model Program (Sternberg, Ritchey, Pegnatore, Wills, & Hill, 1986); the *Hawaii Early Learning Program* (Furano et al., 1979); the *Portage Guide to Early Education* (Bluma et al., 1976); the *Teaching Research Curriculum for Moderately and Severely Handicapped* (Fredericks et al., 1976); Thurman and Widerstrom (1990); and the *Guide to Early Developmental Training* (Tilton, Liska, & Bourland, 1977).

An over-worked teacher is rarely able to duplicate the richness and flexibility found in published curricula. Some uncritically adopt a developmental-maturational approach, turning generalizations about child development into readiness rules: "Indra can't work on walking. She hasn't gone through the crawling stage yet." They turn guidelines for educational sequences into narrow paths: "Now that we have done motor imitation, we will work on vocal imitation." Sometimes they work on simplified developmental-readiness tasks so long that instruction becomes aversive and age-inappropriate (Gaussen, 1984). Children become stuck at the level of nonfunctional, "pseudo-academic" tasks (Garwood, 1982), such as stringing beads and pointing to objects named.

Lastly, stages of "normal" development may not be appropriate for many children with developmental disabilities (Greenwald & Leonard, 1979; Rogers, 1977; Snyder-McLean, McLean, & Etter, 1988). Some children who do not display alleged readiness skills *do have* advanced competencies. This is often true of children with autism. Also, items appropriate for young children *without* developmental disabilities may not be appropriate for children *with* developmental disabilities, especially when they are older. An adolescent with mental retardation may not properly stack rings on a dowel. This may be because the task is less interesting and/or the adolescent is physically unable to do it, rather than a lack of sensorimotor competence. Even if such tasks could provide a valid assessment, they are not appropriate for an older child's curriculum.

Functional-Ecological Perspective   Curriculum developers with a functional-ecological perspective are not convinced one must follow a "normal" developmental-maturational sequence for children with developmental disabilities. What is most important to them is gradually building skills in individualized paths that will help children become more competent members of society as soon as possible.

Examples of curricula with a functional-ecological perspective include Brown et al. (1980); Brown, Evans, Weed, and Owens (1987); Gaylord-Ross and Holvoet (1985); Gold (1975); the *IMPACT* curriculum (Neel & Billingsley, 1989); the *Individualized Curriculum Sequence Model* (Sailor & Guess, 1983); the *Learning in Functional Environments Curriculum* (Stetson, 1985); the *Programmed Environments Curriculum* (Tawney, Knapp, O'Reilly, & Pratt, 1979); and Valletutti and Bender (1985).

Assessment in a functional-ecological approach involves examining congruence between a child's current repertoire and the required competencies and available opportunities for participation in current and possibly future life settings. For instance, an ecological inventory reveals that competent participation in the community consists of major roles (e.g., employee). Roles are analyzed into component activities (e.g., dressing properly, doing the job). Each activity is analyzed into component tasks (e.g., selecting and putting on each item of clothing), and each task is analyzed into chains of actions or even tiny movements (Belmore & Brown, 1978; Brown et al., 1981; Gold, 1980). Assessing across tasks and places, the teacher-task analyst identifies strong and weak behavior links a person needs to improve, and those a person can readily be taught to perform in everyday tasks and activities.

Finally, guidelines on what and when to teach are based on the ideas that: 1) there are typical sequences (not necessarily determined by maturation) through which children acquire skills (Bailey & Wolery, 1984; Cohen & Gross, 1979), and/or 2) certain behaviors are used in performing other behaviors. The progression from earlier to later tasks, or for assembling parts into larger wholes, can be portrayed with "hierarchical task analyses" (Thiagarajian, Semmel, & Semmel, 1974) or "lattices" (Smith, 1981) in which a chain of main tasks is analyzed into chains or hierarchies of subtasks.

Some classroom teachers and staff take the functional approach to the extreme. Apparently believing that tasks can be broken down into such small components that almost anyone can be taught almost anything, their students or clients sometimes work on competencies (e.g., toileting) for which they are simply not ready. Or they work on such small parts of tasks that the purpose and whole are a mystery; the tasks are "too atomized to be of significant value in . . . life's reality contexts" (Valletutti & Bender, 1985, p. ix). Moreover, while they teach functional behaviors, such as doing dishes, some teachers do not analyze children's life environments. Thus, they train students to be workers—to answer work-related questions and perform work tasks—but not how to participate in ordinary social activities, such as games, conversation, religious rituals, and outings in their "natural" environments (Abel, 1989). Finally, some who uncritically use a functional-ecological approach take the organization of a child's life environments as given, rather than determine how they could be altered to better suit a child's needs and capabilities.

Some educators have no specific perspective. They work on skills that supervisors or parents want worked on, that colleagues work on, that strike their fancy ("It's Christmas. Let's learn 'Jingle Bells.'"), or that bother them ("These kids are so clumsy! Let's start a program on motor skills."). This idiosyncratic style is flexible; it serves some of the interests of families and teachers, and expresses teachers' desires to create their own curriculum. However, it does not ensure that children will work on tasks they will be able to learn or that will benefit them in daily life. Moreover, idiosyncratic curricula often become directionless and chaotic.

SOCIALLY INSENSITIVE ASSESSMENT

What is assessment about? It sounds scientific, objective, precise: "Indra's scores put her at the 40th percentile." It has the ring of positive thinking: "We will identify Jerry's strengths, not just needs." Beneath the confident, beneficent phrasing, assessment often involves judging how children "stack up" to models of the "normal" child. Just where does Juan deviate, or fall short (Martin, 1988)? To find out, behaviors and tasks are selected from the model of the standard repertoire; a child's performance is then observed and compared with the model. However, because the model oversimplifies ongoing, environment-connected behavior, so does assessment.

Oversimplification of Assessments

The Sample of Competence and Participation Is Small Observations usually are of short duration and confined to classrooms and clinicians' offices. Different domains are commonly assessed by different persons, and only a handful of items from the domains are assessed. Detailed information possessed by families and others is often not wanted, and may be considered inferior to what clinicians gather (Tomlinson, 1982). In sum, assessments do not depict the range of a child's competence and participation (i.e., functional behavioral repertoire) in daily life.

Assessment in Unusual Environments Assessments are usually conducted in forms of interaction (e.g., tests) by people and in places unfamiliar to the child. When conducted in the classroom or home, the situation still may be contrived or abnormal (Bronfenbrenner, 1977). Recent research shows that some individuals with developmental disabilities reveal many communication competencies in familiar environments. When talking to strangers without disabilities, however, the same persons limit themselves to answering questions in the least sophisticated manner (e.g., "yes" and "no") (Hughes & May, 1986; Yearley & Brewer, 1989). In sum, much assessment information may be invalid; that is, it may fail to identify both needs and competencies.

Samples Include Too Little Ordinary Behavior The common assessment focuses on behaviors that are isolated from normal sequences, nonfunctional, and simplified to a few easy-to-describe steps (Fewell & Rich, 1987). To assess eye-hand coordination, a child might put pegs in holes and stack rings on a dowel, rather than put dishes in a dish drainer and utensils in a drawer. To assess object permanence, a psychologist may hide a toy behind a box to see if the child reaches for it, rather than observing the child searching for things at home. The latter is a more normal use of the knowledge of object permanence, reveals the range of objects to which the idea applies, and shows how the child searches.

Moreover, too little attention is paid to the way a child's performances are tailored to and/or inhibited by environments. One does not learn the extent to which a child is attuned to cues for where things go and when events happen; the events (e.g., sounds, objects) to which a child is more and less attentive; the cues, prompts, and consequences that work best and worst; or alternative ways the child can accomplish the same functions. In the end, assessments provide little information on the size and adaptability of a child's repertoire. Thus, one cannot plan adequate programs that satisfy the child's needs or build on the child's capabilities.

Assessments Rarely Address Membership and Personhood   Many social features of development are unexplored with assessments. One learns little of a child's involvement in the round of daily life, the nature of child–caregiver interactions, or the roles (e.g., member, adversary) allocated to the child. In other words, assessments usually study the child alone rather than the congruence between the child and his or her environments. Program plans, therefore, say little about needed changes in environments.

Assessments Try To Serve Too Many Purposes at Once   As Wolery has argued (M. Wolery, personal communication, June 3, 1991), the same assessment may serve too many purposes at once. Information may be used to: 1) determine if a child is eligible for any services; 2) produce a diagnosis to reduce families' and educators' confusion and make possible third-party reimbursement; 3) make or justify placement decisions; 4) plan a child's curriculum; 5) explain lack of progress; or 6) placate teachers, families, and others. Often, information collected to answer one question (e.g., scores on tests signifying whether a child has a developmental disability) is used inappropriately to answer others (e.g., precisely what a child's needs are).

Findings and Recommendations from Assessments

Findings and recommendations from assessments are commonly self-evident, circular, and vague (Martin, 1988; Pyecha, 1980). Typical reports contain entries such as "This 6-year-old male displays a severe language delay. He is mute except for a few one- and two-word requests." Here, the label—"severe language delay"—attempts to hide people's ignorance of why the child does not talk. Obviously a 6-year-old child who is mute is language delayed. The report goes on to say, "He requires intensive, structured language therapy." Although the words *intensive* and *structured* lend credibility to the report, they are statements of the obvious, but with no details on procedures for language therapy. The teacher will have to depend on the specialist.

Another report reads, "She has had encopresis since the age of 4. It is recommended that she receive toilet training." The words "has had" transform a behavioral deficit into an illness or condition. Again, no details are given for the obvious recommendation of toilet training.

Still another report states, "Ten-year-old Indra makes good eye contact, listens well to instructions, but has poor fine motor control." What is "eye contact"? What might "good" eye contact be? Such terms are vague and say nothing that is not already known.

One reason recommendations are often vague statements of the obvious couched in jargon is that the assessment process provides so little understanding of a child's behavior that assessors cannot do much more than give medical-sounding labels and then cite the kind of "therapy" or "teaching" a child needs. In addition, jargon creates the impression that its users have special knowledge (Bart, 1984; Freeman, 1989). Inadequacies in assessment information and subsequent recommendations lead to inadequacies in program planning.

PROGRAM PLANNING

Program plans generally specify a small number of isolated, oversimplified, nonfunctional, and age-inappropriate behaviors. Descriptions of how to teach each competency are superficial, and long-term issues, such as fluency, generalization, adaptation, and maintenance of skill, are not addressed.

The following are examples of entries from individualized education programs (IEPs) or individualized family service plans (IFSPs): "Indra's fine motor skills will increase from their present developmental age of 2.6 to at least the 3.6 level, on such tasks as three- and four-piece puzzles, stringing large beads, stacking rings . . . ." This list has too few "items" to be a reasonable sample of "fine motor" skills. Furthermore, Indra is 10 years old, which makes these age-inappropriate tasks.

"By the end of the year, Jerry will make eye contact 75% of the time." The words "time" and "eye contact" are ambiguous. Is Jerry supposed to make eye contact when asked or when someone's eyes are nearby? Even if these definitions were clear, it is inappropriate to look at people's eyes "75% of the time."

Problems Associated with Program Plans

Program Plans Are Vague and Shortsighted   Program plans describe daily schedules and name teaching methods, but rarely give needed details, such as the sequence of steps by which behavior will be shaped and the prompts and reinforcers to be used (Weisenfeld, 1986). Sometimes, plans for a behavior state as little information as, "Indra will increase her rate of spontaneous speech to at least five well-formed utterances per 15 minutes." This may be a reasonable rate, but what is "spontaneous speech"? No cues or prompts are needed? What is a "well-formed utterance"? Will "Cookie!" do, or is it counted only if Indra says, "I want a cookie, please"? What instructional methods will be used to increase the rate of speaking? Is anyone going to count all the utterances and then calculate rates?

Because plans are vague, it is unlikely that different people will instruct a child the same way. The result is inconsistent instruction, lack of coordination between school and family, and a lack of progress.

Program Plans Say Little About Next Steps   Program plans usually fail to address: 1) generalization from one environment to another (Billingsley, 1984); 2) how subskills (e.g., visual attention, grasping, and turning an object) will be chained into larger wholes (e.g., stirring soup); 3) how teaching methods will be made more normative (e.g., extensive prompting at first, minimal prompting later); 4) how fluency (e.g., duration, speed, and smoothness) will be improved; and 5) how a child will be taught to integrate competent performances into everyday tasks and activities. Consequently, many children are stuck in the stage of acquisition when they could have made more progress.

Program plans are vague because they stem from assessments that are vague and general. In addition, plans are a formality; they satisfy supervisors trying to satisfy still higher authorities (Lovitt, 1977). Indeed, many teachers judge plans to be a waste of time because changes in class composition, assistance, and family–school relations often make it impossible to carry out the plans.

The Planning Process Is Not Necessarily Beneficent   The planning process is usually not one in which administrators, teachers, assessors, and parents sit down in harmony to decide what a child needs and how to provide services. Although all of these people wish the child well, each has a different agenda. The administrator wants to avoid conflict with parents, but keep costs low; parents want children's skills to improve and may want someone to control problem behavior; teachers and therapists want more assistance and materials, but do not want to be a source of conflict. In the end, plans are like a deal that everyone can live with for the time being (Cutler, 1991, 1993).

SHORTCOMINGS IN INSTRUCTION

Some shortcomings in instruction are handed down from inadequate assessment and program planning; others are fostered by working conditions. Shortcomings include inadequate class structure, counterproductive student–caregiver interaction, discrete activity scheduling, nonfunctional and "abnormal" behaviors, and outmoded and superficial behavior modification techniques.

Inadequate Class Structure

The common special education program is a changing collection of relatively disconnected classes or levels, as evidenced by instructional gaps, lack of entry and exit criteria, and unproductive grouping.

Instructional Gaps   Most programs with which this writer and his colleagues are familiar have gaps in curriculum sequences. There may be no classes that teach newly entered children and/or children with severe disabilities essential skills, such as orienting to the environment, turn-taking, cooperating, communicating, playing, and adaptive skills. Placed in too advanced classes, unprepared children engage in more and more disruptive behavior, the control of which becomes the caregivers' major endeavor. Eventually, these children may be placed in restrictive settings, which might have been avoided had they received proper instruction from the start. Yet, there may be no classes to prepare more competent children for entry into regular education, occupational, or living environments. Thus, much of the effort of teachers, families, and children has led to a dead end, and education becomes busy work.

Lack of Entry and Exit Criteria   Many programs do not use relevant criteria to decide when children are ready to enter or leave a level or class. For example, what sort of communication, attention, commonsense knowledge (e.g., cause-effect), adaptive, and motor skills are needed, and how much problem behavior is allowed? Instead, children are placed, retained, or moved because of families' requests, teachers' complaints of disruptiveness, the absence of a lower or higher class, and staff turnover. Therefore, placement may have little to do with children's needs and teachers' skills.

Unproductive Grouping   Given instructional gaps and a lack of educationally relevant entry and exit criteria, students with severe problem behaviors and/or behavior deficits may be segregated to "contain" the problems. Or, children with the same "condition" (e.g., autism, hyperactivity, cerebral palsy) may be grouped together based on the mistaken notion that they need the same program, or because only certain staff are considered capable of handling them. In consequence, some classes are so heterogeneous with respect to students' strengths and needs that widely different methods are required. Therefore, the class is really many one-to-one teacher–student relationships, rather than a group. However, groupings may be so homogeneous that children have little to imitate except each other's disruptive behaviors, or their disabilities require so much of the caregivers' time that there is no time left for teaching.

Counterproductive Student–Caregiver Interaction

Most facilities and families observed by this writer and his co-workers are characterized by counterproductive child–caregiver exchanges. Caregivers typically reinforce problem behaviors by staring at children or repeatedly telling them to stop. However, caregivers often fail to reinforce desirable behaviors as often, quickly, and strongly as they reinforce problem behaviors. Thus, desirable behaviors remain weak and problem behaviors get worse. Adults become fatigued and pessimistic. One of the highest priorities is to assess and improve exchanges in schools and homes. Otherwise, skillful teaching during lessons has little payoff. (Exchanges are discussed in chap. 5, this volume.)

Discrete Activity Scheduling

The usual school day is divided into lessons. In each, a teacher works on a few behaviors selected from children's program plans (e.g., naming objects, imitation). Also, the schedule is much the same from week to week. A typical morning resembles the following:

8:00–8:30:   Calendar: Students sit in front of a big calendar and name the days of the week, answer questions about the weather, and talk about what they did at home yesterday evening.

8:30–9:00:   Individual desk work: Students work at puzzles and other small motor ⟍

9:00–9:30:   Group language lesson: Students sit in chairs in a row facing the teacher wꜣ. pictures and asks questions.

9:30–10:00:   Free play: Students go to a play area.

While such a schedule could be a reasonable way to organize activities, closer observation may reveal problems, such as isolated behavior and isolated methods.

Isolated Behavior   Most sessions are isolated from one another. That is, students' behaviors in one session do not logically follow from or contribute to other sessions. This is unlike daily life in which current tasks (e.g., putting on a coat) are built on earlier tasks (e.g., selecting a coat), and contribute to later tasks (e.g., buttoning the coat). Separating behaviors this way inhibits building simpler behaviors into larger and more useful sequences, and inhibits generalizing desirable behaviors from one place to another.

Isolated Methods   Teaching methods used in one place and session may be different from methods used in others. During lessons on small motor skills, a teacher may reinforce skillful hand movements, but during language lessons the teacher (overfocusing on language behavior) does not reinforce skillful hand movements at all. In effect, the teacher teaches students not to generalize behavior from one environment to another.

Teaching Nonfunctional and "Abnormal" Behavior

In many programs, numerous tasks are nonfunctional. Examples include working puzzles and stringing beads; matching, sorting, and pointing to pictures; reciting the days of the week; imitating movements, such as patting the head; and putting clothespins around the rim of a can. Such tasks do not contribute to larger tasks and activities and are not expected or required of persons in the family, workplace, or other "natural" environments. Some select these behaviors believing they are necessary to psychosocial development.

Many programs teach behaviors that are "abnormal," age-inappropriate, environment-inappropriate, and disvalued. For example, a 12-year-old looks out of place working four-piece puzzles, identifying pastel animals, or reciting nursery rhymes. Although the youngster may have severe disabilities, the same skills could be acquired with age-appropriate tasks, such as matching hand tools with pictures of tasks in which they are used. In addition, some teachers do not notice how they teach behaviors inappropriate to the environment. For example, they teach students to: 1) make eye contact only in exchange for food, although the "normal" use of eye contact is to initiate interaction or reciprocate another's initiations; 2) answer the same questions day after day, such as "How are you?"; 3) imitate words the student does not understand ("Joey, say, 'hurricane.'"); 4) name, point to, or sort pictures instead of things; and 5) perform parts of a functional task (e.g., hammer nails into a board), but not have an end result.

Finally, students and clients are often taught behaviors associated with disvalued roles. They are rarely taught more than one way to do a task, which results in confusion and incompetence in novel situations. In addition, they are expected to sit quietly and go through trial after trial of the same task (massed practice) for many weeks, put up with teasing and noises from others, and calmly wait while five other children take their turns during a group lesson. Together, these conditions would not be tolerated by typical, self-respecting persons.

Outmoded and Superficial Behavior Modification Techniques

When communities suddenly were required to serve all children with special needs, behavioral psychology became a resource that helped educators remedy a variety of disabling conditions; educate teachers, therapists, and families; and organize classrooms. Today, behavioral concepts and methods are a routine part of special education, even where staff claim they are opposed to "behavior modification." Yet, the brand of behavior modification practiced in most programs is not

ly behavior analysts who showed that environmental events (e.g.,
their effects on behavior; that behaviors must be defined by their
one; and that one must pay careful attention to subtle events such as
aer, 1962; Bijou, 1957; Ferster & DeMyer, 1961; Hewett, 1965; Hol-
nme, Csanyi, Gonzales, & Reches, 1969; Lindsley, 1956; Lovaas &
Wolf, 1967; Sapon & Reeback, 1968; Staats, 1964; Terrace, 1963;
well-intentioned and hard working, many educators practice a superficial
of behavior modification.

Over.   *crete Trial and Massed Practice Format*   Teaching often is done in *discrete trials* (Donn.   .-Walsh, Gossage, LaVigna, Schuler, & Traphagen, 1976). That is, the student pays attention, the teacher presents a cue (e.g., "What is this?"), the teacher prompts if
needed, the student responds to the cue and/or prompt, and the teacher provides a consequence
reflecting the quality of the student's response. *Massed practice*—work on the same behavior over
and over in a session—is usually coupled with the discrete trial format.

The discrete trial and massed practice formats are useful. One can use them to: 1) give practice prior to application (e.g., counting money one more time before entering a store); 2) strengthen
newly discovered weak links in a child's repertoire (e.g., short sessions on grasping objects in
between activities that involve grasping); 3) teach repetitive behaviors (e.g., rolling out dough);
and 4) quickly strengthen attention, cooperation, and turn-taking skills in children with severe disabilities and durable problem behaviors (Hamblin, Buckholdt, Ferritor, Kozloff, & Blackwell,
1971). However, many teachers use the discrete trial and massed practice formats as the main
methods of instruction, and/or when it is no longer appropriate (Mulligan, Lacy, & Guess, 1982).
As a result, potentially rich and varied interaction becomes rigid and aversive, caregivers' creativity is stifled, and children's behaviors do not generalize and are not maintained outside of sessions.

Ineffectively Cuing, Prompting, and Providing Consequences   Few teachers pay enough
attention to the details of teaching (e.g., positioning, tone of voice, timing) and students' responses.
Cues are given when children are not paying attention and/or are engaged in problem behavior.
Cues often involve nagging, ambiguous messages ("Do you want to read?"), or a harsh tone of
voice. In addition, learning is hampered by noise and visual stimulation (e.g., excessive wall decorations). So-called "rewards" do not strengthen the behaviors that obtain them. Examples include
the overused response "good," to which students quickly habituate; tokens not exchanged for anything, therefore having little value; or praise that is wooden or sarcastic. Furthermore, desirable
behaviors are reinforced too late and too seldom. Ineffective prompts are used again and again,
stamping in errors. Moreover, teachers correct students' errors and then let students go on to the
next step or next task instead of having them back up and respond correctly to the cue (i.e., positive
practice). Finally, caregivers talk too much (e.g., giving instructions), as though words will give
knowledge and promote correct responses.

Pseudo Groups   The following lesson is a "group" lesson in name only.

Students are in a row in front of Ms. Tyler. She goes around the group, giving students an
opportunity to respond to questions and materials: "Jerry, what is this?" Sometimes she gives a
turn only to those paying attention; sometimes she just goes from one student to another down
the row. If a student does not respond, Ms. Tyler gives a prompt (e.g., "It's a sheep."). If the
student answers correctly the first time, or finally does so with a prompt, the student is
"rewarded."

The above "group" lesson is common, and it seems appropriate. On closer examination, however, one notes several shortcomings. In general, there is no group process. It is one-at-a-time
teaching with students near each other. When not their turn, students play with their fingers or
pester other students. In time, the lesson becomes a cue for disruptive behavior. In addition, the

teacher often reinforces "off-task" behaviors by telling "offenders" to stop: "Jimmy, are we supposed to be hitting our neighbors?" In a few minutes, almost nothing but problem behavior is being performed and reinforced.

PROGRAM EVALUATION

Evaluation should help determine how well a program is working and why, so that the next steps, such as generalization or problem solving, can be planned. Many shortcomings in assessment are also found in program evaluation. First, evaluation has low priority. It competes with the demands of teaching and managing relationships with parents, supervisors, and other teachers. Moreover, evaluation does not have a clear payoff; there are virtually no consequences if a student does not achieve goals on his or her education plan. Second, program evaluation is generally not something teachers are taught to do. For instance, few teachers know how to judge the effectiveness and efficiency of educational programs, how to conduct functional analyses to determine what fosters and inhibits progress, or how to create plans for solving problems or upgrading programs.

Third, program evaluation provides insufficient information. It usually consists of summaries of teachers' and therapists' cursory observations. Evaluative descriptions are vague (e.g., "Jerry's self-control is much improved."). Relatively few behaviors are evaluated—generally only those on the education plan. Change or lack of change in other important behaviors may not be reported. Moreover, change in behaviors outside teaching environments (e.g., in the home), and the effects of any changes on others (e.g., parents), is usually not determined.

Finally, there are problems of validity even when evaluation is systematic. For instance, a large class of behavior, such as eye-hand coordination, is evaluated with a small number of behaviors, such as the number of puzzles the student can do and the number of blocks the student can stack. Surely, eye-hand coordination implies more than this. Also, evaluation might be done in *contrived* situations (e.g., language skills evaluated in a small room by the therapist). One does not learn of the student's performance anywhere else; perhaps it is better. When standardized tests are used, they summarize performance (e.g., the number of items passed or the student's developmental age); however, the examiner may not describe the student's expressed feelings, effort, or attentiveness. Without such details, test information has questionable implications for a child's education program.

SOCIAL CONDITIONS OF EDUCATORS' ENVIRONMENTS

The social conditions in which special education is conducted hamper the development of excellent programs. In many places, funding varies from year to year. Staff and children come and go. After some years, many administrators and teachers focus only on the short-run, and make changes only in response to pressing problems. Thus, programs often develop with little planning.

Multiple and Conflicting Functions

Education serves contradictory functions, which include fostering psychosocial development, baby-sitting, and taking custody over and controlling persons considered too difficult to handle elsewhere. Clearly, guiding psychosocial development differs from controlling children or providing respite for families. Psychosocial development requires nurturing and self-enhancing interaction; control and custody merely require keeping children quiet. The pressure on teachers from supervisors, families, and other teachers to serve conflicting functions results in confusion, vacillation, and contradictions. Nurturing may be interspersed with punishment, while sessions on functional skills compete with aimless activity.

Overspecialization

Schools receive services from transportation companies, consultants, medical facilities, and therapists. This hinders coordination in several ways. For example, teachers may not get drivers' cooperation in strengthening desirable behavior on the bus. In addition, information and recommendations from consultants may mystify rather than enlighten. Examiners at a medical center may describe a child's difficulties as an illness and recommend drug therapy, with no mechanism for helping teachers coordinate educational and medical plans. Thus, recommendations are "tacked on," with no evaluation of efficacy: "Well, Sam seems to be doing better since he started Ritalin."

Furthermore, services often are provided inefficiently. A social worker or school psychologist making home visits to help parents with problem behaviors may know little about a child's classroom behavior. After home visits, the teacher may not be told what was done or learned. Similarly, the physical therapist usually works with individual children in another room for 30 minutes or so a few times a week. Although the teacher and therapist may chat about how a child is doing, little is done to incorporate the therapist's expertise in the classroom; that is, the therapist does not teach teachers physical therapy. Therefore, the progress children make with specialists is unlikely to generalize to the classroom. In addition, it may be impossible to obtain assessments and consultations when needed. A communication therapist may be available only for short periods, perhaps not when needed. With children coming and going to and from speech, physical, and occupational therapies, classrooms resemble bus stations.

Stigmatization and Social Isolation

Children's problem behaviors and deficits affect their self-concept and place in society as well as that of their teachers and family members (Goffman, 1963). As much as children are subjected to and affected by "societal reaction" to their disabilities, so are their families and teachers who become the object of stares and whispers, are given less-than-satisfactory classrooms, and have separate hours for the gym and cafeteria. Unless teachers' and parents' sense of worth and place are firmly rooted in a supportive personal community, or in beliefs enabling them to come to terms with the situation, many will detach from children, try to force them to become more normal, or be satisfied with keeping them in segregated facilities.

Lack of Leadership and Administrative Support

Directors of special education and school principals, whose positions make them natural leaders, rarely lead. A principal may know little about special needs and regard special education in his or her school as peripheral. Program directors are so encumbered with financial matters, hiring, and complaints that they have little time for program development, for regularly visiting classrooms and reinforcing staff, or for evaluating performance and providing counsel and training. Without leadership and administrative support, many staff feel alone.

Conflict and Lack of Coordination Between Families and Facilities

When families place their children in a program, they may expect a lot, keep a watchful eye on progress, continually evaluate services, and advocate strongly. Sometimes assertiveness is met with defensiveness from staff and administrators who believe resources are scarce and parents are a pain. Escalating conflict ensues, moving from letters to hearings, appeals, and lawsuits. Some parents are passive, thankful for what they have found or believing it is the school's job, not theirs, to educate their children. In this situation, staff and families do not use or create opportunities to share knowledge and skill (Cutler, 1991).

In either case, children's educations seldom involve collaborative assessment, planning, teaching, and evaluation. Parents and staff frequently misunderstand each other's needs, goals, and knowledge. Parents may be excluded from more than minimal participation. Consequently, interaction between children and their teachers and parents becomes quite different, hindering generalization of beneficial change from one environment to another and wasting opportunities to increase progress. In sum, natural collaborators may become or remain adversaries or strangers.

Disempowerment and Alienation from Work

Alienated labor means a worker has little control over the goals or organization of his or her work; the work is specialized and routinized; the worker's knowledge and skill become more limited; and the worker has little control over the results of his or her labor (e.g., is unable to predict outcomes) (Larson, 1980). The effects of alienated labor include difficulty in the worker's understanding of the goals and organization of the work, a sense that one's efforts have little use or meaning, an experience that the "object" worked on seems alien, a feeling of disempowerment, and eventually detachment from the work process and perhaps fellow workers.

The concept of alienated labor applies to many special education programs and, increasingly, to human services workers in general (Arches, 1991; Wolfensberger, 1991). While staff see students as people, specialization and routinization encourage staff to see behavior as raw material to work on—mold and shape. The more the goal of behavior change predominates over nurturing interaction, the more teachers see children as objects. Eventually, some teachers become alienated from the educational process and perhaps from their working self ("What am I doing here?").

Also, specialization renders staff competent in a small portion of the work process. Classroom teachers may not know how to provide therapies, and one therapist does not know what other therapists know how to do. This leaves each with a fear of poorly serving the children and being found incompetent. In time, some staff become passive and others become alienated from colleagues as they guard their turf (i.e., students, methods) in an effort to protect jobs and self-esteem. This hinders the development of coordinated programs.

Finally, although most staff invest a great deal in students, many feel powerless to affect day-to-day conditions, such as the curriculum or class composition (Bart, 1984; Tomlinson, 1982). Administrators may not be able to hold staff accountable for inadequate instruction and lack of progress, and staff may be unable to hold administrators accountable for lack of support. Educators' perceived inability to have an effect results in their belief that it makes no sense to plan long-term program development. This results in a strategy of just getting by, thus completing the vicious circle.

SUMMARY

This chapter describes shortcomings in current practices with respect to the three common human needs discussed in Chapter 1. Two things should be made clear. First, as sensitive and intelligent observers, educators are aware of the shortcomings in special education. Second, shortcomings do not make a case for pessimism. They flow neither from the nature of disabilities nor from educators' and families' lack of effort. Rather, they stem from a flawed model of psychosocial development and stifling working conditions that this book and *Guidelines and Protocols for Practice* try to help remedy.

A major implication of this chapter is that to improve practices, and hence outcomes, a better understanding of psychosocial development is needed (this is discussed in chaps. 3–6, this volume). Educators and families also need a way to empower one another so they can develop coordinated programs in which innovative practices become the standard (see chap. 8, this volume).

REFERENCES

Abel, W. (1989). *The effect of organizational rationalization on social interactions within community-based residential programs for mentally handicapped people.* Unpublished doctoral dissertation, Boston University.

Ames, L.B., Gillespie, C., Haines, J., & Illg, F. (1980). *Gesell developmental schedules* (rev. ed.). Lumberville, PA: Gesell Institute for Human Development Programs for Education.

Arches, J. (1991, May). Social structure, burnout, and job satisfaction. *Social Work, 36*(3), 202–206.

Baer, D. (1962). Laboratory control of thumbsucking by withdrawal of reinforcement. *Journal of the Experimental Analysis of Behavior, 5*, 525–528.

Bailey, D.B., & Wolery, M. (1984). *Teaching infants and preschoolers with handicaps.* Columbus, OH: Charles E. Merrill.

Baker, G.B., & Hacker, P.M.S. (1984). *Language, sense and nonsense.* Oxford, England: Basil Blackwell.

Bart, D.S. (1984). The differential diagnosis of special education: Managing social pathology as individual disability. In L. Barton & S. Tomlinson (Eds.), *Special education and social interests* (pp. 81–121). New York: Nichols Publishing Company.

Bayley, N. (1969). *Bayley Scales of Infant Development.* New York: The Psychological Corporation.

Belmore, K.J., & Brown, L. (1978). A job skill inventory strategy designed for severely handicapped potential workers. In N. Haring & D. Bricker (Eds.), *Teaching the severely handicapped: Volume III.* Columbus, OH: Special Press.

Bijou, S.W. (1957). Methodology for an experimental analysis of young children. *Psychological Reports, 3*, 243–250.

Billingsley, F. (1984). Where are the generalized outcomes? *Journal of The Association for the Severely Handicapped, 9*, 186–200.

Bluma, S.M., Shearer, M.S., Froham, A.H., & Hillard, J.M. (1976). *Portage guide to early education* (No. 12). Portage, WI: Cooperative Educational Agency.

Bricker, D.B. (1986). *Early education of at-risk and handicapped infants, toddlers, and preschool children.* Glenview, IL: Scott, Foresman.

Bronfenbrenner, U. (1977). Toward an experimental ecology of human development. *American Psychologist, 72*, 512–531.

Brown, F., Evans, I.M., Weed, K.A., & Owens, V. (1987). Delineating functional competence: A component model. *Journal of The Association for Persons with Severe Handicaps, 12*(2), 117–124.

Brown, L., Falvey, M., Vincent, L., Kaye, N., Johnson, F., Farra-Parish, P., & Gruenewald, L.C. (1980). Strategies for generating comprehensive, longitudinal and chronological age appropriate, individual educational programs for adolescents and young adult severely handicapped students. *Journal of Special Education, 14*, 199–215.

Brown, L., Pumpian, I., Baumgart, D., Van Deventer, P., Ford, A., Nisbet, J., Schroeder, J., & Gruenewald, L. (1981). Longitudinal transition plans in programs for severely handicapped students. *Exceptional Children, 47*, 624–630.

Brown, R. (1973). *A first language: The early stages.* Cambridge, MA: Harvard University Press.

Cohen, M., & Gross, P. (1979). *The developmental resource: Behavioral sequences for assessment and program planning (Vol. 1).* New York: Grune & Stratton.

Cutler, B.C. (1991). *Families and services in autism: Promises to keep.* Unpublished doctoral dissertation, Boston University School of Education.

Cutler, B.C. (1993). *You, your child, and "special" education: A guide to making the system work.* Baltimore: Paul H. Brookes Publishing Co.

Donnellan-Walsh, A., Gossage, L.D., LaVigna, G.W., Schuler, A.L., & Traphagen, J. (1976). *Teaching makes a difference: A guide for developing successful classes for autistic and other severely handicapped children—Teacher's manual.* California State Department of Education.

Dunst, C.J. (1980). *A clinical and educational manual for use with the Uzgiris and Hunt scales of infant psychological development.* Austin, TX: PRO-ED.

Dunst, C.J. (1981). *Infant learning: A cognitive-linguistic intervention strategy.* Hingham, MA: Teaching Resources.

Erickson, E.H. (1959). Growth and crises of the healthy personality. *Psychological Issues, 1*(1), 50–100.

Ferster, C.B., & DeMyer, M.K. (1961). The development of performance in autistic children in an automatically controlled environment. *Journal of Chronic Diseases, 13*, 312–345.

Fewell, R.R., & Rich, J.S. (1987). Play assessment as a procedure for examining cognitive, communication, and social skills in multihandicapped children. *Journal of Psychoeducational Assessment, 2*, 107–118.

Flavell, J.H. (1963). *The developmental psychology of Jean Piaget.* New York: VanNostrand Reinhold.

Fredericks, H.D., Riggs, C., Furey, T., Grove, D., Moore, W., McDonnell, J., Jordan, E., Hanson, W., Baldwin, V., & Wadlow, M. (1976). *The teaching research curriculum for moderately and severely handicapped.* Springfield, Il: Charles C Thomas.

Freeman, A. (1989). Diagnosis as explanation. *Early Child Development and Care, 44*, 61–72.

Freud, S. (1964). *Standard edition (Vol. 23).* London: Hogarth Press.

Furano, S., O'Reilly, K.A., Hosaka, C.M., Inatsuka, T., Allman, T.L., & Zelsloft, B. (1979). *Hawaii early education profile.* Palo Alto, CA: VORT Corp.

Garwood, G. (1982). (Mis)use of developmental scales in program evaluation. *Topics in Early Childhood Special Education, 1*, 61–69.

Gaussen, T. (1984). Developmental milestones and conceptual millstones: Some practical and theoretical limitations in infant assessment procedures. *Child: Care, Health, and Development, 10*, 99–115.

Gaylord-Ross, R., & Holvoet, J. (1985). *Strategies of educating students with severe handicaps.* Boston: Little, Brown.

Gesell, A., & Amatruda, C. (1969). *Developmental diagnosis.* New York: Harper & Row.

Goffman, E. (1963). *Stigma: Notes on the management of spoiled identity.* New York: Simon & Schuster.

Gold, M. (1975). Vocational training. In J. Wortis (Ed.), *Mental retardation and developmental disabilities: An annual review (Vol. 7).* New York: Brunner/Mazel.

Gold, M. (1980). *Try another way: Training manual.* Champaign, Il: Research Press.

Greenwald, C.A., & Leonard, L.B. (1979). Communication and sensorimotor development of Down's syndrome children. *American Journal of Mental Deficiency, 84*, 296–303.

Hamblin, R.L., Buckholdt, D., Ferritor, D., Kozloff, M., & Blackwell, L. (1971). *The humanization processes.* New York: John Wiley and Sons.

Hewett, F.M. (1965). Teaching speech to an autistic child through operant conditioning. *American Journal of Orthopsychiatry, 35,* 552–560.

Holland, J.G., & Skinner, B.F. (1961). *The analysis of behavior.* New York: McGraw-Hill.

Homme, L., Csanyi, A.P., Gonzales, M.A., & Reches, J.R. (1969). *How to use contingency contracting in the classroom.* Champaign, Il: Research Press.

Hughes, D., & May, D. (1986). Order, rules and social control in two training centres for mentally retarded adults. *Sociological Review, 34,* 158–184.

Johnson-Martin, N.M., Jens, K.G., Attermeier, S.M., & Hacker, B.J. (1991). *The Carolina curriculum for infants and toddlers with special needs.* Baltimore: Paul H. Brookes Publishing Co.

Kamii, C., & DeVries, R. (1974). Piaget for early education. In R.K. Parker (Ed.), *The preschool in action* (2nd ed.). Needham Heights: Allyn & Bacon.

Larson, M.S. (1980). Proletarianization and educated labor. *Theory and Society, 9,* 131–175.

Lindsley, O.R. (1956). Operant conditioning methods applied to research in chronic schizophrenia. *Psychiatric Research Reports, 5,* 118–139.

Lovaas, O.I., & Simmons, J.Q. (1969). Manipulation of self-destruction in three retarded children. *Journal of Applied Behavior Analysis, 2,* 143–159.

Lovitt, T.C. (1977). *In spite of my resistance, I've learned something from children.* Columbus, OH: Charles E. Merrill.

Martin, A. (1988). Screening, early intervention, and remediation: Obscuring children's potential. *Harvard Education Review, 58,* 4, 488–501.

McCarthy, D. (1972). *Manual for the McCarthy scales of children's abilities.* New York: The Psychological Group.

Mulligan, M., Lacy, L., & Guess, D. (1982). The effects of massed, distributed, and spaced trial sequencing on severely handicapped students' performance. *Journal of The Association for the Severely Handicapped, 7,* 48–61.

Neel, R.S., & Billingsley, F.F. (1989). *IMPACT: A functional curriculum handbook for students with moderate to severe disabilities.* Baltimore: Paul H. Brookes Publishing Co.

Neisworth, J.T., & Bagnato, S.J. (1987). *The young exceptional child: Early development and education.* New York: Macmillan.

Phillips, G.M. (1991). *Communication incompetencies: A theory of training oral performance behaviors.* Carbondale, Il: Southern Illinois University Press.

Piaget, J. (1952). *The origins of intelligence in children.* New York: International Universities Press.

Piaget, J. (1954). *The construction of reality in the child.* New York: Basic Books.

Pyecha, J. (1980). *A national survey of individualized educational programs (IEPs) for handicapped children. Vol. 1: Executive summary. Final report.* Washington, DC: Office of Special Education. (ERIC Document Reproduction Service No. ED 199 970)

Risley, T.R., & Wolf, M.M. (1967). Experimental manipulation of autistic behavior and generalization into the home. In R. Ulrich, T. Stachnik, & J. Mabry (Eds.), *Control of human behavior.* Glenview, IL: Scott, Foresman.

Rogers, S. (1977). Characteristics of the cognitive development of profoundly retarded children. *Child Development, 48,* 837–843.

Sailor, W., & Guess, D. (1983). *Severely handicapped students: An instructional design.* Boston: Houghton Mifflin.

Sapon, S.M., & Reeback, R.T. (1968). *Shaping vocal antecedents to productive verbal behavior in a nine year old Mongoloid boy.* Reports from the verbal behavior laboratory. Rochester, NY: University of Rochester.

Sasso, G.M., Reimers, T.M., Cooper, L.J., Wacker, D., Berg, W., Steege, M., Kelly, L., & Allaire, A. (1992). Use of descriptive and experimental analyses to identify the functional properties of aberrant behavior in school settings. *Journal of Applied Behavior Analysis, 25*(4), 809–821.

Schopler, E., & Reichler, R.J. (1978). *Psycho-educational profile: Individualized assessment for autistic and developmentally disabled children: Home treatment program.* Baltimore: University Park Press.

Schopler, E., & Reichler, R.J. (1982). *Teaching strategies for parents and professionals: Individualized assessment and treatment for autistic and developmentally disabled children.* Baltimore: University Park Press.

Schwebel, M., & Ralph, J. (Eds.). (1973). *Piaget in the classroom.* New York: Basic Books.

Sigafoos, J., & Dempsey, R. (1992). Assessing choice among children with multiple disabilities. *Journal of Applied Behavior Analysis, 25*(3), 747–755.

Smith, D.D. (1981). *Teaching the learning disabled.* Englewood Cliffs, NJ: Prentice Hall.

Snyder-McLean, L., McLean, J.E., & Etter, R. (1988). Clinical assessment of sensorimotor knowledge in nonverbal, severely retarded clients. *Topics in Language Disorders, 8*(4), 1–22.

Staats, A.W. (Ed.). (1964). *Human learning.* New York: Holt, Rinehart & Winston.

Sternberg, L., Ritchey, H., Pegnatore, L., Wills, L., & Hill, C. (1986). *A curriculum for profoundly handicapped students: The Broward county model program.* Rockville, MD: Aspen Publishers Inc.

Stetson, F. (1985). *L.I.F.E.: Learning in functional environments: A training program for teachers of severely handicapped students.* Houston: Region IV, Educational Service Center.

Tawney, J.A., Knapp, D.S., O'Reilly, C.D., & Pratt, S.S. (1979). *Programmed environments curriculum.* Columbus, OH: Charles E. Merrill.

Terrace, H.S. (1963). Discrimination learning with and without "errors." *Journal of the Experimental Analysis of Behavior, 6,* 1–27.

Thiagarajian, S., Semmel, D., & Semmel, M. (1974). *Instructional development for training teachers of exceptional children: A sourcebook.* Reston, VA: Council for Exceptional Children.

Thurman, S.K., & Widerstrom, A.H. (1990). *Infants and young children with special needs: A developmental and ecological approach* (2nd ed.). Baltimore: Paul H. Brookes Publishing Co.

Tilton, J.R., Liska, D.L., & Bourland, D. (1977). *A guide to early development training.* Boston: Allyn & Bacon.

Tomlinson, S. (1982). *A sociology of special education.* London: Routledge & Kegan Paul.

Uzgiris, I., & Hunt, J.M. (1975). *Assessment in infancy: Ordinal scales of psychological development.* Urbana: University of Illinois Press.

Valletutti, P.J., & Bender, M. (1985). *Teaching the moderately and severely handicapped. A functional curriculum for communication and socialization. Vol. II* (2nd ed.). Austin, TX: PRO-ED.

Wahler, R.G. (1969). Setting generality: Some specific and general effects of child behavior therapy. *Journal of Applied Behavior Analysis, 2,* 239–246.

Weisenfeld, R.B. (1986). The IEPs of Down Syndrome children: A content analysis. *Education and Training of the Mentally Retarded, 21*(3), 211–219.

White, O.R., & Haring, N.G. (1976). *Exceptional teaching.* Columbus, OH: Charles E. Merrill.

Wolfensberger, W. (1991). Reflections on a lifetime in human services and mental retardation. *Mental Retardation, 29*(1), 1–15.

Yearley, S., & Brewer, J.D. (1989). Stigma and conversational competence: A conversation analytic study of the mentally handicapped. *Human Studies, 12*(1–2), 97–115.

CHAPTER 3

LEARNING THROUGH INTERACTION WITH ENVIRONMENTS

CHAPTERS 3–6 PROVIDE TWO MODELS THAT CAN IMPROVE EDUCATIONAL PRACTICES. ONE SHOWS HOW simpler behaviors are assembled into larger units forming a child's functional behavioral repertoire. The second describes progressive change in competence and social membership (i.e., psychosocial development).

This chapter focuses on an elemental level of the functional behavioral repertoire—namely, respondent reflexes and operant (purposive) actions. It offers suggestions for assessment, program planning, instruction, and evaluation that are applied to the five phases of learning in Chapter 4, this volume.

PSYCHOSOCIAL DEVELOPMENT, FUNCTIONAL BEHAVIORAL REPERTOIRE, INTERACTION, AND LEARNING

The functional behavioral repertoire is the set of behaviors a person uses to participate in the everyday world. It includes acting (e.g., communicating), thinking (e.g., planning), and feeling (e.g., pleasure). The functional behavioral repertoire is not ready-made at birth; it is a lifelong collaborative project. The term *psychosocial development* refers to progressive improvement in one's functional behavioral repertoire, in the person one is perceived to be, and in the membership status one is accorded.

Maturation certainly plays a role in psychosocial development. Yet, much learning is involved, as suggested by the fact that simple movements are gradually assembled into actions, tasks, activities, and roles that are performed in certain places with greater or lesser frequency, skill, duration, and effort.

Behavior, Learning, and Interaction

It may seem unusual to regard feeling and thinking as behavior. Yet, these aspects of behavior, along with acting, change as humans interact with their surroundings. *Learning, therefore, means regular changes in behavior resulting from interaction.*

The crucial words in this definition are "resulting from interaction." Changes due to aging, drugs, illness, or lack of sleep should not be considered learned. Even so, one usually has to look closely to determine what is being learned. Sam, for example, now walks slowly down the hall when Ms. Gonzales holds his hand. But Sam's "improved" walking depends on the restrictive prompts from Ms. Gonzales. The instant she lets go, Sam runs. To determine what children are really learning, therefore, one must identify the events to which they are responding. Sam has not learned to walk slowly; he has learned not to resist Ms. Gonzales's grip.

Learning occurs through interaction—cycles of action and reaction with the physical environment, with others in social exchanges and activities, and with one's own behavior. The following are some examples.

Interaction with Features of the Physical Environment

Indra is hammering nails into soft wood. With each swing, either she misses, bends a nail sideways, or lands a direct hit. Each nail's "reaction" to Indra's swing teaches Indra about the effects of observing, aiming, force, and angles. She uses this information to guide her next hammering actions.

Interaction with Others in Exchanges

Alone in the living room, 6-year-old Bart listens with envy as Mom feeds 2-year-old Maggie in the kitchen. When at last Maggie toddles into the living room, Bart shoves her. Maggie tumbles and yells; Mom runs into the living room and scolds Bart. This teaches Bart that shoving Maggie is a way to get Mom running.

Interaction Within One's Own Behavior Stream

As Bill enters the classroom, Ms. Wright notices her breathing quickens and her abdomen tightens. She responds by telling herself, "I'm tense. Relax." She responds to the self-prescription by relaxing her neck and abdomen, breathing slowly, and visualizing productive interaction with Bill. Tension subsides. This consequence is *reinforcement* (information), teaching Ms. Wright the way to respond in similar circumstances.

The reinforcement Indra gets when nails go straight in, Bart gets when Mom scolds, and Ms. Wright gets when tension subsides is information generated by action—information they can use in choosing how to act in the future. With repetition (practice), the above interactions yield progressive change. Indra swings the hammer hard and straight more often; Bart shoves Maggie more often when Mom is out of sight, but near enough to hear; Ms. Wright notices certain sensations, calls them tension, and relaxes more often.

Principles of learning are statements about the sorts of behavior changes likely to occur under certain conditions (e.g., selectively reinforced features of behavior—skillfulness, effort, speed—are likely to increase). We can use principles of learning, found throughout this chapter and Chapter 4, this volume, to create environments that give children enough incentive and information about the world to be willing and able to change.

Five Phases of Learning

Learning means regular changes in behavior resulting from interaction with the physical environment, and others' as well as one's own behavior. What sorts of changes? A useful distinction is between early and later changes in the learning process. Five kinds of changes, or phases of learning, are acquisition, fluency, generalization, adaptation, and maintenance (Haring, Liberty, & White, 1980; Haring, White, & Liberty, 1978).

Acquisition   Acquisition, or skill building, is the early phase when a person learns which events to take as cues, how to perform the right movements or actions, and how to arrange actions into effective sequences. When reading, acquisition is when a child learns which letter combinations are cues to say specific words, and to read from left to right and from the end of one line to the start of the next.

Fluency   Fluency builds on acquisition. A child who has learned to read many words then learns to say them faster, string them into sentences, omit unnecessary mouth movements and sounds, read for longer periods, and read aloud at a proper level of intensity.

Generalization   The third phase, generalization, refers to the spread of behaviors learned in one environment to other environments. For instance, a child learns to read at home as well as school, stories as well as instructions, from the television screen and billboards as well as pages, and blue and red letters as well as black letters. Generalization implies that a person knows which differences in environments are relevant and which are not relevant to the task at hand.

Adaptation   Adaptation means altering the way a behavior is performed (the form) to suit circumstances. Examples include reading near a window if a light bulb burns out, pointing to each word if the print is small, asking for help in saying a new word, and holding a book open with one hand if the binding is stiff.

Maintenance   Maintenance concerns the durability of behavior when instruction ends. To foster maintenance, one strengthens fluency and adaptation, and gradually fades the amount of prompting and reinforcement.

The typical special education program focuses on acquisition. The usual assessment report, for instance, gives a child's score on a test of reading comprehension, or lists words a child reads, but reveals little about the smoothness, attentiveness, and length of the child's reading episodes, or about the range of materials the child reads. Similarly, program plans specify how to teach new words, but have few suggestions about generalization, fluency, maintenance, and adaptation. All special education practices, from assessment through program evaluation, must focus on the five phases of learning. Otherwise, there will be little improvement in children's competent participation in daily life.

ASSOCIATION OF EVENTS WITH REGULAR CHANGES IN BEHAVIOR

When people interact with their environments, they receive information. Some of this information comes before one performs a behavior, signifying that the next event is going to happen, or that certain actions will have certain consequences. Such antecedent events cue what one feels, thinks, and does next.

Other events, called prompts and obstacles, occur during performance, influencing the manner of the performance. There are several kinds of prompts, including accentuating relevant features of the setting (e.g., making cues and consequences more noticeable); gestures (e.g., pointing to a tool Juan is looking for); instructions (e.g., telling Indra to use her right hand); models (showing how); templates and devices for guiding movements and increasing strength (e.g., holding materials in a vice); and manual, or hands-on, assistance.

In contrast to prompts, some events hinder learning and performance. A teacher may use a manual prompt that is too forceful, a room may be too noisy, there may be no tools to strengthen a child's grip, and areas of a home or classroom may look so similar that children do not notice relevant differences and therefore play where they are supposed to eat, for example.

Other events occur after a response. As consequences, they give informative feedback on effects, such as one's performance was successful (reinforcement), produced pain or loss (punishment), or had no effect (extinction).

Table 3.1 illustrates functional relationships between ongoing behavior and the antecedent events, prompts, obstacles, and consequences that surround it. The next sections examine each functional relationship shown in Table 3.1.

ANTECEDENTS OF BEHAVIOR

Behavior rarely just occurs. Unconditioned stimuli and conditioned stimuli elicit specific movements and feelings—a kind of respondent behavior. Discriminative stimuli, however, initiate actions and thoughts—operant behavior.

Table 3.1.   Functional relationships between ongoing behavior and environment

Antecedents (occasions)	Behavior (feelings, thoughts, actions)	Consequences (provide informative feedback)
Discriminative stimuli provide information about the consequences of next responses.	↑ Prompts (assists) and hindrances including: Accentuating relevant features of settings Gestures Instructions Models Tools, templates, and jigs Manual	Positive reinforcement Negative reinforcement Type I punishment Type II punishment Extinction
Unconditioned stimuli (e.g., thunder) elicit unconditioned responses (e.g., fright).		
Conditioned stimuli (e.g., lightning) provide information about next events (e.g., thunder) and, therefore, elicit conditioned responses (fright).		

Events Can Become Cues Through Respondent Learning

Some events, called *stimuli,* elicit specific movements and feelings called *respondents.* The relationship between a stimulus and an elicited respondent is a *reflex* (Pavlov, 1927).

Unconditioned (Unlearned) Reflexes   Some stimuli elicit respondents, such as attention, pleasure, and pain, without prior learning or training. A person who bumps his or her nose against a door is instantly alert, feels pain, and experiences watery eyes. The bumped nose is an *unconditioned stimulus*—unconditioned because it elicits responses without prior training in nose-bumping. Responses to unconditioned stimuli are called *unconditioned responses* because one does not have to learn to make them in reaction to eliciting stimuli. The connection between an unconditioned stimulus (bumped nose) and an unconditioned response (attention, tears, and pain) is an *unconditioned reflex.*

Conditioned Reflexes   Most stimuli elicit reflexive movements and feelings through experience or training. For example, 1-year-old Brenda is in an early intervention program. She is being fed by Mr. Lee, a new teacher. Each bite of food elicits pleasure in Brenda, revealed in her smiles and giggles. Each bite is an *unconditioned stimulus;* with no prior teaching, food elicits Brenda's pleasure and increased attention (orientation) to the environment. Brenda's pleasure and attention are *unconditioned responses.*

Unlike the food, Mr. Lee elicits no feelings and strong attention in Brenda. His touch, voice, and smell are neutral stimuli, meaning or signifying nothing to Brenda. However, respondent conditioning is taking place while Mr. Lee feeds Brenda.

Each time Mr. Lee gives Brenda a bite of food, it is a *conditioning trial*—an occasion when Brenda experiences food and pleasure at about the same time she experiences neutral stimuli, such as Mr. Lee. After a week of "conditioning," Brenda is immediately attentive and expresses pleasure when she hears Mr. Lee's voice and footsteps, smells his cologne, and is held in his arms.

When previously neutral stimuli (i.e., Mr. Lee's face and voice) elicit the same responses in Brenda (i.e., pleasure and increased attention) that food has elicited all along, the previously neutral stimuli are called *conditioned stimuli*—their ability to elicit responses came only through Brenda's experience. The pleasure and attention elicited by the newly conditioned stimuli are *conditioned responses.* The connections between the newly conditioned stimuli and the newly conditioned responses are *conditioned reflexes.*

The following diagram illustrates what has happened.

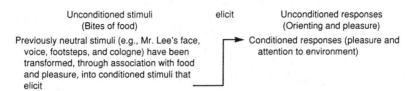

Briefly, many previously neutral and even unnoticed events are, through association, taking on significance or meaning for Brenda (Dawson, Catania, Schell, & Grings, 1979). She is experiencing interaction with Mr. Lee as orderly; she is acquiring knowledge that certain events (e.g., greetings from Mr. Lee) predict or signify what happens next—being held, eating, and feeling pleasure. These antecedent events now evoke the same attention and pleasure that food alone used to evoke.

Social Exchanges and Reciprocal Respondent Conditioning During social exchanges between two people, respondent conditioning happens to both people. Referring to the example above, Brenda is not the only participant whose feelings and attention are being conditioned; Mr. Lee had no previous experience with infants. Consequently, many of Brenda's behaviors, such as wiggling and turning her head, made him uneasy. There was also much about Brenda's appearance and behavior Mr. Lee did not even notice. However, the more Mr. Lee fed Brenda, the more often, faster, and intensely Brenda smiled, giggled, and snuggled up to him. It so happens that being smiled at, giggled at, and snuggled up to are stimuli that have long been able to elicit pleasure in Mr. Lee. The hundreds of associations between Brenda's previously neutral, or (to Mr. Lee) mildly discomforting, behaviors and the pleasure elicited by Brenda's smiles, giggles, and snuggling resulted in Brenda's face, smell, hair color, smile, eye contact, and wiggling eliciting Mr. Lee's attention and pleasure.

Another example of reciprocal respondent conditioning is found in exchanges between Jerry and Ms. Tyler. Jerry's whining and self-injurious behaviors elicit fear and anger in Ms. Tyler. At the same time, the boring tasks, long teaching sessions, and lack of reinforcement from Ms. Tyler make interaction with her painful for Jerry. The frequent associations between Jerry's presence and his disruptive behavior, as well as Ms. Tyler's anger, have left Ms. Tyler feeling angry whenever she is with Jerry, even when he is quiet or when she thinks about him after school. Jerry feels displeasure when he is around Ms. Tyler. In fact, praise and hugs from her make him queasy. Therefore, he stops doing anything that produces praise or hugs from her.

Reciprocal respondent conditioning affects the course of future exchanges. Because Ms. Tyler is an aversive stimulus to Jerry, he tries to escape in ways that she does not like (e.g., turning away). This makes Jerry even more aversive to Ms. Tyler, which results in her behaving harshly to him, therefore making her even more aversive to Jerry. They are caught in a vicious cycle.

However, because Brenda and Mr. Lee bring each other pleasure, each is likely to do even more that makes the other feel good, which further increases their attention and liking of each other. In other words, reciprocal respondent conditioning of people's feelings helps create and sustain interaction patterns that have long-term effects, such as mutual attraction or mutual hostility and avoidance. (See chap. 5, this volume, for a detailed discussion of exchanges.)

Knowledge of Respondent Conditioning

Crucial to the development of social bonds and the acquisition of commonsense knowledge is orienting and experiencing feelings in response to certain people and social activities. Yet, for many children with developmental disabilities, the natural environment has too few events that elicit attention and feeling (Koegel & Koegel, 1988). Indeed, such a deficit is part of the definition of autism. Thus, from the beginning of many children's educations, caregivers need to systematically associate neutral but important stimuli, such as their voices, certain words (come, look, good), facial expressions (smiles), and touch with stimuli that already elicit children's attention and feelings. The following vignette between a mother and her 2-year-old son shows how a parent helps to condition (i.e., make meaningful) previously neutral events.

> Donny splashes water and smiles (he elicits his own response). Mom laughs with him, says, "Splash, splash," and rubs his back (pointing out what he is doing and associating her touch with his pleasure). Mom invites him to do it again ("Donny, again. Again!") and praises him when he does ("Good. Big splash."). Mom helps Donny to make more big splashes that she associates with descriptive words ("Big splash. Big splash."). She hugs him while he is enjoying himself. She then raises his hand to make another splash, which elicits his attention, and shows him her smile and wide open eyes (a facial expression signifying anticipation, as though to say "Here it comes."). This associates her expression with Donny's apparent feelings of anticipation of the big splash. As she brings his hand down to slap the water, she says "Down." Donny again laughs at the splash. Mom repeats this several more times, each time saying "Down" along with the action. Donny raises his own hand. Mom says "Now, down!" Donny slaps the water, and Mom hugs him.

There are numerous opportunities each day to arrange the conditioning of beneficial reflexes, such that caregivers' voices and touch, social activities, and children's actions come to elicit attention and pleasure. However, conditions must be right for respondent conditioning to occur.

The louder the noise, the higher one jumps; the bigger the smile from a person one likes, the warmer one feels. In other words, the greater the *intensity* of a stimulus to which one is paying attention and that has the capacity to affect one, the greater the *magnitude* of one's unconditioned or conditioned response to it (Barry, 1975). Thus, if a teacher wants to get a child's attention or reinforce a behavior, the teacher ought to use stimuli intense enough to elicit strong attention. Perhaps children pay little attention in class and do not learn what instructions and room dividers are supposed to mean because stimuli do not stand out. Assessment and ongoing program evaluation should examine the salience of events in a child's life.

When Randy rocks gently, it takes 5 seconds for Mr. Conklin to feel discomfort. When Randy rocks vigorously, Mr. Conklin is startled immediately. Randy is learning the right way to get a big, quick response from Mr. Conklin. In sum, the greater the *intensity* of an unconditioned or conditioned stimulus (e.g., Randy's rocking), the less time it takes (*latency*) for the unconditioned or conditioned response (Mr. Conklin's startle response) to appear. Thus, if one wants children to respond quickly, one should present salient, meaningful stimuli. A subtle gesture or a meek question (e.g., "Can you come here?") rarely evoke speedy responses.

If lightning were no longer followed by thunder, lightning would no longer signify that thunder is on the way and would eventually lose its capacity to elicit fright. Something like this has begun to happen between Jerry and Ms. Tyler. She has stopped paying so much attention to (and accidently reinforcing) Jerry's whining. Instead, she relaxes when he is disruptive and reinforces desirable behaviors often. She also uses materials and tasks that are interesting to Jerry and stops sessions before he is tired. In other words, Ms. Tyler has enriched Jerry's environment. As a result, Jerry's whining has decreased and happy participation has increased. As Jerry's behavior improves, so do Ms. Tyler's feelings—she no longer dislikes being around him. What accounts for changed feelings?

Respondent Extinction   The answer to the above question is *respondent extinction*. Each time Jerry and Ms. Tyler interact without Jerry whining and fussing, it is a respondent extinction trial—an instance when Ms. Tyler does not experience an association among Jerry's presence, whining, and her perceived helplessness and aggravation. In other words, if conditioned stimuli (Jerry's presence) are experienced over and over in the absence of the unconditioned stimuli (Jerry's disruptive behavior) that give emotional significance to Jerry's presence, then respondent extinction will occur; that is, the conditioned stimuli lose the capacity to elicit conditioned responses. Thus, Jerry's presence no longer means the same thing—aggravation—to Ms. Tyler.

Respondent extinction can be combined with respondent conditioning to replace conditioned emotional responses with new ones. For example, 5-year-old Jessie was physically abused. Through respondent conditioning, she was terrified of her parents and other adults. Several times a day for a month, Jessie's counselor associated her own presence and soothing voice with Jessie's favorite music and ice cream (stimuli that already elicited pleasure in Jessie). Gradually, the counselor was able to get closer to Jessie until eventually she and Jessie could sit and play together with Jessie feeling pleasure rather than fear. Other caregivers then used the same method.

The respondent extinction part of the example involved *disassociating* caregivers from pain and loud voices that elicited Jessie's fear; the new respondent conditioning involved teaching Jessie that the presence of caregivers signified safety and pleasure. Together, the two methods or processes are called *counterconditioning*.

After Jessie's interactions with the counselor and others, a teacher working with Jessie used a forceful manual prompt. Jessie cried and withdrew. Within a week, she was as fearful of adults as before. In sum, reassociations between conditioned stimuli (adults' presence) and ol' unconditioned stimuli (pain at an adult's hand) can keep alive a conditioned reflex (adults' presence elicits fear). In other words, conditioned responses never die; they wait to be elicited. This has two implications. First, assessment and ongoing program evaluation should determine what conditioned reflexes have been established in a child, whether old fears and pains are being restimulated, and whether enough is being done to extinguish or countercondition such responses. Second, to reliably weaken conditioned responses, one has to extinguish them in the presence of many events that can elicit them. Using Jessie as an example, she could be innoculated against potential fear-eliciting stimuli (e.g., frowns, loud requests, angry faces) by gradually exposing her to them, all the while presenting pleasure- or relaxation-eliciting stimuli. In addition, she could be taught to make bold responses in otherwise uncomfortable situations.

Respondent Stimulus Generalization Another important respondent learning process is *respondent stimulus generalization*. Jessie had been afraid of adults who looked, moved, or spoke like those who had abused her. Brenda now smiles and giggles when held by people who have not fed her, especially men who look like Mr. Lee. Likewise, when Jerry and Ms. Tyler were adversaries, Jerry avoided women with whom he had never interacted, and Ms. Tyler was aggravated by students who looked or sounded like Jerry. In sum, the more closely other events resemble unconditioned or conditioned stimuli, the more likely those other events are to elicit similar conditioned responses.

Respondent stimulus generalization often is based on the physical resemblance of stimuli, as in the above examples. Generalization can be based on other factors as well. For example, Jerry's parents, Mr. and Mrs. Hardy, always have an excuse for why they cannot join a group of parents and teachers who support each other and swap ideas. Some teachers think the Hardys are uninterested in their son's education. The fact is, the Hardys become sad when they think about being in a parent-teacher group. How can this be if the Hardys have never been in any such group? The answer is this: The Hardys believe their efforts on Jerry's behalf have been failures, and each failure has made them sad. Joining a parent-teacher group is among those events that resemble one another conceptually; they are all "chances to fail our son." Thus, the *thought* of joining a group (another place to fail) elicits sadness. (Chap. 9, this volume, discusses how to help families with issues such as this.)

Respondent Stimulus Discrimination and Habituation Brenda used to smile at Mr. Perkins, who looks a lot like Mr. Lee (respondent stimulus generalization). She no longer does. The reason is *respondent stimulus discrimination*. Mr. Perkins does not feed Brenda, or do anything else that elicits attention and pleasure from her. Thus, Brenda has learned an important difference between Mr. Perkins and Mr. Lee. Her responses have become discriminated—reserved for places where Mr. Lee and food are to be found. To prevent this from happening, new places and people must occasionally be associated with attention- and pleasure-eliciting stimuli.

Mr. Lee has been feeding Brenda the same food and talking to her the same way for 2 months. Recently, Brenda has become inattentive, and the magnitude of smiling and giggling has lessened. These changes represent *habituation*. Brenda has had her fill. If Mr. Lee continues using the same food and talk, these events will stop evoking any attention and pleasure in Brenda (neutral stimuli). If he persists, they will become aversive and Brenda will start squirming and spitting the food.

Habituation may occur in a *constant* setting. For example, it takes only about 3 minutes of continuous exposure to his or her mother's face for an infant to habituate (Bornstein & Ludemann, 1989). Thus, one should rotate tasks, places, reinforcers, ways of talking, and other events to which one wants children to continue responding. However, if one wants a child to stop responding to an event, one should reduce the intensity of the event and not vary it. For example, Juan frequently ran toward the street as a way of getting Mr. Eaton to chase him. Realizing he was unwittingly reinforcing a behavior he wanted to replace, Mr. Eaton started going after Juan in an unexciting way. In time, Juan habituated to Mr. Eaton's tepid response and it lost its reinforcing effect.

Operant Discrimination Learning

Orienting and feeling (respondents) are reactions *to* the environment. Acting and thinking are purposive. They operate *on* the environment and are termed *operants* (Skinner, 1953). Operant behavior is initiated by *discriminative stimuli* (cues). Cues provide information that: 1) it is now possible to perform certain responses, and/or 2) certain responses will have certain results. When a behavior is performed in response to some events and not others, one can say that *operant stimulus discrimination,* or *stimulus control,* has been achieved (Holland & Skinner, 1961). Below are examples of behavior that is initiated by specific cues.

Learning How To Respond to Threats

Ms. Rogers found that when her son Steven woke up fussy and with little appetite, he would be a "tantrum-throwing monster" by afternoon. She also learned that if she did not ask Steven to do chores and gave him free access to music and snacks, she could avoid Steven's afternoon antics. Now, whenever Steven wakes up with red eyes, has no appetite, and is fussy, Ms. Rogers begins placating him.

Transferring Stimulus Control to Natural Cues

Indra learned the steps in making a sandwich, but needed special cues. For instance, she only opened the refrigerator door and took out cheese and mustard when she saw pictures of cheese and a jar of mustard taped to the door. Also, before she wheeled herself to the bread cabinet, she waited for Mr. Hawkins to point to it.

Mr. Hawkins decided to teach Indra to look for, notice, and respond to natural cues for each step in the task. In practice, he gradually faded the intensity and completeness of the special cues, while directing Indra to respond to natural cues.

The first day, Mr. Hawkins covered the pictures of cheese and mustard with a sheet of tissue paper that was the same color as the refrigerator door. Seeing the pictures through the paper, Indra took out the cheese and mustard as usual. The next day Mr. Hawkins covered the pictures (which he had trimmed in size) with two sheets of smaller tissue paper. Still seeing the faint pictures, as well as the visually larger refrigerator door (the natural cue), Indra got out the cheese and mustard. By the end of the week, a tiny piece of opaque paper was in the spot where the pictures used to be. As Indra began to open the refrigerator, Mr. Hawkins suggested that she remove the paper cue and throw it away.

The above vignettes show that when certain events reliably precede a behavior that is reinforced (or punished), these events may become cues or discriminative stimuli (sometimes called

S+) for a person to perform the previously reinforced (and not to perform the previously punished) behaviors. The next vignette shows how events do not become cues.

What Happens When Words Are Inconsequential

Four children in Mr. MacDuff's class are wandering around the room. "Sit down or you won't get to go to recess," he says with an angry voice. They continue roaming. In a few minutes, Mr. MacDuff repeats the threat. Finally, he leads each child to his or her seat. When it is time for recess, they all go.

   Mr. MacDuff is showing prisms and magnifying glasses. Some children pay attention, but Mr. MacDuff rarely looks, praises, or calls on them. Some are half asleep. They, too, get no reactions from him. Others are "falling" out of their seats or dropping books onto the floor. Mr. MacDuff repeatedly tells them to stop ("Jeff, sit up. Richard! Is that the way to treat your book?").

By the end of the year, no one pays attention to Mr. MacDuff's threats. When he tells them to get ready for a lesson, most students get a drowsy feeling. When he gives an instruction, they ignore it. In brief, Mr. MacDuff taught his students that his facial expressions, words, and tones of voice do not predict *reliable* or *salient* consequences (reinforcing or punishing) for any behaviors. Paying attention versus sleeping, sitting versus roaming, doing tasks versus dropping books are equally likely to be ignored or reinforced.

   This discussion focused on stimulus discrimination (i.e., behaviors happening in response to selected cues). Generalization, the next topic, refers to behaviors spreading to a wider range of cues.

Operant Stimulus Generalization

Referring again to Ms. Tyler, recall that she was irritated not only around Jerry, but around children who looked and sounded like Jerry. This is respondent stimulus generalization. The following vignette illustrates *operant stimulus generalization,* which has to do with the transfer of actions (not feelings) from environments where they were first learned.

Generalized Involvement

When school began, Becky rarely paid attention, cooperated, or took part in Ms. Thatcher's class. However, Ms. Thatcher frequently reinforced even small improvements in her behavior, and by November Becky was participating at a high level.

   Last Monday, Becky began taking Ms. Brookes's math class for an hour a day. By Thursday, Becky was participating at about the same high rate as in Ms. Thatcher's class even though she had not yet received as much reinforcement from Ms. Brookes. It should be noted that Ms. Brookes's class resembles Ms. Thatcher's class in many ways (e.g., female teacher, style of teaching, male aide, blue walls, desk arrangements).

Becky's involvement generalized from Ms. Thatcher's class, where it was first strengthened, to another environment that resembled it. Operant stimulus generalization often occurs without programming. After being instructed to step on the brake pedal in the presence of three or four red traffic lights, we do so on our own in the presence of other red traffic lights. Yet, it is a big mistake and an enormous waste to take generalization for granted. It is a mistake because children with developmental disabilities (as well as other children) do not automatically generalize skills from classrooms to daily life environments and vice versa. It is an enormous waste because the lack of generalization means that teaching has done little to further psychosocial development.

   Why is generalization difficult? There are at least four reasons. First, the materials, interaction format (teachers ask questions, children respond, teachers provide feedback), and the cues, prompts, and reinforcers in teaching environments may differ widely from those in community environments. In crossing streets, for example, Juan is so dependent upon prompts from Mr. Eaton

("Okay. Go!"), that when Mr. Eaton is not there Juan stands at the intersection, unable to use natural cues, such as the sight of other people crossing (models) or signs that flash "walk."

Second, when children do not receive much instruction on adapting behavior to a variety of environments, they are ill-equipped when their usual performances do not work. Knowing how to spread mustard only with a knife, Indra is unprepared for places with no knives.

Third, a child may hesitate to perform a task in a different environment because the child is not sufficiently fluent and because mistakes are aversive, perhaps because of past disapproval or lack of reinforcement for mistakes.

Fourth, a child may not notice or understand the significance of important similarities and irrelevant differences across environments. Juan, for instance, has operated only a few soda machines. For him, the relevant stimulus dimensions are a horizontal row of 2-inch square plastic push panels. When faced with a row of round buttons or a column of square panels, he becomes confused. In sum, because one cannot take generalization for granted, it is important to plan and program it as discussed in the next chapter.

CONSEQUENCES OF BEHAVIOR

Consequences affect how often, where, how fast, how long, how attentively, how skillfully, and how effortfully one performs certain actions and thoughts now and in the future. The following are a few examples:

1. Steven gets cookies for whining at Grandma Anne's house, but not at Aunt Dora's house. This differential reinforcement of whining depending on the location is why Steven whines so often at Grandma Anne's and so seldom at Aunt Dora's.
2. At first, Mr. Jackson reinforced even a few seconds of children's attention. As attention increased, he waited a little longer before reinforcing. This differential reinforcement of longer duration attention resulted in children paying attention for a half hour or more.
3. Ms. Nelson is much more likely to interact with students behaving calmly than with those behaving in a "hyper" fashion. Her differential reinforcement of low intensity behavior accounts for why more of her students are becoming calmer.

The above examples demonstrate that one is more likely to repeat a behavior that was reinforced, to repeat it in places where it was reinforced, and to repeat the forms (e.g., speed, duration, skill, intensity) being enacted at the time of reinforcement. However, one is less likely than before to repeat a behavior that was punished or had no effect, to repeat it in places where it was punished or had no effect, and/or to repeat the forms being enacted at the time the behavior was punished or had no effect.

Operant behaviors (actions and thoughts) can have five kinds of consequences. Each of the five relationships between behaviors and consequences is a *contingency of reinforcement*. Contingency refers to the if-then nature of behavior–consequence relationships: If behavior X is performed, then consequence Y is produced. The five contingencies of reinforcement are:

1. If a behavior is followed by the *delivery* of an event, and the behavior *increases* in strength (e.g., happens more often), then the event is called a *positive reinforcer* and the contingency is called *positive reinforcement*.
2. If a behavior is followed by the *removal,* avoidance, delay, reduction in the duration, or reduction in the intensity of an event, and the behavior *increases* in strength, then the event is called a *negative reinforcer* (or *aversive stimulus*) and the contingency is called *negative reinforcement*.
3. If a behavior is followed by the *delivery* of an event, and the behavior *decreases* in strength, then the event is called a *negative reinforcer* (or *aversive stimulus*) and the contingency is called *Type I punishment*.

4. If a behavior is followed by the *removal,* delay, reduction in the duration, or reduction in the intensity of an event, and the behavior *decreases* in strength, then the event is called a *positive reinforcer* and the contingency is called *Type II punishment.*
5. If a behavior is followed by *no change* in the environment, or by events that are neither positive nor negative reinforcers, and the behavior *decreases* in strength, then the events are called *neutral stimuli* and the contingency is called *extinction.*

Each consequence and contingency is defined *not* by the way it looks, the effect it is supposed to have, or even how it feels to the persons involved. Rather, each is defined by its actual effects on behavior. Problems arise when one fails to define consequences and contingencies by their effects. For example, when Jerry roams the room, Ms. Tyler stares at him. She assumes her facial expression is mildly punishing and will teach Jerry not to roam in the future. If Ms. Tyler counts how many times Jerry leaves his seat each day, she will find that the rate is increasing. Her facial expression is not punishment; rather, her facial expression is positive reinforcement because it strengthens behavior.

REINFORCEMENT CONTINGENCIES

Positive Reinforcement

Some consequences encourage one to perform the same behavior again, in the same place or in similar places, and with the same form. Such events are positive reinforcers. The contingency between a behavior and the positive reinforcer is *positive reinforcement.*

It is misleading to use the term *reward* instead of *positive reinforcer.* Reward implies that one wants, intends to get, or needs the so-called rewarding event. Of course, sometimes one decides one wants something, does something to get it, and is pleased when it arrives. Yet, children rarely tell themselves, "If I whine long enough, Grandma Anne will give me cookies." Similarly, adults do not say, "If I turn the steering wheel to the right, the car will round the corner." Yet, when the car rounds the corner, it positively reinforces prior steering behaviors, just as cookies reinforce whining. In sum, positive reinforcer and positive reinforcement are broader than reward; they include consequent events that strengthen behaviors whether one is aware of the consequences, intends to get them, or is gratified by them.

Kinds of Positive Reinforcers The following is a list of events that may be positive reinforcers for many people under certain conditions.

1. Food and liquids when one is hungry and thirsty.
2. Stimulating activity—the less things change, the less stimulation it takes for behavior to be reinforced.
3. Responses of others that make one feel wanted, needed, loved, protected, important, and competent. Thus, the opportunity to participate in social activities may be as strong of a reinforcer as tangible outcomes (e.g., food).
4. Attention (e.g., being noticed, provoking anger, getting another to respond, getting another to come to us).
5. Having tasks or interactions turn out in a way that signifies that actions have predictable effects, that the world is orderly or fair, or that allow people to go on to the next thing. Examples include keeping track of behavior, provoking reactions from others, ending arguments, and feeling the doorknob turn after grasping and twisting it. Note that the state of affairs at the outcome need not be intense. One barely notices the feel of the stairs under one's feet after each step; yet, the sensations are reinforcers. Imagine what would happen to walking behavior if one did not continually receive informative feedback.
6. Physical contact, such as hugs, caresses, and pats.

7. Approval or praise.
8. Smiles, winks, nods, hand waves, "special" gestures, and facial expressions.
9. Choosing the next task ("Great job, Juan! Now what do you want to work on?"), choosing a place to sit, choosing reinforcers, and deciding on the reinforcement contingency ("How many problems do you want to do?").
10. The opportunity to engage in behaviors considered strange. Many children with developmental disabilities engage in self-stimulation. These behaviors may provide *perceptual reinforcement* (Lovaas, Newsom, & Hickman, 1987); social reinforcement (e.g., attention from adults) (Durand & Carr, 1987); and/or be maintained by neurobiological mechanisms (e.g., some behaviors may increase endorphin levels, thus decreasing pain) (Lewis, Baumeister, & Mailman, 1987). Instead of fruitlessly trying to extinguish or punish "bizarre" behaviors, they should be used to reinforce desirable behavior. For instance, after several minutes of attentive participation, Jerry is invited to spin a plate or feel a piece of silk for 15 seconds—behaviors that he does frequently. In this way, Jerry's attention will increase and self-stimulation will gradually become confined to lessons (Charlop, Kurtz, & Casey, 1990; Sugai & White, 1986; Wolery, Kirk, & Gast, 1985).

Schedules of Reinforcement   Schedules of reinforcement concern details of reinforcement and punishment contingencies. The following are the main schedules of reinforcement and their effects (Ferster & Perrott, 1968; Ferster & Skinner, 1957).

Continuous Schedule   Some behaviors are reinforced (or punished) every time. For instance, toddlers are probably reinforced every time they say a new word in a caregiver's presence. These continuous schedules have three effects. First, continuous schedules yield a relatively fast rate of learning in contrast to schedules in which behavior is reinforced or punished once in awhile— intermittent schedules. To understand this, consider what would happen if parents did not reinforce a young child every time he or she said a new word.

Cindy: (Looks at mother.) Momma.
Mother: Yes, I am Momma.
Cindy: Dadda.
Mother: (No response.)
Cindy: Dadda, Dadda, Dadda, DooDoo.
Mother: Yes, Dadda.
Cindy: DooDoo.

Reinforcement may "work" by stopping a child right after he or she makes a "correct" response, in effect, telling the child, "That's the one!" (Guthrie, 1959). On an intermittent schedule, however, a child makes several correct responses that are not reinforced, several incorrect responses that are not reinforced, and then a correct response that is reinforced. It may take the child a long time to figure out which responses get reinforced and which do not. Thus, it is important to reinforce weak behaviors on schedules that are as continuous as possible.

Second, *continuous schedules sustain reinforced behaviors at a high rate and punished behaviors at a low rate.* At the same time, they produce relatively fast satiation or habituation. Being reinforced every time, one is likely to be full of the reinforcer quicker than if an intermittent schedule is used. Similarly, if one were punished by a mild event (e.g., a reprimand) on a continuous schedule, one might habituate quickly. Thus, to avoid becoming satiated on reinforcers, children should be slowly weaned off continuous schedules and onto intermittent schedules once a behavior occurs at a relatively high rate or is done rather skillfully. Proceeding slowly means, for instance, first reinforcing every response, then (on the average) two out of three responses, then one out of two, one out of three, and so forth.

Third, behaviors that were on a continuous schedule, but are no longer reinforced at all (i.e., are on extinction), are likely to weaken fairly quickly. A common example is the child whose whining for candy at the grocery store is reinforced every time a parent gives in at the checkout counter. If the parent suddenly stops exchanging candy for whining (and instead exchanges candy, or better yet, fruit and hugs, for help with shopping), the child may whine long and loud (an extinction burst), but only for a few trips to the store. The stark contrast between continuous reinforcement for whining and suddenly no reinforcement for whining makes it easy for the child to see that the old contingency is no longer in effect. Thus, whining is no longer worth the effort.

Intermittent Schedule   When a behavior is not reinforced or punished every time, it is on an intermittent schedule. Intermittent schedules have several effects. First, behavior on intermittent schedules increases (if reinforced) or decreases (if punished) more slowly than behavior on a continuous schedule. Second, because the person is receiving less frequent reinforcement or punishment, it takes longer for satiation or habituation to occur. Third, because the person is not used to receiving reinforcement every time, if the behavior is put on extinction, the person may continue to perform the previously reinforced behavior for a long time. Thus, behaviors that have been on an intermittent schedule (e.g., occasionally reinforced whining) may be durable.

Some intermittent schedules are "fixed" and others are "variable." On a fixed schedule, behavior is reinforced when the same (fixed) number of responses is performed (e.g., after every six correct answers), or when a target response happens after a fixed amount of time since the last reinforcement.

Fixed schedules produce a faster rate of behavior as one gets closer to reinforcement, perhaps because each next response is more likely to be reinforced. Fixed schedules also produce a pause after reinforcement, which is longer if more responses are required or if the required interval is longer before reinforcement. Thus, when teachers use fixed schedules (e.g., children have to do the same amount of work, or work for the same amount of time, before they are reinforced), children begin to "work" in earnest only when they get close to the reinforcement. In addition, children are lethargic after reinforcement. This is what happens when sessions are the same length and end with a "big" reinforcer. Fixed schedules, therefore, are not recommended.

Other intermittent schedules are variable. A behavior might be reinforced after a different number of responses (e.g., after four, then after eight, then after three) or after a different interval of time has gone by since the last reinforcement. Because a person cannot predict which response will be reinforced, as on a fixed schedule, and because each response is equally likely to be reinforced, variable schedules produce a more even rate of behavior. Thus, it is probably best to wean children off of continuous schedules and onto variable ones—reinforcement may come after two, five, or just one problem(s).

Reinforcement Depends on Circumstances   Whether an event is a positive reinforcer, neutral event, or punishment, and how much the event strengthens or weakens behavior, depends on several factors (Chandler, Fowler, & Lubeck, 1992). These include deprivation and satiation, background reinforcement and punishment, and concurrent (alternative) schedules. Let us first examine deprivation and satiation.

Ten-year-old Sam walks around school with his arms immobilized in cardboard tubes. Teachers explain that this is a way to prevent Sam from hitting himself.

To observe Sam's behavior without the tubes, an aide removed the tubes, sat Sam at a table, gave him puzzles to work, and walked away. For several minutes, Sam moved puzzle pieces around, occasionally looking up to watch the teachers with other children. He then began moaning softly, and finally hit his head with his knuckles several times. A teacher quickly came over, Sam held out his hand, and the teacher slapped it hard enough to hurt. The teacher walked away.

A few minutes later, Sam hit himself again, held out his hand, and received another slap in exchange. The teachers saw this as an amazing example of moral development: "He is willing to take the punishment. He knows he's doing wrong."

By definition, the slaps were not punishment, as they did not decrease Sam's head-hitting. Each slap was positive reinforcement; it strengthened head-hitting. How can pain be positive reinforcement rather than Type I punishment? The answer is revealed by examining Sam's environment.

Being noticed, talked to, and able to create an effect often are positive reinforcers. Sam rarely has social contact, and few behaviors (except for hitting himself) have immediate and reliable effects. In sum, deprivation is a "setting event" (Bijou & Baer, 1961) or an "establishing operation" (Michael, 1982) that can increase the value of social contact and the ability to have an effect to the point that they may be worth a painful price.

Thus, using extinction, time out (isolation), or corporal punishment alone to decrease undesirable behaviors may actually increase deprivation to the point that a child "uses" undesirable behaviors more often to get social contact or to have an effect of *any* kind. Thus, the early stages of many children's educations should teach simple, desirable behaviors that produce social contact and the experience of having a predictable effect.

This writer once taught 6-year-old Chip, a boy with autism. After about a year, Chip performed self-stimulatory behaviors at a low rate, used many phrases and sentences, did a number of everyday tasks, and engaged in cooperative play. One day, Chip became inattentive, stopped talking, and began engaging in bizarre behavior. I hypothesized that I was not reinforcing Chip enough, and, therefore, increased the frequency. Over the next few days, things became steadily worse. What was going on? The answer is *satiation* and *habituation*. Chip was tired of the same praise, yogurt, hugs, rides on the Big Wheel, and tasks. Instead of substituting these, I gave Chip even more of the same.

The example with Sam shows that deprivation can increase the value of events to the point that aversive events are positive reinforcers. Satiation and habituation, however, weaken the strength of reinforcers. At the extreme, as with Chip, satiation and habituation turn positive reinforcers into aversive stimuli. The implication, again, is that one should rotate reinforcers and tasks before satiation and habituation set in, and teach children to choose their own reinforcers.

Background reinforcement (the hedonic value of the environment) is a second factor determining whether events will be reinforcement or punishment, and how much they will affect behavior (Epling & Pierce, 1990). Imagine a classroom where teachers keep cranky children placated with a steady stream of music, snacks, social contact, and toys (i.e., the environment has high hedonic value for the children). One day, caregivers decide to strengthen the children's cooperation by using praise. Given the amount of background reinforcement, praise is *not* likely to be a strong reinforcer. In fact, children may respond to the new contingency in a way that says, "Who cares about praise? We've got these other goodies." Thus, to increase the reinforcing strength of certain events, one ought to ensure that children do not have much access to them or to other reinforcers. Instead, many reinforcers should be saved for strengthening specific desirable behaviors.

Imagine a child in an impoverished environment where there is little background reinforcement. In this case, events that might otherwise be neutral or even painful, such as reprimands for problem behaviors, may become positive reinforcers that strengthen the problem behaviors. Moreover, if a child's environment is not only impoverished of positive reinforcers, but is aversive (e.g., many difficult tasks), then even bizarre, self-injurious, or aggressive behaviors that bring escape or avoidance will be strongly reinforced. Therefore, to weaken problem behaviors that ordinarily produce reinforcing social contact (e.g., stares from caregivers), one might weaken the value of social contact by *increasing* the amount of background reinforcement. To weaken problem behaviors reinforced by escape or avoidance of aversive events, one might enrich children's environments with toys, music, and games, and reduce the number and difficulty of aversive tasks (Rincover, 1986).

Concurrent reinforcement schedules are a third condition affecting the strength of reinforcers. Situations often contain concurrent schedules; that is, one can invest time and behavior in alternative ways. One might have a choice between reading a funny book, calling a friend on the telephone, doing the laundry, or scrubbing the floors. Each behavior is on a different schedule of reinforcement. Reading a funny book produces more reinforcement for less time and behavior than does scrubbing floors. The difference in the schedules helps to explain why, given the choice, many people choose reading over scrubbing.

Interestingly, the rate of a behavior, or the time spent at a behavior, tends to match the rate of reinforcement for that behavior relative to other behaviors. This is the "matching law" (Herrnstein, 1961); it applies to human behavior in many situations (Martens, Lochner, & Kelly, 1992; McDowell, 1988; Neef, Mace, Shea, & Shade, 1992). In fact, the matching law helps to explain why some behaviors are stronger than others. It can also help to plan effective programs, as illustrated by the following vignette.

Luke's Behavior and Concurrent Schedules

Luke, a 7-year-old boy with autism, was observed in his home for $1^1/_2$ hours each day for 4 consecutive days. He engaged in a number of behaviors, which are listed from most to least frequent: 1) getting into cabinets, refrigerator, and dressers to remove or disarrange contents; 2) playing with water in the bathroom sink; 3) shrieking at the top of his voice; 4) moaning and flapping his hands; 5) playing in a conventional manner with blocks and toy cars; and 6) cooperating with parents' requests.

How does one account for the relative frequencies of each behavior? Does Luke play with toys so seldom and with water so often because he has less skill with toys? Does Luke have a neurological disability that causes his shrieking and flapping? Although these are reasonable suggestions, observation shows how often Luke was *reinforced* for each behavior.

	Average number of episodes per session	Average percentage of episodes reinforced
Getting into things	23	95
Playing in water	19	69
Shrieking	10	43
Moaning and flapping	3	0
Conventional play	<3	0
Cooperation	<3	0

Note that Luke got into the cabinets twice as often as he shrieked. Also note that getting into the cabinets was twice as likely to be reinforced as shrieking. In other words, the frequency of each behavior closely matches the relative rate of reinforcement for that behavior (Kozloff, 1983).

Implications of the matching law are pretty clear. Because the rate of a behavior is likely to match the frequency with which it is reinforced, caregivers must ensure that virtually all reinforcement is for desirable behaviors. Note, too, that when undesirable behaviors are no longer reinforced, the total amount of a child's background reinforcement decreases. This may increase the value of remaining reinforcement, making it easier to strengthen desirable behavior.

The matching law is also useful in program evaluation. If Luke's rate of talking is decreasing, it may be that he is now getting more reinforcement for other behaviors. If so, we can decrease reinforcement for those other behaviors and/or increase reinforcement for talking.

Negative Reinforcement

Negative reinforcement should not be confused with punishment. Punishment weakens behavior, whereas both positive and negative reinforcement *strengthen* behavior. For instance, when Juan skillfully puts on a coat, Mr. Eaton praises him; therefore, Juan's skillful dressing increases. This is positive reinforcement. When Juan goes outside and feels the chilly wind, he pulls the zipper higher and feels relief. In the future, Juan continues to zip up in response to the wind. This contingency is negative reinforcement for zipping. In other words, with positive reinforcement, a behavior receives some event or reaction from the environment (e.g., praise, money, a chance to go on to another activity). With negative reinforcement, a behavior enables one to escape from, avoid, delay, decrease the intensity of, or decrease the duration of events that are aversive.

As with positive reinforcement, one learns to perform negatively reinforced behaviors where they have produced desirable results and soon after events signal that something aversive is coming. One also learns to perform more effective forms of escape and avoidance behavior (e.g., the quickest way to zip). Examples of behaviors that sometimes enable one to escape, avoid, delay, or diminish aversive events include the following:

1. Repeating requests, demands, commands, pleas, and threats because it is aversive when people do not comply the first time.
2. Frowning, whining, begging, or acting sick to get others to leave one alone or to take away or not give aversive tasks. Note that one can use the same behavior both to get positive reinforcers and to get away from aversive stimuli.
3. Making excuses (even to oneself), getting involved in other tasks, misplacing things, or forgetting information to stall, avoid, or escape aversive tasks and situations.
4. Giving in to other people's irritating behaviors so they will stop, or giving in to threatening behaviors so others will not do as threatened.
5. Not making requests of another, not commenting on or even noticing another's behavior to avoid aversive reactions.
6. Pretending to be calm or happy, doing things alone, or accepting others' poor performances to avoid unpleasant let-downs or others acting out.

Many behaviors of children and caregivers are negatively reinforced. For example, children engage in self-stimulation, tantrums, aggression, and even self-injurious behavior to escape or avoid tasks and interaction (Iwata, 1987). Reciprocally, caregivers learn to reinforce problem behaviors because reinforcement temporarily stops those behaviors. This negatively reinforces caregivers for reinforcing children's aversive behavior (Ferster & Perrott, 1968). (Chap. 5, this volume, examines child–caregiver exchanges in detail and suggests how to replace counterproductive exchanges.)

Shaping is the process of guiding change by differentially reinforcing performances in a certain direction. For example, Tammy is no longer reinforced for baby talk, but only for more mature forms of talking; the harder Indra swings the hammer, the deeper the nails go into the wood; the faster he zips, the faster Juan escapes from the chilly wind; the louder Jerry whines, the more likely Ms. Tyler is to let him out of the task; Luke receives more frequent hugs when he engages in creative play with toy cars and houses; Bart gets his parents' attention only when he engages in milder-than-usual yelling; and Sam could be reinforced when he hits himself more gently. Although it may seem strange to intentionally reinforce undesirable behaviors, these behaviors are going to be accidentally reinforced anyway; that is, they will be on variable schedules making them resistant to extinction. More importantly, reinforcing undesirable behaviors when they occur in more appropriate places or forms will shape them in those directions. Two contingencies of reinforcement have been discussed—positive and negative reinforcement. The third and fourth contingencies of reinforcement, Type I and Type II punishment, are also related.

Type I Punishment

Type I punishment should not be confused with negative reinforcement. As discussed, in negative reinforcement, behavior results in escape from, avoidance of, delay of, or diminishing of aversive events, and the behavior is strengthened. In Type I punishment, behavior is followed by aversive events and is weakened; that is, the performance is disrupted and the behavior happens less often, in fewer places, and perhaps with less intensity. For example, a few experiences of running on icy sidewalks and falling are usually enough to completely suppress running on ice.

Type II Punishment

In Type II punishment, behavior results in the removal, delay, or reduction in the quantity, value, or duration of positive reinforcers. As in Type I punishment, the behavior decreases in strength. Examples of Type II punishment include having a child go to his or her room after hitting a sibling (removal of social contact and television), or giving a child less dessert as a result of throwing food during the meal.

Research suggests that Type I and Type II punishment yield the fastest reduction in behavior when: 1) punishment occurs every time the behavior happens; 2) punishment is immediate (making it easier for the person to discriminate the behavior being punished); 3) alternative behaviors in the person's repertoire are frequently reinforced; 4) punishing consequences are strong enough to disrupt or stop the ongoing behavior; and 5) the presence of the punishment contingency is cued in a salient way (e.g., the behavior is punished in particular places and by particular people after a reminder is given) (Axelrod & Apsche, 1983). The apparent effectiveness and simplicity of punishment may tempt caregivers to try it on problem behavior. Yet, punishment is the focus of much controversy.

The main arguments in the debate over aversive and nonaversive methods concern their dehumanizing versus humanizing nature, the reinforcement of those using aversive methods, and the effectiveness and feasibility of both approaches. The debate over aversive and nonaversive teaching is the focus of the next two sections.

Nonaversive Teaching A number of so-called *nonaversive* methods are used to reduce or replace self-injury (e.g., eye gouging, head banging); aggression; self-stimulation (e.g., rocking, mouthing objects); pica (ingesting nonfood items); and other problem behavior. Following are several nonaversive methods.

First, a problem behavior may be put on extinction (discussed later in this chapter); that is, it is no longer positively reinforced (e.g., with attention) or negatively reinforced (e.g., by allowing a child to escape from tasks). At the same time, the child might be reinforced either for: 1) almost any other desirable behaviors (DRO—differential reinforcement of other behavior), or 2) behaviors physically incompatible with the problem behavior (DRI—differential reinforcement of incompatible behavior) (LaVigna & Donnellan, 1986). For instance, Juan is not reinforced for running toward the street, but only for walking, looking at flowers, and talking with teachers both near and away from streets.

Second, the communicative function of problem behavior could be determined (e.g., Jerry hits Ms. Tyler when a lesson has become aversive). The child is then taught desirable alternative ways to serve that function (e.g., raising a hand) (DRA—differential reinforcement of alternative behavior) (Donnellan, Mirenda, Mesaros, & Fassbender, 1984; Durand & Carr, 1992).

Third, the average rate of a problem behavior is determined. The child is then reinforced at the end of every interval in which the behavior was performed at a lower rate (DRL—differential reinforcement of low rates) (LaVigna & Donnellan, 1986). Sam, for instance, hits his head about once per second during episodes that last 3–5 minutes. Now, Sam is observed during consecutive 30-second intervals. Whenever the head-hitting rate during a 30-second interval is less than 1 per second (i.e., less than 30 for the interval), Sam is reinforced. Gradually, Sam is reinforced only if the rate is slower and slower.

Another approach is to determine the average amount of time the child spends between episodes of a problem behavior. The child is reinforced for longer inter-episode intervals (LaVigna & Donnellan, 1986). For instance, between episodes of rocking, Juan sits or stands still for about 10 minutes. Thus, any time he is relatively still for more than 10 minutes, he is reinforced. Gradually, the length of the required nonrocking interval would be increased; that is, the reinforcement schedule is "progressive."

Shaping is a fourth nonaversive method (LaVigna & Donnellan, 1986). For instance, Sam might be reinforced for softer head hits or for shorter episodes of head hitting; Roger might be reinforced for less destructive tantrums.

A fifth method is bringing a problem behavior under stimulus control. This means the child is differentially reinforced (i.e., only reinforced) for performing the behavior in a safer or more appropriate place (Pace, Iwata, Edwards, & McCosh, 1986). For example, Luke made a mess in all of the kitchen drawers; therefore he was given his own kitchen drawer that is painted a different color from the rest. Chip, who frequently spun ash trays and plates, was taught to spin toy tops at his play table.

Sixth, one could strengthen cooperation. This would enable caregivers to interrupt sequences leading to problem behavior (e.g., "Johnny, raise your hand if you need help.") (Davis, Brady, Williams, & Hamilton, 1992; Russo, Cataldo, & Cushing, 1981).

Another method is to increase the hedonic value of the child's environment with toys, music, less difficult tasks, and affectionate contact, so that the child has less incentive to engage in problem behaviors that produce self-stimulation, reprimands, or escape (Horner, 1980).

More selectively, a child could be given so much access to reinforcers for a specific problem behavior that the child is *satiated* and the problem behavior decreases (Rast, Johnson, Drum, & Cronin, 1981). For example, Luke was *invited* to play with water in a special tub (stimulus control) four or five times a day. By week's end, he either declined invitations or left water play sessions, indicating he was satiated. His parents and siblings then started teaching him how to play with toys and games.

Errorless learning (e.g., using the time delay system of prompting described later) is another nonaversive approach. It is especially useful with problem behaviors (e.g., aggression) that result from frustration and/or the loss of expected reinforcement following errors (Hamblin, Buckholdt, Ferritor, Kozloff, & Blackwell, 1971).

Finally, one can teach children *self-control,* including relaxation, counting their behaviors, and self-reinforcement (e.g., for lower rates of problem behavior or for performing alternative behaviors) (Gelfand & Hartmann, 1984; Koegel, Koegel, Hurley, & Frea, 1992; Stahmer & Schreibman, 1992).

Note that nonaversive programs usually combine several of the above methods, either at once or in a sequence (Cooper et al., 1992). For instance, because Sam hits his head only when he is alone, bored, or ignored, the first step might be to enrich his home and school with toys and more pleasant interaction. This would reduce Sam's incentive to hit himself. Furthermore, because one function of Sam's head hitting is communication ("Someone pay attention to me!"), Sam could be taught desirable forms of communication, such as asking for attention or approaching people. Sam could also be reinforced for lower rates of hitting, longer intervals between hitting episodes, and softer hitting. Finally, Sam could be taught to mark a box on a recording sheet he carries with him after each short interval (cued by a bell timer at his desk) in which he has not hit himself. After five hit-free intervals, Sam is allowed to choose a reinforcer from a menu (Fisher et al., 1992).

The nonaversive methods described here are apparently effective in reducing and/or replacing many problem behaviors. The alternatives—aversive methods—should also be examined.

Aversive Teaching   Aversive methods to reduce problem behaviors include: 1) painful electric shock for each episode of a problem behavior (Lichstein & Schreibman, 1976); 2) mild electrical stimulation (Linscheid, Iwata, Ricketts, Williams, & Griffin, 1990); 3) spanking; 4) visual screening (e.g., covering a child's eyes) (Singh & Winton, 1984); 5) physical restraint (Luiselli, Suskin, & Slocumb, 1984); and 6) water mist sprayed on the face (Singh, Watson, & Winton, 1986).

Some argue that aversive methods are degrading and dehumanizing. Persons with developmental disabilities already receive more than their share of deprivation and harsh treatment. In contrast, nonaversive methods help create an interpersonal climate more likely to promote psychosocial development (Guess, Helmstetter, Turnbull, & Knowlton, 1986; LaVigna & Donnellan, 1986).

The counterargument is that while aversive methods are painful, so is surgery for life-threatening illness. Moreover, by quickly decreasing behaviors, aversive methods not only save a child's sight, brain, or life, but increase the quality of life—self-stimulatory, aggressive, and self-injurious behaviors are major reasons why children are put in residential facilities (Hill & Bruininks, 1984).

Finally, so-called nonaversive methods may be aversive. For instance, if differential reinforcement of low rates (DRL) is used, and Sam hits his head too often during an interval, Sam would lose reinforcement. This consequence is supposed to reduce the rate of head hitting. By definition, this is Type II punishment—punishment by removal of reinforcers (Rolider & Van Houten, 1990). Similarly, no longer letting Jerry escape from onerous tasks to extinguish his escape-aggression would be aversive to him. Thus, before one labels a method "aversive" or "nonaversive," one must determine what contingencies are involved.

A second argument against aversive methods is that caregivers are negatively reinforced when punishment suppresses behaviors that caregivers do not like. This might lead to punishment becoming the typical response even to mild problem behaviors (Donnellan & LaVigna, 1990; Ferster & Perrott, 1968). Eventually, caregivers may become more competent at punishing than at teaching desirable behaviors. The social system is then based on coercion and fear.

However, those who would permit aversive methods stress that it should be used by trained and supervised persons following a set of rules concerning assessment, selection of methods, and evaluation of effectiveness (Green, 1990). In addition, reducing children's problem behaviors increases the hedonic value of the environment for caregivers, thus decreasing any incentive to use punishment.

Some argue that nonaversive methods can be effective with virtually all problem behaviors (Donnellan & LaVigna, 1987), whereas aversive methods do not always decrease punished behaviors (Romanczyk & Goren, 1975) and may have destructive side effects, such as aggression, withdrawal, avoidance of those who deliver punishment, anxiety, and a reduction in desirable behaviors (Ferster & Perrott, 1968; Newsom, Favell, & Rincover, 1983).

Some stress that nonaversive methods are more socially acceptable and can be used in ordinary and applied research environments. It is virtually impossible, however, to properly use aversive methods for long (e.g., to punish every time and immediately). Proponents of aversive methods counter that nonaversive methods are just as hard to use (e.g., reinforcing immediately and consistently, not reinforcing problem behavior). Moreover, nonaversive methods may require hundreds of hours and many caregivers. During this time, a child may be hurting himself or herself and others (Paisey, Whitney, & Hislop, 1990).

The arguments presented by each side are equally logical and inconclusive (see Axelrod & Apsche, 1983; Repp & Singh, 1990). In the long run, the arguments may be less important than progress in understanding and preventing problem behaviors that is stimulated by the debate. This writer can only suggest that the severity and durability of many problem behaviors can be avoided if education is started in schools and homes as early as possible. Furthermore, child–caregiver interaction should be assessed and improved in a collaborative fashion (see chap. 5, this volume) to prevent the escalation of punishment and the degradation of social relations as unprepared and unsupported families and teachers try to cope with children's increasingly frustrating problem behaviors.

Extinction

Sometimes, a behavior produces little or no change in or reaction from the environment. For example, Mitchell rubs his eyes and stamps his feet. This is a cue that unless someone turns on music or lets him out of tasks, Mitchell will start running around out of control. Invariably, someone gives in to (and reinforces) Mitchell's threats. This contingency has been going on for years. Realizing that giving in to threats reinforces them, teachers now merely nod at Mitchell when he threatens, or give him a brief smile as if to say "So? Yes?" Or, they walk out of the room, or go on with their own tasks, as though they do not care about Mitchell's act or his running around. More important than putting Mitchell's threats on extinction, teachers differentially reinforce desirable behaviors, such as working at harder tasks for a little longer than before, asking for what he wants, or negotiating not to work on certain tasks.

Consequences are information about the effectiveness of behavior. When behavior does not produce a salient change in the environment, the information is "The preceding behavior does not work," "Things are not as they used to be," or "Try something else."

The effect of extinction depends on several factors. One is the schedule of reinforcement the behavior is on. If a behavior is receiving little reinforcement, it is likely to be weak (seldom occur). Extinction will further weaken it. If, however, a behavior is on a rich schedule (e.g., continuous reinforcement) and is put on extinction, there may be an immediate emotional response and escalation of the behavior, as though the person were trying to get back the usual effect. This is an *extinction burst*. However, if the escalated behavior is not reinforced, it is likely to decrease fairly quickly. Finally, if a behavior is on an intermittent schedule of the variable variety, so that the person cannot tell when the behavior is likely to be reinforced, then the person may continue performing the behavior for a long time, even though it is now on extinction. The following is an example of how behavior on an intermittent schedule (especially a variable schedule) resists extinction.

> Robin used expressions such as "Oh, shut up," "Buzz off," and "Says you" to evoke exciting reactions from her mother, who would reply, "Don't talk to me that way, young lady!" However, her mother reacted this way only once in awhile—when she was tired or when Robin made a lot of rude remarks in a row. In other words, Robin's rude talk was on an intermittent schedule of the variable kind. This taught Robin that while she could not tell which rude remark would be reinforced, eventually reinforcement would come. Thus, Robin made rude remarks all day at a steady rate.
>
> Realizing that Robin enjoyed reprimands, her mother decided to put rude talk on extinction—to make no response at all. The result was that Robin increased the rate of rude remarks, and kept it up day and night, day after day. By the end of the week, just as Robin was getting the message and was about to stop the remarks for a long while, she uttered a nasty swear word. Her tolerance exhausted, her mother yelled. This taught Robin that if she maintained a high rate of rude remarks for a week, and then escalated to nasty words, she would be swiftly reinforced. Mom had to start the extinction process all over.

In sum, if one is going to put on extinction a behavior that used to be on a variable reinforcement schedule, one must never reinforce the behavior, and certainly not when it has escalated.

Extinction is also affected by the strength of alternative behaviors in a person's repertoire. If a child does not know other ways to get what he or she wants, if alternative behaviors are weak, and/or if such behaviors are seldom reinforced anyway, then the child has little alternative but to continue performing the behavior that used to be reinforced. In other words, ignoring a problem behavior is rarely sufficient. One must teach alternative desirable behavior by providing numerous and obvious opportunities; adequate prompts; and quick, frequent, high quality reinforcement (Sprague & Horner, 1992). Thus, if Robin's mother had reinforced even short intervals of nonrude talk, Robin's rude talk would have extinguished more rapidly.

Lastly, it should be noted that caregivers' behaviors may be weakened by extinction: teaching efforts that yield little apparent change, or creative thinking that is ignored. Extinction is possibly a major cause of burnout. That is why methods for providing social-emotional support and recognition ought to be a basic feature of special education programs, as described in Chapter 8 of this volume.

PROMPTS AND OBSTACLES

The proper use of cues and reinforcement may not be enough to improve performance. A child may need assistance producing the right responses. This section examines six kinds of prompts as well as strategies for selecting, introducing, and fading prompts.

What To Prompt

Interaction with the physical environment, with others, and with one's own behavior is in a sequence called a *trial*. A trial has three parts (shown in Table 3.1): antecedents, behaviors, and consequences. A child may need assistance interacting with any of the parts of a trial. For example, a child might not pay attention to cues, or a child may be incapable of performing effective movements. Furthermore, a child may not notice or understand the informational significance of the consequences of his or her actions.

Types of Prompts

There are at least six kinds of prompts: accentuating, gestures, instructions, models, manual, and tools and other aids.

Accentuating   The relevant features of a trial can be made more ear- and eye-catching to attract attention or increase a child's understanding of what he or she is doing. Examples include: using large letters; shining a light on important objects; marking off play versus eating areas with bright contrasting colors; increasing the loudness of requests; using electronic equipment to help a child notice changing muscle tension, or a mirror to help observe posture; using food pictures taped to a refrigerator door to cue the child to open it; and placing small pictures of objects beneath the words for those objects to assist reading. As will be described later in this chapter, such prompts might be *faded* as a child responds to them in a more reliable and fluent fashion. For instance, the pictures beneath the printed words might be gradually covered up. The salience of instructional events can also be increased by reducing background sounds and removing distracting sights.

Gestures   Gesture prompts include a caregiver's nodding, pointing, or looking at places or relevant objects to give the child information about when, how, where, or with what to respond. For example, Luke's mother points to Luke's special drawer, as though to say, "Play over there." Also, she uses conventional arm or head gestures at the same time that she says, "Come here."

Obstacles that hinder gesture prompts include gestures that are vague (the child cannot tell where the teacher is pointing), too fast, or presented with too many other events (e.g., talk, other gestures) so that the child cannot pick out the relevant gesture.

Instructions   Instructions can be classified according to what they instruct a child to do and how the instruction is given. Instructions might tell the child: 1) that he or she can respond ("There are no cars in the street. Walk now."), 2) what response to make ("Now spread the jelly."), 3) what to pay attention to ("Watch my mouth."), and 4) how he or she might respond ("Use both hands.").

Note that instructions can be *full* ("Now put the pillow on the bed.") or *partial* ("Pillow."). Instructions can also be *verbal* (live or tape recorded); *pictorial* (a series of pictures of the steps in clearing a supper table); or *written* (cards that recite rules, such as "First we hang up the coat and then we play."). *Hints* or indirect prompts may also be considered a form of instruction. For example, if Juan does not know the next step while making his bed, Mr. Eaton says, "What do you lay your head on?" Finally, *options* might be provided so that when Jerry is confused by what to do in the play area, Ms. Tyler says, "You could play in the sand box or play with the trucks" (Wolery, Bailey, & Sugai, 1988).

Obstacles regarding instructions include ambient sound or talking on a caregiver's part, making it difficult for the child to discriminate the instruction. Too many words might make it difficult for a child to pay attention, follow, or remember an instruction. Words may be vague and abstract. An instruction spoken too quickly or along with an angry face, posture, or tone of voice might elicit feelings and/or escape behaviors that interfere with attention or correct responding.

Models   Models involve demonstrating all or part of a desired performance. For example, Juan is holding a saw properly with his right hand, but not securing the board with his left. Mr. Eaton says, "Like this," which gets Juan's attention. Then Mr. Eaton puts his own left hand on the board and presses down (a motor model). Juan imitates the model and Mr. Eaton gives him a pat on the back. If Juan had not imitated the motor model, Mr. Eaton could have repeated the motor model and then manually prompted Juan to imitate it.

In addition to imitating caregivers, children learn to imitate desirable behaviors of peers (McGee, Paradis, & Feldman, 1993). For example, Jerry, seated next to Sam, is cued to observe Sam making vertical lines on paper. Then Jerry is cued to hold his own pencil and watch and copy what Sam is doing. At first, Jerry is additionally prompted manually to make lines as Sam is doing. Once he begins to model Sam's drawing, manual prompts are faded (Fowler, 1988; Hamblin et al., 1971).

Obstacles to effectiveness would be models that are presented too quickly, that do not demonstrate enough steps, or that are given when a child is not paying attention.

Manual Prompts   Manual prompts involve physically helping a child to correctly move his or her body. For instance, Mr. Hawkins gently turns Indra's head so she sees relevant cues in a hair brushing task. He guides her hands with his own so she correctly performs the brushing movements. He gently turns her head so she can see how her hair looks—the relevant consequence of brushing.

Manual prompts vary with respect to *completeness* and *restrictiveness.* Regarding completeness, one can manually prompt every single movement in a sequence (e.g., from locating the hair brush to replacing it on the shelf) or only one response (e.g., hand over hand help in brushing). Regarding restrictiveness, or the degree of guidance, one can use a *partial* manual prompt allowing much leeway of movement, or a *full* manual prompt that restricts movement to a certain path. For instance, Ms. Tyler holds Jerry's hand while they draw lines.

Obstacles to effective manual prompting include prompts that are so forceful or restrictive that they elicit pain and escape behavior. Manual prompting might be too partial, giving a child so much leeway that the child makes incorrect responses or makes correct responses too late. Manual prompts also might evoke responses that are undesirable. For example, touching Indra's shoulder to prompt her to move forward may prompt her to turn around and look at Mr. Hawkins. Furthermore, some children have an aversion to being touched or moved.

Tools and Other Aids   Tools, jigs, templates, and devices refer to materials and mechanical and/or electrical means to simplify tasks or increase a child's closeness to objects, range of motion, strength, accuracy, and attention. Examples include eating utensils with special handles; clothing and other materials joined with velcro; microswitches for electrical equipment; a strap for pulling open a refrigerator door; mats with outlines of plates and utensils; stools for standing; partially predrilled holes to facilitate using a screwdriver; a computer or tape recorder that gives cues, instructions, or feedback for each step; and equipment for seating, reaching, turning, and holding things. Naturally, the absence of such assistance is a major obstacle in the lives of persons with developmental disabilities.

Dimensions of Prompting

Prompts vary along the dimensions of intensity, degree of guidance, and the number of steps of a performance that are prompted. Let us first examine each dimension and then the strategies that can help introduce and remove (fade) prompts in a systematic way.

Intensity   Prompts have greater or lesser intensity. For instance, instructions can be given with a loud or soft voice; models and gestures can be presented with more or less energy, flourish, or pizzazz; manual prompts can vary from an almost unfelt touch to actually holding a child's limb; and accentuating can vary from extreme to subtle.

Degree of Guidance Prompts can also afford more or less leeway in responding. Manual prompts can vary from narrowly guiding Juan's arm, hand, and finger when pressing a soda selection button, to merely nudging his arm in the general direction. Ms. Gonzales can model all of the answer Sam is to imitate; for instance, "It's a crow. Say 'crow.'" Or she might use an incomplete prompt (e.g., "It's a cr . . ."), which allows Sam to complete the response. A jig or template can completely guide Luke's utensil-placing movements (e.g., trays with slots the size and shape of utensils), or they can provide only a visual outline.

Number of Steps that Are Prompted Prompting varies with regard to how many steps, and which steps, are prompted. For example, Jerry is skilled at none of the steps in making a bed. Consequently, Ms. Tyler prompts every single step, with models, instructions, and manual help. Juan, however, is skilled at many of the actions in making a sandwich; therefore, Mr. Eaton only manually prompts Juan to open the package of bread, and later uses a partial model to help him slice the sandwich.

Prompting Strategies In view of the dimensions noted above, one needs strategies for deciding which prompts to use, which steps in a task to prompt, and how to introduce and remove (fade) prompts. There are five main strategies: stimulus manipulation, graduated guidance, most-to-least prompting, least-to-most prompting, and time delay.

Stimulus Manipulation Some prompts involve accentuating cues to attract attention and give a child more information about what to do. Accentuations (e.g., brighter lighting) can be gradually removed unless constant accentuation is needed to compensate a sensory disability. Wolery and his colleagues (Wolery et al., 1988) identify three ways to initially accentuate cues and then fade the accentuation. These are stimulus fading, stimulus shaping, and superimposition followed by fading or shaping (Koegel, Egel, & Dunlap, 1980; Lalli & Browder, 1993; Repp, Karsh, & Lenz, 1990; Smeets & Striefel, 1990).

With *stimulus fading,* an *irrelevant* feature of the cue is used to attract the child's attention and cue a differential response. Once the child responds to the accentuated dimensions, the accentuations are faded out, leaving the child responding to more normative and relevant dimensions. For example, to help Luke discriminate his kitchen drawer from others in which he is not to play, Luke's was painted jet black. It could have stayed black, but once Luke was playing only in his drawer, his parents altered the color until Luke's drawer looked the same as the rest. First, they painted his drawer dark grey, then light grey, then very light grey, and so on until it was white like the other drawers. (They also could have painted it white at the outer edge, gradually painting toward the center over a period of a week.)

Similarly, to help Juan discriminate the correct hand tool to pick out of any pair in front of him on the work table, Mr. Eaton placed the target (requested) tool closer to Juan. When Juan began responding correctly to the requests, Mr. Eaton moved the target tool farther away until Juan was responding to the name and not position.

In *stimulus shaping,* a *relevant* dimension of a cue is first accentuated in some fashion and then gradually altered, or shaped, until the child is responding to the cue in its *normative* form. For example, Indra is learning to read. To help her discriminate letters, each is shaped like an object whose name begins with the letter. For instance, the letter "t" looks like a tree. As Indra learns to name and read words written in accentuated letters, their form is gradually shaped into the normative style.

Finally, *superimposition* is the kind of stimulus manipulation Mr. Hawkins used when he pasted pictures of food on the refrigerator door. Each day, he faded the superimposed stimuli until the door itself (the target stimulus) was sufficient to cue Indra to open it.

Graduated Guidance In graduated guidance (Demchack, 1989), a caregiver provides as much or as little prompting as needed at any step in a task. When Juan properly places a dinner plate, but hesitates before placing the fork, Mr. Eaton points to the correct spot. A little further in the sequence, to prevent Juan from placing a cup too far from the right spot, Mr. Eaton increases the restrictiveness of the prompt by grasping Juan's hand, pointing to the correct spot, and moving Juan's hand that is holding the cup to the spot. When it is time to place the next cup, Mr. Eaton tries to fade the manual prompt and use only a gesture (pointing to the next cup and the spot to put it). During the next session on table setting, Mr. Eaton again uses as much or as little prompting as needed.

Because graduated guidance involves adjusting the amount of assistance as needed, it is useful for children who engage in much disruptive behavior when they have either too much leeway or find restriction aversive.

Most-to-Least Prompting   In the system of most-to-least prompting, or decreasing assistance (Miller & Test, 1989), the teacher completes the following steps:

1. Creates a hierarchy of prompts varying in intensiveness and/or restrictiveness
2. Starts instruction with the most intense or most restrictive prompt
3. Gives the prompt before the child makes an error
4. Moves down the hierarchy to a slightly less intense or restrictive prompt as the child does more of a step on his or her own

In using the system of most-to-least prompts, one first conducts a task analysis of how the task is ordinarily done. Then, a hierarchy of prompts from most to least intrusive is developed for *each* step. A set of criteria (Wolery et al., 1988) is created for deciding how competently a child must perform a step before moving to the next, less intrusive prompt. Table 3.2 illustrates part of what such a plan might look like.

The most-to-least system has several advantages. It decreases the number of errors a child makes, decreases the amount of time between the initiating cue and the child's response, and is useful if a child does not imitate well (Schoen, 1986). In general, it may be better to use during the acquisition phase when a child cannot perform the task independently.

Least-to-Most Prompting   In the system of least-to-most prompts, or increasing assistance (Gast, Ault, Wolery, Doyle, & Belanger, 1988), prompting begins at the bottom of the hierarchy of

Table 3.2.   Partial plan for most-to-least prompting for opening a door

Steps	Decreasing prompts				
1. Approach the door.	Hold shoulders and walk to the door.	Hold hand and walk to the door.	Hold hand and walk half way.	Give instruction— "Walk . . ."	Gesture (point).
2. Locate the doorknob.	Turn and aim head toward the knob.	Gently nudge chin toward the knob.	Gesture (point) toward the knob.		
3. Reach for the knob.					
4. Grasp the knob.					

Criteria for movement   In step 1, when the child walks directly to the door with only a very light touch on the shoulder as a prompt, switch from touching the child's shoulder to holding the child's hand. When the child walks directly and quickly to the door with a very light touch on his or her hand as a prompt, begin to fade the prompt (touching the child's hand while walking) about half way to the door.

intensity and/or restrictiveness. If the lowest level prompt is not enough to help a child perform a step more competently, one moves to the next higher level, and so forth until one finds the level that prevents errors. Instruction continues at that level. When the child needs less assistance at a step, the prompt is faded by going down the hierarchy. As with most-to-least prompting, this system requires that a task be analyzed into a sequence of steps. In addition, a series of increasingly intrusive prompts is specified for each step. Finally, criteria are established for deciding when to increase the level of prompting.

For example, in Table 3.2, step 3 of the door opening task is "reach for the knob." Prompts, from least to most, might be:

1. Pointing in the direction of the knob
2. Pointing at and nearly touching the knob
3. Pointing and instruction ("Grasp it.")
4. Modeling and instruction ("Grasp it.")
5. Instruction ("Grasp it.") and gentle nudge to the shoulder
6. Full manual prompt at elbow
7. Full manual prompt of arm and instruction ("Grasp it."), as well as holding and aiming the child's head so that the child is looking at the doorknob

Criteria for moving from a lower level prompt to the next higher level might be based on a child's performance of the correct movements and a chosen *response interval* (Wolery et al., 1988, p. 263) between an initiating cue and the child's response. For instance, if Lucy does not reach for the knob with her right or left hand within 3–5 seconds while looking at it, move from level 1 (pointing in the general direction) to level 2 (pointing at and nearly touching the knob).

The system of least-to-most prompts may not be wise during the early (acquisition) phase of instruction, as it allows a child to make errors. Instead, it may be useful when working to improve fluency (i.e., duration, speed, effort, weeding out unnecessary movements) and generalization.

Time Delay Time delay involves providing a short time between an initiating cue (e.g., "What is this called?") and a subsequent prompt (e.g., modeling the correct answer) (Berkowitz, 1990; Griffen, Wolery, & Schuster, 1992; Lalli & Browder, 1993; Smeets & Striefel, 1990; Touchette & Howard, 1984; Wolery et al., 1988; Wolery, Ault, Gast, Doyle, & Griffen, 1990). Below is an example of how *progressive* time delay was used by Mr. Eaton to teach Juan the names of hand tools.

1. Mr. Eaton puts two tools from a set of five or so on the table in front of Juan. Mr. Eaton waits until Juan looks at the tools, or he cues him to look.
2. When Juan looks at the tools, Mr. Eaton says, "Give me the screwdriver," and simultaneously points to the screwdriver. (The delay is 0 seconds.) If Juan picks up the screwdriver, he is reinforced. If he responds incorrectly several times, or does not respond at all, Mr. Eaton (still presenting the request and the pointing prompt simultaneously) adds another prompt (e.g., manually moves Juan's hand to the named tool). If Juan still make errors on the next trials, Mr. Eaton tries a more powerful reinforcer.
3. After about 10 trials (or perhaps a whole teaching session) at the 0-second delay level, Mr. Eaton gets Juan's attention as before, asks for one of the tools, and waits 1 second before giving the pointing prompt. If Juan responds correctly before the prompt, he is reinforced. If he merely imitates the prompt, he is still reinforced because Mr. Eaton does not want to extinguish imitation. If Juan responds before the prompt, but incorrectly, he may have to be taught to wait for the prompt. If Juan responds incorrectly after the prompt, perhaps more intrusive prompts or stronger reinforcers are needed. Mr. Eaton does not do more than a few trials in a row on picking up the same tool, especially if Juan is making errors.

4. After a block of trials (or a session) with 1-second delay between the request and the prompt, Mr. Eaton increases the delay to 2 seconds, and so on, until Juan reliably and correctly antici-pates the delayed prompt (i.e., responds to the request and not the prompt).

Note that, instead of progressively increasing the number of seconds between the cue and the prompt, Mr. Eaton might use a *constant* time delay interval throughout the instruction (e.g., 4 sec-onds) (Winterling, Gast, Wolery, & Farmer, 1992).

In contrast to the other methods, time delay does not result in a student waiting for (and becoming dependent upon) a prompt. Also, by prompting before errors, it benefits children who become upset and/or for whom errors become "correct" responses (Miller & Test, 1989).

SUMMARY AND IMPLICATIONS

This chapter is based on the idea that learning—a major part of the process of psychosocial devel-opment—occurs as we interact with antecedent events, prompts or obstacles, and consequences that are organized as respondent conditioning trials and operant contingencies of reinforcement in our surroundings. This chapter presents a number of generalizations about learning, such as the following:

1. Through their association with unconditioned stimuli (e.g., being fed), neutral stimuli (e.g., a caregiver's voice) may become conditioned stimuli that elicit attention and feelings (condi-tioned responses).
2. Contingencies of positive and negative reinforcement, Type I and Type II punishment, and extinction yield changes in how often, how fast, how long, how effortfully, where, and how skillfully a child performs operant behaviors.
3. Some antecedent events become discriminative stimuli that signify or "tell" us about the con-sequences of certain actions, and, therefore, become cues to perform reinforcable behaviors and not to perform punishable behaviors or behaviors that are not likely to have any effect.
4. Prompts and obstacles affect the way a child responds to cues, performs ongoing behaviors, and responds to consequences.

Clearly, assessments must provide information on the *kinds* of antecedent events, prompts, obstacles, and contingencies of reinforcement and punishment in a child's environments, and on the child's learning and performance under such conditions. Later chapters in this volume suggest how to obtain assessment information.

REFERENCES

Axelrod, S., & Apsche, J. (1983). *The effects of punishment on human behavior.* New York: Academic Press.

Barry, R.J. (1975). Low-intensity auditory stimulation and the GSR orienting response. *Physiological Psychology, 3,* 98–100.

Berkowitz, S. (1990). A comparison of two methods of prompting in training discrimination of communication book pic-tures by autistic students. *Journal of Autism and Developmental Disorders, 20*(2), 255–262.

Bijou, S.W., & Baer, D. (1961). *Child development I: A systematic and empirical theory.* New York: Appleton-Century-Crofts.

Bornstein, M.H., & Ludemann, P.M. (1989). Habituation at home. *Infant Behavior and Development, 12*(5), 25–29.

Chandler, L.K., Fowler, S.A., & Lubeck, R.C. (1992). An analysis of the effects of multiple setting events on the social behavior of preschool children with special needs. *Journal of Applied Behavior Analysis, 25,* 249–263.

Charlop, M.H., Kurtz, P.F., & Casey, F.G. (1990). Using aberrant behaviors as reinforcers for autistic children. *Journal of Applied Behavior Analysis, 23,* 163–181.

Cooper, L.J., Wacker, D.P., Thursby, D., Plagmann, L.A., Harding, J., Millard, T., & Derby, M. (1992). Analysis of the effects of task preferences, task demands, and adult attention on child behavior in outpatient and classroom settings. *Journal of Applied Behavior Analysis, 25,* 823–840.

Davis, C.A., Brady, M.P., Williams, R.E., & Hamilton, R. (1992). Effects of high probability requests on the acquisition and generalization of responses to requests in young children with behavior disorders. *Journal of Applied Behavior Analysis, 25,* 905–916.

Dawson, M.M., Catania, J.J., Schell, A.M., & Grings, W.W. (1979). Autonomic classical conditioning as a function of awareness of stimulus contingencies. *Biological Psychology, 9,* 23–40.

Demchack, M. (1989). A comparison of graduated guidance and increasing assistance in teaching adults with severe handicaps leisure skills. *Education and Training in Mental Retardation, 24*(1), 45–55.

Donnellan, A.M., & LaVigna, G.W. (1987, December). A note of cautious optimism. *DD Directions, 2.*

Donnellan, A.M., & LaVigna, G.W. (1990). Myths about punishment. In A.C. Repp & N.N. Singh (Eds.), *Perspectives on the use of nonaversive and aversive interventions for persons with developmental disabilities* (pp. 33–57). Sycamore, IL: Sycamore Publishing Co.

Donnellan, A.M., Mirenda, P.L., Mesaros, R.A., & Fassbender, L.L. (1984). Analyzing the communicative functions of aberrant behavior. *Journal of The Association for Persons with Severe Handicaps, 3,* 201–212.

Durand, V.M., & Carr, E.G. (1987). Social influences on "self-stimulatory" behavior: Analysis and treatment application. *Journal of Applied Behavior Analysis, 20,* 119–132.

Durand, M.V., & Carr, E.G. (1992). An analysis of maintenance following functional communication training. *Journal of Applied Behavior Analysis, 25,* 777–794.

Epling, W.F., & Pierce, W.D. (1990). Laboratory to application: An experimental analysis of severe problem behavior. In A.C. Repp & N.N. Singh (Eds.), *Perspectives on the use of nonaversive and aversive interventions for persons with developmental disabilities* (pp. 451–464). Sycamore, IL: Sycamore Publishing Co.

Ferster, C.B., & Perrott, M.C. (1968). *Behavior principles.* New York: Meredith Corporation.

Ferster, C.B., & Skinner, B.F. (1957). *Schedules of reinforcement.* New York: Appleton-Century-Crofts.

Fisher, W., Piazza, C.C., Bowman, L.G., Hagopian, L., Owens, J.C., & Slevin, I. (1992). A comparison of two approaches for identifying reinforcers for persons with severe and profound disabilities. *Journal of Applied Behavior Analysis, 25,* 491–498.

Fowler, S.A. (1988). The effects of peer-mediated interventions on establishing, maintaining, and generalizing children's behavior changes. In R.H. Horner, G. Dunlap, & R.L. Koegel (Eds.), *Generalization and maintenance: Life-style changes in applied settings* (pp. 143–170). Baltimore: Paul H. Brookes Publishing Co.

Gast, D.L., Ault, M.J., Wolery, M., Doyle, P.M., & Belanger, S. (1988). Comparison of constant time delay and the system of least prompts in teaching sight word reading to students with moderate mental retardation. *Education and Training in Mental Retardation, 23*(2), 117–128.

Gelfand, D.M., & Hartmann, D.P. (1984). *Child behavior analysis and therapy* (2nd ed.). Elmsford, NY: Pergamon.

Green, G. (1990). Least restrictive use of restrictive procedures: Guidelines and competencies. In A.C. Repp & N.N. Singh (Eds.), *Perspectives on the use of nonaversive and aversive interventions for persons with developmental disabilities* (pp. 479–493). Sycamore, IL: Sycamore Publishing Company.

Griffen, A.K., Wolery, M., & Schuster, J.W. (1992). Triadic instruction of chained food preparation responses: Acquisition and observational learning. *Journal of Applied Behavior Analysis, 25,* 193–204.

Guess, D., Helmstetter, E., Turnbull, H.R., & Knowlton, S. (1986). *Use of aversive procedures with persons who are disabled: An historical review and critical analysis.* Seattle: The Association for Persons with Severe Handicaps.

Guthrie, E.P. (1959). *The psychology of learning* (2nd ed.). New York: Harper & Row.

Hamblin, R.L., Buckholdt, D., Ferritor, D., Kozloff, M., & Blackwell, L. (1971). *The humanization processes.* New York: John Wiley & Sons.

Haring, N.G., Liberty, K.A., & White, O.R. (1980). Rules for data-based strategy decisions in instructional programs: Current research and instructional implications. In W. Sailor, B. Wilcox, & L. Brown (Eds.), *Methods of instruction for severely handicapped students* (pp. 159–192). Baltimore: Paul H. Brookes Publishing Co.

Haring, N.G., White, O.R., & Liberty, K.A. (1978). *An investigation of phases of learning and facilitating instructional events for the severely handicapped: An annual progress report, 1977–78.* Bureau of Education of the Handicapped, Project No. 443CH70564. Seattle: University of Washington, College of Education.

Herrnstein, R.J. (1961). Relative and absolute strength of response as a function of frequency of reinforcement. *Journal of the Experimental Analysis of Behavior, 4,* 267–272.

Hill, B.K., & Bruininks, R.H. (1984). Maladaptive behavior of mentally retarded individuals in residential settings. *American Journal of Mental Deficiency, 88,* 380–387.

Holland, J.G., & Skinner, B.F. (1961). *The analysis of behavior.* New York: McGraw-Hill.

Horner, R.D. (1980). The effects of an environmental "enrichment" program on the behavior of institutionalized profoundly retarded children. *Journal of Applied Behavior Analysis, 13,* 473–491.

Iwata, B.A. (1987). Negative reinforcement in applied behavior analysis: An emerging technology. *Journal of Applied Behavior Analysis, 20,* 361–378.

Koegel, R.L., Egel, A.L., & Dunlap, G. (1980). Learning characteristics of autistic children. In W. Sailor, B. Wilcox, & L. Brown (Eds.), *Methods of instruction for severely handicapped students* (pp. 259–301). Baltimore: Paul H. Brookes Publishing Co.

Koegel, R.L., & Koegel, L.K. (1988). Generalized responsivity and pivotal behaviors. In R.H. Horner, G. Dunlap, & R.L. Koegel (Eds.), *Generalization and maintenance: Life-style changes in applied settings* (pp. 41–66). Baltimore: Paul H. Brookes Publishing Co.

Koegel, L.K., Koegel, R.L., Hurley, C., & Frea, W.D. (1992). Improving social skills and disruptive behavior in children with autism through self-management. *Journal of Applied Behavior Analysis, 25,* 341–353.

Kozloff, M.A. (1983). *Reaching the autistic child.* Cambridge, MA: Brookline Books. (Originally published by Research Press, 1973.)

Lalli, J.S., & Browder, D.M. (1993). Comparison of sight word training procedures with validation of the most practical procedure in teaching reading for daily living. *Research in Developmental Disabilities, 14,* 107–127.

LaVigna, G.W., & Donnellan, A.M. (1986). *Alternatives to punishment: Solving behavior problems with non-aversive strategies*. New York: Irvington.

Lewis, M.H., Baumeister, A.A., & Mailman, R.B. (1987). A neurobiological alternative to the perceptual reinforcement hypothesis of stereotyped behavior: A commentary on "self-stimulatory behavior and perceptual reinforcement." *Journal of Applied Behavior Analysis, 20*, 253–258.

Lichstein, K.L., & Schreibman, L. (1976). Employing electric shock with autistic children: A review of the side effects. *Journal of Autism and Childhood Schizophrenia, 6*, 163–173.

Linscheid, T.R., Iwata, B.A., Ricketts, R.W., Williams, D.E., & Griffin, J.C. (1990). Clinical evaluation of the self-injurious behavior inhibiting system (SIBIS). *Journal of Applied Behavior Analysis, 23*, 53–78.

Lovaas, O.I., Newsom, C., & Hickman, C. (1987). Self-stimulatory behavior and perceptual reinforcement. *Journal of Applied Behavior Analysis, 20*, 45–68.

Luiselli, J.K., Suskin, L., & Slocumb, P.R. (1984). Application of immobilization time-out in management programming with developmentally disabled children. *Child and Family Behavior Therapy, 6*, 1–15.

Martens, B.K., Lochner, D.G., & Kelly, S.Q. (1992). The effects of variable-interval reinforcement on academic engagement: A demonstration of matching theory. *Journal of Applied Behavior Analysis, 25*, 143–151.

McDowell, J.J. (1988). Matching theory in natural human environments. *The Behavior Analyst, 11*, 95–109.

McGee, G.G., Paradis, T., & Feldman, R.S. (1993). Free effects of integration on levels of autistic behavior. *Topics in Early Childhood Special Education, 13*(1), 57–67.

Michael, J. (1982). Distinguishing between discriminative and motivational functions of stimuli. *Journal of the Experimental Analysis of Behavior, 37*, 149–155.

Miller, U.C., & Test, D.W. (1989). A comparison of constant time delay and most-to-least prompting in teaching laundry skills to students with moderate retardation. *Education and Training in Mental Retardation, 24*(4), 363–370.

Neef, N.A., Mace, F.C., Shea, M.C., & Shade, D. (1992). Effects of reinforcer rate and reinforcer quality on time allocation: Extensions of matching theory to educational settings. *Journal of Applied Behavior Analysis, 25*(3), 691–699.

Newsom, C., Favell, J.E., & Rincover, A. (1983). Side effects of punishment. In S. Axelrod & J. Apsche (Eds.), *The effects of punishment on human behavior* (pp. 285–316). New York: Academic Press.

Pace, G.M., Iwata, B.A., Edwards, G.L., & McCosh, K.C. (1986). Stimulus fading and transfer of treatment of self-restraint and self-injurious behaviors. *Journal of Applied Behavior Analysis, 19*, 381–389.

Paisey, T.J.H., Whitney, R.B., & Hislop, P.M. (1990). Client characteristics and treatment selection: Legitimate influences and misleading inferences. In A.C. Repp & N.N. Singh (Eds.), *Perspectives on the use of nonaversive and aversive interventions for persons with developmental disabilities* (pp. 175–197). Sycamore, IL: Sycamore Publishing Company.

Pavlov, I.P. (1927). *Conditioned reflexes*. Oxford: Oxford University Press.

Rast, J., Johnson, J., Drum, C., & Cronin, J. (1981). The relation of food quantity to rumination behavior. *Journal of Applied Behavior Analysis, 14*, 121–130.

Repp, A.C., Karsh, K.G., & Lenz, M.W. (1990). Discrimination training for persons with developmental disabilities: A comparison of the task demonstration model and the standard prompting hierarchy. *Journal of Applied Behavior Analysis, 23*, 43–52.

Repp, A.C., & Singh, N.N. (Eds.). (1990). *Perspectives on the use of nonaversive and aversive interventions for persons with developmental disabilities*. Sycamore, IL: Sycamore Publishing Company.

Rincover, A. (1986). Behavioral research in self-injury and self-stimulation. *Psychiatric Perspectives on Mental Retardation, 9*, 755–766.

Rolider, A., & Van Houten, R. (1990). The role of reinforcement in reducing inappropriate behavior: Some myths and misconceptions. In A.C. Repp & N.N. Singh (Eds.), *Perspectives on the use of nonaversive and aversive interventions for persons with developmental disabilities* (pp. 119–127). Sycamore, IL: Sycamore Publishing Company.

Romanczyk, R.G., & Goren, E.R. (1975). Severe self-injurious behavior: The problem of clinical control. *Journal of Consulting and Clinical Psychology, 43*, 730–739.

Russo, D.C., Cataldo, M.F., & Cushing, P.J. (1981). Compliance training and behavioral covariation in the treatment of multiple behavior problems. *Journal of Applied Behavior Analysis, 14*, 209–222.

Schoen, S.F. (1986). Assistance procedures to facilitate transfer of stimulus control: Review and analysis. *Education and Training of the Mentally Retarded, 21*, 62–74.

Singh, N.N., Watson, J.E., & Winton, A.S. (1986). Treating self-injury: Water mist versus facial screening or forced arm exercise. *Journal of Applied Behavior Analysis, 19*, 403–410.

Singh, N.N., & Winton, A.S.W. (1984). Effects of a screening procedure on pica and collateral behaviors. *Journal of Behavior Therapy and Experimental Psychiatry, 15*, 59–65.

Skinner, B.F. (1953). *Science and human behavior*. New York: Free Press.

Smeets, P.M., & Striefel, S. (1990). Discrimination training of mirror image stimuli with a delayed-prompt technique: Some critical dimensions of extra-stimulus prompts. *Journal of Experimental Child Psychology, 49*, 275–299.

Sprague, J.R., & Horner, R.H. (1992). Covariation within functional response classes: Implications for treatment of severe problem behavior. *Journal of Applied Behavior Analysis, 25*, 735–745.

Stahmer, A.C., & Schreibman, L. (1992). Teaching children with autism appropriate play in unsupervised environments using a self-management treatment package. *Journal of Applied Behavior Analysis, 25*, 447–459.

Sugai, G., & White, W.J. (1986). Effects of using object self-stimulation as a reinforcer on the prevocational work rates of autistic children. *Journal of Autism and Developmental Disorders, 16*, 471–495.

Touchette, P.E., & Howard, J.S. (1984). Errorless learning: Reinforcement contingencies and stimulus control transfer in delayed prompting. *Journal of Applied Behavior Analysis, 17*, 175–188.

Winterling, V., Gast, D.L., Wolery, M., & Farmer, J.A. (1992). Teaching safety skills to high school students with moderate disabilities. *Journal of Applied Behavior Analysis, 25*, 217–227.

Wolery, M., Ault, M.J., Gast, D.L., Doyle, P.M., & Griffen, A.K. (1990). Comparison of constant time delay and the system of least prompts in teaching chained tasks. *Education and Training in Mental Retardation, 25*(3), 243–257.

Wolery, M., Bailey, D.B., & Sugai, G.M. (1988). *Effective teaching: Principles and procedures of applied behavior analysis with exceptional students.* Boston: Allyn & Bacon.

Wolery, M., Kirk, K., & Gast, D.L. (1985). Stereotypic behavior as a reinforcer: Effects and side effects. *Journal of Autism and Developmental Disorders, 15,* 149–161.

CHAPTER 4

INSTRUCTION ACROSS THE FIVE PHASES OF LEARNING

THIS CHAPTER BUILDS ON THE PRINCIPLES OF LEARNING PRESENTED IN CHAPTER 3. IT SHOWS HOW TO plan, conduct, evaluate, and upgrade instruction to foster the five phases of learning—acquisition, fluency, generalization, adaptation, and maintenance. Changes across the five phases represent improvements in children's functional behavioral repertoires and psychosocial development.

The purpose of this chapter is to introduce concepts that guide assessment, program planning, and ongoing evaluation described in *Guidelines and Protocols for Practice*. For detailed discussions of instruction, the reader should see Bailey and Wolery (1984); Baker and Brightman (1989); Bricker (1986); Cooper, Heron, and Heward (1987); Ferster and Perrott (1968); Haring (1988); Horner, Dunlap, and Koegel (1988); Johnson-Martin, Attermeier, and Hacker (1990); Neel and Billingsley (1989); Snell (1987); White and Haring (1980); and Wolery, Bailey, and Sugai (1988).

ISSUES RELEVANT TO ALL FIVE PHASES OF LEARNING

This section defines the five phases of learning and instruction. It also discusses instructional environments and the proper use of cues, prompts, and reinforcers.

Five Phases of Instruction and Learning

Chapter 3 introduced the five phases of instruction and learning (Haring, White, & Liberty, 1978; Horner et al., 1988; Wolery et al., 1988). Briefly, these are:

Acquisition—the early phase when a child is learning how to perform a task.
Fluency—behavior is performed in a smooth manner and at effective and/or culturally desirable speeds, durations, and intensities.
Generalization—a child transfers behaviors acquired in one environment to new cues and locations.
Adaptation—altering a performance in response to circumstances (e.g., using both hands to pull a heavy door).
Maintenance—behavior remains strong when instruction ends.

Instruction does not need to follow the above sequence. Several weeks into the acquisition phase, for instance, Sam was 90% likely to look at a teacher who called his name. Therefore, he was next taught to generalize the looking response to family members and other teachers. Then he was taught to respond faster and look at speakers for a longer time (fluency).

In addition, different behaviors may be in different phases. Juan is learning to cook with more skill (acquisition); speak in longer and smoother sentences (fluency); model the desirable behavior of age peers (generalization); dress with clothing that has different kinds of buttons, hooks, and snaps (adaptation); and continue attending to tasks even though he gets less reinforcement for it (maintenance). Thus, assessment and ongoing evaluation are used to determine what phase(s) of learning each target behavior is in, and when to shift instruction from one phase to another.

Instruction Environments

Three environments for instruction include routine tasks and activities, incidental-engineered opportunities, and special sessions. Each has advantages and possible disadvantages.

Routine Tasks and Activities The round of daily life is a regular sequence of tasks and longer activities. Routine tasks and activities are a preferred instructional environment. This is so for the following reasons:

1. There are regular and frequent opportunities to participate in social life and learn a variety of behaviors essential for psychosocial development.
2. A child's participation can be varied from partial contributions (e.g., handing someone a spoon) to lengthier contributions (e.g., stirring soup).
3. A child learns about means-end relations (i.e., to accomplish Z, first do X and Y), parts and wholes (e.g., a sandwich consists of bread, filling, and condiment), and conventions (e.g., for eating and playing games).
4. Participation is likely to be noticed, reinforced, supported by available models, and to enhance others' perceptions of the child's competence.
5. Cues, prompts, and reinforcers are normative, "natural," and consistently available. Thus, the problem of generalization from contrived sessions to everyday environments is lessened.
6. Because tasks and activities occur in different conditions (e.g., eating in the kitchen vs. back-yard), adaptation is fostered (Falvey, 1989; Gaylord-Ross & Holvoet, 1985; Hecht, Levine, & Mastergeorge, 1993; Sailor, Goetz Anderson, Hunt, & Gee, 1988).

However, one difficulty with instruction during routine tasks and activities is that some activities are infrequent and occur only in certain places, which limits learning opportunities. Also, there may be interruptions and background noise. Moreover, child–caregiver interaction may be unproductive, and caregivers' teaching skills may be rather weak. These should be assessed and, if necessary, improved before starting instruction in routine tasks and activities (e.g., in the family).

Incidental-Engineered Opportunities Daily life contains many episodes that allow alert caregivers to give instruction that facilitates all phases of learning, as well as children's participation in social life (Ferster, 1967). Four incidental-engineered opportunities are: incidental teaching, mand-model technique, delay procedure, and chain interruption.

Incidental Teaching During incidental teaching, a caregiver either waits for or engineers the situation to encourage a particular response. The caregiver then prompts, reinforces, and/or encourages the child to expand the performance (Dunst & McWilliams, 1988; Hart & Risley, 1975; Stowitschek, McConaughy, Peatross, Salzberg, & Lignugaris/Kraft, 1988; Wolery et al., 1988).

In the following two adventitious opportunities, caregivers found chances to reinforce, prompt, and/or give children cues to try a behavior again in an improved way.

> Ms. Tyler is watching Jerry build a tower with blocks. When he has trouble with the eighth block, she comes over and says, "This is a tall tower. Let me help with this block." She steadies the lower blocks while Jerry stacks the eighth. "Great job!"

> Sam put his plate in the sink, but was not too careful. His mother says, "Thank you, Sam. Here is another one to put in. Now very gently." This helps Sam to improve his skill.

In contrast to adventitious opportunities, the following example shows how Ms. Blake *engineered* the situation to encourage responses that she could prompt and/or reinforce.

Ms. Blake engineered many chances for Becky to emit new or improved responses. For example: 1) she put very little dessert in Becky's dish to encourage asking for more; 2) she "forgot" to pour Becky juice to encourage asking; 3) she put Becky's lunch box in a different place so Becky would look for it or ask for help; and 4) she held out of reach a toy Becky liked, to encourage asking or at least imitating a prompt: "Say, 'Teddy bear, please.'"

The following dialogues illustrate incidental teaching that *expands* a child's behavior so it becomes integrated in conventional social interactions (McLean & Snyder-McLean, 1984).

Indra:	(Holds up a hair ribbon.) Blue ribbon.
Ms. Adams:	Yes! It is blue. Show me something else that is blue. (Generalizing "blue" and creating a form of "show-me" turn-taking.)
Indra:	(Points to Ms. Adams's blouse.)
Ms. Adams:	Mm hm. My blouse is blue. Now, you ask me.
Indra:	(Silence)
Ms. Adams:	Say, "Show me something green." (Prompt.)
Indra:	Show green!
Ms. Adams:	(Smiles and touches Indra's book bag.) This is green!

Steven:	(Looks at the story book page his mother is reading.)
Ms. Rogers:	And then the mouse climbed onto the cat's back. You point to the mouse on the cat's back. (An opportunity for partial participation in the story activity.)
Steven:	(Points correctly.)
Ms. Rogers:	Yes. That is the mouse on the cat's back. And then the cat began to run.
Steven:	Cat run. (Imitates. Expands participation to "informing" Ms. Rogers of the cat's actions.)
Ms. Rogers:	Yes, run! And look! (Points.) Then the cat saw another cat. A black cat. (Pause)
Steven:	(Silence)
Ms. Rogers:	(Points again to the black cat while Steven looks.) Black cat. Say, "Black cat." (Prompt)
Steven:	Black cat.
Ms. Rogers:	Yes! It's a (pause). (Opportunity space)
Steven:	Black cat.

Social life consists of conventional (scripted), collaborative activities, such as conversation and play. The above dialogues show caregivers finding "openings" to start a scripted activity and then helping a child to take a turn. In this way, children learn to respond to specific cues (e.g., hear a question and give an answer). Children also learn about the organization, purpose, and location of the larger activities.

Mand-Model Technique   With the mand-model technique, a teacher inserts a request into a child's ongoing activity and then prompts and/or reinforces the child's response (Goetz & Sailor, 1988). For example, while Luke is playing with toy cars, his mother asks what he is doing, or asks him to show her a red car. This request brings Luke into contact with possibly unnoticed events and helps him generalize into the play environment behaviors he acquired elsewhere (e.g., color naming and participation in a question-answer format). In contrast to incidental teaching, the mand-model technique involves more initiation by a caregiver.

Delay Procedure   In the delay procedure, a teacher identifies spots in a task or interaction where a child could make a request (Halle, Baer, & Spradlin, 1981). The teacher participates in the interaction as usual, but at the preselected spot the teacher interrupts the flow for a few seconds and waits for the child's request. If a request is not forthcoming, the teacher models one. Consider the following:

Instead of asking, Indra holds out her hand and waits for her father to give her the television remote control. Using the delay procedure, Indra's father picks up the control as usual, holds it for Indra to see, but waits 5 seconds for her to request it. When she does not ask, he says, "Say, 'Switcher, please'" (prompt). Indra imitates the prompt and her father gives her the selector (natural reinforcement).

Indra soon understood that the delay signified the need to ask, and began asking before the 5-second cue-prompt interval ended. In a few weeks, she was asking before her father held up the remote control (which produced faster reinforcement). Her father next used the delay procedure to generalize Indra's asking to other environments (e.g., to ask for a piggy back ride or more ice cream).

Chain Interruption   In chain interruption, a caregiver interrupts the child engaged in a sequence and makes a request requiring the child to insert another behavior into the sequence, thus enriching it (Hunt & Goetz, 1988). The following scenario is an example of chain interruption.

As Jerry is leaving the play area, Ms. Tyler says, "You can go back to your desk as soon as you put away the blocks and the picture book." He cooperates and receives the natural activity reinforcement. Later, when Jerry is about to pass her on the way to the playground, Ms. Tyler passively blocks his path so he has to initiate interaction to get her to move. If he does not make eye contact or ask her to move, Ms. Tyler provides a model (e.g., "Jerry, say, 'Move, please.'"). When he imitates, he is naturally reinforced by the opportunity to complete the sequence.

Special Teaching Sessions   Special sessions are all too common in many programs. Some researcher-practitioners believe sessions may inhibit creativity and generalization, and foster fatigue and resistance when sessions involve special times and locations; a limited range of tasks and materials; nonnormative cues, prompts, and reinforcers; and excessive practice (Bryen & Joyce, 1985; Mulligan, Guess, Holvoet, & Brown, 1980). However, special sessions can be useful under the following conditions.

First, if a child is unresponsive, uncooperative, or involved in self-stimulation (Koegel & Koegel, 1988), teaching sessions can be an effective and perhaps necessary environment for initially strengthening responsiveness and turn-taking during simple collaborative tasks. Second, if child–caregiver exchanges are counterproductive, then sessions can be an ideal place to improve them. Third, sessions can help caregivers increase their teaching competence and give children with a history of slow progress the experience of success. Increasing competencies can then be generalized to routine tasks and activities.

Fourth, if a child makes little progress during routine activities and incidental opportunities, teaching sessions could be used as needed for practicing weak behaviors. As weak behaviors increase in strength, the child is taught to generalize them to the right spots in routine tasks and incidental opportunities. Fifth, planning and running sessions may increase cooperation among family members or school staff. For instance, one person teaches while the other takes data or watches other children.

Still, teaching sessions can inhibit psychosocial development unless carefully planned. One must consider how to: 1) use age-appropriate tasks and materials; 2) introduce normative cues, reinforcers, and reinforcement schedules to promote generalization and maintenance; 3) systematically fade prompts; 4) increase adaptation by teaching children to perform tasks in different ways with different materials; and 5) help children generalize and sustain acquired behaviors in other places.

Guidelines for Effective Use of Cues

Avoid repeating cues that do not evoke attention and proper responses; it is usually wise to get a child's attention before giving cues. Events that strongly compete with attention and responding should be removed or lessened, and the tone of voice, pitch, and rhythm of speech that evoke and sustain attention should be considered. For both infants and some children with severe disabilities, "motherese" (high-pitched and exaggerated intonation) evokes and sustains gaze and attention better than the speech ordinarily used with older children (Santarcangelo & Dyer, 1988).

Cues that are salient and unambiguous (clear in action significance) should be used, and important words should be stressed. Rooms should be divided into clearly designated areas (e.g., playing, eating, studying, personal and group space), and places and containers should be provided for toys, food, and clothing.

In the early stages of a child's education, and with inattentive and/or uncooperative children, avoid background talk. Employ talk for cues, prompts, and reinforcement of important behaviors.

It is often useful to provide a break of a few seconds between learning trials. If a child makes an error, is corrected, and then correctly performs the behavior, wait a few seconds and repeat the cue to which the child responded incorrectly, prompting to ensure a correct response to the cue.

Periodically change decorations, schedules, gestures, tone of voice, activities, and seating arrangements to sustain alertness and provide opportunities for generalization and adaptation. To avoid teaching undesirable behavior and errors, be aware of children's responses to different events. For example, are group lessons a place where children are learning to take turns or to pester others?

Guidelines for Effective Use of Prompts and Reinforcers

As much as possible, prompt before errors. During acquisition, it may be wise to use time delay, most-to-least prompting, or graduated guidance (as these decrease the chance of errors), instead of least-to-most prompting. Think of different ways to prompt the same response, and do not continue to use a prompt if a child continues to err or resist.

To identify events that reinforce (increase) behaviors, use observation, experiment, and interviews with persons familiar with the child. Sustain effectiveness by rotating reinforcers (Dunlap & Koegel, 1980), decreasing background access to reinforcers for specific behaviors, and teaching children to select reinforcers (Dyer, Dunlap, & Winterling, 1990; Fisher et al., 1992; Parsons, Reid, Reynolds, & Bumgarner, 1990; Realon, Favell, & Lowerre, 1990). Reinforce immediately, before children engage in another behavior. It is also important to reinforce behaviors that are both in an improved form and are desirable alternatives to and/or physically incompatible with undesirable behavior. Weak behaviors should be reinforced on a continuous schedule. As they accelerate, gradually thin the schedule and move to a variable one. Also, gradually delay reinforcement. When delaying delivery of a "big" reinforcer (e.g., a favorite activity), provide immediate reinforcement with conditioned reinforcers (e.g., praise).

Conditioned Reinforcers   Caregivers need a range of normative reinforcers (e.g., smiling, praising, assenting to requests), otherwise they are left with contrived contingencies, such as tokens, food rewards, and threats (e.g., "If you don't clean up, you can't go out."). Thus, it is important to transform neutral events into conditioned reinforcers.

Events become conditioned reinforcers because they *regularly mediate* or stand between a person's responses and a person's receipt of already reinforcing events (Ferster & Perrott, 1968). For instance, when Luke cleans the supper table, his father smiles and lets him operate the computer. Because his father's smile regularly comes between Luke's cleaning and access to the computer, the smile becomes a conditioned reinforcer that will strengthen many of Luke's behaviors.

Conditioned Reinforcers that Are Situation Specific   Some conditioned reinforcers are confined to a specific situation. For example, Ms. Tyler reinforces children's task performance with tokens (e.g., poker chips) later exchanged for toys and snacks. The tokens are strong conditioned reinforcers, as indicated by the fact that children do many tasks to get them. However, this arrangement happens only in class, which is one reason children seldom perform tasks learned in Ms. Tyler's class anywhere else. Thus, it would be better if Ms. Tyler used conditioned reinforcers found outside of class.

Generalized Conditioned Reinforcers   Some events mediate between many behaviors and subsequent reinforcers. These events are *generalized conditioned reinforcers*. Money is an example—it is obtained by a variety of behaviors and is used to receive many other reinforcers. Thus, it is hard to become satiated on money.

Certain behaviors of caregivers become generalized reinforcers, as illustrated in Table 4.1, which summarizes an analysis in Ferster and Perrott (1968). Table 4.1 shows that children learn which of their interaction initiations produce reliable responses from caregivers and are reliably followed by reinforcers ("After I get Daddy to look at me he will [talk, play, joke] with me."). Caregivers' mediating responses become *generalized* conditioned reinforcers, strengthening *anything* children do to get them. As with money for adults, children are not easily satiated on caregivers' mediating behaviors. Moreover, children may be distressed by punishment or the threat of punishment from caregivers. Part of assessment and ongoing evaluation, therefore, is to find which behaviors of caregivers are generalized reinforcers for a child and which are not.

How To Condition Reinforcers   The general procedure for conditioning reinforcers is to regularly insert otherwise neutral but culturally important events between a child's responses and other known reinforcers. There are many ways to do this.

1. Give children praise, hugs, and pats on the back (initially neutral for some children) just before food, play, and other known reinforcers.
2. Give children stamps, stickers, tokens, check marks, and stars contingent upon desirable behaviors, which children exchange (almost immediately at first) for known reinforcers.
3. Let children wear special hats or buttons signifying that the children later get to engage in reinforcing activities.
4. Teach children to record their own behavior (e.g., to mark a box on a sheet of paper for each task completed or for each interval without self-stimulation). High enough scores for desirable behavior, or low enough scores for undesirable behavior, are then reinforced. In this way, self-attention, self-recording, and self-control can become conditioned reinforcers.
5. Teach children to choose tasks and reinforcers. The opportunity to choose becomes a generalized reinforcer.
6. Regularly respond to children's desirable initiations with known reinforcers, as indicated in Table 4.1. For example, regularly return a child's gaze with a smile and then an invitation to play.
7. Teach children to initiate interaction in desirable ways (e.g., to ask for contact, comfort, play) so that you can provide mediating responses (e.g., smile, and say "Okay"), which then lead to reinforcers.

ACQUISITION

This section examines Jerry's acquisition of skill at hand washing. Later sections trace the progressive changes in Jerry's hand washing, through fluency, generalization, adaptation, and maintenance.

Assessment and Program Planning

Before starting hand washing instruction, Ms. Tyler (Jerry's teacher) and Mrs. Hardy (Jerry's mother) conducted a task analysis. First, they watched how they and several children skilled at

Table 4.1.   Caregivers' behaviors as generalized reinforcers

Child's initiating response	Caregiver's mediating response	Subsequent reinforcers
Calls, looks at, approaches, cooperates with, makes request of, cries at, or takes the hand of caregiver; shows toy or completed task to caregiver.	Turns toward, looks at, smiles at, approaches, goes with child; says, "Yes" or "Okay"; asks "What's wrong?" or "Want to play?"; praises child.	Child is picked up, hugged, given snacks, comforted, or played with.

hand washing accomplish the task, carefully noting *steps, cues* that initiate each step, and natu .. *consequences* produced by completing each step (Winterling, Gast, Wolery, & Farmer, 1992). They summarized observations on a recording form shown in Table 4.2. Note that their analysis shows how what is accomplished at one step (the natural consequence) provides informative feedback (e.g., reinforcement) and also may serve as a cue for the next step.

Next, Jerry's mother and Ms. Tyler used their analysis of how the task is ordinarily done to assess Jerry's performance in school and home bathrooms. Because the bathrooms differed in color, and the shape and location of the sink was different, they could learn how these events affected Jerry's performance. Ms. Tyler had Jerry wash his hands twice—before a snack and after finger painting. Jerry's mother took notes on the recording form. After playing in the yard at home, Jerry washed his hands with his mother while Ms. Tyler took notes. Their notes described Jerry's performance on each of the already identified steps on Table 4.2.

To initiate hand washing, Jerry was brought to the sink and asked to wash his hands. At each step of the task, whomever was with him *waited* to see how he responded to "natural" cues (e.g., the sight of the faucet). If he did not notice the cue or began to respond incorrectly (e.g., spinning the bar of soap), he was prompted to perform the proper responses. The least intrusive prompt was used at first (e.g., pointing to the faucet) to find out what kinds of prompts and the degree of prompting Jerry seemed to need. Jerry was praised often for cooperating.

Finally, Ms. Tyler and Mrs. Hardy summarized their notes as follows:

1. Jerry did not notice and did not respond correctly to natural cues for each step.
2. Jerry did respond correctly on some steps when prompted with instructions (e.g., "Look at the soap."), gestures (e.g., pointing to the faucet), or models (e.g., turning off the faucet).
3. On some steps (e.g., lathering), Jerry needed a partial manual prompt (e.g., gently holding his arms at the elbows).
4. Jerry noticed more salient consequences (e.g., lathered hands), but not subtle ones (e.g., well-rinsed hands).

Table 4.2. Recording form for task analysis of hand washing

Cues	Responses	Consequences
See cold water faucet on right side of sink.	Reach for and grasp faucet.	See and/or feel faucet in hand.
See and/or feel faucet in hand.	Turn handle counter-clock-wise.	See, hear, and feel handle turn and water flow.
See, hear, and feel water flow.	Adjust flow.	See, hear, and possibly feel flow.
See, feel, and hear adjusted flow.	Remove hand from faucet and pick up soap.	Visual track of hand to soap; feel soap in hand.
Feel soap in hand.	Bring left and right hands together under flowing water.	See and feel hands in water.
See and feel hands in flowing water.	Rub hands together while holding soap.	Feel and see hands rubbing with soap.
Feel and see hands rubbing with soap.	Replace soap on sink.	Visual track of hand with soap.
See soap replaced on sink.	Put hands under flowing water and rinse and/or rub.	Feel and see water, and feel changing texture of skin.
Feel and see water and changing texture of skin.	Reach for and turn off faucet.	See and feel handle turn and flow cease.
See water flow cease.	Reach for towel.	

other tasks revealed that Jerry could perform the component actions of hand
(reaching, grasping, turning objects, rubbing hands together). This meant that he
...ot need special practice sessions on components.
...e sustained Jerry's effort and attention.

Ms. Tyler and Mrs. Hardy used the assessment information to plan instruction on acquisition. They decided to: 1) work on hand washing at routine times and places; 2) use progressive time delay prompting (i.e., after giving a cue, waiting a specified and gradually increasing number of seconds before prompting) combined with the graduated guidance strategy (using as much of a prompt as needed); and 3) reinforce with praise and hugs during instruction, and with snacks and reinforcing activities after instruction. The last instructional decision concerned teaching Jerry to assemble component task steps into an effective sequence; that is, which method of chaining to use. The next section describes four possibilities.

Strategies for Chaining

Human conduct is organized in sequences of varying lengths—opening a door, making a sandwich, playing a game, or cleaning a whole house. Chaining is a method for teaching people to perform component behaviors in a sequence, and to assemble components in an effective or conventional order. There are two traditional chaining methods. In *forward chaining,* a student learns to do the first step; then the first and second steps in a row; then the first, second, and third steps in a row; and so forth until the student can do them all.

In *backward chaining,* a student watches while the teacher demonstrates all but the last step. The student then notices the cues provided by the previous steps (e.g., what an almost made bed looks like), and performs the last step (putting the pillows in place). When the student can do the last step without help, the teacher demonstrates all but the last two, helps the student do the second to last (new) step, and the student performs the last (already learned) step. The process continues backward down the chain until the student can do the whole chain starting with the first step.

Recently, two more chaining methods have been introduced that are more effective than forward or backward chaining in teaching some tasks. In *whole task* (or *total cycle*) *instruction,* a student performs all of the steps in a task in the conventional order during each session. The student is prompted as needed at any step (Gaylord-Ross & Holvoet, 1985; Wilcox & Bellamy, 1982). Gradually, prompts are faded. However, some tasks have so many steps that attention weakens when the whole task method is used. Thus, a fourth method can be employed—*shorter total cycle programming.* This method involves the following steps: 1) a long task is divided into a series of subtasks, 2) the student is taught all the steps in one subtask via the whole task method, and 3) in later sessions the next subtasks are added in forward chaining fashion (McWilliams, Nietupski, & Hamre-Nietupski, 1990). For example, doing the dishes might be divided into subtasks such as: 1) filling the sink with soapy water, which consists of a series of even smaller steps; 2) loading the sink with dishes; 3) washing the dishes; 4) rinsing; and 5) stacking the dishes. In shorter total cycle programming, a student might be taught the first shorter cycle (filling the sink with soapy water), then the first shorter cycle plus the second shorter cycle (loading the dishes), then the first two cycles plus the third shorter cycle, and so forth.

The effectiveness of these four methods of chaining depends on current skills and task organization. Some tasks have high organization—one step flows into the next. For instance, rinsing a plate closely follows soaping the plate. This is because cues for rinsing (e.g., water) are nearby; only a few movements are needed to shift from soaping to rinsing, and the transition from soaping to rinsing is part of other tasks. In tasks with high organization, the whole task and shorter total cycle chaining methods are probably better choices than forward or backward chaining (Briggs & Naylor, 1962; Naylor & Briggs, 1963). This may be because forward and backward chaining divide organized tasks into contrived segments.

When tasks have low organization, and especially when components are difficult for a student, forward or backward chaining may be better than the whole task method. Indeed, when the end of a task is distant from the first steps, backward chaining appears especially effective. A possible explanation is that because backward chaining begins with instruction on the last step, a student always knows where he or she is going and can adjust performance in the early steps to meet the goal. If the whole task method is used with a long task, a student might not know where his or her early behaviors are leading, and any early errors could produce more errors along the way (Wightman & Lintern, 1985; Wightman & Sistrunk, 1987). However, the above findings are not the last word; there is much ongoing research on these issues. Moreover, a child's performance and preference for different chaining methods can be assessed.

Ms. Tyler and Mrs. Hardy elected the whole task method because hand washing has high organization and Jerry is skilled enough at component actions that the task may not have to be divided into subtasks. For Indra, shorter total cycle programming may be necessary because she has difficulty performing actions within steps.

Ongoing Evaluation

While working together, either Ms. Tyler or Mrs. Hardy took notes guided by the task analysis form (Table 4.2) while the other taught. When alone, they summarized observations on the form after the session. Evaluative information included Jerry's responses to natural cues; his performance at each step; prompts used and Jerry's response to prompts (e.g., if a manual prompt got him started, did he complete the step on his own?); whether Jerry noticed and responded to the consequences of each step; and his involvement (attention, cooperation, effort, enjoyment). Comparing recordings over time, they determined: 1) the steps at which Jerry was more competent; 2) how long each step took; 3) how smoothly he moved from one step to another; 4) how long attention, effort, and enjoyment lasted; and 5) weak spots in any steps.

On this basis, they decided that Jerry needed extra practice on putting soap gently back in the dish (rather than throwing it); therefore, they had special sessions on gently replacing many objects (including soap). The practice improved Jerry's soap replacing actions in the hand washing task. After 6 weeks, Jerry was doing the entire task with virtually no assistance. Ms. Tyler and Mrs. Hardy concluded it was time to think about fluency.

FLUENCY

Fluency refers to how quickly, naturally, smoothly, and how long a sequence is done. Although Jerry needed little prompting to perform the required actions in hand washing, his performance was not fluent. He spent 2–3 minutes lathering; did not turn the water all the way off; added unnecessary or inappropriate behaviors to the routine (e.g., spinning the soap dish); and sometimes left before he was done. The following are ways Mrs. Hardy and Ms. Tyler altered instruction to increase fluency.

First, they increased *efficiency*. Carefully observing Jerry's performance using Lin and Browder's format (1990), they identified five "operations" whose improvement would decrease fatigue while increasing speed and persistence. The five "operations" are as follows.

1. Because Jerry spent extra time *searching* for the soap, they accentuated the cue by using a bright pink bar.
2. Because Jerry spent time looking from one faucet to the other before *selecting* one, they gave him practice choosing the right faucet before each session. During the task itself, they reinforced reaching for the right faucet.
3. Jerry struggled to turn the faucet on and did not turn it off all the way. Therefore, he got practice on *grasping* and *turning* objects during incidental-engineered opportunities (e.g., squeezing a ball, twisting jar lids).

4.   Jerry spent much time soaping his hands because he held the bar in one hand while rubbing it on the other. Using a smaller bar and prompting him to grip it with both hands, the effectiveness of Jerry's *hold* was increased.
5.   Rinsing took so long because Jerry *inspected* what he was doing. Therefore, rinsing was analyzed into smaller steps: hold both hands under water, rub palms together, rub back of each hand with the palm of the other, and remove hands from water. Jerry was taught to use these steps every time, until the rinsing cycle was so automatic he did not have to inspect it.

In addition, Jerry's *speed* was shaped by reinforcing efficient movements that were accomplished quickly.

To *delete inappropriate behaviors,* when the action was performed (e.g., Jerry reached for the soap dish to spin it), the action was inhibited and he was prompted to perform the correct task step. Then he had to back up one or two steps in the sequence and re-do the sequence without the inappropriate behavior.

A final fluency goal was to *increase the amount of time* Jerry spent participating in the task. His incentive was increased by raising the value of the reinforcers he received after hand washing. Moreover, he did not receive these reinforcers (e.g., story) unless he finished the task.

GENERALIZATION

In 3 more weeks of teaching, Jerry's fluency in hand washing markedly improved. However, ongoing evaluation revealed that hand washing had not generalized. For example, Jerry would not wash hands for anyone but his mother or Ms. Tyler, he was confused by the green pine-scented soap and antique faucets at Grandma's house, he fussed about washing at a restaurant, and he did not wash in response to hands covered with food. In sum, Jerry needed work on generalization.

Fostering Generalization

Generalization involves transferring behaviors acquired in one environment to other environments. This section suggests how to facilitate and/or directly promote generalization.

Teach Behaviors Likely To Generalize   At least 10 criteria suggest which behaviors are likely to generalize. They are:

1.   Behaviors that are functional, expected, or frequently called for in other environments.
2.   Behaviors likely to have frequent opportunities and reinforcement in other environments
3.   Behaviors capable of being taught by persons in other environments
4.   Behaviors of wide applicability
5.   Behaviors likely to be neither punished nor involved in conflicting contingencies (e.g., reinforced by some people and punished by others)
6.   Behaviors that are age-appropriate and culturally appropriate
7.   Behaviors for which naturally occurring cues, prompts, reinforcers, and reinforcement schedules are already sufficient
8.   Behaviors a child performs competently and adapts (i.e., performs in various ways) depending on circumstances
9.   Behaviors for which there are available models in other environments
10. Behaviors relevant to environments in which the child is a frequent participant (Day & Horner, 1986; Fox, 1989; Haring, 1988; Stewart, Van Houten, & Van Houten, 1992)

Ms. Tyler's and Mrs. Hardy's selection of hand washing was a good one; it satisfied all of the above criteria.

Teach in Natural Environments   Instruction during routine tasks, activities, and incidental-engineered opportunities avoids some difficulties of generalization from special sessions (Sailor et al., 1988). If one cannot teach in natural environments, however, one may simulate them. For instance, because Luke is disruptive in barber shops, caregivers are teaching him how to get a haircut in school with a teacher wearing a barber jacket and Luke wearing a cloth covering while sitting in a chair in front of a mirror. However, teaching in both simulated and "natural" conditions may not exhaust the variations a child will confront in daily life. Therefore, one needs to directly promote generalization.

Teach a High Level of Competence and Fluency   Increase skill and fluency to the point that the child's performance is judged skillful by others and, therefore, may be reinforced. Teaching essential steps and problem steps to the point of "overlearning" (e.g., through repeated drill) may be helpful. For example, Juan's slow response to the employee taking his order in a fast food restaurant erodes the interaction sequence. The employee then makes a face communicating that Juan is odd, which subsequently upsets Juan. Having identified the weak spots in the sequence, Mr. Eaton and Juan have practice sessions in which Juan responds almost automatically. For instance: 1) in response to "Order please" or "Can I take your order?", Juan says "I'll have (names of items)"; 2) in response to "Will there be anything else?", Juan says "No, that's all"; and 3) in response to "That'll be (payment owed)," Juan gives $10 to the cashier.

Teach Related Skills   When a performance does not work in a new environment, one still might be successful if one can call on related skills (Liberty, Haring, White, & Billingsley, 1988). Thus, Juan is taught several ways to order fast food: verbally, pointing to items on a menu, and showing an employee food pictures Juan carries in his pocket. Likewise, Mrs. Hardy and Ms. Tyler reason that if Jerry cannot find the bathroom at a restaurant, his competence will be improved if he can ask for directions.

Teach How To Respond to a Range of Likely Situations   This section describes *general case instruction* (Albin & Horner, 1988; Chadsey-Rusch & Halle, 1992; Horner, McDonnell, & Bellamy, 1986; Repp & Karsh, 1992), which has the following steps: identify and describe environments where a child may be expected to perform the behavior, select environments for teaching generalization and environments for probing generalization, provide instruction to promote generalization, and probe for generalization in untrained environments.

Identify and Describe Environments   To identify and describe environments where a child may be expected to perform the behavior, the following questions should be answered. Where is Juan likely to eat out in the future? How does one order at fast food restaurants versus sit-down restaurants? What are the scripts or steps; the cues, prompts, and consequences for each step; and the levels of proficiency required? What are the similarities and differences *across* environments? Where is Jerry likely to wash his hands? What are the different sorts of doors, faucets, soaps, towels, and arrangements of objects?

Select Environments   Within the list of environments where a performance will be useful, select environments for instruction on generalization and environments for probing (testing) how much generalization has occurred. Regarding Juan's eating out, instruction is to be at McDonald's and at Sal's Pizzeria. Probe environments will be Burger King and Vinnie's Little Villa. For Jerry's hand washing, Ms. Tyler and Mrs. Hardy chose the school restroom and a bathroom at home for instruction, and the kitchen sink at home, the kitchen and bathroom at Grandma's house, and a restroom at McDonald's to probe generalization.

Provide Instruction To Promote Generalization   Following are three guidelines for promoting generalization to the untrained (probe) environments. *First, teach a child which cues to respond to (S+) and which cues not to respond to (S-).* Mr. Eaton teaches Juan to notice, distinguish, and understand the significance of: 1) the person who takes the food order (S+: approach this person) versus cooks, managers, and maintenance workers (S-: do not order from these persons); and 2) tables that are clean and unoccupied (S+: eat here) versus tables that are occupied or dirty (S-: do not eat here, try another table). Similarly, Mrs. Hardy and Ms. Tyler teach Jerry the difference between: 1) dirty hands (S+: wash them) and clean hands (S-: no need to wash them);

2) a bottle of detergent with soap in it (S+: turn this over and squeeze) and one that is empty (S-: just rinse your hands); 3) a hot water faucet that works (S+: turn it) versus one that does not work (S-: try the other faucet); and 4) restrooms with a sign for males (S+: go in) and those with a sign for females (S-: find the male restroom).

Second, use multiple examples (exemplars) of relevant cues (S+s and S-s) during instructional sessions (Hughes, 1992; Winterling et al., 1992). In addition to distinguishing employees who take orders and other staff, Mr. Eaton teaches Juan to: 1) order from men, women, and people of different ethnicities; 2) respond to many functionally equivalent cues ("What'll you have?"; "Can I help you?"; "Order, please."; "Next.") the same way; 3) use different menus written on the wall, printed on one sheet, or printed on folded pages; and 4) find the cashier, napkins, straws, and trash containers.

Similarly, Ms. Tyler and Mrs. Hardy help Jerry to: 1) distinguish different kinds (exemplars) of dirty hands—muddy, greasy, dabbed with mustard; 2) locate soap and towels at different places in bathrooms; 3) use different soap dispensers and towels; 4) wash in different sinks; and 5) enter restrooms with various signs for male and not restrooms with various signs for female. During instruction, a range of examples are covered so that children are likely to adapt performance to differences in environments.

Third, when a student responds properly to a range of common examples, teach exceptions. For instance, Juan orders food from the counter of a take-out restaurant, and from a table at a sit-down restaurant. Now, he learns to order at a drive-through restaurant, a snack bar, and a street vendor. Once Jerry uses different sinks, he is taught to wash hands in the yard with a hose or from a bucket. These "exceptions" require somewhat different behaviors. For example, at a drive-through restaurant, Juan has to give his order to a microphone.

Probe for Generalization in Untrained Environments   When a student responds to a range of common examples and exceptions, generalization to probe environments is examined (Lalli & Browder, 1993). For example, Juan's performance is assessed at Burger King, and on another day at Vinnie's Little Villa. Having taught Jerry to wash hands at school and home, Jerry's performance is now assessed at Grandma's house and at the McDonald's restroom.

During probe sessions, the same data are taken as during initial assessment and ongoing evaluation of acquisition and fluency-building, using a recording form such as the one shown in Table 4.2. It is important to note strong and weak spots in the sequences and to suggest ways to improve performance. For example, Juan's performance at Burger King broke down when he was asked other questions, such as "What's up, pal?" Either Juan needs to learn to answer such questions, or Mr. Eaton needs to increase Juan's fluency so much that Juan is not distracted. Performance also may be weak because a student does not know how to adapt to a range of circumstances. In the restroom at McDonald's, Jerry's performance eroded when he faced a liquid soap dispenser.

In sum, the strategy in general case instruction is to teach in one group of environments; probe generalization to the other group of environments; identify strong and weak spots, or error patterns, in the probe environments; diagnose the trouble and suggest remedies; try the remedies; and probe some more. As performance in probe environments improves, a decision is made when to stop the cycle.

Several other methods, not as comprehensive as general case instruction, can also promote generalization. These are sequential modification, introducing natural contingencies, teaching loosely, teaching others, teaching a child to mediate his or her own generalization, and partial participation.

Teach Sequential Modification   General case instruction is probably needed when a performance has many steps and is to be performed in many environments. However, generalization of simple and/or circumscribed tasks may be accomplished with *sequential modification* (Haring, 1988). Sequential modification involves teaching a behavior in one environment (e.g., using free-standing water fountains with a lever handle); probing for generalization to another environment (e.g., free-standing water fountains with a push button); identifying and remedying weak performances in the first probe environment; probing in a second environment (wall-mounted fountains with a lever handle) and improving weak spots as needed; and continuing to probe, teach, and probe in new places until a child is competent in a range of environments.

Introduce Natural Contingencies It is best to use materials, cues, prompts, reinforcers, and reinforcement schedules found in the environments where a child's performance is expected to generalize. When an instructional environment is not normative, one can normalize it as skill and fluency increase (Haring, 1988). Specifically, one may gradually: 1) reinforce less with contrived reinforcers, such as food and tokens, and more with praise, smiles, and hugs; 2) praise, smile, and nod as do persons in environments for generalization (i.e., without so much enthusiasm); 3) shift from immediate and continuous reinforcement schedules to intermittent reinforcement with praise, smiles, nods, and activities that normatively follow performances; 4) shift from accentuated cues and intrusive prompts to normative ones; 5) position oneself farther from the child while doing the task; and 6) introduce materials from environments for generalization (e.g., plastic spoons and printed napkins from McDonald's).

Teach Loosely Generalization is inhibited by a limited number of cues and materials and if a child only knows how to respond in limited ways. Teaching loosely (Haring, 1988), however, can promote generalization. In particular, one regularly: 1) initiates a performance and its steps in varying ways; 2) conducts instruction in different rooms, at different tables, and with a child sitting in different places; and 3) encourages a child to perform steps in novel ways (e.g., taking bread out of the package with one hand, two hands, a fork), and to perform whole sequences in different orders.

Teach Others By collaborating, Ms. Tyler and Jerry's mother avoid many difficulties of generalizing Jerry's performance from school to home, and vice versa (Kozloff, 1983). Because Jerry's performance affects other persons as well, some of these people may join instruction on generalization. For example, at home, Jerry's father is nearby while Mrs. Hardy teaches Jerry. This way, Jerry associates his father with the activity. In coming days, Jerry's father will fade into the teaching (first reinforcing Jerry, then prompting and reinforcing, and then cuing) while Jerry's mother fades out. Later, one parent teaches Jerry's siblings and others to work with Jerry (Fowler, 1988; Kozloff, 1983; Stewart et al., 1992). It is also useful to enlist support of persons in community environments. For instance, Mr. Eaton prepares the manager at a fast food restaurant for Juan's arrival and suggests how Juan can be cued and prompted.

Teach a Child To Mediate Generalization A child can facilitate generalization in several ways (Haring, 1988; Irving, Erickson, Singer, & Stahlberg, 1992; Koegel & Koegel, 1988; Koegel, Koegel, Hurley, & Frea, 1992; Stahmer & Schreibman, 1992), including self-recording, self-reinforcement, reciting or reading instructions, following pictured steps, and applying problem-solving methods such as trying a different way or soliciting help.

Partial Participation Partial participation promotes generalization, increases involvement in the social world, and improves others' judgments of a child's competence. These may result in a child playing more valuable roles in school and family. Facilitating partial participation involves: 1) identifying behaviors in a child's repertoire (actions, tasks), which, if performed at the right time and place, would increase participation in daily life; 2) identifying spots in the round of routine tasks and activities where the child can perform identified behaviors; 3) adapting tasks and/or materials so the child can more easily participate; 4) planning how to invite participation and how to provide cues, prompts, and reinforcement; 5) instructing others to follow the plan; 6) implementing the plan; and 7) generalizing the same partial participation to other spots and/or using chaining methods to increase the amount of participation (Baumgart et al., 1982).

Following the above steps, Mrs. Hardy and Ms. Tyler gradually increase Jerry's participation by inviting him to turn on the hot and cold water faucets while his mother washes dishes; squeeze detergent into the dish water; rub a sponge across several plates, which he enjoys so much he sticks around to rinse a few cups; and find the dish towel. In the backyard, Jerry's father invites him to turn on the faucet, rub the sponge on the car fenders and doors, and hose the car off. After a month of instruction on generalization, the data indicate that Jerry successfully washes his hands in many environments. This indicates that it is time to work on adaptation.

ADAPTATION

Adaptation refers to performance that is altered in response to environments. What does Jerry do if soap is not in the usual spot on the sink, or if soap is in a dispenser that has a handle that does not come back up by itself? Although increasing skill, fluency, and generalization may increase the adaptability of his performances, Jerry may benefit from special instruction.

Adaptation is fostered by gradually altering situations. With the example of hand washing, this means: 1) tightening the faucet and prompting Jerry to turn harder; 2) putting the soap dish under the sink and prompting Jerry to look for it; 3) giving Jerry practice using a pump dispenser and then introducing it where bar soap used to be; 4) pushing the handle of the pump dispenser down so far that Jerry has to grasp it with one hand and pull the handle up with the other; 5) standing Jerry in front of a high sink and prompting him to use a handy stool; 6) putting the stool in the bathroom closet and prompting him to find it; and 7) prompting Jerry to rearrange the environment himself (e.g., move the soap to different places and then use it). In addition, adaptation is increased by continuing to invite Jerry to use components of hand washing (e.g., using faucets, rinsing) in a variety of tasks and activities.

MAINTENANCE

Maintenance refers to durability. The work on acquisition, fluency, generalization, and adaptation is largely wasted if hand washing deteriorates when instruction on other skills becomes more prominent. However, behavior is likely to be more durable if a student's performance of task components is strong, the overall task is fluent, and the task is performed in many environments in adapted ways.

Additional methods can develop maintenance. For instance, Ms. Tyler and Mrs. Hardy: 1) prevent dependence on frequent reinforcement by thinning the reinforcement schedule until Jerry only receives an occasional nod while washing; 2) prevent dependence on contrived reinforcers by replacing them with normative activity reinforcers ("Clean hands! Now you can sit on the couch."); 3) delay reinforcement by increasing and varying the time between completion of tasks and subsequent enjoyable activities; 4) teach Jerry to wash in response to natural cues, such as dirty hands; 5) teach Jerry to reinforce himself ("All clean! Now yogurt."); 6) teach Jerry to monitor his own performance (e.g., to cue and/or describe what he is doing, and to notice and correct improper behaviors ["No spinning now."]); 7) inspect Jerry's hands at unpredictable times, reinforcing if they are clean and prompting him to wash them if they are not (Dunlap & Plienis, 1988); and 8) begin to see Jerry as a more skillful member of family and school systems, and provide him with a more advanced role (e.g., someone expected to keep himself clean and contribute cleaning actions to routine tasks and activities).

SUMMARY

This chapter describes how progress can be fostered in a student's functional behavioral repertoire by programming the changes labeled acquisition, fluency, generalization, adaptation, and maintenance. Particular attention is given to environments for instruction (routine tasks and activities, incidental-engineered opportunities, and special teaching sessions), the creation of conditioned reinforcers, and general case instruction.

REFERENCES

Albin, R.W., & Horner, R.H. (1988). Generalization with precision. In R.H. Horner, G. Dunlap, & R.L. Koegel (Eds.), *Generalization and maintenance: Life-style changes in applied settings* (pp. 99–120). Baltimore: Paul H. Brookes Publishing Co.

Bailey, D.B., & Wolery, M. (1984). *Teaching infants and preschoolers with handicaps.* Columbus, OH: Charles E. Merrill.

Baker, B.L., & Brightman, A.J. (1989). *Steps to independence: A skills training guide for parents and teachers of children with special needs* (2nd ed.). Baltimore: Paul H. Brookes Publishing Co.

Baumgart, D., Brown, L., Pumpian, I., Nisbet, J., Sweet, M., Messina, R., & Schroeder, J. (1982). The principle of partial participation and individualized adaptations in educational programs for severely handicapped students. *Journal of The Association for the Severely Handicapped, 7*(2), 17–27.

Bricker, D. (1986). *Early education of at-risk and handicapped infants, toddlers, and preschool children.* Glenview, IL: Scott, Foresman.

Briggs, G.E., & Naylor, J.C. (1962). The relative efficiency of several training methods as a function of transfer task complexity. *Journal of Experimental Psychology, 64,* 505–512.

Bryen, D.N., & Joyce, D.G. (1985). Language intervention with the severely handicapped: A decade of research. *Journal of Special Education, 19,* 7–39.

Chadsey-Rusch, J., & Halle, J. (1992). The application of general case instruction to the requesting repertoires of learners with severe disabilities. *Journal of The Association for Persons with Severe Handicaps, 17*(3), 121–132.

Cooper, J.O., Heron, T.E., & Heward, W.L. (1987). *Applied behavior analysis.* Columbus, OH: Charles E. Merrill.

Day, H.M., & Horner, R.H. (1986). Response variation and the generalization of dressing skills. *Applied Research in Mental Retardation, 7,* 189–202.

Dunlap, G., & Koegel, R.L. (1980). Motivating autistic children through stimulus variation. *Journal of Applied Behavior Analysis, 13,* 619–627.

Dunlap, G., & Plienis, A.J. (1988). Generalization and maintenance of unsupervised responding via remote contingencies. In R.H. Horner, G. Dunlap, & R.L. Koegel (Eds.), *Generalization and maintenance: Life-style changes in applied settings* (pp. 121–142). Baltimore: Paul H. Brookes Publishing Co.

Dunst, C.J., & McWilliams, R.A. (1988). Cognitive assessment of multiply handicapped young children. In T. Wachs & R. Sheehan (Eds.), *Assessment of developmentally disabled children* (pp. 105–130). New York: Plenum.

Dyer, K., Dunlap, G., & Winterling, V. (1990). Effects of choice making on the serious problem behaviors of students with severe handicaps. *Journal of Applied Behavior Analysis, 23,* 515–524.

Falvey, M.A. (1989). *Community-based curriculum: Instructional strategies for students with severe handicaps* (2nd ed.). Balitmore: Paul H. Brookes Publishing Co.

Ferster, C.B. (1967). Arbitrary and natrual reinforcement. *Psychological Record, 17,* 341–347.

Ferster, C.B., & Perrott, M.C. (1968). *Behavior principles.* New York: Meredith Corporation.

Fisher, W., Piazza, C.C., Bowman, L.G., Hagopian, L., Owens, J.C., & Slevin, I. (1992). A comparison of two approaches for identifying reinforcers for persons with severe and profound disabilities. *Journal of Applied Behavior Analysis, 25*(2), 491–498.

Fowler, S.A. (1988). The effects of peer-mediated interventions on establishing, maintaining, and generalizing children's behavior changes. In R.H. Horner, G. Dunlap, & R.L. Koegel (Eds.), *Generalization and maintenance: Life-style changes in applied settings* (pp. 143–170). Baltimore: Paul H. Brookes Publishing Co.

Fox, L. (1989, September). Stimulus generalization of skills and persons with profound mental handicaps. *Education and Training in Mental Retardation, 24*(3), 219–229.

Gaylord-Ross, R., & Holvoet, J. (1985). *Strategies of educating students with severe handicaps.* Boston: Little, Brown.

Goetz, L., & Sailor, W. (1988). New directions: Communication development in persons with severe disabilities. *Topics in Language Disorders, 8*(4), 41–54.

Halle, J.W., Baer, D.M., & Spradlin, J.E. (1981). An analysis of teachers' generalized use of delay in helping children: A stimulus control procedure to increase language use in handicapped children. *Journal of Applied Behavior Analysis, 14,* 389–409.

Haring, N.G. (1988). *Generalization for students with severe handicaps: Strategies and solutions.* Seattle: University of Washington Press.

Haring, N.G., White, O.R., & Liberty, K.A. (1978). *An investigation of phases of learning and facilitating instructional events for the severely handicapped: An annual progress report, 1977–78.* Bureau of Education of the Handicapped, Project No. 443CH70564. Seattle: University of Washington, College of Education.

Hart, B., & Risley, T. (1975). Incidental teaching of language in the preschool. *Journal of Applied Behavior Analysis, 8,* 411–420.

Hecht, B.F., Levine, H.G., & Mastergeorge, A.B. (1993). Conversational roles of children with developmental delays and their mothers in natural and semi-structured situations. *American Journal on Mental Retardation, 97*(4), 419–429.

Horner, R.H., Dunlap, G., & Koegel, R.L. (Eds.). (1988). *Generalization and maintenance: Life-style changes in applied settings.* Baltimore: Paul H. Brookes Publishing Co.

Horner, R.H., McDonnell, J.J., & Bellamy, G.T. (1986). Teaching generalized skills: General case instruction in simulation and community settings. In R.H. Horner, L.H. Meyer, & H.D. Fredericks (Eds.), *Education of learners with severe handicaps: Exemplary service strategies* (pp. 289–314). Baltimore: Paul H. Brookes Publishing Co.

Hughes, C. (1992). Teaching self-instruction utilizing multiple exemplars to produce generalized problem solving among individuals with severe mental retardation. *American Journal on Mental Retardation, 93*(3), 302–314.

Hunt, P., & Goetz, L. (1988). Teaching spontaneous communication in natural settings through interrupted behavior chains. *Topics in Language Disorders, 9*(1), 58–71.

Irving, A.B., Erickson, A.M., Singer, G.H.S., & Stahlberg, D. (1992). A coordinated program to transfer self-management skills from school to home. *Education and Training in Mental Retardation, 27,* 241–254.

Johnson-Martin, N.M., Attermeier, S.M., & Hacker, B.J. (1990). *The Carolina curriculum for preschoolers with special needs.* Baltimore: Paul H. Brookes Publishing Co.

Koegel, R.L., & Koegel, L.K. (1988). Generalized responsivity and pivotal behaviors. In R.H. Horner, G. Dunlap, & R.L. Koegel (Eds.), *Generalization and maintenance: Life-style changes in applied settings* (pp. 41–66). Baltimore: Paul H. Brookes Publishing Co.

Koegel, L.K., Koegel, R.L., Hurley, C., & Frea, W.D. (1992). Improving social skills and disruptive behavior in children with autism through self-management. *Journal of Applied Behavior Analysis, 25*(2), 341–353.

Kozloff, M.A. (1983). *Reaching the autistic child.* Cambridge, MA: Brookline Books. (Originally published by Research Press, 1973.)

Lalli, J.S., & Browder, D.M. (1993). Comparison of sight word training procedures with validation of the most practical procedure in teaching reading for daily living. *Research in Developmental Disabilities, 14,* 107–127.

Liberty, K.A., Haring, N.G., White, O.R., & Billingsley, F. (1988). A technology for the future: Decision rules for generalization. *Education and Training in Mental Retardation, 23*(4), 315–326.

Lin, C., & Browder, D.M. (1990). An application of the engineering principles of motion study for the development of task analyses. *Education and Training in Mental Retardation, 25*(4), 367–375.

McLean, J., & Snyder-McLean, L. (Eds.). (1984). Strategies of facilitating language development in clinics, schools, and homes. *Seminars in Speech and Language, 5*(3), 159–266.

McWilliams, R., Nietupski, J., & Hamre-Nietupski, S. (1990). Teaching complex activities to students with moderate handicaps through the forward chaining of shorter total cycle response sequences. *Education and Training in Mental Retardation, 25*(3), 292–298.

Mulligan, M., Guess, D., Holvoet, J., & Brown, F. (1980). The Individualized Curriculum Sequencing Model (I): Implications for research on massed, distributed, or spaced trial training. *Journal of The Association for the Severely Handicapped, 5,* 325–336.

Naylor, J.C., & Briggs, G.E. (1963). Effect of task complexity and task organization on the relative efficiency of part and whole training methods. *Journal of Experimental Psychology, 65,* 217–224.

Neel, R.S., & Billingsley, F.F. (1989). *IMPACT: A functional curriculum handbook for students with moderate to severe disabilities.* Baltimore: Paul H. Brookes Publishing Co.

Parsons, M.B., Reid, D.H., Reynolds, J., & Bumgarner, M. (1990). Effects of chosen versus assigned jobs on the work performance of persons with severe handicaps. *Journal of Applied Behavior Analysis, 23,* 253–258.

Realon, R.E., Favell, J.E., & Lowerre, A. (1990). The effects of making choices on engagement levels with persons who are profoundly mentally handicapped. *Education and Training in Mental Retardation, 25*(3), 299–305.

Repp, A.C., & Karsh, K.G. (1992). An analysis of a group teaching procedure for persons with developmental disabilities. *Journal of Applied Behavior Analysis, 25,* 701–712.

Sailor, W., Goetz, L., Anderson, J., Hunt, P., & Gee, K. (1988). Research on community intensive instruction as a model for building functional, generalized skills. In R.H. Horner, G. Dunlap, & R.L. Koegel (Eds.), *Generalization and maintenance: Life-style changes in applied settings* (pp. 67–98). Baltimore: Paul H. Brookes Publishing Co.

Santarcangelo, S., & Dyer, K. (1988). Prosodic aspects of motherese: Effects on gaze and responsiveness in developmentally disabled children. *Journal of Experimental Child Psychology, 46,* 406–418.

Snell, M.E. (Ed.). (1987). *Systematic instruction of persons with severe handicaps* (3rd ed.). Columbus, OH: Charles E. Merrill.

Stahmer, A.C., & Schreibman, L. (1992). Teaching children with autism appropriate play in unsupervised environments using a self-management treatment package. *Journal of Applied Behavior Analysis, 25,* 447–459.

Stewart, G., Van Houten, R., & Van Houten, J. (1992). Increasing generalized social interactions in psychotic and mentally retarded residents through peer-mediated therapy. *Journal of Applied Behavior Analysis, 25,* 335–339.

Stowitschek, J.J., McConaughy, E.K., Peatross, D., Salzberg, C.L., & Lignugaris/Kraft, B. (1988). Effects of group incidental training on the use of social amenities by adults with mental retardation in work settings. *Education and Training in Mental Retardation, 23*(3), 202–212.

White, O.R., & Haring, N.G. (1980). *Exceptional teaching* (2nd ed.). Columbus, OH: Charles E. Merrill.

Wightman, D.C., & Lintern, G. (1985). Part-task training for tracking and manual control. *Human Factors, 27,* 267–284.

Wightman, D.C., & Sistrunk, F. (1987). Part-task training strategies in simulated carrier landing final approach training. *Human Factors, 29,* 245–254.

Wilcox, B., & Bellamy, G.T. (1982). *Design of high school programs for severely handicapped students.* Baltimore: Paul H. Brookes Publishing Co.

Winterling, V., Gast, D.L., Wolery, M., & Farmer, J.A. (1992). Teaching safety skills to high school students with moderate disabilities. *Journal of Applied Behavior Analysis, 25,* 217–227.

Wolery, M., Bailey, D.B., Jr., & Sugai, G.M. (1988). *Effective teaching: Principles and procedures of applied behavior analysis with exceptional students.* Boston: Allyn & Bacon.

CHAPTER 5

STRUCTURED EXCHANGES AS A CONTEXT FOR LEARNING AND PSYCHOSOCIAL DEVELOPMENT

EXCHANGES ARE A PERVASIVE FORM OF SOCIAL LIFE BY WHICH PEOPLE ACCOMPLISH GREETINGS, CONversations, teaching sessions, work projects, religious services, and other activities (Blau, 1964; Homans, 1961). They are the context and the means by which connections to others are established and sustained, a functional behavioral repertoire is developed, and psychosocial development progresses. Indeed, life satisfaction is powerfully influenced by the quality of exchanges in families, schools, neighborhoods, and workplaces. Yet, many caregivers pay too little attention to exchanges. While trying to stop tantrums or obtain correct responses during lessons, they unwittingly engage in the kinds of exchanges that teach children to throw worse tantrums and make more errors. Moreover, many caregivers try to work on complex skills before children have even learned to pay attention and take turns.

GENERALIZATIONS ABOUT SOCIAL INTERACTION

Most traits that define humanness and individuality are achieved through social interaction. For example, during early exchanges, infants and young children learn to attend to voices and faces; take turns; imitate; and perform "conventionalized acts," such as pointing and requesting (Bakeman & Adamson, 1986). Indeed, the behavior organizing effect of exchanges is evident in the first months when, among other patterns, the infant extends a foot, smiles, and giggles before the anticipated toe tickle.

Orderly Exchanges

Interaction between infants and caregivers, and even between adults who have just been introduced, is often awkward at first. With repetition, exchanges become familiar, regular in form, almost "scripted" (Crais, 1990; Duncan & Farley, 1990; Nelson, 1986). With practice, participants develop commonsense knowledge of different exchanges (e.g., play, request-consent, conflict) and learn to interact in each one. The following exchanges are easily recognized.

Dad: Bart, put this wrapper in the trash, please.
Bart: No. I don't want to.
Dad: Bart! I said, put this in the trash!
Bart: (Starts to walk away.)
Dad: Come back here! I'm talking to you!
Bart: (Starts to run away, grinning.)
Dad: (Becomes very angry.)

Bart and his father are enacting the *rewarded noncompliance* (or nagging) exchange. The father makes a request, Bart does not cooperate, and the father repeats himself, which probably reinforces Bart's noncooperation. If Bart finally cooperates, it will reinforce the father's nagging.

Following is another kind of exchange.

Fern:	(Attentively drying dishes. Looks at Ms. Wright.)
Ms.Wright:	Wow! You are working so hard!! I love it!
Fern:	(Looks up and smiles; then places a dried plate on the stack.)
Ms. Wright:	Yes! You did that very gently.
Fern:	(Smiles and picks up another plate.)
Ms. Wright:	A blue plate.
Fern:	Buh-luh.
Ms. Wright:	Blue. Very good, Fern! Show me another blue plate.
Fern:	(Points to another blue plate.) This.
Ms. Wright:	Yes! It is blue.

Fern and Ms. Wright are performing *mutual reward* exchanges during a routine activity. Each one's actions positively reinforce, and in turn are positively reinforced by, the other's actions. Thus, each one's reinforced behaviors will increase, as will their fondness for each other and the activity.

Initiations and Reciprocations   During an exchange episode, each person takes at least one turn. The following display illustrates the turns of an exchange episode—initiating cue and reciprocating consequence—in the rewarded noncompliance (nagging) exchange.

Father: Initiates exchange by making a request of Bart (cue).	→	Bart: Responds to (reciprocates) his father's initiating request with a verbal refusal and by walking away, which are aversive for the father.	→	Father: Responds to (reciprocates) Bart's uncooperative response by repeating the request, which reinforces Bart's prior uncooperative response and gives Bart a cue for another uncooperative response.

There are many ways to initiate exchanges. For instance, one can ask questions, make requests, give commands, threaten, make invitations, appear to need help, perform behavior that is aversive to the other, perform behavior pleasing to the other, or stop what one is doing to give the other a chance to respond. Technically, *exchange initiations are cues for another to take a turn.* (Cues are discussed in chap. 3, this volume.)

The first person's initiating action (e.g., request) is followed by the other's *reciprocation*. Reciprocations include answering or not answering a question; cooperating or not cooperating with a request; accepting or declining an offer; providing or not providing help; giving in to, ignoring, or punishing the first person's aversive behavior; or ignoring or reinforcing the first person's desirable behavior. Note that the second person's reciprocating response to the first person's initiation serves as reinforcement, punishment, or extinction of the first person's initiation. For example, Bart's father's request is followed by Bart's noncooperation, which the father experiences as an aversive (punishing) consequence. Bart's noncooperation, however, is followed by nagging from the father, which is a positive reinforcer for Bart.

Single Exchanges and Sequences of Exchanges   Social interaction may involve one or two exchanges, as in the example of Bart and his father. However, interaction often involves several exchanges assembled into activities, such as lessons, chores, meals, games, and conversations. Notice that the series of exchanges creates the larger activity; at the same time, participants' sense of the developing activity guides performance of future exchanges in it. For instance, in Fern's and

Ms. Wright's interaction, each mutually rewarding exchange contributes to a larger activity—a pleasant lesson on doing dishes. At the same time, Fern's and Ms. Wright's sense that they are engaging in a pleasant lesson influences *how* they interact during the next exchanges in the lesson.

It is important to be mindful of both the separate exchanges and the larger activity being created. A less observant teacher, for instance, judges an ongoing lesson to be a disaster. The teacher then becomes hypersensitive to undesirable behaviors, unwittingly reinforces those behaviors, and produces the expected disaster. A more observant teacher notices when exchanges are not handled well and uses the assessment to improve the next exchanges and, therefore, the lesson.

Learning To Take Turns The first time Fern and Ms. Wright made eye contact while doing the dishes was coincidental; so was Ms. Wright's reciprocating praise. Now they enact their parts in mutual reward exchanges as if the exchanges were familiar. With repetition, participants interpret actions of the other person as cues to take a reciprocating turn. Participants also learn what sorts of actions to perform during their turns. For example, Ms. Wright learned that when she praises Fern, Fern continues and intensifies her desirable behavior. This is reinforcing for Ms. Wright. Hence, Ms. Wright sees Fern's desirable behaviors as a cue not just to reciprocate, but to reciprocate with enthusiastic praise.

Types of Exchanges

No two episodes are exactly alike; there is variation in facial expression, posture, and what is said. Yet, the *kind* of behavior each person performs, defined by effects on the other person (e.g., reinforcement, punishment, extinction), may be the same. For example, there are many ways Bart's father can make requests of Bart, many ways Bart can be uncooperative, and many ways his father can repeat requests, but all are variations of the same form or pattern—rewarded noncompliance. Thus, countless superficially different interactions become a small set of exchange types. Each yields specific changes in participants.

Reciprocal Teaching-Learning Process

During exchanges, each person's initiating or reciprocating actions may serve as: 1) unconditioned or conditioned stimuli that elicit emotional and attentional responses in the other person; 2) cues or discriminative stimuli that set the occasion for the other to respond; 3) prompts or hindrances; and 4) reinforcing, punishing, or extinguishing consequences the other person receives. Such consequences teach the other person whether, when, and how to behave in future exchanges (Blau, 1964; Hamblin, Buckholdt, Ferritor, Kozloff, & Blackwell, 1971; Homans, 1961; Kozloff, 1983, 1988; Patterson, 1980, 1982; Patterson & Reid, 1984). Thus, the more people interact, the more teaching and learning occur. The following interaction between Steven and his mother illustrates reciprocal (two-way) teaching-learning in a series of rewarded coercion exchanges. Steven's mother, Ms. Rogers, is pushing the shopping cart while 7-year-old Steven walks with her. Steven was behaving well until they reached the aisle with the cookies.

Steven: (Grabs a bag of cookies.) Deeze! Want deeze! (Steven's loud whining command is a conditioned stimulus that elicits pain in Ms. Rogers. What will onlookers think?)

Ms. Rogers: No. You eat too much of that stuff. Put them back. (By not complying with Steven's command, Ms. Rogers has put it on extinction.)

Steven: Cookie! Want cookie! (Ms. Rogers's face reddens. Because his first command was not reinforced, Steven escalates to yelling, which is coercive to Ms. Rogers; she feels unable to tolerate it.)

Ms. Rogers: Okay. Calm down. You can have a small package, but you must promise to be good. Okay? (Ms. Rogers escapes Steven's coercive yelling by promising him cookies. This positively reinforces yelling. It teaches him that yelling, not whining, is the better way to get cookies and other things he wants. Because they immediately precede cookies, Ms. Rogers's red face and promises are being turned into generalized reinforcers for Steven. [See chap. 4, this volume.])

Steven: (Stops yelling and wipes tears from his cheeks.) Okay. (Steven stops his aversive behavior.)

Ms. Rogers: (Feels relief. Hands Steven a package of cookies. By stopping his yelling at this moment, Steven negatively reinforces Ms. Rogers for having given in. This teaches her that the way to stop Steven's and possibly other children's coercive behaviors is to give something to them.)

Consider the short-term and long-term changes that occur between Steven and his mother. Short-term changes occur during or right after episodes. For instance, when Steven grabs the cookies, demands, and yells, it elicits pain in Ms. Rogers. The removal of such behavior produces relief. Similarly, being told that he cannot have what he wants elicits pain in Steven, whereas receiving promises and cookies elicits pleasure.

Respondent conditioning trials and operant contingencies of reinforcement (described in chaps. 3 and 4, this volume) are embedded in exchanges. Thus, repetition of a certain exchange has predictable long-term effects. For example:

1. Steven yells more often and Ms. Rogers gives in more often.
2. Steven learns more ways to coerce Ms. Rogers (response generalization) and uses coercion in more places with more people (stimulus generalization).
3. Facial expressions and promises by Ms. Rogers that signify she will soon give in become generalized conditioned reinforcers for Steven.
4. Ms. Rogers learns more ways to give in to stop Steven's coercion and gives in in more places and to more children (generalization).
5. Steven becomes more skillful at coercion and Ms. Rogers becomes more skillful at escaping by giving children whatever stops their coercive behaviors (shaping).
6. They perform the rewarded coercion exchange more often.
7. Ms. Rogers develops dislike for Steven, shopping, tasks, and places where this exchange happens (respondent conditioning).
8. Ms. Rogers's and Steven's relationship is increasingly adversarial.

A year from now, an assessment report will say Steven has a disorder of impulse control. The report will say nothing of the thousands of rewarded coercion exchanges in which Steven was accidentally taught to use aversive behaviors to get what he wants. In other words, *a child's behavioral repertoire suggests the exchanges in which the child has been participating.* This is why assessments must describe exchanges in a child's school and home, and why individualized education programs for children and individualized family service plans for families must specify how to replace counterproductive exchanges and increase productive ones.

Durability

Some exchanges persist even when people want to change. This is known as durability. There are several sources of durability, including reinforcement; coercion; fatigue; unacceptable alternatives; norms, beliefs, and self-perceptions; and defense mechanisms.

Reinforcement   When an exchange involves reinforcement for one or both persons, both people repeat their usual roles when the occasion arises, as this yields more reinforcement. This applies to Fern and Ms. Wright, who positively reinforce each other's behavior. It also applies to Steven and Ms. Rogers. Steven receives cookies for yelling and Ms. Rogers receives respite from Steven's yelling after she gives him cookies. Thus, the next time Steven is in the cookie aisle, he will demand and yell and Ms. Rogers will give in. Even mutually aversive exchanges such as a fight may involve reinforcement. For instance, a caregiver sees a student's hitting as aggression and punishes the student so that the student backs off. The caregiver's use of punishment is negatively reinforced by respite from the next "aggressive" behavior from the student.

In sum, exchanges usually enable participants to receive positive reinforcers or to escape and avoid aversive events. Even when exchanges yield discomfort or distress in the long run, short-term reinforcement ("success") encourages people to continue, sometimes to a destructive level. As Patterson points out:

> If the key socializing agent . . . becomes shaped to maximize short-term payoff, then the family is truly distressed. It means that the key agent is likely to overplay aversive events to induce immediate short-term changes. At the same time, she is likely to underplay the use of positive reinforcers to produce long-term changes. (1980, p. 26)

Coercion   Coercion is another source of durability, as shown by the following vignette.

> Ms. Reed decided to stop reinforcing Sally's tantrum-threatening behaviors. The next time Sally made a face and moaned, Ms. Reed ignored it and walked away. Sally did not give up, however. When reinforcement for moaning did not come, she escalated to a major tantrum. Ms. Reed became frightened and gave in despite her earlier decision. "Okay. Easy! Stop yelling . . . That's good. Let's go to the play area for awhile."

Ms. Reed thinks that requiring Sally to stop yelling before she can play will teach Sally not to yell. In fact, giving in *after* Sally escalates to yelling teaches Sally to yell as a way of forcing Ms. Reed to offer the play area. It also teaches Sally to use escalation to discourage Ms. Reed from trying to improve exchanges. This pattern (one person changes behavior, the other escalates to worse behavior, and the first person gives in) helps explain how people learn helplessness and develop quick-fix strategies for solving problems. It is hard for caregivers to withstand escalation in a child's coercive behavior when they get little encouragement, advice, or hands-on assistance.

Fatigue   Whether from the effort of teaching, childrearing, or other labor, fatigue is a source of durability. One may not have the energy to think of or try ways to improve interaction. Thus, families and teachers may need to improve exchanges in small steps, while also receiving assistance and respite.

Unacceptable Alternatives   Ms. Reed continues with her usual method of responding to threats and tantrums because she: 1) does not know it is okay to walk away from a child who is screaming; 2) does not notice that Sally's screaming comes in several forms, some more desirable than others; 3) does not know how to shape screaming in desirable directions by reinforcing shorter episodes or lower intensities; and 4) is afraid that trying alternatives may be risky. The same problem applies to children. If they do not have skills to perform desirable alternative behaviors, they may continue undesirable behaviors that have paid off, even if these behaviors are on extinction. Thus one has to find simpler behaviors to reinforce, and teach children difficult behaviors in small steps.

Norms, Beliefs, and Self-Perceptions   Although some exchanges are distressing, people may believe that: 1) they should not expect any better; 2) the other's behavior should be tolerated; and 3) acting differently (e.g., requiring that a child earn certain reinforcers) would be unfair. These sustain destructive exchanges while making people feel better in the short-run.

Defense Mechanisms   Exchanges may be durable because "defenses" against discomfort reduce the incentive to make substantial change. "Defenses" include: 1) *selective inattention* ("I rarely reinforce undesirable behavior."); 2) *denial* ("Punish Bud? I never punish Bud!"); 3) *rationalization* ("Maybe I do punish Bud, but he needs it."); 4) *distortion* ("I do not give in to threats. I just do not want her to be sad."); 5) *distraction and sublimation*—eating, spending a lot of time in the teachers' lounge, decorating—to dampen pain of counterproductive exchanges and avoid thinking about them.

Development of Productive and Counterproductive Exchanges

In some classrooms and homes, interaction is increasingly cooperative and mutually rewarding. Members see each other as collaborators. Their positive responses to one another (smiles, compliments, touch) are generalized reinforcers. In other environments, interaction is increasingly conflictual. Members learn to threaten, coerce, punish, nag, obstruct, and withdraw. They see each other as adversaries. In addition, the negative responses they provoke (anger, expressions of pain) are generalized reinforcers.

Emergence and Crystallization of Mutual Reward   An understanding of how mutual reward versus conflict crystallizes into a way of life could promote productive exchanges and halt a trend toward durable destructive ones. This description of early child–caregiver exchanges draws on the work of Abidin, Jenkins, and McGaughey (1992); Ainsworth, Blehar, Waters, and Wall (1978); Bakeman and Adamson (1986); Bakeman and Brown (1977); Barnard and Bee (1979); Brazelton, Tronick, Adamson, Als, and Wise (1975); Caldwell and Bradley (1978); Cohn and Tronick (1987, 1988); Dunham and Dunham (1988); Farran, Kasari, and Jay (1986); Fernald and Kuhl (1987); Field (1987); Field, Healy, and LeBlanc (1989); Gusella, Muir, and Tronick (1988); Hyche, Bakeman, and Adamson (1992); Jarvis, Myers, and Creasey (1989); Marfo (1992); Martin (1981); Newson (1978); Olson, Bates, and Bayles (1982, 1985, 1989); Patterson (1982); Patterson and Reid (1984); Pettit and Bates (1989); Rutter and Durkin (1987); Stevenson, VerHoeve, Roach, and Leavitt (1986); van de Rijt-Plooij and Plooij (1993); and White and Watts (1973).

A set of child–caregiver interactions called *positive involvement* (Pettit & Bates, 1989) or *reciprocity* (Jarvis et al., 1989) starts a trend of mutual reward. First, caregivers frequently smile at, touch, vocalize, play with, hold, and caress the infant or young child. Moreover, they do so with the precise actions and timing that complement the child's smiling at, attending to, vocalizing, cooperating with, approaching, and displaying security in the presence of caregivers. For example, a child reaches out to a parent who then picks up the child; or the child looks at the teacher and vocalizes, and the teacher smiles and vocalizes back. These episodes of mutual reward increase in frequency and become the form by which activities such as dressing, feeding, playing, and conflict resolution (e.g., "You can play as soon as you finish eating.") are accomplished.

Second, caregivers provide frequent opportunities for the infant and young child to participate in daily activities (see the discussion on incidental teaching in chap. 4, this volume). For example, a parent raises a spoon and waits for the child to look at and reach for it, or gives the child clear signals that it is the child's turn (e.g., "Now you give *me* one."). This brings the child into activities as a *collaborator*.

Third, caregivers tailor cues to children's capabilities (or caregivers' cuing behavior is shaped by children's relative responsiveness). For example, a teacher says a child's name to get his or her attention; smiles with wide open eyes; moves objects so the child notices; and uses the tone of voice, pitch, and rhythm (e.g., motherese) that sustain attention (Fernald & Kuhl, 1987).

Fourth, caregivers respond as if children's behaviors are purposeful and relevant to the activity. For example, a parent understands a turned away head is a sign that the child does not like the food offered. The parent comments ("Oh, you don't want applesauce?") and removes it. Thus, the child learns that he or she can affect the environment in ways that get pleasant rather than angry reactions.

Emergence and Crystallization of Conflict Exchanges   In contrast to mutual reward, increasing coercion, nagging, threats, and withdrawal may be started by "negative involvement." In particular, there is less reciprocal smiling, vocalizing, touching, snuggling, and attending between infant or young child and caregivers. This is associated with a decreasing rate of smiling from the child and an increasing rate of gaze aversion, withdrawal, aggression, and anxiety around or ambivalence toward caregivers.

For example: 1) a child's reaching out is seen as a demand and is rejected; 2) a child gazes at a teacher and vocalizes, but it is not noticed; 3) a parent vocalizes at the child, but the child is engrossed in something else (i.e., initiations are not synchronized with the child's behavior); 4) a teacher vocalizes in a steady stream, not giving the child a chance to vocalize in return, or feeds the child without giving the child a chance to watch and grasp the spoon; and 5) a caregiver's cues are not tailored to a child's preferences and capabilities (e.g., instructions are too fast, have a harsh tone, and include words the child does not understand). In sum, there is less reciprocal affection, fewer chances for the child to collaborate in activities, and poor timing between each person's initiations and reciprocations.

In addition, there is increasing aversive interaction. An infant's perceived demands and a young child's perceived uncooperativeness prompt caregivers to use threats (e.g., "If you drop any more food, I'll take your dinner away."); punishment (e.g., "Stay in your room all day and cry."); nagging (e.g., "If I have to tell you once more!"); and harsh tones of voice (e.g., "Get over here!"). Some children respond to this style in ways caregivers see as increased demands and uncooperativeness. A caregiver then reacts with even more aversive responses (Martin, 1981). When depressed, a caregiver and infant or young child may spend much time in states of reciprocal anger-protest or disengagement-withdrawal. Indeed, Field remarks that the "sharing of negative states . . . by . . . depressed mothers and their infants suggests a contagion effect of negative mood" (Field et al., 1989, p. 370). In sum, children and caregivers gradually perfect a pattern of mutual dissatisfaction. Each demands what the other will not give or does not know how to give, and each delivers what the other does not want. Routine activities become opportunities for more conflict.

Mutual Reward versus Conflict Exchanges   A trend of mutual reward versus conflict is shaped by several factors. One is children's illnesses and developmental disabilities. For instance, parents of children with pulmonary disorders and parents of infants with craniofacial deformities are *less likely* than parents of moderately ill children and infants without facial deformities to respond to children's cues, and to hold, affectionately touch, smile at, look at, laugh with, and vocalize with their children (Barden, Ford, Jensen, Rogers-Salyer, & Salyer, 1989; Jarvis et al., 1989). In the case of children with pulmonary disorders, parents' rates of positive involvement appeared to decrease over time. And in the case of infants with craniofacial deformities, parents' relatively low rates of positive responses to their children were complemented by children's low rates of smiling at parents. Thus, some parents and children begin a relationship with a relatively low rate of mutually rewarding exchanges—a pattern that this author suspects is strongly affected by parents' initial shock, lack of support, and hospital procedures that separate parents and infants.

Yet, a child's developmental disability alone is not sufficient to impair early child–caregiver interaction. For instance, children with hearing impairments and language delays are "as likely to establish a positive, reciprocal, and secure relationship with their mothers as . . . hearing toddlers" (Lederberg & Mobley, 1990, p. 1602). Thus, some illnesses and developmental disabilities may be more "normal" and less traumatizing to parents, involve less hospital separation, and make it easier for parents to adapt their caregiving to their children's capabilities (e.g., using vision and touch to manage exchanges with children who have a hearing impairment).

A child's temperament combined with a caregiver's tolerance can also affect emerging exchanges. When children who are loud, active, easily aroused, and/or unsoothable are paired with caregivers with a similar high-strung temperament, caregivers' tolerance may be exceeded quickly and often. This can result in caregivers nagging, giving in, or punishing to stop behavior they find aversive. The result is that children's "aversive" behavior may intensify and become durable (Bell, 1979; Bell & Chapman, 1986).

Caregivers' perceptions of children's behavior affect developing exchanges. For instance, parents who rate their 2-year-old child as "troublesome," "unresponsive" to the mother, and "unsociable" (hard to control, frequently expressing anger) may adopt a coercive and nagging style and try to restrict the child's activities. Some children react with more troublesome behavior. By the age of 6, children are rated by their caregivers as highly negative, noncompliant, impulsive, aggressive, anxious, or socially withdrawn (Olson et al., 1989). Perhaps through a similar process, parents who perceive their children as aggressive at 4 years of age were likely to have seen their children as temperamentally difficult between 6 and 24 months of age (Pettit & Bates, 1989).

External factors can also affect child–caregiver interaction For example, social support (e.g., assistance, approval, a sympathetic ear) from a spouse, relatives, and friends is associated with mutually rewarding mother–infant exchanges (Hann, 1989). Lack of support from a spouse, however, is associated with a young mother's lower rate of vocalizing with her infant (Culp, Applebaum, Osofsky, & Levy, 1988).

There is much discussion of the contribution made by children, caregivers, and the family and school environment to child–caregiver exchanges (Dodge, 1990; Lytton, 1990; Wahler, 1990). Still, it is clear that early patterns (reciprocity vs. conflict) often become durable. Thus, child–caregiver exchanges should be assessed as early as possible, focusing on involvement or reciprocity. Moreover, caregivers of children with disabilities should receive training as soon as possible in structuring mutual reward exchanges and avoiding or restructuring conflict exchanges (Bromwich, 1981; Kirkham, 1993; Seifer, Clark, & Sameroff, 1991; Tannock, Girolametto, & Siegel, 1992).

COUNTERPRODUCTIVE AND PRODUCTIVE EXCHANGES

Some exchanges are counterproductive; they involve conflict, pain for one or both persons, and yield change contrary to people's better interests. Productive exchanges, however, involve mutual reward; they engender more pleasant feelings and beneficial change in both participants. (The term *reward* is used in this section to mean exchanges; the term *reinforcement* retains its precise sense and is used when exchanges are analyzed.) Table 5.1 lists counterproductive exchanges and productive mutual reward alternatives.

Counterproductive (Conflict) Exchanges

Counterproductive exchanges involve conflict and pain. That is, one person wants what the other does not give, or one gets what he or she does not want. Furthermore, these exchanges are short-term solutions that turn difficulties into desperate situations. As Fingarette points out, "One choice, one act leads to another. We do not foresee, we do not intend the long-term pattern, but a series of individual quick-fix solutions may lead us into one" (1988, p. 103).

Rewarded Coercion   Rewarded coercion involves one person doing something another person does not like. For example, Mr. Pitt tells Jeff that he cannot go outside. Jeff throws himself to the floor, yelling and kicking. Mr. Pitt's abdominal muscles tighten, and his face and posture display shock, embarrassment, fear, or anger. He stares at Jeff, communicating displeasure, repri-

Table 5.1   Productive and counterproductive exchanges

Counterproductive (conflict) exchanges	Productive (mutual reward) alternatives
Rewarded coercion	Unrewarded coercion
Rewarded threat	Unrewarded threat or earning
Rewarded noncompliance or nagging	Single signals or cooperation training
Aversive methods	All of the above and below
Lack of opportunities for desirable behavior	Plenty of opportunities for desirable behavior
Improper prompts and/or assistance	Proper prompts and/or assistance
Lack of rewards for desirable behavior	Plenty of rewards for desirable behavior

mands him, tries to calm him with explanations, offers an activity to soothe him, or finally lets Jeff go out—perhaps adding, "As soon as you calm down."

Some of Mr. Pitt's escape reactions reinforce Jeff's coercive behavior; Jeff is commanding and receiving attention, predictable consequences (having an effect), and perhaps goodies as well. His feelings are temporarily changed by the reinforcement, and his tantrum stops or softens. This negatively reinforces Mr. Pitt's "giving-in" escape behaviors. Thus, both Jeff's coercive behaviors and Mr. Pitt's escape behaviors are reinforced.

Several long-term changes result from repetition of rewarded coercion exchanges. First, each person performs the usual behavior more often. Also, because each person's behavior is in response to cues from the other, the exchange happens more often. Second, with repetition, Jeff becomes skillful at having tantrums in ways and environments that yield the quickest, most certain, and best reinforcers. Likewise, Mr. Pitt becomes skillful at giving in to Jeff's tantrums (e.g., giving Jeff the "right" response). Third, mutual reward exchanges happen less often because Mr. Pitt and others give Jeff fewer chances and less reinforcement for desirable behavior. This is because Jeff is aversive to be around. The lack of opportunities and reinforcement for desirable behavior, however, leaves Jeff with little alternative but coercive behavior.

Fourth, when Jeff becomes satiated on Mr. Pitt's and others' usual reinforcements, he will *not stop* tantrumming, but will escalate and/or try other coercive behaviors until people try new and (to Jeff) more reinforcing ways of getting Jeff to stop. At the same time, when people get used to Jeff's current kind of tantrum, or decide not to give in anymore, Jeff will escalate; if people then give in, it teaches Jeff to escalate until others cannot bear his tantrums. Eventually, Jeff is seen and treated as an adversary.

Rewarded Threat   The following is an example of rewarded threat.

When Tommy was 3 years old, he broke things and hit people when he did not get his way. Such behavior was coercive to teachers and family, who reinforced Tommy's aggression by giving him some item or activity to stop the behavior. Over the years Tommy participated in the rewarded coercion exchange repeatedly, always with the same effects.

Without reflecting on it, Tommy's family and teachers learned cues predicting when Tommy's aggression was about to start—a look on Tommy's face, restlessness, or poor appetite. Unwittingly, they reacted to threatening cues as they had reacted to aggression—with reinforcement. "Is something bothering you?", "Okay, you've done enough math," or allowing him to watch television.

The placating (avoidance) responses from others did reduce the frequency of Tommy's threatened aggression. Also, by not aggressing, Tommy negatively reinforced people for reinforcing his threats. In time, Tommy gained (was given) much control over his home and classroom; all he had to do was threaten aggression.

Repetition of the rewarded threat exchange yields long-term changes. First, the exchange happens more often and in more places. Second, the frequency and skill of Tommy's threats and others' placations rises. Lastly, productive exchanges decrease, as few want to interact with Tommy. This further weakens his competence and participation in daily interactions and activities. Eventually, caregivers' " . . . avoidance activities take on a momentum of their own . . . . (T)he avoidance pattern becomes easier and easier, more and more spontaneously favored in response to a variety of threatening or anxiety-producing situations" (Fingarette, 1988, p. 109). In sum, caregivers buy temporary peace and safety by placating Tommy. The price Tommy pays for the short-run reinforcement of threats is an impoverished functional behavioral repertoire and little psychosocial development. When his threats are too draining and incompetencies too burdensome, he may be removed from the home or school.

Rewarded Noncompliance   In a rewarded noncompliance exchange, an adult's initiation (e.g., request, question) is followed by a child's uncooperative response. This is aversive to the initiator, who then repeats himself or herself, usually in more exciting (reinforcing) ways. The child may respond to each repetition by further noncooperation. Eventually, the adult may give up. This, along with prior nagging, reinforces the child's whole series of uncooperative responses. If and when the child cooperates, perhaps because the adult's nagging is now aversive or the adult has threatened the child, the adult is reinforced for all of the nagging. In time, the adult's nagging is frequent and durable, as is the child's uncooperative and inattentive behavior. Unaware of these adult–child exchanges, an outsider may see the child as having a hearing impairment, receptive language deficit, or personality disorder.

Aversive Methods   Aversive methods can be one-sided and mutual. In the *one-sided* use of aversive methods, a child does something that a caregiver does not like. The caregiver reacts either by punishing the child (e.g., spanking, insults) or by taking away positive reinforcers. This interrupts or stops the child's behavior and perhaps elicits a display of discomfort. These effects reinforce the use of aversive methods. With repetition, the caregiver uses aversive methods more often, and the child may become withdrawn and anxious.

In the *mutual* use of aversive methods, the "punishment" is neither fast, consistent, nor hard enough to stop the child's behavior for long. Immediately or soon thereafter, the child escalates the "punished" behavior (e.g., throws a worse tantrum), or uses counter-aggression (e.g., biting) to punish the caregiver for the punishment. This surprises the caregiver and/or makes the caregiver stop, which reinforces the child's counter-aggression. Eventually, the caregiver punishes the child again, and another round begins. Each person experiences reinforcement when the other expresses hurt or temporarily stops the aversive behavior. In time, mutually aversive exchanges occur in longer series (fights), intensity escalates (Patterson, 1980), and the two people become skillful at provoking and hurting each other. Also, as Patterson says, "First the mother and then the rest of the family arrive at a point where they are punishing each other for substantial proportions of their total interactions. This is presumably a sign of incipient breakdown in the family system" (1980, p. 42).

The same may be said of the long-term use of aversive methods in schools. When a child's problem behavior (shaped in severity by the aversive exchanges) is finally considered too frequent or difficult to contain, the child may be removed from school.

Lack of Opportunities for Desirable Behavior   Another counterproductive exchange involves a caregiver who does not notice or does not provide a child with opportunities to perform desirable behavior. Perhaps the caregiver does not see opportunities in the round of daily life where the child can join in (e.g., cooking). Or, the caregiver may not notice desirable behaviors or believe that efforts to involve the child would have much effect. Perhaps the adult is too tired. The result is minimal development of a child's functional behavioral repertoire. The caregiver exerts less effort in the short-run, but more in the long-run.

Improper Prompts   A child's response may be too slow or in error, but instead of properly prompting the child to make a better response, the adult: 1) gives no prompt, which teaches the child that erroneous responses are either correct or permissible; 2) uses prompts that interfere with attention to cues (e.g., loud instructions or forceful manual prompts); 3) does not draw the child's attention to relevant cues; or 4) prompts the child to repair an error, but does not have the child back up, observe the original cues, and make a correct response without a prompt. Thus, the child merely learns to imitate the prompt. The result of improper prompting is that the child remains dependent upon prompts and improves little. The adult perceives his or her efforts as futile and gives the child simpler tasks or more extensive prompting, which may stifle psychosocial development.

Lack of Rewards   A child's desirable behavior may not be reinforced because adults: 1) dislike the child; 2) stay away from the child; 3) pay little attention to what the child is doing; 4) do not notice desirable behavior; 5) notice desirable behavior, but believe it does not deserve reinforcement; 6) believe that behaviors are either good or bad, so if the child has a mild tantrum, the adult will not try to shape lower intensity tantrums by reinforcing it; 7) reinforce too late; or 8) "reinforce" with events that are not reinforcers (e.g., praise that is wooden or sarcastic).

If behaviors are weak to begin with, they will stay that way, and if they are occurring at a fairly high rate, the lack of reinforcement will weaken them. Moreover, the lack of reinforcement for desirable behaviors means that the hedonic value of the child's environment is low. This increases the child's incentive to perform undesirable behaviors that are more likely to be reinforced.

Exchange Clusters   Sometimes there are only a few counterproductive exchanges in a school or family. For example, a child habitually whines for dessert. In many environments, several kinds of counterproductive exchanges occur frequently while mutual reward exchanges are infrequent.

The following example suggests how a situation might go from okay to intolerable. Early in the school year, a few children whine and a few others engage in self-stimulatory behavior. With little prior training and no on-site coaching on exchanges, the teacher accidentally reinforces such behaviors by telling children to stop. As rewarded coercion exchanges and children's undesirable behaviors increase, the teacher becomes tired and less tolerant. Consequently, the teacher fails to notice and reinforce desirable behaviors, prompts with less skill, nags, and gives easier tasks to avoid children's whining (i.e., rewarded threat). Children then make more errors and whine to get attention or escape tasks. Eventually, most of the interaction consists of the teacher trying to control undesirable behavior in the context of nagging, rewarded coercion, and rewarded threat exchanges. At times, the teacher is punitive—using a harsh tone of voice, insults, painful manual prompts, and spanking. Although such a situation can be remedied, it is easier to prevent the situation by knowing what each exchange looks like, paying attention to ongoing exchanges, and knowing how to replace counterproductive with productive exchanges.

Productive (Mutual Reward) Alternatives to Counterproductive Exchanges

In mutual reward exchanges, one person initiates with a behavior that is reinforcing to the other person, and that person reciprocates in a way reinforcing to the first person. The following vignettes illustrate how caregivers can structure mutual reward exchanges to replace counterproductive ones.

Randy is constantly in motion, making faces and noises, drumming with his pencils, spinning books on his desk top, or running around the room. After 2 days at a developmental disabilities clinic, Randy was diagnosed with attention deficit hyperactivity disorder and medications were prescribed. It is not clear whether there is anything in Randy's brain chemistry that accounts for his hyperactive behavior. However, one thing is certain—Randy's hyperactive behavior gets a lot of reinforcement in the coercion, threat, and nagging exchanges, such as "Randy! Sit still. Where are you going? Come back here. I said, come here! Cut that out. Leave that alone. Stop running . . . ." Even worse, Randy gets few opportunities and little reinforcement for desirable behaviors.

After careful observation, analysis, and planning, Randy's parents and teachers altered the exchanges with him. Whenever he is sitting calmly for as little as 30 seconds (his average is about 45 seconds), paying attention to his work or to desirable behavior of other children, or is occupied in any constructive way, they reinforce it with praise, a smile, or a soft touch. That is, they look for and reinforce desirable behavior rather than looking for and reinforcing behaviors they do not like. As the average duration of Randy's attentive behavior increases, they wait a little longer before reinforcing him; that is, they *shape* longer intervals of attentive behavior. In addition, they give Randy many chances each day to earn reinforcers by engaging in desirable behavior in the form of simple chores, doing favors, and answering questions.

When he becomes hyperactive (e.g., leaves his seat and runs around), parents and teachers no longer reinforce this behavior by telling him to come back or running after him. Instead, they pay attention to someone else's desirable behavior. If Randy returns to his work or to some other desirable activity in *less* time than before, they reinforce this by saying, "That was great the way you came back so soon!" In fact, teachers let Randy run and get into things as reinforcers for having engaged in desirable behavior.

By first replacing counterproductive exchanges with productive ones, rather than first giving medication, caregivers learn how much of Randy's behavior is the result of social interaction rather than a disorder. At the same time, caregivers learn what exchanges yield productive behavior in Randy. The next example shows one way to replace the nagging exchange with cooperation training or single signals.

Bart's father realized that getting angry and repeating requests when Bart did not cooperate was teaching Bart not to cooperate or pay attention. Bart's father decided to restructure exchanges with him. Each day he asked Bart to do 10 different simple tasks. Many were the same each day; that is, they were Bart's daily job. If Bart cooperated more quickly and with less back talk or more skill than usual, his father reinforced Bart with praise and the opportunity to put a check mark on a special chart on the refrigerator. When Bart earned three check marks he could choose back-up reinforcers, such as wrestling with his father, video games, or looking at skateboard magazines. If Bart did not cooperate better than usual, his father walked away. If one of Bart's sisters was nearby, his father made the same request of her and reinforced her for cooperating. This showed Bart the effects of cooperation versus noncooperation.

In a few days, Bart caught on. Not only was he more cooperative, but the nature of Bart and his father's relationship started to change. They sought out one another rather than avoided one another. Indeed, Bart performed some tasks without being asked, for which he was soundly reinforced.

With the above examples in mind, let us look at the short- and long-term changes that result from repeating mutual reward exchanges.

1. In the short-term, each person's behavior receives a reinforcing reaction from the other person. Being reinforced, each person expresses his or her feelings by smiling, assuming more relaxed postures, thanking the other, and/or continuing the reinforced behavior. Such return expressions of pleasure are reinforcing to the one who delivered the reinforcement, thus completing the productive cycle.
2. Because each person's behavior is reinforcing to the other and reinforced by the reaction of the other, each person performs his or her part in the exchange more often. In fact, through respondent conditioning, mutual sentiments of liking become stronger. Also, the exchange happens more often and perhaps becomes a familiar part of the classroom or family.
3. Counterproductive exchanges decrease as each person feels more respect, sympathy, and liking for the other and is less reinforced by displeasing or injuring the other.
4. Each person's skill at mutually rewarding exchanges increases. Parents and teachers become better at initiating, prompting, and reinforcing children's desirable behavior because certain ways of doing so yield more smiling and repetitions of desirable behaviors. Also, children become more skillful at engaging in behavior that gets the fastest, most frequent, and strongest reinforcement from caregivers.
5. Each person generalizes reinforced behaviors to other environments. For example, what teachers do when restructuring exchanges with Randy, they may do in exchanges with others. Also, what Randy learns during mutual reward interaction with teachers and parents, he generalizes to other locations and interactions with other adults.
6. Overall, the family and classroom are more pleasant and foster improvement in each person's functional behavioral repertoire and psychosocial development.

INCREASING PRODUCTIVE EXCHANGES
AND REPLACING COUNTERPRODUCTIVE EXCHANGES

Efforts to improve children's skills, manage problem behaviors, and foster psychosocial development are futile without a foundation of productive exchanges. How much can a child learn during instruction if the child neither pays attention nor has skill at taking turns? How can a student learn daily life tasks if he or she is unwittingly punished for errors and if opportunities to contribute are not noticed? How long will caregivers be motivated to teach anything if counterproductive exchanges breed fatigue and a sense that "things" are out of control?

Research by this author and his colleagues indicates that some of the fastest and most important changes in children, parents, teachers, and their relationships come from improving exchanges (Kozloff, 1988; Kozloff et al., 1988; Kozloff, Helm, & Cutler, 1987). As caregivers learn how exchanges work, observe exchanges, increase productive exchanges, and restructure counterproductive exchanges, they become more confident, energetic, and skillful; children become more attuned to what is going on, more cooperative, less disruptive, and able to learn more difficult skills such as imitation, talking, and self-help.

The following are steps this author and his colleagues teach families, teachers, therapists, and administrators. The steps ought to be a routine part of assessment, program planning, instruction, and program evaluation, as discussed in *Guidelines and Protocols*. Each step takes several days to a week or more to institute. As later steps are started, earlier ones are upgraded.

Step 1: Determine What Is Reinforcing and Aversive

What events are reinforcers for children? By identifying events that are already reinforcers, as well as those that might be used as reinforcers, teachers and families can initiate productive exchanges with Grandma's law (Homme, 1967): "As soon as you put away your toys, we can (wrestle, read, color, make sandwiches, and so forth)." In addition, they will know when they are accidentally reinforcing undesirable behaviors (e.g., by staring) and will be better prepared to reinforce a range of desirable behaviors without satiating children.

In addition to positive reinforcers, it is important to identify aversive events—events that disrupt a child's behaviors, elicit escape and avoidance responses, or weaken behaviors that precede the events. Examples include certain tasks and activities, words, tones of voice, facial expressions, gestures, places, objects, touching, sounds, and colors. With this knowledge, caregivers can increase the hedonic value of interaction by removing aversive events (e.g., not using threatening tones of voice). In addition, caregivers can desensitize children to aversive places, events, or tasks by exposing them to these things in small doses with a lot of reinforcement.

Generally, to determine what is reinforcing and aversive, one uses interviews and direct observation with caregivers (see chaps. 9 and 10, this volume). Parents and teachers should be alert to events such as: 1) a child behaves a certain way to receive something versus behaving to escape from, delay, or avoid; 2) a child expresses pleasure versus displeasure in receiving or anticipating; 3) a child talks about a topic with enjoyment versus distaste; 4) a child asks for something versus refuses or never mentions it; and 5) once an object or activity is received, there is an increase versus a decrease in the frequency of the behaviors that resulted in receipt of the object or activity. Positive reinforcers and aversive events that are identified should be summarized using guidelines such as those shown in Table 5.2 (see also Form 7, *Recording Conditioned Stimuli, Positive Reinforcers, and Aversive Stimuli* in Section II of the companion to this volume, *Guidelines and Protocols*).

Caregivers should also identify events that are positive reinforcers and aversive stimuli for themselves. Certain behaviors of children may be aversive because of when or where they happen (e.g., self-stimulatory behavior in the grocery store). Others may be aversive because they interfere with the caregiver's activities, are judged dangerous or injurious, or embarrass the caregiver. At

Table 5.2.   Recording Conditioned Stimuli, Positive Reinforcers, and Aversive Stimuli

Please list the conditioned stimuli, positive reinforcers, and aversive stimuli for the child who is being assessed.

1. Actions the child performs or has the opportunity to perform:

2. Tasks the child performs or is given:

3. Activities the child participates in or has the opportunity to participate in:

4. Objects:

5. Sounds:

6. Visual stimuli (e.g., television programs, pictures, passing cars):

7. Tactile and kinesthetic stimuli (e.g., swinging, touch, heat, cold):

8. Responses from particular others, especially responses that may be generalized reinforcers because they regularly mediate between a child's behavior and the child receiving other known reinforcers (e.g., praise, gaze, touch, invitations ["Want to play?"], consent ["Okay"], being approached, being yelled at):

(continued)

Table 5.2   (*continued*)

9. Places (e.g., stores, car, rooms, in chair):

10. Mental imagery (e.g., of eating, of playing, of performing certain tasks):

11. Edibles:

12. Subtle or general features of environments (e.g., predictability; things being "in their place"; events happening "on time"; tasks being challenging, flexible, functional, cooperative, or involving certain muscle groups):

the same time, certain behaviors of children are reinforcing to caregivers. Examples might include smiling; coming to the adult when he or she calls the child's name; competencies, such as dressing and communicating in a conventional way; and traits, such as attentiveness and cooperativeness.

Caregivers ought to identify behaviors of children that are positive and negative reinforcers for them and describe forms of the behaviors that are more reinforcing or aversive. For instance, does a child have to communicate in well-formed utterances, or are fair approximations reinforcing? Does a child have to pay attention for 10 minutes, or is a little improvement over the usual 5-minute span reinforcing? Is any sort of tantrum quite aversive, or does the degree of aversiveness depend on the loudness or length? Such a list will remind caregivers of behaviors to look for, encourage, and reinforce (including undesirable behaviors to shape in a more desirable direction).

Step 2: Describe Ongoing Exchanges

Before developing plans to improve exchanges, caregivers should spend a week or so observing interaction, learning how often different exchanges occur, and describing episodes of some exchanges in detail. It is important to observe a child's exchanges with adult caregivers, siblings, and peers with whom the child has frequent contact. (Methods of direct observation are presented in chap. 10, this volume; assessment of exchanges is described in Form 3 of *Guidelines and Protocols.*)

Counting Exchanges   Teachers and family members can observe interaction for several days between and during routine activities, such as meals and lessons. The point is to learn how often different exchanges occur and the conditions in which they occur. For example, the rewarded coercion exchange might occur most often when caregivers are busy or tired; the mutual reward exchange may occur more often during play activities. A simple recording form, such as that shown in Figure 5.1, can be used to count exchanges.

Caregivers may be able to count one or two different exchanges. For instance, a teacher might count how often he or she reinforces desirable behavior and nags when children do not cooperate.

Recording Form for Counting Exchanges

If exchanges are happening at a fairly low rate, you might be able to identify and record each one (continuous event recording). If many exchanges are happening one after another, as during a task or activity, time sampling may be more feasible. For example, divide the observation period into consecutive 30-second intervals and record the first exchange that happens in an interval. Record exchanges by putting a hash mark (//) to the right of the exchange. Use initials to indicate different caregivers who are interacting with children. Do **not** try to observe and count all of the following types of exchanges at once. Instead, begin with a few, such as reinforcement for desirable behavior versus reinforcement for coercive behavior. At another time, you may count a different exchange, such as nagging.

1. Adult gives child opportunity for desirable behavior.
2. Adult fails to give child opportunity for desirable behavior.
3. Adult reinforces child's desirable behavior.
4. Adult fails to reinforce child's desirable behavior.
5. Adult reinforces child's coercive behavior.
6. Adult reinforces child's threat of coercive behavior.
7. Adult does not reinforce child's coercive or threatening behavior; instead, he or she encourages and reinforces a desirable alternative behavior.
8. Adult uses aversive methods.
9. Adult uses effective prompt.
10. Adult fails to use effective prompt.
11. Adult nags when child does not cooperate.
12. Adult does not nag when child does not cooperate.

Figure 5.1   Recording form for counting exchanges.

However, because instruction and other activities preclude more self-observation and recording, it is good for teachers and parents to team up and observe one another. Later, they may review and summarize the record as shown by the following.

Summary of Exchanges in Ms. Reed's Class
Observed During a 3-Hour Period by Ms. Wright

Rewarded coercion: Children engaged in 50 episodes of whining, self-stimulation, tantrums, and hitting other children. Ms. Reed reinforced these behaviors 25 times (50%) by telling children to stop, staring at children, giving them easier work, and so forth. (Ms. Reed's comment: "I was more likely to notice and reinforce these behaviors later in the period as I became tired.")

Nagging: Ms. Reed gave 48 exchange initiations, consisting of requests and questions. Children did not cooperate 24 times (50%). She reinforced noncooperation 16 times (67%) by repeating herself. (Ms. Reed's comment: "I was most likely to nag if children had been uncooperative earlier.")

Cooperation training: Children cooperated with requests and questions 24 times (50%). Ms. Reed reinforced cooperation with praise, hugs, and sometimes activities only 12 times (50%). In sum, she reinforced noncooperation more often than cooperation.

Lack of reinforcement for desirable behavior: Randy was never reinforced when he was sitting quietly. Sarah was only reinforced twice when she was not rocking. Out of the eight times that Sally had to wait for something (e.g., snack, going outside) she only moaned four times, but Ms. Reed reinforced her only once (25%). (Ms. Reed's comment: "I am more likely to notice and reinforce the desirable behaviors of children whom I like or when I am not feeling tense.")

The above analysis clearly notes the improvements that are needed.

Narrative Recording   In addition to counting different exchanges, it is useful to describe typical episodes in greater detail to see how they are performed, and, therefore, gain more control of one's actions. For example, Luke's mother writes:

> Here is how we do the nagging exchange in our house. I say to Luke, "How about helping me make the beds?", and he says, "Naw. Don't want to. Mike do it." This makes me angry. I puff myself up and say, "I want you to help me. Don't say I don't want to!" I see that he gets a kick out of my reaction, but I am so mad that I ask again. He gives me another excuse, and then I give up. I guess it rewards him when I repeat myself and then let him out of doing what I ask.

After repeated observations and descriptions, the patterns become clearer, and productive alternatives begin to suggest themselves.

Step 3: Suggest Changes and Carry Out Those that Seem Easiest

Given a picture of exchanges in the family and school and an understanding of principles of learning and exchange, parents and teachers work together to suggest how to increase mutual reward exchanges and replace counterproductive exchanges. Suggestions are written and included in children's individualized education programs (IEPs) and individualized family service plans (IFSPs). The following are some examples.

Ms. Reed's Initial Plans for the Classroom

I will be on the lookout even for little things children do that I like (e.g., speaking clearly, asking for what they want in a pleasant voice, playing constructively, cooperating with requests). I will reinforce these with smiles, hugs, telling children how good their behavior makes me feel, and allowing them to choose the next activities.

Also, I will give children lots of chances each day to follow simple requests, such as turning lights on and off, opening and closing doors, and putting plates on the table. If children cooperate better than usual, they will be reinforced with praise and activities, such as play, reading, and other events. If they do not cooperate, I will ask and reinforce another child.

The Peppers' Plan for Improving Betty's Bedtime Behavior

To give Betty more control, we will teach her to read the clock so she can tell when it is time for bed. We could even give her choices about the time to go to bed. Also, Betty can choose the story book, who she wants to put her to bed, and what she would like to drink.

We will signal the time to go to her room by saying, "Bedtime, Betty." If she goes in more happily and quickly and with less prompting than usual, she gets a big hug. Then she gets her story, drink, and a tuck. We will stay with her until she is settled in (or up to 10 more minutes). Then we will leave the room. If she whines or yells, we will not go back in. Other things to try might be: reinforcing Betty after every few minutes that she is quiet, reinforcing her in the morning for a better than usual bedtime, or letting her read to herself for a certain number of minutes after we leave the room.

When initial plans are going well, new ones can be developed.

Step 4: Increase Reinforcement of Desirable Behavior

One of the first and easiest changes toward desirable behavior is to increase the mutual reward exchange by noticing and reinforcing other adults' and children's desirable behaviors, especially behaviors that are newer, weaker, improved, and/or alternatives to undesirable behaviors. This means increasing how often, how warmly, how quickly, and the number of ways others are reinforced. One can even set obtainable goals, such as, "Today, I am going to reinforce my teacher's aide at least 10 times when she reinforces children's desirable behaviors; I will reinforce Jeff at least 10 times when he is not making noises, Sally at least 5 times when she smiles, and Randy at least 20 times when he is moving more slowly than usual."

At the same time, one ought to ignore behaviors that are merely irritating. For instance, instead of telling Sarah to stop rocking, her teacher might pay attention to another student who is sitting still. Instead of commenting on Sally's "bad mood face," her parents might go about their business and pay attention to her when her expression improves. The practice of increasing reinforcement for desirable behavior should be sustained. However, earlier behaviors might be reinforced slightly less often and new ones more often.

Step 5: Examine the Round of Daily Life

Typical days are divided into major portions, such as morning, afternoon, and evening. Major portions consist of activities, such as having meals, evening activities, and getting ready for bed. Activities consist of tasks, such as preparing food, eating, and cleaning up. If caregivers examine the way a child's daily life is organized, they can find ways to involve the child in more exchanges and tasks and hence increase the child's competence. (This topic is discussed in detail in chap. 6, this volume, and in *Guidelines and Protocols*.)

Step 6: Develop and Operate on the Basis of a Set of Rules

When created collaboratively, rules enable participants to clarify likes and dislikes and orient themselves to something larger and more permanent than feelings. Several kinds of rules can be established: 1) general rules for everyone in all places and activities (e.g., no hitting, no toys left on the stairs); 2) rules for specific places and activities (e.g., walking in the cafeteria, cleaning the table before going outside to play); and 3) rules for certain people (e.g., if Sarah wants to rock, she can rock in her rocking chair after she earns the privilege). Once established, rules can initiate (cue) or prompt desirable behavior.

Step 7: Strengthen Cooperation

Caregivers can strengthen cooperation by noticing and reinforcing it and not reacting to uncooperative responses. If needed, programs to increase cooperation can be planned. Such a program to strengthen cooperation might involve giving children a certain number of simple tasks each day, reinforcing improvements in cooperation, and ignoring noncooperation. It is best if adults and children discuss tasks to be done and reinforcers they think will increase cooperation. Contracts and record keeping systems can then be created.

Step 8: Systematically Replace Problem Behaviors

A guideline is not to think about getting rid of a child's problem behaviors, but to help the child perform alternative behaviors. The effort to replace problem behaviors is facilitated by taking the role of observer and thinking about how to productively respond to problem behaviors; not trying to be perfect in dealing with problem behaviors; reinforcing oneself for changing one's behaviors; and getting hands-on assistance, coaching, and reinforcement. The following vignette is an example of how teachers and parents, working together, replaced many problem behaviors in a child whose membership in the family was becoming more tenuous by the day.

Rudy

Four-year-old Rudy's large repertoire of obnoxious behaviors drove his parents way down the road to distraction. Rudy spent his days yelling, slamming doors, going from one room to another making messes, tearing and scribbling on wallpaper, kicking, spitting, throwing food, and constantly changing television channels, to mention a few behaviors. At the same time, Rudy rarely talked or engaged in everyday chores and adaptive routines. Although diagnosed with autism, his behavioral excesses and deficits could not be explained by autism alone.

Observation showed that Rudy's undesirable behaviors were reinforced by adults' immediate, high intensity, and frequent reactions, such as yelling or telling him to stop; they nagged and talked to Rudy so much that their voices had little meaning, and they rarely gave Rudy chances to participate in and be reinforced for everyday tasks.

Using this assessment information, the first thing Rudy's teachers and parents did was stay alert for behavior they wanted to see more of, and then immediately responded with praise and hugs. Knowing he liked to color (especially on wallpaper), his parents (with Rudy's help) set up a special place at home for Rudy to play, as an alternative to running and making messes. Several times a day they initiated play on coloring, puzzles, cutting and pasting, and other things Rudy enjoyed, and reinforced him frequently. After a few weeks, they began leaving play sessions for longer periods of time, and then came back, to teach Rudy to play independently.

Parents and teachers noticed that Rudy had caught on to the "your turn/my turn" structure of exchanges, and so they began playing little games, such as "You give me a crayon and I give you one," and "You point to one thing in a picture and I point to another." With exchanges such as these as a context, they began to introduce different behavior contents, such as imitating one another and doing tasks together. Gradually, they began working on talking (e.g., asking for bites of food or for other reinforcers, and naming objects).

The kinds of productive exchanges happening during these sessions were also structured during everyday environments. Using incidental-engineered instruction, Rudy's parents and teachers taught him to ask for things he wanted, to set his place at the table before he could eat, and to help clean up before he could go outside. The more skillful he became, the more of each task he could do by himself and the more new tasks were introduced.

Whenever he intentionally made a mess, Rudy had to clean it up before he could do anything else. Whenever he kicked doors or furniture at home, he was immediately sent to his room and not allowed to come out until he had been quiet for a few minutes. However, such behaviors rarely happen any more, perhaps because Rudy is becoming so competent at other ways to be a member of his family and school.

SUMMARY

This chapter shows how: 1) exchanges are organized, 2) exchanges produce predictable short-term and long-term change in behaviors and relationships, 3) early child–caregiver exchanges can set in motion a trend of increasing mutual reward or conflict, and 4) exchanges in schools and families can be improved by following a series of steps. Because exchanges are the major context in which the functional behavioral repertoire develops or fails to develop, exchanges must be considered in all special education practices. Assessment must describe exchanges in a child's life environments, and program planning must suggest ways to improve exchanges. An early goal of instruction is to establish productive exchanges with children to bring them into the social world; ongoing evaluation must monitor the quality of these exchanges.

REFERENCES

Abidin, R.R., Jenkins, C.L., & McGaughey, M.C. (1992). The relationship of early family variables to children's subsequent behavioral adjustment. *Journal of Clinical Child Psychology, 21*(1), 60–69.

Ainsworth, M.D.S., Blehar, M.C., Waters, E., & Wall, S. (1978). *Patterns of attachment.* Hillsdale, NJ: Lawrence Erlbaum Associates.

Bakeman, R., & Adamson, L.B. (1986). Infants' conventionalized acts: Gestures with mothers and peers. *Infant Behavior and Development, 9,* 215–230.

Bakeman, R., & Brown, J. (1977). Behavioral dialogues: An approach to the assessment of mother-infant interaction. *Child Development, 48,* 195–203.

Barden, C.R., Ford, M.E., Jensen, A.G., Rogers-Salyer, M., & Salyer, K.E. (1989). Effects of craniofacial deformity in infancy on the quality of mother-infant interaction. *Child Development, 60,* 819–824.

Barnard, K.E., & Bee, H.L. (1979). The assessment of parent-infant interaction by observation of feeding and teaching. In T.B. Brazelton & H. Als (Eds.), *New approaches to developmental screening of infants.* New York: Elsevier/North Holland.

Bell, R.Q. (1979). Parent, child, and reciprocal influences. *American Psychologist, 34,* 821–826.

Bell, R.Q., & Chapman, M. (1986). Child effects in studies using experiments with brief longitudinal approaches to socialization. *Developmental Psychology, 22,* 559–603.

Blau, P.M. (1964). *Exchange and power in social life.* New York: John Wiley & Sons.

Brazelton, T.B., Tronick, E., Adamson, L., Als, H., & Wise, S. (1975). Early mother-infant reciprocity. In M.A. Hofer (Ed.), *The parent-infant relationship* (pp. 137–155). London: Ciba.

Bromwich, R. (1981). *Working with parents and infants: An interactional approach.* Baltimore: University Park Press.

Caldwell, B.M., & Bradley, R.H. (1978). *Manual for the home observation for measurement of the environment.* Little Rock: University of Arkansas.

Cohn, J.F., & Tronick, E.Z. (1987). Mother-infant face-to-face interaction: The sequence of dyadic states at 3, 6, and 9 months. *Developmental Psychology, 23*(1), 68–77.

Cohn, J.F., & Tronick, E.Z. (1988). Mother-infant face-to-face interaction: Influence is bidirectional and unrelated to periodic cycles in either partner's behavior. *Developmental Psychology, 24*(3), 386–392.

Crais, E.R. (1990). World knowledge to word knowledge. *Topics in Language Disorders, 10*(3), 45–62.

Culp, R.E., Applebaum, M.I., Osofsky, J.D., & Levy, J.A. (1988). Adolescent and older mothers: Comparison between prenatal and maternal variables and newborn interaction measures. *Infant Behavior and Development, 11,* 353–362.

Dodge, K.A. (1990). Nature vs nurture in child development: It is time to ask a different question. *Developmental Psychology, 26*(5), 698–701.

Duncan, S., Jr., & Farley, A.M. (1990). Achieving parent-child coordination through convention: Fixed- and variable-sequence conventions. *Child Development, 61,* 742–753.

Dunham, P., & Dunham, F. (1988). Effects of mother-infant social interactions on infants subsequent contingency task performance. *Child Development, 61,* 785–793.

Farran, D.C., Kasari, G., & Jay, S. (1986). *Parent/caregiver involvement scale.* Chapel Hill: Frank Porter Graham Development Center, University of North Carolina.

Fernald, A., & Kuhl, P. (1987). Accoustic determinants of infant preference for mother's speech. *Infant Behavior and Development, 10.* 279–293.

Field, T. (1987). Affective and interactive disturbances in infants. In D. Osofsky (Ed.), *Handbook of infant development* (2nd ed.) (pp. 972–1005). New York: Wiley-Interscience.

Field, T., Healy, B., & LeBlanc, W.G. (1989). Sharing and synchrony of behavior states and heart rate in nondepressed versus depressed mother-infant interactions. *Infant Behavior and Development, 12,* 357–376.

Fingarette, H. (1988). *Heavy drinking.* Berkeley: University of California.

Gusella, J., Muir, D., & Tronick, E.Z. (1988). The effect of manipulating maternal behavior during an intervention on three- and six-month-olds' affect and attention. *Child Development, 59*(4), 1111–1124.

Hamblin, R.L., Buckholdt, D., Ferritor, D., Kozloff, M., & Blackwell, L. (1971). *The humanization processes.* New York: John Wiley & Sons.

Hann, D. (1989). A systems conceptualization of the quality of mother-infant interaction. *Infant Behavior and Development, 12,* 251–263.

Homans, G.C. (1961). *Social behavior: Its elementary forms.* New York: Harcourt, Brace and World.

Homme, L. (1967). *A behavior technology exists—here and now.* Paper presented at the Aerospace Education Foundation's "Education for the 1970's" seminar, Washington, DC.

Hyche, J.K., Jr., Bakeman, R., & Adamson, L.B. (1992). Understanding communicative cues of infants with Down syndrome: Effects of mothers' experience and infants' age. *Journal of Applied Developmental Psychology, 13,* 1–16.

Jarvis, P.A., Myers, B.J., & Creasey, G.L. (1989). The effects of infants' illness on mothers' interactions with prematures at 4 and 8 months. *Infant Behavior and Development, 12,* 25–35.

Kirkham, M.A. (1993). Two-year follow-up of skills training with mothers of children with disabilities. *American Journal on Mental Retardation, 97*(5), 509–520.

Kozloff, M.A. (1983) *Reaching the autistic child.* Cambridge, MA: Brookline Books. (Originally published by Research Press, 1973.)

Kozloff, M.A. (1988). *Productive interaction with students, children, and clients.* Springfield, IL: Charles C Thomas.

Kozloff, M.A., Helm, D.T., & Cutler, B.C. (1987). Parent training: Working to increase normalization and prevent institutionalization. In J. Mulick & R. Antonak (Eds.), *Transitions in mental retardation* (pp. 70–93). Norwood, NJ: Ablex.

Kozloff, M.A., Helm, D.T., Cutler, B.C., Douglas-Steele, D., Wells, A., & Scampini, L. (1988). Training programs for families of children with autism or other handicaps. In R.DeV. Peters & R.J. McMahon (Eds.), *Social learning and systems approaches to marriage and the family* (pp. 217–250). New York: Brunner/Mazel.

Lederberg, A.R., & Mobley, C.E. (1990). The effect of hearing impairment on the quality of attachment and mother-toddler interaction. *Child Development, 61,* 1596–1604.

Lytton, H. (1990). Child and parent effect in boys' conduct disorders: A reinterpretation. *Developmental Psychology, 26*(5), 683–697.

Marfo, K. (1992). Correlates of maternal directiveness with children who are developmentally delayed. *American Journal of Orthopsychiatry, 62*(2), 219–233.

Martin, J.A. (1981). A longitudinal study of the consequences of early mother-infant interaction: A microanalytic approach. *Monograph of the Society for Research on Child Development, 46*(3), Serial Number 190.

Nelson, K. (Ed.). (1986). *Event knowledge: Structure and function in development.* Hillsdale, NJ:Lawrence Erlbaum Associates.

Newson, J. (1978). Dialogue and development. In A. Lock (Ed.), *Action, gesture and symbol.* London: Academic Press.

Olson, S.L., Bates, J.E., & Bayles, K. (1982). Maternal perceptions of infant and toddler behavior: A longitudinal construct validation study. *Infant Behavior and Development, 5,* 397–410.

Olson, S.L., Bates, J.E, & Bayles, K. (1985). Mother-child interaction and children's speech progress: A longitudinal study of the first two years. *Merrill-Palmer Quarterly, 32,* 1–20.

Olson, S.L., Bates, J.E., & Bayles, K. (1989). Predicting long-term developmental outcomes for maternal perceptions of infant and toddler behavior. *Infant Behavior and Development, 12,* 77–92.

Patterson, G.R. (1980). Mothers: The unacknowledged victims. *Monograph of the Society for Research on Child Development, 45*(15), Serial Number 186.

Patterson, G.R. (1982). *Coercive family processes.* Eugene, OR: Cataglia.

Paterson, G.R., & Reid, J.B. (1984). Social interaction processes within the family: The study of the moment-by-moment family transactions in which human development is embedded. *Journal of Applied Developmental Psychology, 5,* 237–262.

Pettit, G.S., & Bates, J.E. (1989). Family interaction patterns and children's behavior problems from infancy to four years. *Developmental Psychology, 25*(3), 413–420.

Rutter, D.R., & Durkin, K. (1987). Turn-taking in mother-infant interaction: An examination of vocalization and gaze. *Developmental Psychology, 23*(1), 54–61.

Seifer, R., Clark, G.N., & Sameroff, A.J. (1991). Positive effects of interaction coaching on infants with developmental disabilities and their mothers. *American Journal on Mental Retardation, 96*(1), 1–11.

Stevenson, M.B., VerHoeve, J.N., Roach, M.A., & Leavitt, L.S. (1986). The beginning of conversation: Early patterns in mother-infant vocal responsiveness. *Infant Behavior and Development, 9,* 423–440.

Tannock, R., Girolametto, L., & Siegel, L.S. (1992). Language intervention with children who have developmental delays: Effects of an interactive approach. *American Journal on Mental Retardation, 97*(2), 145–160.

van de Rijt-Plooij, H.H.C., & Plooij, F.X. (1993). Distinct periods of mother-infant conflict in normal development: Sources of progress and germs of pathology. *Journal of Child Psychology and Psychiatry, 34*(2), 229–245.

Wahler, R.G. (1990). Who is driving the interaction? A commentary on "Child and parent effects in boys' conduct disorders." *Developmental Psychology, 26*(5), 702–704.

White, B.L., & Watts, J.C. (1973). *Experience and environment.* Englewood Cliffs, NJ: Prentice Hall.

CHAPTER 6

FUNCTIONAL BEHAVIORAL REPERTOIRE AND PSYCHOSOCIAL DEVELOPMENT

FEATURES OF SPECIAL EDUCATION THAT INHIBIT THE EFFORTS OF TEACHERS AND FAMILIES TO MEET children's needs were identified in Chapter 2, this volume. It specifically noted that assessments often are done in unusual environments, fail to describe children's participation in daily life, and are summarized with vague and/or superficial statements. Program plans lack detail and do not address long-term issues (described in chap. 4, this volume), such as fluency, generalization, adaptation, and the maintenance of gains. In addition, instruction often involves isolated, age-inappropriate, nonfunctional skills, and overuses massed practice and contrived reinforcement contingencies. Finally, program evaluation describes little of a child's functional behavioral repertoire and fails to show how progress is facilitated or hindered by school, family, and community environments. At the same time, professionals and families work in conditions of unpredictability, overspecialization, lack of leadership, conflicting functions, isolation, stigmatization, alienated labor, and little coordination between schools and homes.

Educators and families of children with disabilities cannot substantially improve educational practices and working conditions (and therefore cannot do much more to foster psychosocial development) unless they are guided by a better understanding of behavior organization and psychosocial development. The purpose of this chapter is twofold. The first purpose is to replace the model of the standard behavioral repertoire described in Chapter 2—a model that reduces action and membership to abstract categories—with a model of the functional behavioral repertoire, which depicts how behavior is organized as children interact with their surroundings. The second purpose is to remedy some educators' one-sided use of developmental-maturational, functional-ecological, or lack of curriculum guidelines by offering a model of psychosocial development that synthesizes current work in developmental psychology, experimental learning, sociology, and special education.

FUNCTIONAL BEHAVIORAL REPERTOIRE

The functional behavioral repertoire is the portion of a person's repertoire enabling him or her to competently participate in his or her surroundings. The word "participate" means that a person's behavior is oriented to, guided by, and fits into social interactions, tasks, and activities. For instance, Luke listens for the sound of the table being set, enters the kitchen, and sits down. Participation, or involvement, therefore is one aspect of the functional behavioral repertoire to assess. One can, for example, describe Luke's: 1) proximity to events; 2) attention; 3) reactions to common cues and consequences; and 4) roles in family and school (e.g., onlooker, disrupter, partial participant, real helper).

"Competence" means a person's behavior contributes to the accomplishment of tasks, activities, or interactions. For example, when Luke stacks the supper dishes, he watches his own actions, gently puts one plate on top of another, promptly stacks the next plate, and does not add too many extra movements. In other words, he performs conventionally correct and effective movements and actions in a fluid sequence, and he performs the right movements and actions at the right places and times.

Organization of the Functional Behavioral Repertoire

Increasing competence and participation imply four kinds of changes in the functional behavioral repertoire. These include: 1) using certain behaviors to achieve certain ends or functions (e.g., making eye contact to produce a smile from another); 2) performing a behavior in different ways (e.g., speaking more often and more fluently); 3) performing some behaviors in select environments (discrimination) and other behaviors in a range of environments (generalization); and 4) assembling component behaviors into different and/or longer sequences.

Regarding the fourth change noted above, the functional behavioral repertoire consists of movements assembled into longer chains of actions, which are then organized into tasks, ordered as activities, and combined into roles. Any competently completed sequence (e.g., drying dishes) serves a function. Internally, sequences consist of steps or "spots" at which portions of the overall function or work are accomplished. Generally, the work at most spots can be performed by a "class" of functionally equivalent behaviors. Furthermore, sequences can be adapted to circumstances by rearranging and/or adding steps.

A "whole" has characteristics that the separate parts do not have, specifically *organization*. For instance, one may know how to jump, run, bounce the ball, raise arms, and look at the hoop, but one cannot play competent basketball by performing the actions separately. One must arrange these actions into sequences, such as passing, shooting, and rebounding, which are performed at the right spots in plays, at the right locations on the court, and according to the rules of the game. Just as performing isolated behaviors does not yield a competent basketball player, teaching isolated skills does not produce a more competent child. Therefore, the functional behavioral repertoire must be portrayed and improved as sequences (assemblies) of ongoing behaviors in various contexts.

Sequences of Different Length   People perform countless movements in their daily lives, not in random fashion, but in sequences. A larger sequence (e.g., preparing a meal) is composed of smaller ones (e.g., getting ingredients, slicing carrots); the smaller ones (slicing carrots) are composed of still smaller ones (holding the knife, moving the knife across the carrot). The arrangement is much like a set of boxes within boxes. Obviously, the ordering of smaller parts creates the larger whole. At the same time, the ongoing larger sequence or whole is a context that guides the performance of the smaller actions, giving them a purpose, location, and form (Barker, 1963, 1968). Movements, actions, tasks, activities, and larger units are useful concepts in assessing, planning for, teaching, and evaluating children's functional behavioral repertoires.

Movements   A close look shows that a person's behavioral repertoire consists of movements (flexion, extension, rotation) of the head, eyes, hands, arms, legs, trunk, and so forth. Some movements are respondent (i.e., elicited by unconditioned and conditioned stimuli); others are operant (i.e., cued by discriminative stimuli). It could be said that the functional behavioral repertoire is assembled from the ground up; we come into life moving and then learn to assemble movements into actions, tasks, activities, and roles.

Actions   Movements are combined into short sequences known as actions. Actions are more than arrangements of movements, they are also purposeful and functional and influenced by their consequences. In other words, acts involve both *what* is accomplished (the function) and *how* it is accomplished (the manner or form) (Catania, 1973; Lee, 1987). For example, Juan coordinates movements of his head and eyes into the act of looking to bring his baseball cap into view (the out-come); he next arranges movements of his eyes, arm, and hand into the act of reaching to produce physical contact with the cap; he then organizes movements of wrists and fingers into the act of grasping the cap by the bill to prepare it for being put on; and, finally, he looks in the mirror while placing the cap on his head.

Tasks   A task is a sequence of actions. For example, Juan is assembling actions into the task of putting on a cap. Next, he will find his tape player and insert a tape. Note that at this level of organization (task), some tasks contain more action steps than others. Also note that the tasks in a person's functional behavioral repertoire are a product of opportunities in the person's life environments. In some classrooms, adolescent students work puzzles, string beads, and roll Play Doh. In other classrooms, students use the same actions to perform functional tasks, such as preparing meals.

Activities   An activity is several tasks performed in a sequence. Juan is getting ready to leave his room—the next activity might be breakfast, followed by cleaning up, and then riding to school. Note that having a child perform a task (e.g., putting on a cap) outside of the usual activity context (getting dressed) for purposes of assessment or skill building may be experienced as meaningless or confusing. This is because events that precede, accompany, and follow the out-of-context task are unusual. The implication is that assessment and teaching should take place in environments that are as usual as possible.

Larger Units   Behaviors are organized into even larger patterns than activities. For instance, tasks and activities are assembled into major portions of a day, such as getting ready to leave the house in the morning, morning work, lunch break, afternoon work, supper, evening time, and bed-time. Major portions are organized into typical days (e.g., Blue Monday, "Thank-God-It's-Friday"), and days are arranged into weeks. Furthermore, actions, tasks, and activities are assembled into the roles that one performs in different physical and social environments. One of the largest units of behavior may be a stage of psychosocial development. Note that stages, such as preschool and adolescence, are largely products of the social organization of families, schools, communities, and cultures.

Figure 6.1 illustrates the organization of the functional behavioral repertoire. It shows how movements are assembled into feeding actions in the task of eating soup within the activity of having a meal during an evening portion of a typical day. All of this is part of the role that a person plays in a stage of psychosocial development. The upward arrows indicate that larger sequences are created by assemblies of smaller component sequences within them. The downward arrows show that an ongoing sequence is a behavioral context that guides (canalizes) the way that one assembles the components.

Sequences, Spots, and Classes   Nearly all sequences accomplish some amount of work. At the end of an action, one's hand is in contact with the doorknob; at the end of a task, a sandwich is ready for eating. Each behavior in a sequence, therefore, does a portion of the overall work. Indeed, certain behaviors must be in the sequence and performed at certain locations so that next steps and the overall sequence can be accomplished. Thus, sequences consist of *spots* (Pike, 1954)—places, steps, or locations—where portions of the work are done.

There may be several ways to do the work at a particular spot. The set of functionally equivalent ways is a *class* (Catania, 1973; Lee, 1987; Pike, 1954). For example, when making a sandwich, one task requires getting out the bread. This can be done by reaching into the package with either one hand or both hands, dumping out several slices, or digging out slices with a fork. There are also alternative ways to perform one's turns in exchanges. Initially, an infant greets a parent by turning his or her head to the parent. Gradually, the class of greeting actions expands to include smiling, waving hands, kicking feet, vocalizing, calling the parent's name, and saying hello in various ways. In general, *the size of a class grows as a function of both maturation and adaptation to changes in environments.*

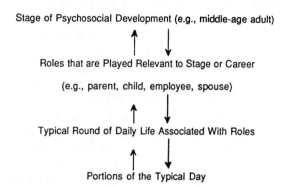

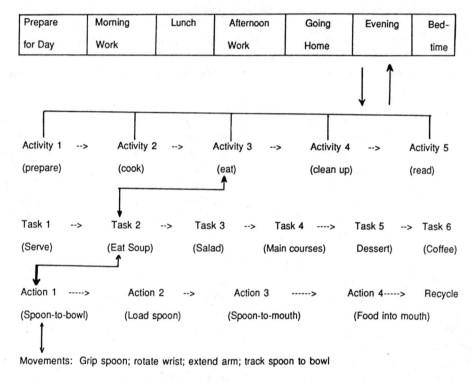

Figure 6.1. Organization of the functional behavioral repertoire.

Furthermore, spots or steps often can be assembled in different ways that have about the same outcome. During the early morning portion of a typical day, for instance, one has to bathe, dress, toilet, eat, and collect money, wallet, and car keys. Typically, one uses the bathroom first, showers, dresses, eats, and gets one's belongings; however, one could eat first and then shower, or eat and then get dressed. Different sequences work, although some are more efficient than others. Again, adaptation (rearranging behavior into alternative sequences) is promoted by changes—something novel, unfamiliar, perhaps more difficult—within or across environments.

One also learns to use established sequences to serve new purposes (Thelen, 1985). For instance, Indra reaches for, grasps, and picks up crackers to eat. In the near future, she will use a similar sequence to put coins in a soda machine. This is an example of *differentiation;* a new kind of order emerges out of the old. Just how a new sequence emerges can be understood by noting: 1) how one behavioral part is adjusted to another (e.g., reaching makes grasping possible), and 2) how behavioral parts are adjusted to the environment (e.g., the grip that puts a cracker in one's mouth must be altered to fit a coin in a soda machine slot) (Gottlieb, 1991).

Implications for Practices

There are several implications to the idea that sequences are assemblies of smaller sequences, and that any sequence consists of a function (work) that is accomplished, as well as spots, classes, and alternative orderings. First, a child is not likely to competently perform longer sequences unless he or she can perform the parts. Therefore, one must identify the movements, actions, and tasks that constitute strong versus weak components in a child's repertoire. At the same time, it may be easier for a child to learn some components if instruction occurs in usual environments (e.g., shoelace tying with real shoes when it is time to dress, rather than lacing boards after lunch).

Second, many behaviors can be made functional by integrating them in tasks that are part of a child's everyday world. For example, Luke pats table tops and counters so often that it seems weird. However, he could use patting in the task of making hamburger patties, smoothing sheets, fluffing pillows, and comforting the cat.

Third, one is reminded to focus on the correct level of behavior organization. Indra used to take a long time to eat. Mr. Hawkins began setting a timer for 20 minutes, praising Indra when she beat the clock, and removing her plate when she did not. The result was that Indra rarely beat the clock, but learned to shriek in response to the Type II punishment. Mr. Hawkins's program did not work because it focused on a feature of the eating activity (duration) when the problem was at the lower level of actions; that is, Indra had a hard time scooping with a spoon and spearing with a fork. Had Mr. Hawkins improved these smaller sequences by working on fluency, Indra would have eaten faster without extra reinforcement (and certainly without punishment) contingencies.

Fourth, the more ways a person can perform the work at any spot (i.e., the larger the person's classes of behavior), the more adaptable and competent is the person's behavioral repertoire. For instance, if a snack bar has no knives, Juan can effectively fill the mustard-spreading spot if he knows how to use spoons or straws. But, if the classes in a child's repertoire contain few alternative ways to do the same work, even a small change from the usual environment may erode performance. Thus, assessment and ongoing program evaluation must determine how a child tries to accomplish the same tasks in different conditions. If one finds that Juan can unscrew only those jar lids that are moderately large and loose, one ought to help him increase the size of his jar opening class.

Fifth, the more ways a child knows how to *add* and *rearrange* behaviors into equally effective sequences, the more adaptable the child's functional behavioral repertoire will be. If Juan's cap is not in the usual place, his dressing activity will not "fall apart" if he knows how to insert a new spot ("looking for my cap") in the old sequence. Again, assessment and ongoing evaluation should focus on how a child adapts sequences to fit circumstances; and during instruction, the child should be exposed to slightly different conditions to encourage him or her to rearrange sequences.

Similarly, we ought to be interested in whether a child prefers or has an easier time arranging behaviors in one order as opposed to another order. It makes little sense to insist that Indra wash and dress before breakfast if she would be happier and more cooperative if she ate first.

PSYCHOSOCIAL DEVELOPMENT

Psychosocial development is neither the unfolding of an already written biological plan nor the one-sided molding of a child's behavior by the environment. Psychosocial development is an ongoing collaborative achievement, a progression of reciprocal developments in a child and in the child's environments. In the best circumstances, a child is learning to be a more competent participant at the same time that caregivers are learning how to provide an environment congruent with the child's changing needs, preferences, competencies, and capacities.

Canalization

Canalization is a process in which development is constrained, promoted, and guided by environments. Originally used in biology (Waddington, 1970), the concept applies to psychosocial development as well. The following quotation from Thelen (1989) expresses this idea: "development proceeds not as the progressive revelation or elaboration of already existing schemata, programs, or plans, but as the opportunistic marshalling of the available components that best befit the task at hand . . . ." (p. 947).

Maturation and Canalization   Maturation of bones, muscles, organs, and the nervous system increases a child's capabilities to perform behaviors with an improved form (e.g., reaching with more precision) and to combine components into sequences (e.g., movements of head, eyes, arms, and legs assembled into crawling). However, capabilities become competencies only through action in environments. The following quotation expresses the basic idea. "Development is function driven to the extent that anatomical structure and neurological mechanisms exist only as components until they are expressed in a context" (Thelen, 1989, p. 947). For example, competent crawling is fostered by objects and places to crawl toward and surfaces to crawl on. Appropriate communication requires frameworks of social interaction that teach a child how to assemble sounds into communicative acts and when to insert them during conversations.

At the same time, *competence increases capacity* (Inhelder & Piaget, 1958). As Indra learns to feed herself crackers, it increases her capacity to operate soda machines and to benefit from instruction on more difficult sorts of hand-eye-object coordination. Thus, assessment and ongoing evaluation must identify the increased capacities for learning and performance made possible by a child's current competence.

Canalization of the Functions of Behavior   Environments provide functions or ends for action—things to see, get to, and manipulate; places to go; responses of others to influence. "(T)he development of (a) child's actions starts from a state of no intentionality and goal-directedness and is gradually canalized toward culturally acceptable and prescribed forms of goal-setting and goal-attainment" (Valsiner, 1987, pp. 147–148). Below is an example of how exchanges—one feature of an environment—transform movements into purposive actions that the child then uses to participate in the exchanges.

> Brenda is an infant with Down syndrome. Along with other parents, her mother is taking a course at Brenda's early intervention center on how to create mutual reward exchanges involving reciprocity or positive involvement to foster social bonding and teach children essential social skills, such as turn-taking.
>
> Brenda and her mother sit facing each other on the living room floor. When Brenda looks at her mother, her mother opens her eyes wide and coos at Brenda, who then smiles. After four exchanges of this sort, her mother inserts another component into the routine. She holds up a set of keys and shakes them. Brenda turns her head, gazes at the jingling keys and wiggles her arms in excitement. Brenda's mother interprets her reflexive arm movements as a *communicative act*—a request for the keys. "Oh, you want these? Here." Her mother puts them in the hand that is closest to her. Brenda jingles the keys for a while and then drops them. Her mother holds up the keys and shakes them again, which elicits more reflexive attention and arm waving from Brenda. Again, her mother puts the keys in the hand closest to her.
>
> After 20 more exchanges, which are also learning trials, Brenda purposefully reaches for the keys with the hand that is closest to her mother and she clearly looks for the keys when her mother is not holding them up. In other words, by regularly eliciting and then reinforcing Brenda's reflexive attention and arm movements, her mother has transformed them into purposive actions that fit the turn-taking exchanges.

Canalization of the Form of Behavior   Environments not only canalize the functions of behavior, they also help to mold behavior into forms for accomplishing the different functions. This is described using the example of Brenda and her mother.

As time goes by, Brenda's mother does not reinforce just any sort of attention and arm movements from Brenda, she reinforces only the more fluent and conventional forms (e.g., arm movements in which Brenda points to what she seems to want). Thus, the mother's differential reinforcement of increasingly conventional gesturing, combined with Brenda's increasing strength and control over her eyes and limbs, gradually canalize Brenda's behavior toward culturally acceptable forms. (Fogel, 1981; Fogel & Thelen, 1987)

In general, environments canalize the forms of behavior in two ways. First, they *prevent* or *inhibit* and *differentially encourage* some forms over others. For instance, a preschooler might be prevented from riding his tricycle in the living room, but given opportunities, cues, prompts, and reinforcement for riding in the basement or yard.

Second, environments provide *templates* or frameworks. For instance, the routine order of conversational interaction is a social template that helps participants assemble attending, listening, and talking.

Canalization of the Functional Behavioral Repertoire

Different levels of the functional behavioral repertoire are canalized in different levels of environments, as shown in Figure 6.2. Figure 6.2 illustrates four points. First, as with the functional behavioral repertoire, *environments are organized as larger and more encompassing units* "that are nested within one another—episodes within episodes, subordinate ones and superordinate ones" (Gibson, 1979, p. 102). For example, cues, prompts, obstacles, and consequences are embedded in the physical environment and in the behaviors of others, and these often occur in exchanges with others. Exchanges, in turn, occur in routine tasks, activities, and portions of typical days in a larger round of daily life.

Second, behavior is in direct contact with and is *immediately* affected by the microscopic units of the person's environment (e.g., cues, prompts, obstacles, and consequences). At the same time, behavior is indirectly affected by the macroscopic or encompassing units (Bronfenbrenner, 1979). For instance, the regular division of labor in a school (the large unit) determines whether everyone, or only the language specialist, provides children with explicit instruction on communication. Thus, the division of labor indirectly, but nonetheless strongly, influences what, where, and how quickly children learn to communicate.

Third, each level of an environment canalizes an associated level of participants' repertoires. At a microscopic level, cues, prompts, and consequences in the physical environment shape participants' operant actions and conditioned reflexes. At a middle range level, exchanges shape participants' social competencies. Finally, at a macroscopic level, the way a school or community provides or denies children opportunities to participate promotes or inhibits children's ability to develop the competence to play valued roles.

Fourth, a child's current behavior and course of development help to create the very environments that canalize his or her development (Cairns, 1991). For instance, a caregiver's teaching skills shape a child's behavior, but the child's behavior reciprocally shapes the caregiver's teaching skills. Ms. Wright is energetic and skillful when teaching because her efforts are quickly and reliably reinforced by beneficial changes in her students. "The child alters the environment and in turn is altered by the changed world he or she has created" (Laosa, 1989, p. 454).

Psychosocial development, therefore, is a lifelong progression of reciprocal changes in a child's functional behavioral repertoire and in the child's environments as the child becomes an increasingly competent participant. Of course, psychosocial development does not necessarily occur or continue. Psychosocial development depends on whether environments are congruent with a child's needs, preferences, competencies, and capacities.

Respondent and Operant Conditioning in the Physical Environment The physical environment canalizes development by providing templates for assembling sequences. For example,

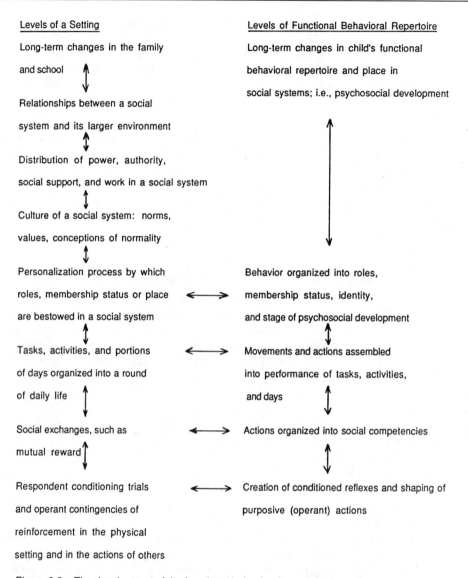

Figure 6.2. The development of the functional behavioral repertoire in environments.

dwellings, parks, and cities are structured such that they can be understood and used as routes. They contain channels, direction and location markers, prompts, and reinforcers.

The following is an example of canalization as Indra interacts with features of her physical environment. Indra is learning how to wheel down sidewalks and navigate her way to the duck pond. She moves hundreds of muscles in action sequences, such as turning the wheels and observing passing cars. She organizes the actions into tasks such as avoiding potholes and going up hills. How do Indra's movements become organized into competent actions and tasks? The answer is found at the intersection between her behavior stream and relevant features of the physical environment (see chap. 3, this volume, for more detail on operant learning).

Through thousands of microscopic interactions, Indra develops practical knowledge of the park; she becomes a skilled navigator. Her behavior is better adapted to the cues, prompts, hindrances, and consequences from the physical environment. She has learned to: 1) look for and notice features relevant to her tasks at hand; 2) select her next behavior in light of the cues; 3) look for, notice, and use possible prompts; 4) assemble component behaviors into functional sequences;

5) repeat sequences that had reinforcing consequences, and stop performing those sequences that have simply not worked; and 6) comprehend (perhaps even represent) the park as a set of routes (Gauvain, 1993).

Available space and kinds of objects also have a strong influence on behavior development (Wohlwill & Heft, 1987). For example:

1. When a room contains only large items such as chairs, tables, tricycles, and toy houses, children might use the items in novel ways, and engage in cooperative and physically active behaviors.
2. When children have a lot of play equipment, they engage in solitary play or form small groups for parallel and cooperative play, and they tend not to share.
3. When children have little play equipment, they share, cry, engage in aimless behavior, switch to less popular items, run and chase, observe one another and make physical contact, stay in closer proximity, and compete and fight.
4. When children have more space, they chase and flee and use materials in novel ways (e.g., make chair trains).
5. When children have less space, they push, hit, cry, scream, watch one another without playing, and engage in stereotypic behaviors (e.g., finger sucking).
6. The creation of separate areas for crafts, large motor, and quiet activities promotes the use of play materials and decreases aimless and stereotypical behavior (Eisert, Kulka, & Moore, 1988; Ichinose & Clark; 1990; Levy & McLeod, 1977; McAfee, 1987; Smith & Connolly, 1980; Speigel-McGill, Bambara, Shores, & Fox, 1984).

By definition, persons with developmental disabilities have a more difficult time adapting to features of their physical environment. They may not be as able to notice important cues; the physical environment may not contain sufficient prompts and may contain obstacles; and "natural" consequences may be hard to notice, slow in coming, and too infrequent to stamp in effective behaviors. Part of assessment, planning, and instruction, therefore, is to examine and then adapt the physical environment to help children come into contact with and use those features that could cue, prompt, and provide informative consequences.

Reinforcement Embedded in the Behaviors of Other People Each person's vast repertoire of nods, winks, hand waves, postures, facial expressions, and vocalizations are part of the respondent conditioning trials and operant contingencies of reinforcement that affect the behavior of others. During the course of many interactions, other people's facial expressions become conditioned stimuli that elicit a child's increased attention and pleasure; hand movements become cues for a child to approach; movements of the eyes and nods of the head become prompts that guide arm movements while a child does a task; and certain words constitute approval that increases the frequency and form of the behavior occurring at the time of reinforcement.

Of course, the behaviors of particular persons may be more, or less, congruent with a child's needs. Thus, when assessing and making plans to improve a child's competence, it is essential to assess caregivers' competence at teaching (discussed in *Guidelines and Protocols*).

Increasingly Complex Forms of Social Organization Surroundings contain both physical structures and social structures (e.g., exchanges) that canalize development.

> A context or situation is not defined solely or even necessarily by the physical setting (e.g., livingroom, sidewalk) or by person combinations (e.g., child and mother, child and sibling); rather, it is constituted of what people are doing and when and where they are doing it. (Laosa, 1989, p. 458)

Social environments are organized into forms or structures of collaboration. The forms have many names—*formats* (Bakeman & Adamson, 1986; Bruner, 1983), *scripts* (Crais, 1990; Nelson, 1986; Schank & Abelson, 1977), *scaffolds* (Wood, 1980), *conventions* (Duncan & Farley, 1990; Smetana, 1989), and *frames* (Fogel, 1977; Goffman, 1974). The social-interactional forms have much in common. They are solutions to "coordination problems" (who does what, when, where, how fast, how well, for how long) that arise during dressing, feeding, and other activities (Duncan & Farley, 1990); they introduce "strong, expectable regularities in the respective actions of participants" (p. 743); they become traditional and obligatory; and they involve a regular set of materials, places, participants, cues, prompts, consequences, and series of steps. Thus, as with structures in the physical environment (e.g., hallways, stairs, arrangements of furniture), social forms constrain and guide (canalize) participants' development. The social forms that will be examined in this section include exchanges, conventional tasks and activities in the round of daily life, the personalization process, cultural features, and social structure.

Exchanges   Exchanges are an elementary form of social organization in which participants take turns providing one another with cues, prompts, and consequences. Chapter 5, this volume, shows how exchanges in the form of rewarded coercion, nagging, rewarded threat, mutual reward, and aversive methods gradually teach participants when it is their turn and how to perform their respective turn parts in the exchange. For instance, Luke's parents do not allow him outside in winter without a coat, but do give him a choice of coats and differentially praise him for selecting certain ones ("Oh, your raincoat! Good choice."). Barney is ignored when he screams for dessert, but is differentially praised for more articulate asking. The structure of an exchange is a canalizing influence on the feelings (conditioned responses) and social competencies of participants.

Conventional Tasks and Activities   Both solitary behavior and exchanges with others occur in a round of daily life in schools and families. Figure 6.3 illustrates how tasks, activities, and portions of a day constitute part of a round of daily life.

How does canalization occur within and across units of daily life? The answer is this: To the extent that a child participates in tasks and activities, and to the extent that these are congruent with the child's learning needs, the child receives cues, prompts from others, and consequences (e.g., reinforcement) that help to stamp in his or her actions. Moreover, the regularity of everyday tasks and activities guides the child's insertion of particular behaviors at particular points. Juan, for instance, is taught to put on underpants, undershirt, socks, shirt, slacks, shoes, jacket, and cap, in that order. Below is an example of the structure (regularity) of a routine activity canalizing a child's development.

Ms. Blake is looking at a story book with Danielle. While Ms. Blake describes the pictures, 5-year-old Danielle stares into space and taps the pages. Danielle gets Ms. Blake to turn pages by wagging her head from side to side or by saying "Eh! Eh!" Ms. Blake has done the picture book activity with so many children that it is scripted (Schank & Abelson, 1977); it has a regular sequence of steps where each person performs specific behaviors during a turn. In Ms. Blake's opinion, Danielle is following the script appropriate for a 1-year-old child.

Typical day				
Morning work	Lunch	Afternoon work	Evening	Sleep

$\updownarrow$

One portion of a typical day: Afternoon work						
Activity 1: General cleanup			Activity 2: Wash and dry clothes			
Task 1: Dust furniture	Task 2: Sweep floor	Task 3: Vacuum rugs	Task 1: Separate clothes	Task 2: Load washer	Task 3: Load dryer	Task 4: Fold clothes

Figure 6.3   Organization of daily life.

Based on the assessment, Ms. Blake now uses verbal and manual prompts to get Danielle to look at and touch the pictures (rather than tap the pages), and models prompts to get Danielle to name the objects ("Look! A duck. [Points.] You touch the duck. That's right. Duck. Now you say duck."). In addition, she helps Danielle turn the pages, or prompts Danielle to say "Turn page," but only after most of the objects on a page have been named.

Within 3 weeks, Danielle has stopped staring at the ceiling, tapping pages, wagging her head, and saying "Eh! Eh!" Instead, she precisely points and correctly names objects, and she either turns pages herself or asks Ms. Blake to turn them when they have been completed. In summary, Danielle's competent participation in the activity has been canalized by the constraints and guidance embedded in the script.

Meals are another major canalizing form of social organization. For instance, a child learns about where meals happen; where snacking takes place; foods for different occasions; which utensils to use; rules for serving, requesting, and handling food; how to position plates and utensils on the table; and how to assemble component movements and actions into eating sequences (Connolly & Dalgleish, 1989; Valsiner, 1987).

The round of daily life as a canalizing environment has several implications for practice. In particular, one should examine: 1) the extent and competence of a child's participation in routine tasks and activities; 2) how much opportunity the child is given to participate, and whether and where more opportunities could be given; and 3) whether tasks and activities are conducted in a way that promotes the child's competence (e.g., Are cues clear, prompts appropriate, reinforcement effective?).

Personalization Process   Children are not automatically granted selfhood, membership, and a place in the social world. These are bestowed by members of families, schools, workplaces, and other social systems as part of what has been called the personalization process (Henry, 1966). The personalization process (introduced in chap. 1, this volume) has several features.

First, members of society develop a conception of a newcomer's place, worth, competence, and potential membership. If a child looks "right" and displays such socially significant behaviors as attentiveness, respect, self-control, ability to communicate, and adaptive skills, others may perceive the child as being like them (a member), treat the child with a certain amount of deference and sensitivity, provide some of what the child needs and wants, protect the child from injury, and, in effect, give the child the chance to perform valued roles in the social system's round of daily life (Bronfenbrenner, 1979).

If, however, a child is perceived to be lacking the significant symbols of membership—the right sort of body and behavioral repertoire—the child may be regarded as "abnormal," threatening, "retarded," "grotesque," or incompetent. In this case, other members may feel little or no obligation to provide a valued place and respectful treatment. Instead, the child may be seen as an adversary or someone to pity. Or, the child may not be allowed membership at all.

It can be asserted, therefore, that one's self-image develops on the basis of others' reactions. The labels others use (e.g., smart girl, poor thing); their facial expressions and tones of voice; and their rewarding or punishing, helping or hindering, offering or denying chances to participate in daily life are all messages that a child may *internalize*. Eventually, the child may respond to him- or herself as the child has experienced others responding to him or her. Through respondent conditioning, the child's body, clothing, and name become conditioned stimuli that elicit pleasure or pain, self-satisfaction or self-loathing.

Finally, the child's self-image affects his or her behaviors (Garfinkel, 1967; Goffman, 1963, 1971; Mead, 1934). People seem to act in ways that confirm, maintain, or fulfill their self-image. For instance, if Indra sees herself as a good student, she will act as such to maintain and augment the self-image of a good student. If, however, she learns to see herself as incompetent and pitiful, then, in the absence of easier, more rewarding alternative self-images and roles, she may act as such to maintain that image and role. After all, it is the only perception she knows.

Therefore, an important part of assessment is to examine the personalization processes in a child's environments. What are the socially significant symbols that define competence, value, and membership? How do others apparently perceive the child, judging by the way they talk to and about the child, reinforce or punish the child, and give or fail to give the child chances to contribute? What roles does the child appear to be playing? Clown? Member in good standing? Adversary? Finally, how might such processes be altered so as to foster psychosocial development?

Cultural Features   Every social system has a cultural side consisting of rules and norms, values, ideas of what is expected of typical persons and members, and what is not preferred or is prohibited. The cultural side of a social system guides all of the units of organization described above. For instance, teachers' images of what constitutes a competent child and rules about appropriate behavior influence how much they reinforce versus punish, the tasks they teach, and the sort of daily life they provide. Likewise, families differ in the age at which, and the skill with which, children are expected to toilet, bathe, dress, talk, use the telephone, cross the street, and set the table. Families and ethnic groups also differ in the frequency and nature of children's contacts with relatives, rules about adults' authority, the number of siblings in the family, religious tenets, and the importance of family routines, which means there will be different expectations about children's interactions with different classes of adults, sharing and playing with other children, and participating in religious and other family activities.

Therefore, an important part of assessment is to describe the cultural side of a child's present and potential future environments. What competencies are required to have a place as a valuable member or a member with potential? What rules are members expected to follow regarding communicating wants, cleanliness, sharing, and contributing to routine tasks? Which behaviors are considered peculiar, shameful, and disgusting?

Social Structure   Another unit of organization in schools, families, and other social systems is social structure. Social structure includes the way work is organized; how rewards, power, and authority are distributed; and the ways members try to control or influence one another's conduct.

Social structure is a large template that guides and limits just about everything that goes on in a social system. For instance, if the division of labor in a family is such that the wife and mother does most of the housekeeping and child rearing, she may feel alienated and resentful. If her husband earns the majority of the income, however, he may feel entitled not to have to help around the house. The clash created by the division of labor sets them up for mutually aversive exchanges (e.g., blaming) and for other counterproductive exchanges with their children (Henry, 1971).

The following are specific features of power, authority, and division of labor to consider when working with families, classrooms, and children. First, consider how tasks and activities are accomplished. What is the division of labor like? Is it highly *specialized* so that certain people do only certain jobs? Is it *routinized* so that tasks are the same day after day? Is it *inflexible* so there is little or no negotiation of who does what or how tasks are done? Is it *exploitative* so that some people do more of the labor (especially the "dirty work") than others? If so, members' functional behavioral repertoires will be limited and they may have little understanding of the overall organization of daily life. Moreover, those who are overworked and/or exploited—for example, the mother who does most of the housework, the teacher who is given the "difficult" children that other teachers refuse to work with—may feel stress, resentment, and alienation that is expressed as anger and/or detachment.

However, a division of labor that teaches people to perform many parts (e.g., therapists teach teachers language therapy), varies the routine, offers many ways to do the same tasks, and allows members to discuss and negotiate who does what and for how long is likely to yield greater motivation, a better understanding of the system, and a sense of purpose and meaning.

A second consideration with power, authority, and the division of labor is the amount of power people have in making decisions. Does one class of people (males, principals, directors of education) make decisions for others about what tasks to perform, how to perform them, how to evaluate performance, and what the consequences will be for different behaviors? If so, those with less control may again feel resentment, alienation, and engage in behaviors to escape, avoid, or delay doing what those in power want them to do. When, however, members (including children) have a greater share in the decision-making process, they develop a sense of ownership of the tasks and outcomes, as well as authenticity about their participation.

A final consideration is the climate of social influence. How do adults try to influence one another's and children's conduct? Do they inform others of their feelings and desires, negotiate, and notice and reinforce behaviors that they like? Or, do they keep quiet, harbor resentments, nag, whine, threaten, and punish? If the latter is the case, then the social system is likely to be aversive, which probably fosters mutual punishment, secrecy, and withdrawal.

It is not enough to examine the features of schools and families that have a direct effect on children (e.g., the physical environment, exchanges, tasks). One must also assess and suggest improvements in broader features that affect caregivers' feelings, sense of ownership, level of stress, and efficiency. How might the division of labor, relations of power, and methods of social influence be improved? Some of the answers are suggested in Chapter 8, this volume.

Members' Relationships with the Larger Community   Much of what occurs within schools and families is affected by access to, integration in, and use of persons, organizations, and networks offering emotional support, advice, respite, and classroom or home assistance. An equally important part of assessment and program planning involves describing parents' and teachers' relationships with their larger environments and how they might be empowered to effect change.

Long-Term Changes in Schools and Families   The course of change is a canalizing influence on further developments. If caregivers become more competent teachers, exchanges between caregivers and students become more productive, students participate more often in everyday affairs, and students perform a more valuable role in the social system, it is likely that the beneficial *direction* of change will promote even more beneficial changes. A course of increasingly counterproductive changes, however, is likely to promote desperate choices and even worse outcomes.

Two implications of the fact that the direction of change fosters more change are clear: 1) caregivers need training and support as early as possible; and 2) when trying to improve the overall situation in a home or school, it is wise to identify the feature that, if changed, would have the greatest payoff to members with the least effort and in the shortest time. In the experience of this author, improving caregiver–child exchanges is that feature.

Ongoing Congruence and Psychosocial Development

A child's behavior develops in a productive direction within any level of an environment only if the environment *fits* (is congruent with) the child's current needs, preferences, competencies, and capacities. Does the physical environment provide appropriate opportunities for action, templates (e.g., routes), cues, prompts, and reinforcement? Are others competent at teaching? Are exchanges primarily of the mutual reward variety? Are routine tasks and activities structured so the child frequently participates? Is the child seen and treated as a valued member with potential? If so, the result will be improvements in the actions, social competencies, and tasks canalized by each level of the environment.

The next question is: Are environments *adjusting* in a way that is commensurate with the child's changing repertoire? In particular, are caregivers: 1) identifying the child's increasing competencies and capacities; 2) altering cues, materials, prompts, and consequences to increase the child's skill, fluency, generalization, adaptation, and maintenance of gains (the subjects of chap. 4, this volume); and 3) providing the child with opportunities to participate in more complex interaction formats, tasks, activities, and roles that are moderately challenging and within the child's reach (Bronfenbrenner, 1979; Laosa, 1989; Odom, 1983; Redding, Morgan, & Harmon, 1988; Vygotsky, 1978; White, Kaban, Shapiro, & Antonucci, 1977; White & Watts, 1973; Wolf & Gardner, 1981)?

One must use ongoing evaluation to answer these questions about ongoing congruence because *the functional behavioral repertoire develops only as much as environments encourage.* This means that if a child's interaction with the world is confined to occasional cues and consequences, then the child's repertoire will remain limited to isolated responses. If the child frequently participates in lengthy series of exchanges (e.g., games, conversations), the child's repertoire will expand to include interaction and play competencies. Thus, it is essential to plan how to increase the *levels* of environments in which a child participates.

The idea of congruence between a child's changing needs, capacities, and competencies, and the constraints and opportunities provided by the child's environments leads to the following prescription: To describe psychosocial development, one has to keep track of the fit between development in a child's functional behavioral repertoire and commensurate changes in the child's environments. The purpose of initial assessment is to describe the adequacy of the current fit. The purpose of program planning and instruction is to improve the fit. Finally, the purpose of ongoing program evaluation is to see if planned improvements are occurring and what differences they are making in a child's psychosocial development.

A MODEL OF PSYCHOSOCIAL DEVELOPMENT

The model of psychosocial development presented in this section is based on four assumptions. First, behavior is best depicted as live performances in environments, rather than abstract categories. Second, psychosocial development is a complex interconnection of behaviors. Third, psychosocial development is an ongoing collaborative achievement. Finally, optimum psychosocial development occurs through participation in natural, everyday interactions.

Behavior as Performances in Environments

The model of psychosocial development portrays (and is designed to foster) competence and membership in children. Thus, behaviors are grouped into categories based not on physical appearance, the age at which they ordinarily appear, or with reference to inferred mental structures and processes. Instead, each cluster of behaviors, or *competency area*, is defined by what the behaviors do for a child and by the environment in which they are typically acquired and/or used (e.g., physical environment, exchanges, collaborative tasks) (Baker & Hacker, 1984; Bijou, 1977; Ochs & Schieffelin, 1979; Wittgenstein, 1958).

Psychosocial Development as Complex Interconnections Among Behaviors

Psychosocial development is not the addition of one behavior after another to a child's repertoire. There are complex interconnections among behaviors. Behaviors may become increasingly skillful, fluent, discriminated, generalized, adapted, and durable, usually at different rates and in different places. Some, in addition, become part of longer sequences guided by the structure of their environments (e.g., scripted tasks). Many behaviors facilitate the emergence and/or coordination of other behaviors. For instance: 1) as walking becomes fluent (e.g., faster), there is a "phase shift" (Fogel & Thelen, 1987) to where the child is suddenly running; 2) in crawling, the orientation of head and eyes to distant objects motivates locomotion while reaching forward steers the body (Goldfield, 1989); and 3) the development of almost any behavior (e.g., standing) increases the child's capacity to perform new behaviors (e.g., climbing). Thus, assessment, planning, instruction, and ongoing evaluation must be concerned with the multiple ways a behavior might be used, the environments where it might be performed, other behaviors that it might facilitate, and other behaviors that might facilitate it.

Psychosocial Development as an Ongoing Collaborative Achievement

Neither a child's functional behavioral repertoire nor the child's environments are things which, once set in motion, continue in that direction. Competence, participation, identity, roles, membership, place, and congruence are *temporary achievements*. Similar to plates spinning on the ends of sticks, one has to work to keep them there. Thus, ongoing evaluation (discussed in *Guidelines and Protocols*) is an essential ingredient in effective programs.

Optimum Psychosocial Development Through Participation in Everyday Interactions

In contrast to contrived lessons, practice, and drills designed to stamp in rules and skills, the natural environment is a configuration that provides more information, more challenge, and makes more behaviors possible (Bloom, 1970; Bronfenbrenner, 1979; Brown, 1973; Piaget, 1973; Schacter, 1979). In addition, teaching in the natural environment lessens problems such as the lack of generalization of behaviors to new places, satiation and habituation, and teaching nonfunctional tasks.

Qualitative Change in the Functional Behavioral Repertoire

No model of psychosocial development can perfectly depict the process of qualitative change in the functional behavioral repertoire that results from a child's participation in complex environments. That is, a "perfect" model does not exist if "perfect" means it includes everything that happens and in just the way it happens. Nor can guidelines for assessment and planning derived from a model of psychosocial development perfectly prescribe what to assess and teach and at what time. Rather than a rigid mold, Figure 6.4 provides a model that acts as a sort of searchlight. This model

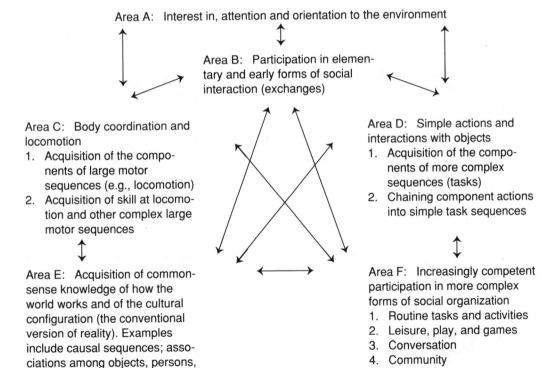

Figure 6.4   Model of children's psychosocial development.

sheds light on aspects of development and pathways of instruction that have not received enough prominence.

Figure 6.4 shows the interrelationships among a number of competency areas. Each area consists of many behaviors or items that are operationalized in the *Child Assessment and Programming Guide* (*CAPG*) in the companion to this volume, *Guidelines and Protocols*. Each of these areas is discussed on the following pages.

Area A: Interest in, Attention and Orientation to, the Environment   Ordinarily, children are interested in and pay attention and orient themselves to their environments. Children are "built to seek and receive information from the periphery" (Thelen, 1989, p. 948). Even young infants watch movements of their own hands, turn to locate the source of sounds, and visually follow moving objects. *Generalized responsivity* (Koegel & Koegel, 1988), *attunement* (Rasmussen, 1986), and increasingly skillful ways of *exploring* and observing the environment (Daniel & Lee, 1990; Gibson, 1988; Palmer, 1989) are important conditions for further development of the functional behavioral repertoire (Clausen & Sersen, 1983; Graham, Anthony, & Zeigler, 1983; Koegel & Koegel, 1988). Thus, it makes sense to strengthen such behaviors, if necessary, at the start of children's educations.

Area B: Participation in Elementary and Early Forms of Social Interaction   At first, an infant's behavior is generated and guided by biological forces and inherited patterns. Soon, movements become adapted to cues, prompts, and consequences from the physical surroundings. In her crib, for instance, the infant learns to turn her head to the left and receive a pleasant color sensation, or to bend her elbow, reach toward her face, and put her fingers into her mouth. Yet, she knows next to nothing about social interaction. She does not know what to do when her mother says, "Are you hungry?"

Within weeks, the child discovers that she is involved in exchanges. For example: 1) the hungry baby cries and a parent feeds her (service-request/service-provision), and 2) the parent calls the baby's name, the baby turns to the parent, and the parent smiles and hugs the baby (request for attention/attentive response).

With repetition (practice), caregivers and children learn to distinguish the interaction forms—both episodic exchanges (e.g., "You give me one and I give you one.") and longer series of exchanges (e.g., play activities, teaching sessions, meals). They also learn how each form is structured or scripted and how to participate. For example, children learn to: 1) initiate interaction in conventional ways; 2) effect changes in others' behaviors in conventional ways; and 3) respond to adults' and others' initiations by looking, laughing, or imitating. Each person's way of initiating and reacting to the other's behavior becomes increasingly skillful, regular, predictable, and durable (Bakeman & Adamson, 1984, 1986; Cohn & Tronick, 1987, 1988; Crais, 1990; Kaye & Fogel, 1980; Paulson & Kymissis, 1988; Stevenson, VerHoeve, Roach, & Leavitt, 1986). Moreover, the behaviors children learn in the context of exchanges (e.g., self-feeding), they soon use independently.

Exchanges bring children into the social world. They help children contact relevant features of their physical environments, and provide scaffolds or templates to help them transform movements into purposive actions and to assemble actions into collaborative sequences (e.g., meals and conversations). The education of many children (e.g., those who are uncooperative, inattentive, disoriented, withdrawn) should begin by involving them in exchanges that will prepare them for the regularities of social life.

Area C: Body Coordination and Locomotion   Building on their interest and attention, as well as their ability to orient themselves to events, children learn to use their bodies as instruments; that is, as means for interacting with and gaining more experiences from their environments (Gibson, 1979). As Rochat (1989) notes, "from the earliest age infants are actors and, in particular, explorers of their environment" (p. 871). For example, they learn to hold their heads erect and to turn them from side to side; to raise, extend, and flex their arms and legs; and to coordinate different sets of movements into standing and walking (Bernstein, 1967; Fogel & Thelen, 1987; Goldfield, 1989; Thomas, 1984; von Hofsten, 1989). Such elementary large motor coordination and locomotion sequences make it possible to move through the environment, which: 1) produces still more experience through which children acquire commonsense knowledge of movements, momentum, weight, surfaces, paths, and routes (Jansson, 1990); 2) sustains children's interest and attention; and 3) increases the size of their "life-world" (Schutz, 1970) from crib to whole house to neighborhood.

Area D: Simple Actions and Interactions with Objects   Facilitated by large motor body coordination and locomotion, interest and attention, and exchanges with others, children learn to perform simple actions and interactions with objects; for example, reaching, holding, grasping, squeezing, turning, scooping, and pushing. Gradually, they learn to combine (chain) elementary actions into *projects* of simple task sequences, such as stacking, fitting, filling, opening, building, and reaching (Palmer, 1989).

Area E: Acquisition of Commonsense Knowledge   In the process of moving through their environments, interacting with themselves, objects, and other persons, children acquire commonsense knowledge of how the world works and culture's way of rendering "reality." Commonsense knowledge is practical knowledge; it is acquired through action rather than recitation (Friedman, 1990).

Examples of commonsense knowledge include: 1) events that do not occur by chance, but are the result of antecedent events or causes (e.g., pull the string and the toy appears) (Piaget, 1954); 2) category schemes expressed in words (e.g., types of things and their attributes—things to eat, things that hurt, things that roll) (Henry, 1971); 3) conventional rules concerning how to eat, dress, point things out, and make requests (Duncan & Farley, 1990); 4) time (e.g., short vs. long, soon vs. later) (Friedman, 1990); 5) space (e.g., paths, landmarks) (Gauvain, 1993; Kermoian & Campos, 1988; Messick, 1988; Siegel, Kirasic, & Kail, 1978); and 6) roles and identities (e.g., sex, value, membership, competence).

Commonsense knowledge is organized in forms shared by members of groups. The forms include *scripts* ("First we get dressed. Then we have breakfast."), *prescriptions* ("To turn the light off, pull the switch down."), *recipes* ("A sandwich has bread, mustard, and cheese."), *visual images* (e.g., cognitive maps), *explanations* ("The vase fell because the dog bumped it."), *rules* ("We never go outside with wet hair."), and *category schemes* (e.g., kinds of times, places, persons, objects, and activities). The forms serve as ways of organizing, mapping, representing, and communicating experience (Bauer & Mandler, 1989; Bauer & Thal, 1990; Schank & Abelson, 1977; Slackman, Hudson, & Fivush, 1986), and as frameworks or templates that guide independent and collaborative action (Schutz, 1970; Wolf & Gardner, 1981). For instance, participants use shared script knowledge of how a game is played to guide their own and each other's actions.

Area F: Increasingly Competent Participation in More Complex Forms of Social Organization   Assuming good fit or congruence, a child's progress in these various competency areas will foster upward adjustments in other people's assessments of the child's competence and in the opportunities that it provides. For instance, the child will be invited to participate in lengthy conversations and games, perform complex tasks, and take part in community environments. Reciprocally, as the child participates in more complex forms of social life, his or her competence and stock of knowledge increase.

PRACTICES BASED ON MODELS OF THE FUNCTIONAL
BEHAVIORAL REPERTOIRE AND PSYCHOSOCIAL DEVELOPMENT

Imagine that Jerry's, Indra's, and Juan's caregivers have collaboratively planned and instituted a new family-school-community program based on models of the functional behavioral repertoire and psychosocial development. Such a program is outlined on the following pages.

Assessment

Assessment is guided by the importance of congruence between each child's needs, competencies, and capacities, and how each child's environments are organized. Thus, assessment, program planning, instruction, and program evaluation are individualized and address both children and their environments (described in *Guidelines and Protocols*).

With respect to each child's functional behavioral repertoire and psychosocial development, caregivers describe (1) a child's performance in all of the competency areas described above in the model of psychosocial development (2) during a variety of routine tasks, activities, and social interactions (3) under a range of everyday conditions (4) supplemented by observations during special assessment sessions. The aim is to identify: common weak spots in sequences where performance breaks down (which might require special practice); common strong sequences and strong spots in sequences (which the child could be taught to use more often and in more places); alternative ways the child can perform the "work" at different spots (i.e., the size of classes) and alternative ways the child can rearrange sequences depending upon the environment; and the cues, prompts, and consequences the child seems to need and prefer.

Regarding children's environments, caregivers describe the precise ways that physical features, adults' teaching competence, child–caregiver exchanges, the round of daily life tasks and activities, the personalization process, the division of labor, and caregivers' relationships with the community promote or hinder children's psychosocial development and caregivers' efforts. Assessments are conducted by teachers, family members, and therapists, relying primarily on direct observation (see chap. 10, this volume) and interviews of one another (see chap. 9, this volume). Observations start at the "core" of each child's world in the home and school, and over the course of a month or so they move outward to restaurants, homes of relatives, parks, and grocery stores.

Having described children's behaviors in the "real world" and having formulated questions that they cannot answer ("Why does Jerry's performance break down if he is interrupted and has to restart a task?"), caregivers seek advice from specialists outside the program (e.g., in the developmental disabilities field).

Program Planning

Building on assessment information, the purpose of program planning and instruction is to improve the fit between each child's functional behavioral repertoire and environments. Each child's individualized education program (IEP) includes competencies desired by families and teachers, as well as competencies expected in potential future instructional, living, and working environments. The competency objectives are arranged in a tentative longitudinal curriculum sequence guided by considerations of demonstrated capability (e.g., moderate skill at some of the component behaviors of a selected task), functionality or usefulness, and the way different behaviors and competency areas facilitate one another, as suggested by the model of psychosocial development in Figure 6.4 and the criteria for task selection (see Form 14, "Criteria for Selecting Competencies To Improve" in Section II of the companion to this volume, *Guidelines and Protocols*).

Plans also include specific ways to improve child–caregiver exchanges in home and school, features of the physical environment, adults' teaching competence, methods of scheduling and performing tasks and activities such that children can be easily included, ways of improving caregivers' perceptions of the children's membership and capability, and caregivers' access to support and concrete assistance.

Most teaching occurs during routine tasks and activities at school and home, using materials, cues, prompts, reinforcers, and reinforcement schedules that are as usual as possible. Some behaviors are jointly worked on at home and school (e.g., cooperation, locomotion, communication); others are worked on separately (e.g., dressing at home, handwriting at school) with plans made for future generalization.

Special sessions at home and school are used to improve "basic" competencies, or to remedy "weak links" that figure into many routines (e.g., teaching Indra to hold an object with one hand and manipulate it with the other). Instead of working on the same tasks over and over, practice is distributed throughout the day. Moreover, children are taught to use the same behaviors in different environments to increase generalization and adaptation.

Program Evaluation

Ongoing evaluation involves tracking improvements in the fit between children's functional behavioral repertoires and their surroundings. Are suggested improvements being made in physical environments (e.g., less noise), and are there subsequent improvements in children's attention? Are suggested improvements being made in parent–child and teacher–child exchanges, and are there concomitant improvements in children's cooperation and problem behaviors?

Whenever evaluation reveals a child's increasing competence at a behavior, caregivers alter environments to promote fluency, generalization, adaptation, and maintenance (described in chap. 4, this volume). They also teach children to use the behavior to serve additional functions, to insert the behavior into other sequences, and to combine it with other behaviors to form new sequences.

At the same time, caregivers determine whether environments are adjusted to accommodate and further encourage children's progress by raising their conceptions of the children's competence, raising their expectations for the children, inviting the children to participate in more complex tasks and activities, and moving away from nonnormative methods.

When ongoing evaluation indicates a lack of development in children and/or in environments, a problem-solving strategy is followed. However, when a child has made so much progress within an instructional environment (class) that further psychosocial development requires a qualitatively different environment, the child is promoted, as described below.

Instructional Goals and Methods

This section illustrates some of the implications of the models of the functional behavioral repertoire and psychosocial development for instruction. There are two main contending answers to the question of where children with disabilities should receive education. The more traditional approach is to attempt to provide a series of educational experiences that, depending on a child's age, competencies, and needs, may begin with separate special education classes and progress to regular education classes (Davis, 1989; Kauffman, 1989; Walker & Bullis, 1991). Since the early 1980s, a second approach has emerged. Advocates of this approach stress the importance of including, and as much as possible *fully integrating,* children with disabilities into regular education from the beginning of children's educations (Biklen, 1992; Gaylord-Ross, 1989; Guralnick, 1979; Sailor et al., 1989; Stainback & Stainback, 1990, 1992). It is likely that continuing research will reveal which of the two contending (and future) approaches yields the best outcomes for children and their caregivers and under what conditions. Important research and thinking on this matter includes that of Baker and Zigmond (1990); Buysse and Bailey (1993); Evans, Salisbury, Palombaro, Berryman, and Hollowood (1992); Fuchs, Fuchs, and Fernstrom (1993); Goldstein, Kacszmarek, Pennington, and Shafer (1992); Haring and Breen (1992); Hundert and Hopkins (1992); Hunt et al. (1993); Kamps et al. (1992); and McGee, Paradis, and Feldman (1993).

Whether programs move from special classes to regular eduction, include children in regular education from the beginning, or have an alternative design, the psychosocial development of children such as Jerry, Indra, and Juan will be fostered by a curriculum that has at least three groups or levels of instructional goals and methods—initial, intermediate, and advanced—as suggested by the earlier work of Bruno-Golden (1977) and Hamblin, Buckholdt, Ferritor, Kozloff, and Blackwell (1971). In schools where children progress from special to regular education, each group of goals and methods might constitute a different class with associated family and community participation. If, however, children are integrated in preschools and regular education classes from the beginning, the three groups will suggest to caregivers the kinds of instructional goals and methods that will help children with disabilities to learn with and from their age peers in regular education. In either environment, assessment information is used to identify the appropriate starting group of goals and methods for a child. As the child learns to participate in the forms of social interaction that characterize his or her current group and becomes more competent at specified curriculum tasks, caregivers will begin to work on the next group. The following are brief descriptions of each group of goals and methods. They should be seen as illustrations of how the models of the functional behavioral repertoire and psychosocial development can be used to create an effective curriculum among the many that are possible.

Initial Group   The initial group of goals and methods is for children whose functional behavioral repertoires are insufficient. Not only are they largely incompetent on items in competency areas E and F in Figure 6.4, but they display profound deficits even in the early areas of A and B. Specifically, they do not pay much attention to their environment; frequently fail to cooperate with requests; avoid and/or do not know how to participate in many of the elementary forms of social interaction; use little speech; do not know how to take care of their needs; and spend much time in self-stimulatory behavior, throwing tantrums, or aggressing to communicate their preferences and dislikes. In terms of psychosocial development, they are "outsiders" in the culture.

The overarching goal of the initial group is to bring children into the conventional world of daily life—to get them interested in and oriented to it; interacting with and learning from the physical environment; participating in and learning the forms of elementary interaction ("You do this and I do that."); and acquiring commonsense knowledge of time, space, cause-effect, and social interaction.

Initial teaching methods with some children may not be normative due to the high frequency and durability of behaviors that interfere with learning (e.g., self-stimulation, noncooperation), the children's short attention, the few events that are positive reinforcers, and the large amount of assistance they need. The major features of teaching include the following:

1. Desirable behaviors are reinforced as soon and as often as possible. If necessary, food reinforcers are used.
2. At the start of a child's education, an emphasis is placed on learning to participate in elementary forms of interaction, such as responding to one's own name, responding to requests such as "Look," and approaching others. (See competency area B of the *Child Assessment and Programming Guide* [CAPG] in *Guidelines and Protocols* for more examples.)
3. As a child progresses, new contents are added to the elementary interactions. For instance, children work on large motor items (e.g., bending and flexing limbs, walking, throwing and kicking a ball); small motor items (e.g., picking up and grasping objects, placing objects in containers, stacking objects, unscrewing jar lids, turning pages); attention to stationary and moving objects; vocalizing; motor and vocal imitation (e.g., imitating sounds, syllables, simple words, actions); simple communication (e.g., asking for things, greeting, asking questions); and simple chores and adaptive tasks (e.g., washing and drying hands and face, helping to set the table for a meal). (See competency areas A, B, C, D, and F of the *CAPG* in *Guidelines and Protocols*.)
4. Much instruction occurs in the context of play (with manipulatable toys, balls, swings). Some teaching may be done in one-to-one sessions to establish interaction, contain and replace certain problem behaviors (e.g., whining), and provide extra practice on components of tasks. As a child becomes more competent on an item during teaching sessions, the competency is generalized to other school, family, and community exchanges and tasks.
5. At first, children alternate between short sessions (either special teaching sessions or routine tasks) in which they work on behaviors that are more difficult or less enjoyable, followed by opportunities to play. As competence and participation increase, play time may be decreased and session time gradually increased.

6. Errors and problem behaviors are prevented as much as possible, and more correct or desirable responses are requested and/or prompted (certainly reinforced). In this way, problem behaviors become detached from their usual cues while desirable behaviors become attached. When errors or certain problem behaviors occur, positive practice is used. That is, the child is encouraged to perform part of the sequence again, leading to the point at which the error or problem behavior occurred. Then the child is encouraged to make an alternative response.

7. Chaining methods (see chap. 4, this volume) are employed to increase the number of steps a child performs in a sequence (e.g., placing more puzzle pieces; retrieving, using, and then putting away materials).

8. Many activities in a child's round of daily life are arranged such that they occur in pairs, with a short amount of a less enjoyable activity followed by a more enjoyable activity. At home, for instance, Jerry can have a snack after his hands are washed, and he can have a bath after he has put away some of his toys.

9. As a child's participation and competence improve, food reinforcers are gradually replaced with social reinforcers, activity reinforcers, and perhaps token reinforcers (e.g., poker chips exchanged for snacks and activities).

10. Age peers who do not have disabilities help children with disabilities to initiate and reciprocate exchanges (e.g., take turns), imitate, communicate, play, and perform other routine tasks and activities (Goldstein et al., 1992; Hanline, 1993; Jolly, Test, & Spooner, 1993; Peck, Donaldson, & Pezzoli, 1990). (See items F14–F26 of the *CAPG* in *Guidelines and Protocols.*)

11. Families receive training in the classroom and at home. At the same time, educators learn from parents those instructional methods parents have found to work and not to work well with their children. Parents and teachers work together to plan joint and separate teaching programs.

The initial group of goals and methods is probably the best choice for Jerry.

Intermediate Group   Children move to the intermediate group of goals and methods when they have learned to participate effectively and enjoyably in elementary forms of interaction, including teaching sessions. Also, at this point, most severe problem behaviors have been markedly reduced, and children are fairly competent at tasks worked on in the initial group. For example, they can name, point to, and ask for many objects; imitate sounds, words, and actions; attend to most lessons and activities for at least 20 minutes; and complete a variety of small motor and large motor tasks.

The specific objectives of the intermediate group are to: 1) teach skills for participating in the round of daily life at home and in school—skills such as waiting your turn, attending in a group, following rules, and cooperating in a group activity (see items F40–F52 of the *CAPG* in *Guidelines and Protocols*); 2) further improve imitation, speech, and task competence in the round of daily living; and 3) generalize children's competencies to other environments (e.g., the bus, the playground, neighbors' homes, and the store (see items E33–E34 and F34–F39 of the *CAPG* in *Guidelines and Protocols*).

Major teaching methods in the intermediate group are as follows:

1. The classroom is divided into areas for working, eating, and playing. Each area is clearly marked with rugs and bookcases. Certain behaviors are expected and others are prohibited in each area. The work area has both individual desks and large tables for group activities. Similar areas are created in the home.

2. A set of general rules is established for the school and home, posted on the walls, and repeated often. Examples include: "No hitting," "Raise your hand for help," and "Put toys away before going outside." (See items E31 and E32 of the *CAPG* in *Guidelines and Protocols*.)

3. When a child becomes a new member of a class, his or her performance in everyday tasks and activities is noted (e.g., how the child enters the room, puts away coat and lunch box, greets

others, gets materials, works independently and with others). (See items F10–F12 of the *CAPG* in *Guidelines and Protocols*.) Strong and weak links are identified, as are problem behaviors, for special attention.

4. During the school day, children learn in several environments, including individual desk work (e.g., handwriting); one-to-one sessions for practice in a specified area (e.g., speech or small motor coordination); small group lessons (e.g., cooperative tasks); and large group lessons or activities (e.g., blackboard, snacks, games). Harder activities are followed either by time in the play area (during which children are taught how to play with their peers) or by an easier or pre-ferred activity.

5. Children's attention, persistence, completion of tasks, rule following, and working on individ-ual goals may be strengthened with a token system. One version (Bruno-Golden, 1977) involves dividing activity time (usually 15 minutes) into consecutive 3-minute intervals. Each child has a recording sheet at his or her desk that has boxes for each of the 3-minute intervals. At the end of each interval, a timer rings and the teacher reinforces those children who were following the rules, working, and participating, by praising them, commenting on desirable behavior, and putting a check mark in the box. Those children who did not receive praise and a check mark are told what they can do during the next interval to earn a check mark.

   At the end of the activity, children receive another check mark if they finish their assigned work. Children can exchange check mark scorings for the opportunity to buy or rent items from the "store" (e.g., fruit, books) or to perform the roles of leader, storekeeper, milkperson, or messenger. Gradually, the check mark system is faded out as children learn to notice and control their own behaviors. The teacher still provides praise and brief commentary, and the children still earn the activity reinforcers. Also, the amount of work, the length of the activi-ties, and the size of the intervals are increased. Families may be using a similar token system at home.

6. Children are taught to control their own behavior and make decisions about the instructional process. For instance, they learn relaxation techniques, how to set performance objectives, self-recording, and self-reinforcement (Stahmer & Schreibman, 1992).

7. Assistance is solicited from restaurant managers and shopkeepers, and children are taken to many community environments to generalize and adapt what they have learned at school and at home. As with the initial group, children with and without disabilities learn to play, commu-nicate, and perform school and community activities together.

It seems that the intermediate group of goals and methods best suits Indra's needs.

Advanced Group   The advanced group is for children who perform few problem behaviors, display strong classroom skills, and have made much progress on communication; that is, they dis-play many of the socially significant symbols of membership competence. The overall goal of the advanced group is to fill gaps in children's repertoires, help children to use their skills in everyday environments, and prepare them for entry into future education environments and/or employment.

Juan was adopted by the Silva family at the age of 12. He now lives in a house instead of an institution. Before school started, his team (including parents, teacher, and others) undertook the assessment task of learning how competent Juan was in relation to the expectations, opportunities, exchanges, tasks and activities, cues, prompts, hindrances, and consequences in his new round of daily life. It was agreed that he should enter a regular sixth grade class with special attention given to the advanced group of goals and methods.

Specific objectives in the advanced group include: 1) teaching children to participate in more complex forms of social interaction, such as games (*CAPG* item F26); 2) teaching children more advanced language forms (e.g., describing ongoing behavior, recounting experiences, correctly using prepositions and tenses, and repairing interaction difficulties [*CAPG* items F28–F33]); 3) increasing the number and complexity of routine tasks that children perform (e.g., preparing a meal [*CAPG* item F7] and grocery shopping [*CAPG* item F37]); 4) teaching reading; 5) generalizing competencies to everyday environments; and 6) working with caregivers in new environments (e.g., junior high schools) to help integrate the children. As in the two earlier groups, families and peers are intimately involved in planning and carrying out instructional activities.

Many methods used in the intermediate group are used in the advanced group as well; that is, children select more of their tasks and reinforcers and record their own behaviors; and reinforcement contingencies tend to be "natural" or normative. In addition to group tasks and activities, children may be taught in one-to-one teaching sessions, or in very small groups, to work on individual needs.

SUMMARY

This chapter presents two models that can improve education practices and outcomes. The model of the functional behavioral repertoire shows how behaviors are assembled into larger sequences as children interact with larger units of their environments. The model of psychosocial development describes the progression of changes in children's competence and participation in relation to congruent changes in the opportunities for learning and participation afforded by their environments.

This chapter ends with a description of a program based on the ideas presented in this and earlier chapters. Unlike the common programs described in Chapters 1 and 2, the new program for Jerry, Indra, and Juan is aimed at promoting psychosocial development by adapting environments to the children's current needs, competencies, and capacities, while simultaneously teaching children the behaviors that will improve participation in their environments.

REFERENCES

Bakeman, R., & Adamson, L.B. (1984). Coordinating attention to people and objects in mother-infant and peer-infant interactions. *Child Development, 55,* 1278–1289.

Bakeman, R., & Adamson, L.B. (1986). Infants' conventionalized acts: Gestures with mothers and peers. *Infant Behavior and Development, 9,* 215–230

Baker, G.B., & Hacker, P.M.S. (1984). *Language, sense and nonsense.* Oxford, England: Basil Blackwell.

Baker, J.M., & Zigmond, N. (1990). Are regular education classes equipped to accomodate students with learning disabilities? *Exceptional Children, 56,* 515–526.

Barker, R. (Ed.). (1963). *The stream of behavior.* New York: Appleton-Century-Crofts.

Barker, R. (1968). *Ecological psychology.* Stanford, CA: Stanford University Press.

Bauer, P.J., & Mandler, J.M. (1989). One thing follows another: Effects of temporal structure on 1–2-year olds' recall of events. *Developmental Psychology, 25,* 197–206.

Bauer, P.J., & Thal, D.J. (1990). Scripts or scraps: Reconsidering the development of sequential understanding. *Journal of Experimental Child Psychology, 50,* 287–304.

Bernstein, N. (1967). *The coordination and regulation of movements.* London: Pergamon Press.

Bijou, S.W. (1977). Practical implications of an interactive model of child development. *Exceptional Children, 44,* 6–14.

Biklen, D. (1992). *Schooling without labels.* Philadelphia: Temple University Press.

Bloom, L. (1970). *Form and function in emerging grammars.* Cambridge, MA: MIT Press.

Bronfenbrenner, U. (1979). *The ecology of human development.* Cambridge, MA: Harvard University Press.

Brown, R. (1973). *The first language.* Cambridge, MA: Harvard University Press.

Bruner, J.S. (1983). *Child talk: Learning to use language.* New York: Norton.

Bruno-Golden, B. (1977). *A teacher's use of behavior modification in the classroom.* Unpublished manuscript, Boston University Department of Sociology, Boston.

Buysse, V., & Bailey, D.B., Jr. (1993). Behavioral and developmental outcomes in young children with disabilities in integrated and segregated settings: A review of comparative studies. *Journal of Special Education, 26*(4), 434–461.

Cairns, R.B. (1991). Multiple metaphors for a singular idea. *Developmental Psychology, 27*(1), 23–26.

Catania, A.C. (1973). The psychologies of structure, function, and development. *American Psychologist, 28,* 434–443.

Clausen, J., & Sersen, E.A. (1983). The orienting response and intellectual retardation. In D. Siddle (Ed.), *Orienting and habituation: Perspectives in human research* (pp. 505–522). New York: John Wiley & Sons.

Cohn, J.F., & Tronick, E.Z. (1987). Mother-infant face-to-face interaction: The sequence of dyadic states at 3, 6, and 9 months. *Developmental Psychology, 23*(1), 68–77.

Cohn, J.F., & Tronick, E.Z. (1988). Mother-infant face-to-face interaction: Influence is bidirectional and unrelated to periodic cycles in either partner's behavior. *Developmental Psychology, 24*(3), 386–392.

Connolly, K., & Dalgleish, M. (1989). The emergence of tool-using skill in infancy. *Developmental Psychology, 25*(6), 894–912.

Crais, E.R. (1990). World knowledge to word knowledge. *Topics in Language Disorders, 10*(3), 45–62.

Daniel, B.M., & Lee, D.N. (1990). Development of looking with head and eyes. *Journal of Experimental Child Psychology, 50,* 200–216.

Davis, W. (1989). The Regular Education Initiative debate: Its promises and problems. *Exceptional Children, 55,* 35–37.

Duncan, S., Jr., & Farley, A.M. (1990). Achieving parent-child coordination through convention: Fixed- and variable-sequence conventions. *Child Development, 61,* 742–753.

Eisert, D., Kulka, L., & Moore, K. (1988). Facilitating play in hospitalized handicapped children: The design of a therapeutic play environment. *Children's Health Care, 16,* 201–208.

Evans, I.M., Salisbury, C.L., Palombaro, M.M., Berryman, J., & Hollowood, T.M. (1992). Peer interactions and social acceptance of elementary-age children with severe disabilities in an inclusive school. *Journal of The Association for Persons with Severe Handicaps, 17*(4), 205–212.

Fogel, A. (1977). Temporal organization in mother-infant face-to-face interaction. In R. Schaffer (Ed.), *Studies in mother-infant interaction* (pp. 119–152). London: Academic Press.

Fogel, A. (1981). The ontogeny of gestural communication: The first six months. In R. Stark (Ed.), *Language behavior in infancy and early childhood* (pp. 17–44). New York: Elsevier/North Holland.

Fogel, A., & Thelen, E. (1987). Development of early expressive and communicative action: Reinterpreting the evidence from a dynamic systems perspective. *Developmental Psychology, 23*(6), 747–761.

Friedman, W.J. (1990). Children's representations of the pattern of daily activities. *Child Development, 61,* 1399–1412.

Fuchs, D., Fuchs, L.S., & Fernstrom, P. (1993). A conservative approach to special education reform: Mainstreaming through transenvironmental programming and curriculum measurement. *American Educational Research Journal, 30*(1), 149–177.

Garfinkel, H. (1967). *Studies in ethnomethodology.* Englewood Cliffs, NJ: Prentice Hall.

Gauvain, M. (1993). The development of spatial thinking in everyday activity. *Developmental Review, 13,* 92–121.

Gaylord-Ross, R. (Ed.). (1989). *Integration strategies for students with handicaps.* Baltimore: Paul H. Brookes Publishing Co.

Gibson, E. (1988). Exploratory behavior in the development of perceiving, acting, and acquiring knowledge. *Annual Review of Psychology, 39,* 1–41.

Gibson, E.J. (1979). *The ecological approach to visual perception.* Boston: Houghton Mifflin.

Goffman, E. (1963). *Stigma: Notes on the management of spoiled identity.* New York: Simon & Schuster.

Goffman, E. (1971). *Relations in public.* New York: Harper & Row.

Goffman, E. (1974). *Frame analysis.* New York: Harper & Row.

Goldfield, E.C. (1989). Transition from rocking to crawling: Postural constraints on infant movement. *Developmental Psychology, 25*(6), 913–919.

Goldstein, H., Kaczmarek, L., Pennington, R., & Shafer, K. (1992). Peer-mediated intervention: Attending to, commenting on, and acknowledging the behavior of preschoolers with autism. *Journal of Applied Behavior Analysis, 25,* 289–305.

Gottlieb, G. (1991). Experimental canalization of behavior development: Theory. *Developmental Psychology, 27*(1), 4–13.

Graham, F.K., Anthony, B.J., & Zeigler, B.L. (1983). The orienting response and developmental processes. In D. Siddle (Ed.), *Orienting and habituation: Perspectives in human research* (pp. 371–430). New York: John Wiley & Sons.

Guralnick, M. (Ed.). (1979). *Early intervention and the integration of handicapped and nonhandicapped children.* Baltimore: University Park Press.

Hamblin, R.L., Buckholdt, D., Ferritor, D., Kozloff, M., & Blackwell, L. (1971). *The humanization processes.* New York: John Wiley & Sons.

Hanline, M.F. (1993). Inclusion of preschoolers with profound disabilities: An analysis of children's interactions. *Journal of The Association for Persons with Severe Handicaps, 18*(1), 28–35.

Haring, T.G., & Breen, C.G. (1992). A peer-mediated social network intervention to enhance the social integration of persons with moderate and severe handicaps. *Journal of Applied Behavior Analysis, 25,* 319–333.

Henry, J. (1966). Personality and aging—with special reference to hospitals for the aged poor. In J.C. McKinney & F.T. DeVyver (Eds.), *Aging and social policy* (pp. 281–301). New York: Meredith.

Henry, J. (1971). *Pathways to madness.* New York: Random House.

Hundert, J., & Hopkins, B. (1992). Training supervisors in a collaborative team approach to promote peer interaction of children with disabilities in integrated preschools. *Journal of Applied Behavior Analysis, 25*(2), 385–400.

Hunt, P., Haring, K., Farron-Davis, F., Staub, D., Rogers, J., Beckstead, S.P., Karasoff, P., Goetz, L., & Sailor, W. (1993). Factors associated with the integrated educational placement of students with severe disabilities. *Journal of The Association for Persons with Severe Handicaps, 18*(1), 6–15.

Ichinose, C.K., & Clark, H.B. (1990). A review of ecological factors that influence the play and activity engagement of handicapped children. *Child and Family Behavior Therapy, 12*(3), 49–76.

Inhelder, B., & Piaget, J. (1958). *The growth of logical thinking from childhood to adolescence.* New York: Basic Books.

Jansson, G. (1990). Non-visual guidance of walking. In R. Warren & A.H. Wertheim (Eds.), *Perception and control of self-motion* (pp. 507–521). Hillsdale, NJ: Lawrence Erlbaum Associates.

Jolly, A.C., Test, D.W., & Spooner, F. (1993). Using badges to increase initiations of children with severe disabilities in a play setting. *Journal of The Association for Persons with Severe Handicaps, 18*(1), 46–51.

Kamps, D.M., Leonard, B.R., Vernon, S., Dugan, E.P., Delquadri, J.C., Gershon, B., Wade, L., & Folk, L. (1992). Teaching social skills to students with autism to increase peer interactions in an integrated first-grade classroom. *Journal of Applied Behavior Analysis, 25,* 281–288.

Kauffman, J.M. (1989). The Regular Education Initiative as Reagan-Bush education policy: A trickle down theory of education for the hard to teach. *Journal of Special Education, 23,* 256–278.

Kaye, K., & Fogel, A. (1980). The temporal structure of face-to-face communication between mothers and infants. *Developmental Psychology, 16*, 454–464.

Kermoian, R., & Campos, J.J. (1988). Locomotor experience: A facilitator of spatial cognitive development. *Child Development, 59*(4), 908–917.

Koegel, R.L., & Koegel, L.K. (1988). Generalized responsivity and pivotal behaviors. In R.H. Horner, G. Dunlap, & R.L. Koegel (Eds.), *Generalization and maintenance: Life-style changes in applied settings* (pp. 41-66). Baltimore: Paul H. Brookes Publishing Co.

Laosa, L.M. (1989). Social competence in childhood: Toward a developmental, sociocultural relativistic paradigm. *Journal of Applied Developmental Psychology, 10*, 447–468.

Lee, V.L. (1987, Fall). The structure of conduct. *Behaviorism, 15*(2), 141–148.

Levy, E., & McLeod, W. (1977). The effects of environmental design on adolescents in an institution. *Mental Retardation, 15*, 28–32.

Lewis, M., & Rosenbaum, L. (Eds.). (1974). *The effect of the infant on its caregiver.* New York: John Wiley & Sons.

McAfee, J.K. (1987). Classroom density and the aggressive behavior of handicapped children. *Education and Treatment of Children, 10*, 134–145.

McGee, G.G., Paradis, T., & Feldman, R.S. (1993). Free effects of integration on levels of autistic behavior. *Topics in Early Childhood Special Education, 13*(1), 57–67.

Mead, G.H. (1934), *Mind, self, and society.* (C.W. Morris, Ed.), Chicago: The University of Chicago Press.

Messick, C.K. (1988). Ins and outs of the acquisition of spatial terms. *Topics in Language Disorders, 8*(2), 14–25.

Nelson, K. (Ed.). (1986). *Event knowledge: Structure and function in development.* Hillsdale, NJ: Lawrence Erlbaum Associates.

Ochs, E., & Schieffelin, B.B. (1979). *Developmental pragmatics.* New York: Academic Press.

Odom, S.L. (1983). The development of social interchanges in infancy. In S.G. Garwood & R.R. Fewell (Eds.), *Educating handicapped infants* (pp. 215–254). Rockville, MD: Aspen Publishers, Inc.

Palmer, C.F. (1989). The discriminating nature of infants' exploratory actions. *Developmental Psychology, 25*(6), 885–893.

Paulson, C.L., & Kymissis, E. (1988). Generalized imitation in infants. *Journal of Experimental Child Psychology; 46,* 324–336.

Peck, C.A., Donaldson, J., & Pezzoli, M. (1990). Some benefits nonhandicapped adolescents perceive for themselves from their social relationships with peers who have severe handicaps. *Journal of The Association for Persons with Severe Handicaps, 15*, 241–249.

Piaget, J. (1954). *The construction of reality in the child.* New York: Basic Books.

Piaget, J. (1973). *To understand is to invent.* New York: Grossman Publishers.

Pike, K.L. (1954). *Language in relation to a unified theory of the structure of human behavior.* Glendale, CA: Summer Institute of Linguistics.

Rasmussen, J. (1986). *Information processing and human machine interaction: An approach to cognitive engineering.* New York: Elsevier/North Holland.

Redding, R.E., Morgan, G.A., & Harmon, R.J. (1988). Mastery motivation in infants and toddlers: Is it greatest when tasks are moderately challenging? *Infant Behavior and Development, 11*, 419–430.

Rochat, P. (1989). Object manipulation and exploration in 2- to 5-month-old infants. *Developmental Psychology, 25,* 871–884.

Sailor, W., Anderson, J.L., Halvorsen, A.T., Doering, K., Filler, J., & Goetz, L. (1989). *The comprehensive local school: Regular education for all students with disabilities.* Baltimore: Paul H. Brookes Publishing Co.

Schacter, F.F. (1979), *Everyday mother talk to toddlers.* New York: Academic Press.

Schank, R.C., & Abelson, R.P. (1977). *Scripts, plans, goals, and understanding.* Hillsdale, NJ: Lawrence Erlbaum Associates.

Schutz, A. (1970). *On phenomenology and social relations.* (H.R. Wagner, Ed.). Chicago: The University of Chicago Press.

Siegel, A.W., Kirasic, K., & Kail, R.V., Jr. (1978). Stalking the elusive cognitive map: The development of children's representations of geographic space. In I. Altman & J. Wohlwill (Eds.) *Children and the environment* (pp. 223–257). New York: Plenum.

Slackman, E.A., Hudson, J.A., & Fivush, R. (1986). Actions, actors, links, and goals: The structure of children's event representations. In K. Nelson (Ed.), *Event knowledge: Structure and function in development* (pp. 47–69). Hillsdale, NJ: Lawrence Erlbaum Associates.

Smetana, J. (1989). Toddlers' social interactions in the context of moral and conventional transgressions in the home. *Developmental Psychology, 25*(4), 499–508.

Smith, P.K., & Connolly, K.J. (1980). *The ecology of preschool behavior.* Cambridge, England: Cambridge University Press.

Speigel-McGill, P., Bambara, L.M., Shores, R.E., & Fox, J.J. (1984). The effects of proximity on socially oriented behaviors of severely multiply handicapped children. *Education and Treatment of Children, 7*, 365–378.

Stahmer, A.C., & Schreibman, L. (1992). Teaching children with autism appropriate play in unsupervised environments using a self-management treatment package. *Journal of Applied Behavior Analysis, 25*, 447–459.

Stainback, W., & Stainback, S. (Eds.). (1990). *Support networks for inclusive schooling: Interdependent integrated education.* Baltimore: Paul H. Brookes Publishing Co.

Stainback, S., & Stainback, W. (Eds.). (1992). *Curriculum considerations in inclusive classrooms: Facilitating learning for all students.* Baltimore: Paul H. Brookes Publishing Co.

Stevenson, M.B., VerHoeve, J.N., Roach, M.A., & Leavitt, L.A. (1986). The beginning of conversation: Early patterns in mother-infant vocal responsiveness. *Infant Behavior and Development, 9*, 423–440.

Thelen, E. (1985). Expression as action: A motor perspective on the transition from spontaneous to instrumental behaviors.

In G. Zivin (Ed.), *The development of experssive behavior: Biology-environment interactions* (pp. 221–248). New York: Academic Press.

Thelen, E. (1989). The (re)discovery of motor development: Learning new things from an old field. *Development Psychology, 25*(6), 946–949.

Thomas, J.R. (Ed.). (1984). *Motor development during childhood and adolescence*. Minneapolis, MN: Burgess.

Valett, R. (1972). Developmental task analysis and psychoeducational programming. *Journal of School Psychology, 10,* 127–133.

Valsiner, J. (1987). *Culture and the development of children's action*. New York: John Wiley & Sons.

von Hofsten, C. (1989). Motor development as the development of systems: Comments on the special section. *Developmental Psychology, 25*(6), 950–953.

Vygotsky, L.S. (1978). *Mind in society*. Cambridge, MA: Harvard University Press.

Waddington, C.H. (1970). *Towards theoretical biology, Vol. 1*. Chicago: Aldine.

Walker, H.M., & Bullis, M. (1991). Behavior disorders and the social context of regular class integration: A conceptual dilemma? In J.W. Lloyd, N.N. Singh, & A. Repp (Eds.), *The regular education initiative: Alternative perspectives on concepts, issues, and models* (pp. 75–93). Dekalb, IL: Sycamore Publishing Co.

White, B.L., Kaban, B., Shapiro, B., & Antonucci, J. (1977). Competence and experience. In I.C. Uzgiris & F. Weizman (Eds.), *The structuring of experience*. New York: Plenum.

White, B.L., & Watts, J.C. (1973). *Experience and environment*. Englewood Cliffs, NJ: Prentice Hall.

Wittgenstein, L. (1958). *Philosophical investigations*. New York: Macmillan.

Wohlwill, J., & Heft, H. (1987). The physical environment and the development of the child. In D. Stokols & I. Altman (Eds.), *Handbook of environmental psychology* (pp. 281–328). New York: John Wiley & Sons.

Wolf, D., & Gardner, H. (1981). On the structure of early socialization. In R.L. Schiefelbush & D.D. Bricker (Eds.), *Early language: Acquisition and intervention* (pp. 287–327). Baltimore: University Park Press.

Wood, D.J. (1980). Teaching the young child: Some relationships between social interaction, language, and thought. In D.R. Olsen (Ed.), *The social foundations of language and thought* (pp. 280–296). New York: Norton.

CHAPTER 7

FAMILIES OF CHILDREN
WITH DEVELOPMENTAL DISABILITIES

Human nature seems to possess a peculiar kind of toughness and many-sidedness, since it overcomes everything which it approaches or which it takes into itself . . . (Goethe, 1949, p. 303)

THIS CHAPTER COMPLETES THE DISCUSSION OF PSYCHOSOCIAL DEVELOPMENT BY EXAMINING FAMILIES of children with disabilities. These families are on a journey unknown to families of children without disabilities. Initial challenges include the realization that their child is not as healthy as they hoped, and the discovery of the extraordinary amount of care the child requires. They also must deal with the distancing reactions of strangers, friends, and even relatives. Furthermore, most families do not know what to expect; where to receive services; or how to nurture, teach, and care for their child.

DEFICIENCIES IN SERVICES AND UNDERSTANDING OF FAMILIES

The "backstage" talk of many professionals reveals a belief that family histories are horror stories, that unproductive family patterns are nearly impossible to improve for long, and that the quality of family life largely reflects parents' intelligence and mental health. These are false and harmful notions (Feldman, Gerstein, & Feldman, 1989; Sonnenschein, 1981). They justify minimal services, sustain social distance, and overlook the fact that families generally have received little support. The following corrective generalizations are supported by much research.

Strength in Adversity

Raising children with disabilities is often difficult. Yet, a large proportion of families say their lives are enriched. Many relate how marriages have become stronger, and how they have developed sensitivities, strengths, and competencies of which they did not think they were capable (Cutler, 1991; Turnbull, Blue-Banning, Behr, & Kerns, 1986). Even for families who have handled the situation on their own for many years, social support, respite care for children, and coaching to manage productive exchanges yield much improvement in children's and parents' skills, moods, and relationships (Baker, Landen, & Kashima, 1991; Cutler, 1991; Jennings, 1990; Kirkham, 1993).

In addition, what some professionals hear as guarded or "nervous" speech patterns are usually reactions to mixed messages from professionals (e.g., "We want to help," along with facial expressions that say, "We also think you're a little nuts.") (Schopler & Loftin, 1969). Moreover, some families' perceived "pushiness" and hostility, which are often too readily diagnosed as part of an antisocial personality, are understandable (perhaps healthy) responses to disempowerment. In the experience of this author and his colleagues, spending several 24-hour days caring for children with disabilities inhibits the tendency to make hasty generalizations about families.

Services

Families of children with disabilities may want or need reassurance, information, coaching, or special equipment. Although families feel heartened when they receive these things, professional services can disempower them (Berger, 1990; Francell, Conn, & Gray, 1988). First, families and their networks of friends and relatives are usually at the periphery of the official educational system. They provide information, approve plans, receive reports, and attend parent-teacher meetings. Yet, little is done in the typical program to equip families with skills and opportunities to collaborate with staff on assessment, planning, teaching, and program evaluation. Second, families are seldom assisted to find resources, such as social support and in-home assistance, or taught skills, such as "behavior management" and self-relaxation, early enough to reduce the strain of caregiving (Bailey, Blasco, & Simeonsson, 1992; Cutler, 1991). After problem behaviors have become impossible to handle, families may receive palliative respite care, a few in-home consultations, therapy for an ailing marriage, or a residential placement for the child.

Finally, just as the work of teachers and the repertoires of children are fragmented by overspecialization (see chap. 2, this volume), families are dissected into "problems" to be "serviced" by separate consultants and agencies. In the end, some families become dependent on the palliatives. This author is convinced that the expertise and good intentions of professionals cannot adequately replace the nurturing, socializing, and personhood-bestowing functions that historically have been served by families and their friends, relatives, and associates. Moreover, with timely family-centered (rather than strictly child-centered), solution-oriented (rather than problem-oriented), parent-empowering (rather than parent-placating), collaborative (rather than professionally directed), long-term (rather than crisis-managing) assistance, the overwhelming majority of families can remain the primary locus of children's psychosocial development (Dunst, Trivette, & Deal, 1988).

Knowledge of Families Is Never Complete

One cannot identify all of a child's competencies, needs, learning requirements, and preferences. The same applies to any family. Interviews, questionnaires, home observations, even parents' diaries do not tell the whole story. Thus, one cannot presume to know more about what families need than family members themselves. In sum, it is a good idea to *ask families*, "What might we do (e.g., what resource might be obtained, what skill might be improved) that could have the greatest, most helpful effect right now?"

EARLY CHALLENGES, RESPONSES, AND CHANGES

The birth of a child with a disability often produces shock, confusion, grief over losing the "idealized" child, guilt from the nagging possibility of having done something wrong, and envy (Featherstone, 1980).

A child's disabilities are basically deficits in age-appropriate and culturally desired behavior, as well as excesses of problem behavior. These may create a stressful environment, especially when a child is unresponsive, temperamental, engages in repetitive behaviors, requires unusual caregiving, makes little progress, and the family receives too little help (Bray, Coleman, & Bracken, 1981). A child's disabilities mean that parents have a great deal of work in taking care of the child (Gallagher, Beckman-Bell, & Cross, 1983; Wilton & Renaut, 1986). Some parents (generally those with too little support) feel their lives are grinding work with no end in sight. In addition, there is often increased financial cost in caring for the child, as well as a slowing of career development and a lack of participation (usually by the mother) in the labor force (Breslau, 1983; Turnbull, 1978).

There is conflicting evidence regarding the effects of early challenges on mothers and fathers. Some researchers have found that fathers initially idealize the child and/or have greater optimism for the child's future (Carver & Carver, 1974), but that later a smaller proportion of fathers than mothers adapt to the child (Molsa & Ikonen-Molsa, 1985). Other researchers have found that mothers report more symptoms of distress, perhaps because they typically have more work to do and take a more "realistic" view (DeMyer, 1979; Goldberg, Marcovitch, MacGregor, & Lojkasek, 1986).

Societal Reaction

Some parents of children with disabilities feel they have lost their place in the community. Beyond an absence of social support, they report rejection. How does this happen? Each society has a set of socially significant symbols of membership, including competencies, possessions, and life circumstances, by which people judge one another's value. As a child acquires socially significant symbols at culturally right times of life, others see the child as being similar to them, competent, desirable, and protectable. They provide approval, shield the child from vulnerabilities, and offer valued roles. The child may interpret such treatment in a way that becomes part of the self-image. "I am a valuable person—a member in good standing." (See chaps. 1 and 6, this volume, for a description of the personalization process by which people bestow membership and personhood on one another.)

It seems that a healthy, competent child is a socially significant symbol of parents' competence and membership. If their child displays a socially acceptable body and behavioral repertoire, others infer that the parents have good genes, share the same values, and have skills to teach their child proper behavior. Thus, the parents are seen as members in good standing.

Conversely, a child's developmental disabilities may reduce parents' self-esteem and weaken their claim to a valuable place. Knowing what the symbols of membership are, some parents may question whether they themselves measure up. Many families, in addition, experience societal reaction that involves: 1) negative assessments of parents' competence; 2) blaming parents for the child's disability; 3) negative reactions to the child (e.g., stares, a refusal to let the child play with "normal" children); and 4) meddling. These responses imply that others question the parents' fitness, value, and membership (Darling, 1979; DeMyer, 1979; Weiss, 1991).

Because most people like to see themselves as compassionate, what explains the negative reactions to those whose lives are clearly difficult? In this author's opinion, it has to do with vulnerability. Many people are shocked when they see a child with a disability. Their sense of how things are supposed to be is strained, and they are frightened. People often decrease vulnerability by increasing distance (e.g., ignoring, not helping, believing and/or communicating that the family is fundamentally different from other families). The alleged differences explain the child's disability, make the universe orderly, and allow the audience to feel that it could not happen to them.

With repeated experience of societal reaction, some parents lose the sense that they are still bonded to others through common origins, consciousness, and destiny. If they internalize distancing reactions, they may question their competence, feel guilty, and be ashamed of their child's disabilities and problem behaviors. In addition, some families become isolated from the community and are suspicious of anyone who offers help (Featherstone, 1980; Gallagher et al., 1983).

Increased Vulnerability

The usual vulnerabilities of parents are increased when they have a child with serious disabilities. The fear of what will happen if they become ill and when they die cannot be escaped by more life insurance because the issue is who will care for their child (Hallum & Krumboltz, 1993; Weiss, 1991). In addition, parents may become economically vulnerable as they seek help, socially vulnerable to whispers and the lack of invitations, and generally vulnerable to those who claim to know the answers. In families where the main breadwinner, often the father, is away most of the day, the caregiver at home may feel vulnerable to the possibility that she or he is unable to perform childrearing and housekeeping tasks. The strain may lay the groundwork for counterproductive exchanges with the child and for emotional and marital difficulties.

Finding Help

Parents usually search for professionals who can tell them what is wrong and what to expect, help the child, or refer them to the right places. When children have certain physical problems, the explanation, help, and predictions are usually straightforward. Yet, it is different when a child is diagnosed with mental retardation, autism, or emotional disabilities. It is not clear why the child is not developing "normally" or what is the best course to follow. Thus, uncertainty is an early challenge for many parents. Moreover, there are usually too few people to assess their child and provide services.

The inadequacies in assessment and referral drive many parents to make the rounds from family physician, to neurologist, psychiatrist, allergist, psychologist, school counselor, and around again (Cutler, 1991). Whereas many parents report timely and adequate help, others are dissatisfied. They point to: 1) diagnoses, referrals, and recommendations that are self-evident, equivocal, and vague; 2) professionals' view of them as inept and having little useful information; 3) a limited role in decision making; 4) restricted access to records; 5) false encouragement; 6) professionals' seeming lack of interest; and 7) lines of questioning that plant seeds of suspicion that they caused their children's disabilities (Caplan & Hall-McCorquodale, 1985; Darling, 1979; DeMyer, 1979; Francell et al., 1988; Petr & Barney, 1993; Weiss, 1991).

Difficulties with professionals may continue as a child grows older. Parents may not receive practical information on community services and managing their child, may not be treated seriously as providers of information, and may continue to receive negative evaluations of their competence and mental health (Cutler, 1991; Darling, 1979; Longo & Bond, 1984). Therefore, it may take a special effort to contact some families and spark their interest in collaborative assessment, program planning, and teaching. Moreover, it is essential that service providers present themselves and their assistance in a way that encourages trust and confidence. (See chaps. 8 and 9, this volume, for a discussion of this topic.)

STRESS AND COPING

Current thinking on stress and coping sheds light on the course of family life. Figure 7.1 shows that some life events are *potential stressors*—"events occurring in the environment or in the body that make an emotional or task demand on the individual" (Hobfoll, 1988, p. 16); for example, actual or anticipated injury and illness, economic vulnerability, overload of childrearing tasks (Cleary & Mechanic, 1983), childrearing combined with marital and housekeeping tasks (Solomon, 1986), strain in marital relations (Weiss, 1991), and the birth of a child with a disability.

Yet, most potential stressors do not engender "strain" (overtaxing of resources) by themselves. Intervening variables include the magnitude of an event—a slight hearing impairment versus total deafness (Palfrey, Walker, Butler, & Singer, 1989)—and the appraisal of the event. A person may regard an event as more or less dangerous, imminent, masterable, bearable, chronic, predictable, and indicative of negative commentary on the person's or family's worth and competence (Lazarus & Folkman, 1986).

When events are seen as threatening, strain or the stress reaction can appear as rapid pulse and respiration, arousal, excitement, and perhaps fear or panic (Frankenhaeuser, 1986). Intense and/or prolonged strain is sometimes followed by psychosomatic and emotional disorders, such as heart disease and depression (Levi, 1981).

Individually and collaboratively, people *cope* with stressors and strain with fairly predictable results. At one extreme, emotional support, assistance, and active problem solving foster a sense of control, instill hope, increase self-esteem, and enable one to overcome or bear stressful circumstances. At the other extreme, chronic denial, worry, blaming, social isolation, self-narcotization

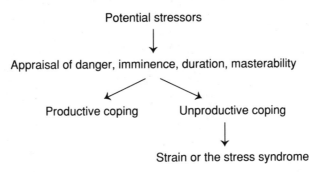

Factors affecting the chances of being faced with stressors, as well as the type and magnitude of stressors: Social class, nature of child's disabilities, and social support

Potential stressors

Appraisal of danger, imminence, duration, masterability

Productive coping   Unproductive coping

Strain or the stress syndrome

Factors affecting appraisal and coping with potential stressors and strain: Social support; enjoyable, self-enhancing events; social class; past and current experiences of mastery; competence; perceived vulnerability; philosophy; job flexibility; family structure; and health

Figure 7.1. Model of the stress and coping process.

(e.g., over-absorption in work), and frantic problem solving are less productive and/or more costly in overcoming or bearing challenges (Frese, 1986; Pearlin & Schooler, 1978). When unproductive methods are habitual, emotional resources may dwindle; social support for a blaming or withdrawn person or family may decrease; and effective coping weakens, perhaps leading to hopelessness.

Finally, exposure, appraisal, and efforts to cope with stressors and strain are influenced by *social support* (Hobfoll, 1988; Telleen, Herzog, & Kilbane, 1989); enjoyable, self-enhancing events (Cohen & Hoberman, 1983); social class (Dohrenwend & Dohrenwend, 1981); past and current experiences of mastery (Hobfoll, 1988); and personal competence, such as teaching and solving problems (Hansson, 1986).

The birth of a child with a disability is a potential stressor. So are distancing reactions of relatives, the load of caregiving, efforts to find services, and strain on family routines (Brotherson & Goldstein, 1993). If families appraise these as more or less dangerous, insurmountable, awful, unjust, and stigmatizing, they may feel more or less strain. The amount of coping resources in relation to the degree of strain either enables a family to productively deal with stressors, or produces frantic unproductive behavior or immobilization. In sum, professionals and families can identify potential and actual stressors. Such knowledge can empower families to handle stressors and strain more productively.

Table 7.1 identifies challenges or potential stressors faced by many families, and resources that may be available. It also identifies early experiences of families and suggests how families may change over time.

CHALLENGES AND RESOURCES

Nature and Severity of a Child's Disability

Different disabilities imply different challenges. Children with vision and hearing impairments or mental retardation may be less responsive than children without these disabilities. This may make it harder to establish reciprocal positive exchanges (see chap. 5, this volume), determine a child's wants and needs, and assess how well a child is being satisfied (Barden, Ford, Jensen, Rogers-Salyer, & Salyer, 1989; Hyche, Bakeman, & Adamson, 1992; Jarvis, Myers, & Creasey, 1989).

Table 7.1.   Challenges and changes in families of children with developmental disabilities

Challenges and resources inside and outside the family	Early challenges, responses, and changes	Possible long-term changes
The child's disability and behavioral repertoire	Dealing with early challenges, such as shock, grief, work load, and financial costs	Parent–child exchanges
Availability and use of services		Degree of participation in the community
Job flexibility	The extent of, and members' responses to, societal reaction	Organization of household routines
Stigma versus acceptance		Marital relationship
Degree of vulnerability	Changes in vulnerability	Degree of family integration
Social support	Experiences with professionals	Sensitivity and reactivity
Parents' health		Energy and fortitude
Parents' philosophy		Degree of assumed personal responsibility
Competence		Assessment of self, spouse, child, and family
Uplifting events		Emotional well-being
Social class		Effects on siblings
		Authenticity versus alienation
		Durability of coping methods
		Child's behavioral repertoire and social place in relation to family members' abilities to adequately care for the child

Children with autism, mental retardation, or cerebral palsy may, in addition, require much supervision and physical labor (Gallagher et al., 1983; Sloper & Turner, 1993); increase financial expenditures; present parents with emergencies; and make it harder for parents to develop their careers and, especially in the case of the mother, participate in the labor force (Breslau, 1983).

In addition, the more limited a child's functional behavioral repertoire is and the more slowly it develops, the more care must be provided for more years, and, therefore, the more fatigued parents may become (DeMyer, 1979; Wilton & Renaut, 1986). Finally, a child's irritability and problem behaviors affect how often family members experience aversive events, how much control they believe they have over their lives, and how much work they have to do (Bray et al., 1981).

Availability and Use of Services

Families often report difficulty obtaining adequate and timely respite care, transportation, babysitting, in-home assistance, and information (Cutler, 1991; Cutler & Kozloff, 1987; Darling, 1979). Consequently, a child's disruptive behaviors may worsen, and parents may become overly fatigued, lonely, and unable to properly satisfy their own and their children's needs (Fogan & Schor, 1993).

Job Flexibility

Many children with disabilities frequently and unpredictably disrupt daily routines. There may be medical emergencies, or a child may be sent home because of disruptive behavior. Flexible employment schedules make it easier for parents to meet unscheduled challenges. Inflexibility makes parents more vulnerable to unpredictable events, increases the workload, and strains family relationships.

Degree of Vulnerability

Humans often feel vulnerable to what they cannot control, including other people's opinions, the economic system, mortality, and illness (Henry, 1973). Common vulnerabilities can be intensified and additional ones may emerge when a family member has a disability. Parents may feel vulnerable to medical emergencies and problem behaviors, changes in school funding, the availability of baby-sitters and respite care, and professionals who control important resources and their children's future (Weiss, 1991).

Along with their peers who have learned the standard ways to handle vulnerability (e.g., buying life insurance), some parents of children with disabilities focus on "getting by" rather than making long-range plans. They may give in to (reinforce) problem behaviors rather than risk changing parent–child exchanges; they may pretend their children's schooling is adequate instead of working to improve it. Such methods are easy to understand given the lack of resources available to many; yet, these methods all but ensure their vulnerability.

Social Support

Social support includes praise, encouragement, hands-on assistance, and advice from spouses, friends, relatives, and others in a social network. The literature suggests that social support helps to maintain behavior change and buffers negative effects of stressful events. Social support is associated with lower rates and severity of depression and physical pain, reduced use of medication, and greater activity levels in persons confronted with stressful events (Cohen & Syme, 1985; Pilisuk & Parks, 1986; Shapiro, 1989; Telleen et al., 1989).

Some research shows that mothers of children with disabilities receive significantly *less* social support than mothers of children without disabilities (Wilton & Renaut, 1986). Other studies indicate that parents receive much *informal* support from friends, other parents, and church members. This decreases strain and increases emotional and physical well-being, family integration, perception of social acceptance, and assessments of their children's competence (Bristol, 1984; Bristol, Gallagher, & Schopler, 1988; Crnic & Greenberg, 1990; Dunst et al., 1988; Wallander, Varni, Babini, DeHaan et al., 1989). One study (Jennings, 1990) found that support from in-laws was a strong predictor of a mother's rating of the family's overall capability to cope. Another study (Kazak, Reber, & Carter, 1988) showed that larger and less dense social networks (i.e., networks that contain many people who do not necessarily know one another) are associated with families' lower stress, perhaps because parents anticipate that if one source is not available, others will be. Thus, it may be helpful for parents to be members of networks with other families of children with disabilities (Petr & Barney, 1993).

Social support implies that one is valuable, normal, and not alone. When it involves appreciation, especially from a spouse, it raises self-esteem, buffers stress, and reduces the probability of depression (Vanfossen, 1986). When it involves good advice and hands-on assistance, it reduces the caregiving load, increases effectiveness, and improves parents' assessments both of their competence and the difficulty of caring for their child. Thus, helping spouses to recognize and appreciate each other's efforts, and increasing access to timely advice, opportunities for companionship, and in-home coaching may be beneficial (Fogan & Schor, 1993; Krauss, 1993).

Stress Reduction

Emotionally uplifting events are stress buffers (Cohen & Hoberman, 1983). Movies, music, sports, hobbies, receiving a raise, watching one's child in a school play, and listening to a spouse describe his or her own satisfaction elicit pleasure and signify that life is worthwhile.

Parents' health is also a factor that affects coping. Parents' health affects their appraisal and tolerance of difficulties, ability to receive and use resources, need for social support, ability to cope with or overcome challenges, and the feasibility of working collaboratively with educators (Turnbull & Turnbull, 1986).

Another important factor in reducing stress is parents' perceptions of competence. Skill at problem solving, help-seeking, communication, teaching, and self-management are empowering. They increase self-reliance and the effectiveness of responses to stressors (Hansson, 1986; Teele, 1981; Wallander, Varni, Babini, Banis, & Wilcox, 1989). Thus, training for new families (e.g., on productive exchanges with children) and ongoing training on how to assess children and teach a variety of skills should be common features of school programs.

Social Class

Members of different social classes (defined by income, occupation, education, and area of residence) have access to different types and amounts of resources (Zuchman, 1982). Yet, higher social class is not necessarily associated with less stress, as wealthier parents may receive less financial support from governments and more educated parents may have a greater awareness of the long-term consequences of their children's disabilities (Singer & Farkas, 1989). Still, wealthier and/or more educated parents may have the time and money to acquire services, professional contacts that give them access to service providers, and mastery experiences and interaction skills that enable them to persuade providers (Wallander, Varni, Babini, Banis et al., 1989).

However, low-income and minority families are just as likely as all other families to actively seek help (Teele, 1981), and to love, have high expectations for, and interact productively with their children. This may be because low-income and minority parents often have extensive social networks and clear rules regarding behavior and discipline (Rosenthal, Groze, & Curiel, 1990).

Regardless of social class, collaboration between special educators and families ought to help parents identify, receive, use, and create resources (e.g., information libraries, meeting rooms in churches, networks of assistance-swapping among families [described in chap. 8, this volume]).

Philosophy of Life

Each person and perhaps each family has a way to make sense of their life's events. A philosophy of life consists of at least three features: handling the existential facts, locus of control, and explanatory style.

Existential Facts   We suffer, we are fallible, we are mortal, and we are responsible for the meaning of our lives. These are the facts of life presented in Christian and Buddhist scriptures (David-Neel, 1978), the philosophy of Arthur Schopenhauer (1906), existentialism (Frankl, 1969), and the writings of behavioral scientists (Ellis & Harper, 1975; Kobasa, 1979). All counsel that the way one handles the existential facts influences moods, actions, and life course. For instance, a person who recognizes the place of suffering in the world is empowered to withstand disappointments and feel compassion for himself or herself and others. A person who denies that suffering is a natural part of life, and sees himself or herself or the family as singled out, increases suffering by being depressed or bitter at "the injustice of it all."

A person who accepts fallibility ("I try to be a good teacher, but, of course, I make many mistakes.") is protected from too much pride and demanding too much of himself or herself and others. A person who insists perfection is possible and necessary, however, is likely to drive himself or herself mercilessly and judge himself or herself harshly at inevitable failures.

A person who lives life as a visit may be less worried about time's passing, and may be graced by blessings ("She finally can use a spoon!") and less bothered by little things ("Food all over your dress again? Oh, well."). A person who clings to life as a possession that may be taken away at any moment may feel anxious much of the time and receive little pleasure from everyday events. Finally, those who define the meaning of life by their actions (e.g., endeavoring to accomplish tasks or to realize values such as truth and compassion) may accept difficulties as personally meaningful and challenging, rather than undue burdens.

Many parents of children with severe disabilities receive little help from family, friends, and professionals. Yet, many of these parents are energetic and hopeful, consider themselves valuable, display a ready wit, and regard their children as a source of pleasure as well as tears. In contrast, this author and his colleagues have known some parents who are chronically depressed and angry, regard their children as "all but unrelieved burdens," and see themselves as failures, even though their children have mild disabilities (Cutler, 1991; Kozloff et al., 1988).

Income, competence, and social connections influence family life, but do not account for everything. Parents with confidence and hope, whether poor or wealthy, are more accepting of disappointments, their own and others' imperfections, and the responsibility to make something of their lives. They appear to be sustained by the belief that their situation will be all right, and by membership in religious or kinship groups that will not let them down. This writer and his colleagues refer to such traits as *moxie* (courage and determination) (Kozloff et al., 1988). Kobasa (1979) calls such parents *hardy*. Parents who are unaccepting of their situation appear to believe that bad things are not supposed to happen to decent, smart, hard-working people; solutions can be bought or should be provided by society; their children's disability is a negative comment on their own fitness and place in the world; and they are alone and singled out for destruction.

It is not clear whether parents' attitudes exist before or are acquired after the birth of their children. Either way, it is important to understand how parents make sense of troubles and where they place responsibility for improving their lives. It may be important to help some families see that they have control over the meaning of and, therefore, their emotional responses to events (see chap. 9, this volume).

Locus of Control   Locus of control refers to a person's perception of how much control he or she has over events (Lefcourt, 1981). Persons who see positive or negative events as potentially under their control have an *internal* locus of control; those who view events as beyond their control have an *external* locus of control. In answer to the question, "Do you think you could improve your child's education by attending PTA meetings and speaking out?", a person with an internal locus of control would say, "Of course! How else am I going to improve her program?" An external locus of control would result in the answer, "I doubt it. Teachers do what they want."

People with internal loci of control are more likely than those with external loci of control to: try to gain control of their life; be less content with information they have; pay attention to relevant cues; exhibit more self-control; and report less anger, despair, and anxiety (Folkman, Lazarus, Dunkel-Shetter, DeLongis, & Gruen, 1986; Lefcourt, 1976; Margalit, Raviv, & Ankonina, 1992; Pearlin & Schooler, 1978).

Explanatory Style   Explanatory or attributional style refers to how a person accounts for negative and positive events (Peterson & Villanova, 1988). It consists of beliefs about the location of the cause of events, how global (widespread) the causes are, and how stable (short-term vs. long-term) the causes are. A person with an internal attributional style believes positive and negative events are caused by his or her own actions or traits—"It's because I'm (tough, smart, weak, stupid)." In contrast, a person with an external attributional style believes he or she is not the cause—"It was luck, God, her, or them."

Whether one has an internal or external attribution style, one may see causes as temporary ("I was a lousy teacher last week, but next week will be different!") or stable ("I'm a lousy teacher. I always have been and probably always will be.").

Furthermore, attributions may be specific or global. A specific attribution would be: "My poor teaching hinders Jerry's speech training, but I'm good at teaching him to dress." A global attribution would be: "My (poor teaching, bad luck, laziness, moodiness) has hurt much of my own and Jerry's life."

The most harmful attributional style is one in which negative events are attributed to internal, stable, and global causes (expressing self-blame, pessimism, hopelessness, and catastrophizing) (Seligman et al., 1988). In contrast to persons whose attribution of negative events is external, temporary, and specific, persons with an internal, stable, and global style report more anxiety and depression, illness, visits to physicians, unhealthy habits, future stressful events, a lower likelihood of taking steps to combat illness and other stressors (passivity), and lower efficacy in coping and changing unhealthy habits (Robins, Block, & Peselow, 1990; Zuroff, Igreja, & Mongrain, 1990).

Relevance of Philosophies for Families   The philosophy that encourages solution-oriented, resource-obtaining, stress-reducing, and self-enhancing appraisal and coping is one in which: 1) causes of negative events are seen as external (little self-blame), temporary, and specific; 2) the locus of control is internal ("I can do something about this!"); and 3) difficulties are opportunities for self-enhancement, commitment, and involvement. However, families may be hampered by a philosophy that involves self-blame; a belief that they cannot effect beneficial changes; and a perception of difficulties as chronic, global, and alien burdens. Still, one must remember that a person's and family's philosophy is a product of circumstance. Those who have not had resources to master troubles, or whose efforts have had negative outcomes, are more likely to develop a pessimistic philosophy. More importantly, later experience in identifying personal strengths and mastering events (e.g., training and support) can change a person's philosophy and reduce symptoms of emotional distress (Hobfoll, 1988; Roberts, Joe, & Rowe-Hallbert, 1992; Seligman et al., 1988).

FAMILIES' EFFORTS IN DEALING WITH EXTRAORDINARY CHALLENGES

A family's style of coping, combined with new and continuing challenges, can foster beneficial or counterproductive changes.

Structured Exchanges Between Parents and Children

Exchanges between parents and young children with disabilities can either hinder or promote the development of productive and mutually rewarding interactions. Infants and children with disabilities may initiate less interaction, make less eye contact, less competently engage in turn-taking, be less active and vocal, provide less feedback, learn more slowly, and resist being held more than infants and children without disabilities (Bailey & Wolery, 1984; Hyche et al., 1992; Jarvis et al., 1989; Levi-Shiff, 1986; Marfo, 1992). Consequently, some parents' efforts to interact may, from the beginning, receive less reinforcement. In addition, if children are temperamental and hard to soothe, parents may experience interaction as aversive.

Without advice and coaching, counterproductive patterns can become habitual. Indeed, in this author's experience with families with and without children with disabilities, only a small percentage of families are characterized primarily by productive exchanges. As in schools, family interaction often involves parents reinforcing disruptive and uncooperative behaviors and frequently not reinforcing desirable behaviors. Such patterns not only inhibit children's psychosocial development, but increase the load of problem behaviors and deficits the family has to deal with. Thus, one of the highest priorities is to help parents institute productive exchanges as early as possible and replace counterproductive with productive exchanges at any time (Booth, Mitchell, Barnard, & Speiker, 1989; Bromwich, 1981; Mahoney & Powell, 1988; Rosenberg & Robinson, 1988; Seifer, Clark, & Sameroff, 1991).

Participation in the Community versus Isolation

The more a family participates in the community, the more they receive resources, experience belonging, and expose children to typical environments. Many families stay involved with relatives, friends, co-workers, teachers, and other parents. They manage to shop, eat out, go to church, and vacation together. Other families become increasingly isolated or "insular" (Featherstone, 1980; Wahler, 1980). Their isolation is driven by:

1. Friends and relatives disassociating after the birth of the child (Morton, 1985)
2. Strained interaction with relatives (Barber, Turnbull, Behr, & Kerns, 1988)

3. Mothers being confined to the home and strained by the demands of multiple roles
4. The inability of families to count on baby-sitting, respite, and in-home assistance (Cutler, 1991)
5. The lack of invitations to other people's homes or their own reluctance to invite others into their home
6. Parents' reluctance to expose themselves and their children to societal reaction
7. The short school day and school year

Organization of Household Routines

Many families negotiate adjustments in the division of labor. In some families, however, a child's problem behaviors and deficits, the ages and number of siblings, the rigidity of the division of labor, too little support, and parents' fatigue result in much noise, routine activities starting late, difficulty teaching the child, and dissatisfaction. Often, parents can increase the efficiency of routines by small changes. For instance, a child can be bathed and dressed after breakfast, or no one eats supper until the trash is taken out. After making a few changes, parents get used to the idea that the round of daily life is flexible, and suggest improvements on their own.

Marital Relations

Marital relations do not inevitably suffer as a result of a child's disabilities. Although some studies point to more marital problems in families of children with disabilities (Bristol et al., 1988; DeMyer, 1979; Schilling, Schinke, & Kirkham, 1985), others suggest that spouses' satisfaction with marital life is increased by mutual emotional and instrumental support (Weiss, 1991). Therefore, it is useful for some parents to become alert to marital exchanges (e.g., support, praise, willingness to compromise) and to factors that influence interaction (e.g., the division of labor, expectations).

Family Integration

Family integration refers to members sharing activities and being supportive and involved in each other's lives. The collaborative effort to meet challenges can increase family integration. However, integration can be weakened by the disruption of routines, little external support leading to fatigue, and changes in the needs and roles of siblings as they mature (Friedrich & Friedrich, 1981; Wilton & Renaut, 1986). Weakened family integration increases loneliness, engenders alienation, and reduces the quality of life. It may be important to help families examine family integration and find ways to increase or sustain it (Fogan & Schor, 1993).

Sensitivity and Reactivity

When challenges exceed resources (e.g., a child's problem behaviors worsen), parents may become hypervigilant. The more sensitive they become, the more likely they are to respond unproductively. It is useful to help parents follow a problem-solving sequence—observing (perhaps taking notes), relaxing, waiting, and planning—rather than emotionally reacting to difficulties.

Energy and Fortitude

Most parents' energy remains sufficient to meet challenges. Their energy level is associated with hands-on assistance, an extended-day and extended-year program for their child, validation of their efforts, and time to engage in enjoyable activities. In the absence of resources, some become increasingly fatigued. Clearly, it is important to help parents obtain resources that will sustain energy. Moreover, it is important to show parents from the beginning that collaboration can decrease their load and energize them.

Effects on Siblings

Some studies show that, with regard to self-concept, behavior problems, and social competence, siblings of children with disabilities are comparable to siblings of children without disabilities (Dyson, 1989; Lobato, Faust, & Spirito, 1988). Other studies indicate that siblings report more negative interactions with mothers and have poorer adjustment scores than siblings of children without disabilities (e.g., they are more anxious and depressed, they perceive themselves to be less competent). Such adjustment scores are associated with their satisfaction with their parents' differential treatment of them and their brothers or sisters with a disability (McHale & Gamble, 1989).

Therefore, although siblings provide services (baby-sitting, handling problem behaviors, taking over housekeeping chores), there is the potential for overwork, resentment, and a decrease in activities with peers, which may hinder psychosocial development. These ought to be considered during assessment and ongoing program evaluation.

Degree of Assumed Responsibility

Many parents accept their limits of energy, time, and knowledge. Some, however, believe they are responsible for moment-to-moment behaviors of their child and their child's future. If their child throws a tantrum, they believe it is because they did something wrong. Moreover, they see their child's deficits as evidence of their ineptitude, weakness, or guilt.

This author does not know how a moderate versus extreme belief in responsibility emerges, but believes that the more parents know about child development, disabilities, the learning process, and the effects of the social environment on mood, belief, and behavior, the more reasonable presumptions of personal responsibility will be. (Chap. 9, this volume, discusses interviewing methods that can foster a more reasonable assumption of personal responsibility.)

Assessments of Self, Child, Family, and Future

Parents' perceptions reflect and sustain their daily life. For example, parents may have self-encouraging and self-approving beliefs about their competence and worth (DeMyer, 1979); see their child as a member and a source of pleasure, pride, family integration, and personal meaningfulness (Friedrich & Friedrich, 1981); and expect their child to make progress and be able to live a more independent life (Wilton & Renaut, 1986).

There are at least two methods for helping parents to improve their assessments of their children. One is to help them identify beneficial changes in their children, desirable features of family life, and personal strengths (see chap. 9, this volume). A second, discussed previously, is to help empower parents with skills for making changes.

Emotional Well-Being

Along with the usual periods of distress that humans experience, many parents sustain vitality, optimism, self-regard, and emotional stability. These, no doubt, are facilitated by successful experiences and by support from spouse, friends, and associates (Bristol et al., 1988; Wallander, Varni, Babini, DeHaan et al., 1989). Some parents, however, experience extreme tension, anxiety, and depression.

It is beneficial to help parents understand that their distress is "normal" in their circumstances (rather than a sign of weakness) and to take active steps to increase well-being through relaxation, exercise, participation in organizations, setting aside time to discuss feelings with spouses, and working to improve their children's education.

Authenticity and Attachment

Work seems authentic when it allows one to be creative or to be of service, and when it is self-pacing and has predictable outcomes. Alienated labor makes some people feel dominated and driven and insignificant or expendable, which leaves them with less energy and inclination to gratify others and with a desire to escape or avoid work. Although usually applied to some factory and office work, and even to teaching (as discussed in chap. 2, this volume), the concept of alienated labor is relevant to parenting children with disabilities. For example, some parents feel controlled by coercive behaviors and believe they have little impact on children's long-term development. In time, they may perceive their efforts, child, household, spouse, and even themselves as alien. "Who am I? Where am I? What is going on?" They feel angry, desperate, and invest less time and effort in family life.

Empowerment and participation are remedies for alienation. Thus, many parents are helped by a better understanding of disabilities, learning, and teaching; how to increase resources; how to evaluate and improve services; and how to become involved with other parents.

Durability of Unproductive Coping Methods and Undesirable Changes

Undesirable changes may become habitual and durable. This can occur through short-run payoffs, coercion, norms and beliefs, and protection.

Short-Run Payoffs   Some parents are exposed to a range of aversive events that occur at a high rate (e.g., problem behavior). They are likely to repeat whatever enables them to escape or avoid such events. For instance, some parents learn to give in to coercive behavior because it brings temporary relief. Others are satisfied by small increases in educational services because they end the hassle with school administrators. In the absence of skill at handling difficulties in a proactive manner (e.g., planning how to improve parent–child exchanges), parents may cling to old ways of reacting that afford relief.

Coercion   When efforts to improve a situation are met with punishment, some people give in and return to former behaviors. For instance, if parents decide to stop reinforcing tantrums, children may escalate the intensity or duration so much that parents give in to their demands. After several perceived failures of this sort, parents may stop trying to improve exchanges. Similarly, parents can coerce one another to maintain existing patterns. Coming home to a whining child, a father may say to the mother, "I don't care what we agreed to do when he whines. Give him a bath—anything to quiet him!" Thus, the mother's efforts to improve the situation may be weakened.

Service providers, too, sometimes use coercion. When parents criticize what is going on in the classroom or request more services, they may be met with tormenting choices; for example, "Sure, you can get a residential placement for Mitch, but only if you give up custody" (McManus & Friesen, 1986), or "Well, we could send him to a school about 200 miles away."

Norms and Beliefs   A third source of durability is norms and beliefs about proper conduct. If a woman believes it is a mother's (more than a father's) job to take care of children, she may continue to play the caregiving role on her own even though it is exhausting her. Likewise, parents may make few requests of their children, settle for inadequate performances, or reinforce problem behaviors because they believe their children should be given nothing but tender loving care. Some parents are reluctant to make changes because they believe their situation is as it is meant to be and change is beyond their control.

In addition, to the extent parents do not see alternative ways to solve problems, or do not see alternatives as within reach, they may develop a "get through the day" strategy that all but ensures things will stay the same.

Protection   After years of looking for help and not finding it, some parents protect themselves in the following ways:

1. Feeling they have little more to give, or that little more can be done, some family members become advocates for others. Such people may be reluctant to engage in collaborative work with educators because they have so much else to do.
2. Some people believe they have only experienced failure, and they do not get along with fami-

lies in similar situations. In response to invitations to join a parent program, or to try a certain teaching method, they reply, "It won't work" or "We've already tried that." This enables them to protect themselves from more perceived failure.

3. Some families are angry with professionals and are reluctant to work with them if given the chance. They may be protecting themselves from more frustration and subordinate roles in relationships. (Chaps. 8 and 9, this volume, discuss ways to build trust and confidence.)

A Child's Place in the Family

A child's behavioral repertoire affects other members' abilities to adequately cope and provide for the child. Many families are characterized by growing complementarity. That is, family members receive sufficient support and assistance, they become better able to satisfy a child's learning requirements and preferences, problem behaviors decrease, and the child acquires competencies enabling him or her to play more valued roles.

In some families, however, there is growing strain between what members need and get, and between what they are called on to do and the resources they have. For instance, skill deficits, boredom, illness, confusion, and counterproductive exchanges result in some children's problem behaviors becoming worse while their desirable behaviors fail to improve enough to compensate for other family members' decreasing energy. Even if a child's health or repertoire does not become worse, the child's growth results in louder noises, bigger messes, and more energy needed to care for him or her. Some parents believe they are unable to master or even adapt to the strain. They also believe the situation has adverse effects on their marriage and other children. Such an assessment may foster pessimism, increased vigilance, and exhaustion. In addition, a parent may become ill or so exhausted that he or she no longer feels able to be a good parent.

Some children perform the "last straw" behavior—a behavior beyond the family's strained coping repertoire. The last straw might be aggression, one too many episodes of running away, or one too many nights of keeping everyone up by yelling. Parents may believe there is no longer a fit between what their child does and needs, and what they can handle and provide. Efforts may then be made to find an outside placement (Blacher & Hanneman, 1993; Sherman & Cocozza, 1984).

IMPLICATIONS FOR COLLABORATION WITH FAMILIES

The above sections should increase the reader's understanding of family members' ongoing efforts to handle everyday tasks and extraordinary challenges using the personal, family, and external resources at their disposal. The following list discusses implications for collaboration with families, especially in the preparation of individualized family service plans (IFSPs).

1. Negative presumptions about families should be avoided. Most families identify ways that they are enriched by their children and that marriages and family integration are strengthened. Indeed, some research suggests that "Families of children with mental retardation appear to resemble comparison families more often than not" (Koller, Richardson, & Katz, 1993, p. 332). Apparent hostility to some professionals is likely to reflect past and present disempowering interactions with professionals rather than parents' antisocial personalities. Timely help engenders remarkable beneficial changes in parents, children, and family life.

2. Services ought to empower rather than do for or placate families. They should be preventive and educational rather than palliative and therapeutic; enacted in homes, classrooms, churches, playgrounds, and libraries (i.e., natural environments) rather than clinics and offices. In addition, they should enlist friends, relatives, other parents, neighbors, and co-workers (i.e., natural networks) rather than only be provided by unfamiliar professionals.

3. Many parents benefit from the chance to verbalize feelings and understandings in an environment that accepts these as natural and human (e.g., with a nonjudgmental and empathetic

consultant or with a group of other parents). Supportive listening and honest sharing foster the mutual trust, openness, and self-confidence needed for effective collaboration.

It is also helpful for parents to tell (or construct) their own story. Some family members will recount the family history as one of failure, incompetence, and negative changes. Although it is important to empathize, it is also important to help families identify successes and beneficial changes, and to see that through collaboration they will acquire resources enabling them to produce a future that is not a continuation of the past.

4. Parents' vast knowledge of their children and family should help guide assessment, program planning, instruction, and program evaluation. Among other things, parents have a good idea of what is reinforcing to their children, which teaching methods work well and which do not, and what resources would benefit the family. Although much information can be obtained through semiformal interviews and questionnaires, it is essential to get a picture of family life that parents generate on their own through journals and recording forms that ask open-ended questions, such as "How is a typical day organized?" and "Please spend a few days making a list of Juan's behaviors that you like and want him to keep doing, as well as those you do not like and want him to stop."

5. What are the family's challenges? By what methods does the family cope, and how successfully, both from an observer's and the family members' points of view? What do they think they need to master or better cope with challenges, and how might they acquire these?

6. How flexible are work schedules? How available is support from neighbors and relatives who might provide transportation, baby-sitting, or preparation of an evening meal?

7. What relationship do parents have with other relatives? Do they receive emotional support, hands-on help, and sound advice? Do they receive criticism? Do they feel abandoned? How might relations be improved if desired by parents? Group meetings for grandparents, aunts, and uncles of children with disabilities may help them share and come to terms with disappointment, and learn satisfying ways to nurture children with disabilities.

8. What is the family's workload, including household, childrearing, and employment tasks? How satisfying and negotiable is the division of labor? How might families alter the division of labor to balance the load?

9. Help parents identify vulnerabilities; assess the danger, likelihood, and masterability of negative events; and obtain resources needed to avoid or handle such events. If, for instance, their own mortality is a concern, parents could be helped to plan for the future through guardianships, trusts, and working to improve their children's educations.

10. Assess and, if beneficial, work to increase the social support available to families. Determine what parents want and/or need—to be listened to, good advice, information, respite, hands-on assistance, recognition. How often do they get what they want or need in relation to how often they want it? To what extent do they listen and express appreciation for each other? How many other people can they count on for help? Who might be brought into their social network—other parents of children with disabilities, high school and college students, church members, neighbors? What might parents offer others?

11. Virtually all families can benefit by learning how to assess the competence of their children's performance and the quality of family and classroom exchanges, plan teaching programs and a long-term educational sequence, teach a variety of competencies and replace problem behaviors, initiate and sustain productive exchanges, follow a problem-solving sequence, relax, reinforce themselves, and locate information and support. Parents are likely to be the best judges of which competencies have the highest priority.

12. Examine the family's philosophy regarding existential facts, locus of control, and attribution, as evidenced in their accounts of family life and forecasts for the future. How might parents be helped to see that they should not be blamed, that they may be exaggerating the stability

and reach of those factors that seem to cause negative events, and that they can have more control with increased competence and support?

13. What are the family's assessments of a child's disability and functional behavioral repertoire as a workload, including problem behavior, behavioral deficits they must accommodate, disruptions of routines, and emergencies? What differences are there between family members' perceptions? What, if changed, might yield the greatest improvement in the overall caregiving load with the least cost—increasing certain of the child's competencies, altering the division of labor, reducing certain problem behaviors?

14. What was the nature of early parent–child interaction? To what extent was the child soothable, inviting, responsive, or rejecting? What are the parents' views of how early exchanges led to current exchange patterns? What are current parent–child exchanges like? How might they be improved?

15. What is the nature of family participation in the community? That is, where do members go, how often, and what do they get (e.g., relief, opportunities to teach their child, opportunities to be alone with a spouse or to do things as a family)? How satisfied are they with how often and how they participate? What factors interfere with, and what factors might increase participation, such as baby-sitting, the child's problem behaviors, societal reaction, and information on the availability of organizations?

16. How is the household organized? That is, how regularly are routine tasks completed, how well are they done, how much work is involved, how much noise and commotion is there, how easy is it to find things and to teach, how satisfied are members, and what steps might be taken to improve household organization?

17. Regarding the spousal relationship, how often do the partners praise versus ignore, negotiate versus blame, and lend a hand without being asked? How satisfied is each parent with his or her interaction? What would he or she like to improve? How might each parent go about it?

18. In single-parent families, to what extent does the parent receive social support and hands-on assistance from relatives and friends? If beneficial, could parents be linked to resource networks?

19. Regarding family integration, how often does the family share different activities (e.g., listen to music, play games, go out, plan teaching programs)? How much do members feel appreciated by others? How much do members feel they understand each other's needs, feelings, and perceptions? How might family integration be increased, if desired?

20. How sensitive and alert are family members? Do they quickly, unwittingly, and unproductively react to problematic events, such as a child's problem behavior or a spouse's or relative's unkind remark? How might parents be helped to become calmer, distance themselves from aversive events, and plan how to respond?

21. How much energy do parents believe they have for different tasks—teaching, general caregiving, spousal relationship, working to obtain or improve services? What are the sources of depletion versus recharging? How can energy be increased? Can energy be increased by altering the division of labor, having more pleasant experiences, receiving reinforcement from a partner, or finding an extended day program for a child?

22. To what extent do parents believe they are responsible for their child's desirable and undesirable behaviors and future? To what extent do they believe that what their child does or does not do reflects their essential personality; that is, reveals the kind of person they are? Would it be useful for parents to recognize the actual limits of anyone's ability to effect change in others, and the limits of time, energy, and knowledge?

23. What are the parents' assessments of themselves (skills, traits), their child (skills, traits, problem behaviors), the family, and the future (e.g., their child's likely life circumstances, their ability to provide for their child)? Do their assessments seem to be overly negative and pessimistic? What changes and resources might improve their assessments?

24. What is the nature of the parents' emotional well-being? How often, how severe, and how incapacitating are tension, anxiety, or depressed moods? What kinds of help do distressed parents receive? How might distress be decreased and support increased?

25. To what extent do parents appear invested in and attached to family life versus alienated and detached? What are the sources of detachment and alienation? Can these be remedied?

26. What makes unproductive coping methods durable? Examples include short-term rewards, coercion, beliefs and norms, lack of perceived alternatives, and defenses against further injury. To what extent do parents recognize these as obstacles to beneficial change? How can parents be empowered so that the sources of durability are weakened?

27. What are family members' perceptions of their capacity to continue to provide for and/or cope with their child's disability? What appears to be needed to improve their child's competencies and participation as well as other members' capacities?

REFERENCES

Bailey, D.B., Jr., Blasco, P.M., & Simeonsson, R.J. (1992). Needs expressed by mothers and fathers of young children with disabilities. *American Journal on Mental Retardation, 97*(1), 1–10.

Bailey, D.B., Jr., & Wolery, M. (1984). *Teaching infants and preschoolers with handicaps.* Columbus, OH: Charles E. Merrill.

Baker, B.L., Landen, S.J., & Kashima, K.J. (1991). Effects of parent training on families of children with mental retardation: Increased burden or generalized benefit. *American Journal on Mental Retardation, 96*(2), 127–136.

Barber, P.A., Turnbull, A.P., Behr, S.K., & Kerns, G.M. (1988). A family systems perspective on early childhood special education. In S.L. Odom & M.B. Karnes (Eds.), *Early intervention for infants and children with handicaps: An empirical base* (pp. 179–198). Baltimore: Paul H. Brookes Publishing Co.

Barden, C.R., Ford, M.E., Jensen, A.G., Rogers-Salyer, M., & Salyer, K.E. (1989). Effects of craniofacial deformity in infancy on the quality of mother-infant interaction. *Child Development, 60,* 819–824.

Berger, B. (1990, July/August). New issues in child development. *Society,* 7–9.

Blacher, J., & Hanneman, R. (1993). Out-of-home placement of children and adolescents with severe handicaps: Behavioral intentions and behavior. *Research in Developmental Disabilities, 14,* 145–160.

Booth, C.L., Mitchell, S.K., Barnard, K.E., & Speiker, S.J. (1989). Development of maternal social skills in multiproblem families: Effects on the mother-child relationship. *Developmental Psychology, 25*(3), 403–412.

Bray, N.M., Coleman, J.M., & Bracken, M.B. (1981). Critical events in parenting handicapped children. *Journal of the Division for Early Childhood, 3,* 26–33.

Breslau, N. (1983). Care of disabled children and women's time use. *Medical Care, 21,* 620–629.

Bristol, M. (1984). Family resources and successful adaptation to autistic children. In E. Schopler & G. Mesibov (Eds.), *The effects of autism on the family* (pp. 289–310). New York: Plenum.

Bristol, M.M., Gallagher, J.J., & Schopler, E. (1988). Mothers and fathers of young developmentally disabled and nondisabled boys: Adaptation and spousal support. *Developmental Psychology, 24*(3), 441–451.

Bromwich, R.M. (1981). *Working with parents and infants: An interactional approach.* Baltimore: University Park Press.

Brotherson, M.J., & Goldstein, B.L. (1992). Time as a resource and constraint for parents of young children with disabilities: Implications for early intervention services. *Topics in Early Childhood Special Education, 12*(4), 508–527.

Caplan, P.J., & Hall-McCorquodale, I. (1985). Mother-blaming in major clinical journals. *American Journal of Orthopsychiatry, 55,* 345–353.

Carver, J., & Carver, N. (1974). *The family of the retarded child.* Syracuse, NY: Syracuse University Division of Special Education and the Center on Human Policy.

Cleary, P.D., & Mechanic, D. (1983). Sex differences in psychological distress among married people. *Journal of Health and Social Behavior, 24,* 111–121.

Cohen, S., & Hoberman, H.M. (1983). Positive events and social supports as buffers of life change stress. *Journal of Applied Social Psychology, 13,* 19–25.

Cohen, S., & Syme, S.L. (Eds.). (1985). *Social support and health.* New York: Academic Press.

Crnic, K.A., & Greenberg, M.T. (1990). Minor parenting stresses with young children. *Child Development, 61,* 1628–1637.

Cutler, B.C. (1991). *Families and services in autism: Promises to keep.* Unpublished doctoral dissertation, School of Education, Boston University, Boston.

Cutler, B.C., & Kozloff, M.A. (1987). Living with autism: Effects on families and family needs. In D.J. Cohen, A. Donnellan, & R. Paul (Eds.), *Handbook of autism and pervasive developmental disorders* (pp. 513–527). New York: John Wiley & Sons.

Darling, R.B. (1979). *Families against society: A study of reactions to children with birth defects.* Beverly Hills: Sage Publications.

David-Neel, A. (1978). *Buddhism: Its doctrines and its methods.* New York: St. Martin's Press.

DeMyer, M.K. (1979). *Parents and children in autism.* Washington, DC: Winston.

Dohrenwend, B.S., & Dohrenwend, B.P. (1981). Socioenvironmental factors, stress, and psychopathology. *American Journal of Community Psychology, 9,* 128–165.

Dunst, C.J., Trivette, C.M., & Deal, A.G. (1988). *Enabling and empowering families: Principles and guidelines for practice.* Cambridge, MA: Brookline Books.

Dyson, L. (1989). Adjustment of siblings of handicapped children: A comparison. *Journal of Pediatric Psychology, 14*(2), 215–229.

Ellis, A., & Harper, R.A. (1975). *A new guide to rational living.* Englewood Cliffs, NJ: Prentice Hall.

Featherstone, H. (1980). *A difference in the family.* New York: Basic Books.

Feldman, D., Gerstein, L.H., & Feldman, B. (1989). Teachers' beliefs about administrators and parents of handicapped and nonhandicapped students. *Journal of Experimental Education, 58*(1), 43–54.

Fogan, J., & Schor, D. (1993). Mothers of children with spina bifida: Factors related to maternal psychosocial functioning. *American Journal of Orthopsychiatry, 63*(1), 146–152.

Folkman, S., Lazarus, R.S., Dunkel-Shetter, C., DeLongis, A., & Gruen, R.J. (1986). The dynamics of a stressful encounter: Cognitive appraisal, coping, and encounter outcomes. *Journal of Personality and Social Psychology, 50*, 992–1003.

Francell, C.G., Conn, V.S., & Gray, D.P. (1988). Families' perception of burden of care for chronic mentally ill relatives. *Hospital and Community Psychiatry, 39*, 1296–1300.

Frankenhaeuser, M. (1986). A psychobiological framework for research on human stress and coping. In M.H. Appley & R.A. Trumbull (Eds.), *Dynamics of stress* (pp. 101–116). New York: Plenum.

Frankl, V. (1969). *The will to meaning.* New York: New American Library.

Frese, M. (1986). Coping as a moderator and mediator between stress at work and psychosomatic complaints. In M.H. Appley & R.A. Trumbull (Eds.), *Dynamics of stress* (pp. 183–206). New York: Plenum.

Friedrich, W.N., & Friedrich, W.L. (1981). Psychological assets of parents of handicapped and nonhandicapped children. *American Journal of Mental Deficiency, 85*, 551–553.

Fuchs, V.R. (1986). Sex differences in economic well-being. *Science, 232*, 459–464.

Gallagher, J.J., Beckman-Bell, P., & Cross, A.H. (1983). Families of handicapped children: Sources of stress and its amelioration. *Exceptional Children, 50*, 10–19.

Goethe, J.W. von (1949). *Goethe's autobiography* (R.O. Moon, Translator). Washington, DC: Public Affairs Press.

Goldberg, S., Marcovitch, S., MacGregor, D., & Lojkasek, M. (1986). Family responses to developmentally delayed preschoolers: Etiology and the father's role. *American Journal of Mental Deficiency, 90*, 610–617.

Hallum, A., & Krumboltz, J.D. (1993). Parents caring for young adults with severe physical disabilities: Psychological issues. *Developmental Medicine and Child Neurology, 35*, 24–32.

Hansson, R.O. (1986). Relational competence, relationships, and adjustment to old age. *Journal of Personality and Social Psychology, 50*, 1050–1058.

Henry, J. (1973). *On sham, vulnerability and other forms of self-destruction.* New York: Vintage Books.

Hobfoll, S.E. (1988). *The ecology of stress.* New York: Hemisphere Publishing Corporation.

Hyche, J.K., Jr., Bakeman, R., & Adamson, L.B. (1992). Understanding communicative cues of infants with Down Syndrome: Effects of mothers' experience and infants' age. *Journal of Applied Developmental Psychology, 13*, 1–16.

Jarvis, P.A., Myers, B.J., & Creasey, G.L. (1989). The effects of infants' illness on mothers' interactions with prematures at 4 and 8 months. *Infant Behavior and Development, 12*, 25–35.

Jennings, S.E. (1990). *Understanding differences in families with developmentally disabled children: A stress and coping approach.* Unpublished doctoral dissertation, Boston University, Boston.

Kazak, A.E., Reber, M., & Carter, A. (1988). Structural and qualitative aspects of social networks in families of young chronically ill children. *Journal of Pediatric Psychology, 13*(2), 171–182.

Kirkham, M.A. (1993). Two-year follow-up of skills training with mothers of children with disabilities. *American Journal on Mental Retardation, 97*(5), 509–520.

Kobasa, S.C. (1979). Stressful life events, personality, and health: An inquiry into hardiness. *Journal of Personality and Social Psychology, 37*, 1–11.

Koller, H., Richardson, S.A., & Katz, M. (1993). Families of children with mental retardation: Comprehensive view from an epidemiological perspective. *American Journal on Mental Retardation, 97*(3), 315–332.

Kozloff, M.A., Helm, D.T., Cutler, B.C., Douglas-Steele, D., Wells, A., & Scampini, L. (1988). Training programs for children with autism or other handicaps. In R.DeV. Peters & R.J. McMahon (Eds.), *Social learning and systems approaches to marriage and the family* (pp. 217–250). New York: Brunner/Mazel.

Krauss, M.W. (1993). Child-related and parenting stress: Similarities and differences between mothers and fathers of children with disabilities. *American Journal on Mental Retardation, 97*(4), 393–404.

Lazarus, R.S., & Folkman, S. (1986). Cognitive theories of stress and the issue of circularity. In M.H. Appley & R.A. Trumbull (Eds.), *Dynamics of stress* (pp. 63–80). New York: Plenum.

Lefcourt, H.M. (1976). *Locus of control.* New York: John Wiley & Sons.

Lefcourt, H.M. (1981). *Research with the locus of control construct: Volume 1: Assessment methods.* New York: Academic Press.

Levi, L. (Ed.). (1981). *Society, stress and disease. Volume IV: Working life.* New York & Toronto: Oxford University Press.

Levi-Shiff, R. (1986). Mother-father-child interactions in families with a mentally retarded young child. *American Journal of Mental Deficiency, 91*, 141–149.

Lobato, D., Faust, D., & Spirito, A. (1988). Examining the effects of chronic disease and disability on children's sibling relationships. *Journal of Pediatric Psychology, 13*(3), 389–407.

Longo, D.C., & Bond, L. (1984). Families of the handicapped child: Research and practice. *Family Relations, 33*, 57–65.

Mahoney, G., & Powell, A. (1988). Modifying parent-child interaction: Enhancing the development of handicapped children. *Journal of Special Education, 22*(1), 82–96.

Marfo, K. (1992). Correlates of maternal directiveness with children who are developmentally disabled. *American Journal of Orthopsychiatry, 62*(2), 219–233.

Margalit, M., Raviv, A., & Ankonina, D.B. (1992). Coping and coherence among parents with disabled children. *Journal of Clinical Child Psychology, 21*(3), 202–209.

McHale, S.M., & Gamble, W.C. (1989). Sibling relationships with disabled and nondisabled brothers and sisters. *Developmental Psychology, 25*(3), 421–429.

McManus, M.C., & Friesen, B.J. (Eds.). (1986). *Families as allies: Conference proceedings.* Portland, OR: Research and Training Center to Improve Services for Severely Emotionally Handicapped Children and Their Families, Portland State University.

Molsa, P., & Ikonen-Molsa, S.A. (1985). The mentally handicapped child and family crisis. *Journal of Mental Deficiency Research, 29,* 309–314.

Morton, K. (1985). Identifying the enemy: A parent's complaint. In H.R. Turnbull & A. Turnbull (Eds.), *Parents speak out: Then and now* (pp. 143–148). Columbus, OH: Charles E. Merrill.

Ostrander, S.A. (1984). *Women of the upper class.* Philadelphia: Temple University Press.

Palfrey, J.S., Walker, D.K., Butler, J.A., & Singer, J.D. (1989). Patterns of response in families of chronically disabled children: An assessment of five metropolitan school districts. *American Journal of Orthopsychiatry, 59*(1), 94–104.

Pearlin, L.I., & Schooler, C. (1978). The structure of coping. *Journal of Health and Social Behavior, 19,* 2–21.

Peterson, C., & Villanova, P. (1988). An expanded attributional style questionnaire. *Journal of Abnormal Psychology, 97*(1), 87–89.

Petr, C.G., & Barney, D.D. (1993). Reasonable efforts for children with disabilities: The parents' perspective. *Social Work, 38*(3), 247–254.

Pilisuk, M., & Parks, S.H. (1986). *The healing web: Social networks and human survival.* Hanover, NH: University Press of New England.

Roberts, M.W., Joe, V.C., & Rowe-Hallbert, A. (1992). Oppositional child behavior and parental locus of control. *Journal of Clinical Child Psychology, 21*(2), 170–177.

Robins, C.J., Block, P., & Peselow, E.D. (1990). Cognition and life events in major depression: A test of the mediation and interaction hypotheses. *Cognitive Therapy and Research, 14*(3), 299–313.

Rosenberg, S.A., & Robinson, C.C. (1988). Interactions of parents with their young handicapped children. In S.L. Odom & M.B. Karnes (Eds.), *Early intervention for infants and children with handicaps: An empirical base* (pp. 159–177). Baltimore: Paul H. Brookes Publishing Co.

Rosenthal, J.A., Groze, V., & Curiel, H. (1990). Race, social class, and special needs adoption. *Social Work, 35*(6), 532–539.

Schilling, R.F., Schinke, S.P., & Kirkham, M.A. (1985). Coping with a handicapped child: Differences between mothers and fathers. *Social Science and Medicine, 21,* 857–863.

Schopenhauer, A. (1906). *The world as will and idea* (5th ed.). London: Paul, Trench, Trubner and Company.

Schopler, E., & Loftin, J. (1969). Thinking disorders in parents of young psychotic children. *Journal of Abnormal Psychology, 74,* 3281–3287.

Seifer, R., Clark, G.N., & Sameroff, A.J. (1991). Positive effects of interaction coaching on infants with developmental disabilities and their mothers. *American Journal on Mental Retardation, 96*(1), 1–11.

Seligman, M.E.P., Castellon, C., Cacciola, J., Schulman, P., Luborsky, L., Ollove, M., & Downey, R. (1988). Explanatory style change during cognitive therapy for unipolar depression. *Journal of Abnormal Psychology, 97*(1), 13–18.

Shapiro, J. (1989). Stress, depression, and support group participation in mothers of developmentally delayed children. *Family Relations, 38,* 169–173.

Sherman, B.R., & Cocozza, J.J. (1984). Stress in families of the developmentally disabled: A literature review of factors affecting the decision to seek out-of-home placements. *Family Relations, 33,* 95–103.

Singer, L., & Farkas, K.J. (1989). The impact of infant disability on maternal perception of stress. *Family Relations, 38,* 444–449.

Sloper, P., & Turner, S. (1993). Risk and resistance factors in the adaptation of parents of children with severe physical disabilities. *Journal of Child Psychology and Psychiatry and Allied Disciplines, 34*(2), 167–188.

Solomon, Z. (1986). Three Mile Island: Social support and affective disorders among mothers. In S.E. Hobfoll (Ed.), *Stress, social support, and women* (pp. 85–97). Washington, DC: Hemisphere Publishing Corporation.

Sonnenschein, P. (1981). Parents and professionals: An uneasy relationship. *Teaching Exceptional Children, 14,* 62–65.

Teele, J.E. (1981). *Mastering stress in child rearing: A longitudinal study of coping and remission.* Lexington, MA: D.C. Heath.

Telleen, S., Herzog, A., & Kilbane, L. (1989). Impact of a family support program on mothers' social support and parenting stress. *American Journal of Orthopsychiatry, 59*(3), 410–419.

Turnbull, A.P. (1978). Moving from being a professional to being a parent: A startling experience. In A.P. Turnbull & H.R. Turnbull (Eds.), *Parents speak out: Growing with a handicapped child.* Columbus, OH: Charles E. Merrill.

Turnbull, A.P., Blue-Banning, M., Behr, S.K., & Kerns, G.M. (1986). Family research and intervention: A value and ethical examination. In P.R. Dokecki & R.M. Zaner (Eds.), *Ethics of dealing with persons with severe handicaps: Toward a research agenda* (pp. 119–140). Baltimore: Paul H. Brookes Publishing Co.

Turnbull, A.P., & Turnbull, H.R. (1986). *Families, professionals, and exceptionality: A special partnership.* Columbus, OH: Charles E. Merrill.

Vanfossen, B.E. (1986). Sex differences in depression: The role of spouse support. In S.E. Hobfoll (Ed.), *Stress, social support, and women* (pp. 69–84). Washington, DC: Hemisphere Publishing Corporation.

Wahler, R.G. (1980). The insular mother: Her problems in parent-child treatment. *Journal of Applied Behavior Analysis, 13,* 207–219.

Wallander, J.L., Varni, J.W., Babini, L., Banis, H.T., & Wilcox, K.T. (1989). Family resources as resistance factors for psychological maladjustment in chronically ill and handicapped children. *Journal of Pediatric Psychology, 14*(2), 157–173.

Wallander, J.L., Varni, J.W., Babini, L., DeHaan, C.B., Wilcox, K.T., & Banis, H.T. (1989). The social environment and the adaptation of mothers of physically handicapped children. *Journal of Pediatric Psychology, 14*(3), 371–387.

Weiss, S.J. (1991). Stressors experienced by family caregivers of children with pervasive developmental disorders. *Child Psychiatry and Human Development, 21*(3), 203–216.

Wilton, K., & Renaut, J. (1986). Stress levels in families with intellectually handicapped preschool children and families with nonhandicapped preschool children. *Journal of Mental Deficiency Research, 30,* 163–169.

Zuchman, E. (1982). *Child disability in the family.* New York: World Rehabilitation Fund.

Zuroff, D.C., Igreja, I., & Mongrain, M. (1990). Dysfunctional attitudes, dependency, and self-criticism as predictors of depressive mood states: A 12-month longitudinal study. *Cognitive Therapy and Research, 14*(3), 315–326.

CHAPTER 8

COORDINATED AND EMPOWERING PROGRAMS

DRAWING ON RECENT RESEARCH AND THIS AUTHOR'S OBSERVATIONS IN MANY SCHOOLS, THIS CHAPTER suggests ways of organizing special education that can help staff and families obtain the resources they need to foster children's psychosocial development. It also offers guidelines for putting these ideas into practice.

PROGRAM ORGANIZATION

The efforts of special educators and families to bring children with disabilities into the social world are thwarted in part by the way many programs are organized. For example, comprehensive assessment, planning, and instruction are inhibited by overspecialization, the isolation of staff, and lack of coordination with families. Additionally, the lack of leadership, on-site assistance, and reinforcement for effective teaching leave staff without clear performance standards or much incentive to use new methods. Finally, the perception of unpredictable resources and the inability of staff and families to substantially improve program organization and development breed vulnerability, pessimism, and apathy. This section describes organizational features that can help educators and families to collaboratively create excellent programs. The areas examined include methods of fostering a shared mission, establishing connections to the community, positive administration, ownership and empowerment, newsletters and materials development, libraries, peer or mentor assistance, teaming, and group training.

Psychosocial Development as a Shared Mission

The core of an educational program for children with disabilities should be the mission to increase their psychosocial development. This means helping children acquire functional skills. It also means helping people in family, school, and community environments perceive children with disabilities as persons who deserve respect, protection, and the opportunity to participate as community members in good standing.

A focus on psychosocial development may have several beneficial effects. One, it gives persons with different jobs in a program a common orientation that can increase the sense of community and the incentive to interact with others (Rosenholtz, 1989). It also provides a framework for evaluating current practices and planning change. For instance, members of the program may feel obliged to determine if the curriculum has gaps regarding psychosocial development, and if so, how they can be filled by adding classes, integrating children into regular education, and providing community instruction. Moreover, psychosocial development as a mission suggests conduct norms and performance evaluation criteria that program members are likely to see as relevant (Gibson,

Ivancevich, & Donnelly, 1985). Examples of such norms include teaching functional, age-appropriate behaviors; paying attention to subtle cues and prompts; and working on fluency, generalization, adaptation, and maintenance, as well as acquisition. Finally, the mission could be used to select staff with skills and outlooks that are compatible with the program's mission.

Connections to the Larger Community

School-based programs are often insulated from community life. Instruction occurs in classrooms 6 hours a day, 5 days a week, 10 months a year. Insulation leaves staff with little incentive to incorporate competencies children need for participation in the outside world. In addition, it makes staff vulnerable to shortages of money, ideas, materials, and support, which inhibits their investing in program development. Insulation also fosters the erroneous notion that teachers alone are largely responsible for beneficial change in children. This leads to some staff becoming vulnerable to criticism from those who do not see that a child's psychosocial development requires collaboration among many caregivers. One long-term goal, therefore, is to establish connections between school, families, and community to increase resources and options for program development (Morril, 1992; Pavalko, 1988). Below are examples of home-school-community connections.

1. Religious groups, age peers and older students without disabilities, senior citizens, and grandparents can assist in class, prepare materials, and be friends who help children with disabilities in, for example, community participation. They also can provide families with baby-sitting, teaching assistance, or help with cooking and transportation. In addition, they can take part in after-school, weekend, or summer programs (Cole, Vandercook, & Rynders, 1988; Haring & Breen, 1992; Home and School Institute, 1985; Platt & Platt, 1980; Schleien, Heyne, & Briehan Berken, 1988; Schleien, Rynders, & Mustonen, 1988).
2. Business and fraternal organizations can provide funds, materials, and opportunities for community instruction (e.g., environments for work on generalization and adaptation) (Nietupski, Hamre-Nietupski, Houselog, Donder, & Anderson, 1988).
3. "District wide 'cadres'" (California Research Institute, 1991, p. 7) of parents, college teachers, fundraisers, physicians, and staff of other programs can consult individually or as members of a standing committee (e.g., help to plan new classes and review program development) (Gardner, 1992).
4. Presence in the community can be increased through *newsletters* and *presentations* to schools, businesses, and voluntary organizations. Moreover, staff members and parents might appear on community cable television to describe their program.
5. Not only is family involvement necessary to children's psychosocial development, but the passage of PL 99-457 (Education of the Handicapped Act Amendments of 1986) requires that communities work to increase participation of and services to families (Early Intervention Program for Infants and Toddlers with Handicaps, 1989; Meisels, 1989). The fact that parents have intimate knowledge of their children's learning and development, that parents generally provide most of their children's socialization experiences, and that family is the only thing most children can depend on should mean that families be seen as equal partners in all aspects of their children's educations. Also, interested families can help in classrooms, program development, and family assistance networks.

Positive Administration

Administrators can help staff and families foster psychosocial development in many ways, as suggested by Nietupski et al. (1988).

1. Administrators can organize large meetings with the purpose of evaluating the program and soliciting suggestions for program development.

2. As leaders, administrators can develop and articulate the mission of the program and disseminate position papers, as well as summaries of group meetings for all to share.

3. Administrators can organize meetings of teachers, families, specialists, cafeteria workers, or regular educators. During these meetings, members can articulate their perception of the program mission, examine their current and potential contributions, and identify resources needed to do their jobs better.

4. Administrators can select as staff those whose attitudes and skills are consistent with the program mission and organization (e.g., teaming). In addition, they can provide opportunities for staff to evaluate and change roles in the program. For instance, a communication therapist with a strong desire to be a classroom teacher might be given the chance to try that position. Helping staff re-examine and select their own roles increases the sense of autonomy and personal investment, decreases the need to transfer poor performers, and may decrease turnover (Wright, 1990).

5. Administrators can increase their presence, support, and reinforcement of staff as an antidote to staff isolation and vulnerability. Wright (1990, p. 129), for instance, advocates "management by walking around" as a way to offer timely emotional support and reinforce competent performance. Recognition can also be given during group meetings and through articles in newsletters. Support from a principal is especially important as "The principal gives sometimes subtle but nonetheless strong messages about the legitimacy of project operations in the school . . ." (McLaughlin, 1991, p. 66). Thus, principals should be included in all phases of program development.

Ownership and Empowerment

As McClure points out, "every decision about learning and instruction that can be made by a local school faculty should be made by that faculty" (1991, p. 235). There are four reasons to organize programs so staff and families have major responsibility for planning, developing, and running their program. First, autonomy increases job satisfaction and personal investment (Bennis, 1989; Eicher & Thompson, 1986; Forester, 1982; Schein, 1985; Smylie, 1988). Second, when administrators whose training is in administration and regular education plan and supervise special education activities, it lowers their credibility and produces resentment in staff. Third, administrators usually do not have time to plan and supervise all activities. Fourth, the conventional form of administration—in which administrators supervise and make decisions for staff—is "seldom, if ever, found to be related to school and teacher effectiveness" (Griffin, 1991, p. 245).

Working together, staff and families generally have and/or can develop the expertise needed to accomplish the following activities (Oja, 1991; Timm & Rule, 1981):

1. Planning, evaluating, and revising the curriculum for children, including entry and exit criteria, target competencies, and practices (e.g., assessment, instruction) for each class

2. Designing teams of teachers, therapists, and families for each class.

3. Assisting one another in classrooms and homes through peer or mentor coaching (discussed later in this chapter)

4. Conducting training programs (discussed later in this chapter)

5. Soliciting participation of community members

6. Operating newsletters, hotlines, and support networks

In addition to increased responsibility and autonomy, it is wise to institutionalize the recognition of members' contributions. It ought to become common practice, for instance, for members to positively comment on one another's competencies and contributions to the mission. Recognition can also be provided through newsletters, position papers on the future of the program, and awards for excellence. In addition, people can be *invited to contribute*. Cafeteria workers, for example, ought to be invited to help plan instruction on using the cafeteria. Finally, important information should be available to every member of the program (e.g., on the program mission, a handbook describing the current organization of the program and its practices, whom to call for help, and upcoming events).

Newsletters and Materials Development

A regular newsletter can serve important functions. It can be a means for attracting volunteers and funding from the community. It can also be used to solicit and disseminate ideas within the program and to community organizations. Moreover, it can be a means for recognizing people's ideas and services, documenting program developments as a way to foster a sense of accomplishment, and informing members of current and upcoming events. Newsletters might be put out by a small group consisting, for instance, of a secretary and an interested parent. Their tasks might include soliciting items for inclusion, funding for printing and mailing, and advertising.

Innovative ideas and practices should be in written and, perhaps, videotape form. Important materials include position papers describing the mission; operating manuals describing each class; summaries of recent literature (e.g., on prompting strategies); training program curricula; how transdisciplinary teams operate; and protocols and forms for assessment, program planning, and program evaluation. A *curriculum committee* of staff, parents, and administrators could shape such materials into a handbook that documents progress, symbolizes collective effort, facilitates the spread of innovations, and is used to train new participants.

Libraries

A program library can be a source of pride and a resource for ideas. A library might include program materials; journals (e.g., *Journal of The Association for Persons with Severe Handicaps,* the *Journal of Applied Behavior Analysis,* and *Topics in Language Disorders*); reprints of articles all members should be familiar with; newsletters about other organizations; and videotapes of assessment and instructional methods.

Peer or Mentor Assistance

Program members can provide social support, help networks, and on-site performance evaluation and coaching through the program.

Social Support   Social support includes encouragement and a sympathetic ear. One format for providing social support is *one-to-one interviews* between staff members and administrators on a regularly scheduled and/or as-needed basis. During interviews, an administrator and staff member can evaluate the program, discuss the staff member's performance, and identify resources the staff member needs to be more effective. Families can also provide social support to one another. For example, experienced families can help new families handle anxiety and confusion, instill hope and a sense of belonging, and offer advice on childrearing (Fitzgerald & Fischer, 1987; Fitzgerald & Karnes, 1987).

Help Networks   Families often can benefit from child care assistance, a ride to the doctor's office, or help with chores when especially busy. Classroom teachers often benefit from an extra person to take data, help teach, or prepare materials. A help network can make these types of assistance more dependable. A network might consist of families, staff members, senior citizens, high school and college students, and voluntary organizations.

The first step in creating a network is to contact all staff and families to determine the assistance needed. At the same time, staff, families, and possible resource persons in the community are asked what assistance they can offer. Second, information about providers and users is compiled into lists. Third, users are sent a copy of the list of providers. In addition, the network is advertised in the newsletter. A useful complement to a resource network is a *telephone hotline* used by families and staff for support and advice during and after school hours.

On-Site Performance Evaluation and Coaching Useful evaluations of teaching performance are rare. The typical evaluation is conducted after difficulties have become problems. It usually involves a superior documenting the alleged shortcomings of someone in a subordinate position. This often leads to those being evaluated making efforts to appear more competent, which they cannot sustain, and to evaluators giving good evaluations simply to avoid conflict. Moreover, the evaluation is usually not followed by coaching or training.

Performance evaluation with on-site coaching that is provided on a regular (e.g., biweekly) or as-needed basis would be an important part of a program. Teachers, therapists, and parents working as pairs or larger teams draw on written materials describing expected practices and help each other to increase skills. The relationship between the one providing and the one receiving evaluation and coaching would either be a *peer* relationship, in which partners have equal experience but different skills, or a *mentoring* relationship, in which one has more experience and skill than the other (Kram, 1985). The benefits of regular evaluation and coaching include the development of shared conduct norms and evaluation criteria, a decrease in isolation and ineffective work, and an increase in program quality and honesty about the need for help. Several partnerships are possible.

1. Experienced parents help new parents institute productive exchanges and teach in the home.
2. Experienced teachers mentor new teachers in all practices from assessment through program evaluation (Demchak, Kontos, & Neisworth, 1992; Hundert & Hopkins, 1992).
3. Therapists train classroom teachers and parents in a transdisciplinary team (discussed later in the chapter).
4. Persons in a training program coach one another.

Willerman, McNeely, and Koffman (1991) describe three phases of performance evaluation and coaching. In phase one, partners discuss the trainee's performance goals and plan the evaluation. For instance, Ms. Reed indicates to Ms. Wright, the mentor, that she wants to improve the way she handles problem behaviors. As a start, Ms. Wright will observe two lessons a day for 2 days, take notes on Ms. Reed's exchanges with children, and provide coaching if asked. In phase two, Ms. Wright will make the site visits, record observations, and provide coaching (e.g., suggestions and demonstrations). In phase three, soon after the observation, Ms. Wright will present her data. She should stress Ms. Reed's skillful performances as well as those to improve. Ms. Reed may ask for advice on how to relax when children are disruptive and for suggestions for handling tantrums. Ms. Reed and Ms. Wright then develop a plan to help Ms. Reed meet her goals. The plan might include readings on exchanges and problem behavior, analyzing videotapes, and on-site coaching.

A longer mentoring relationship was used by this author and his colleagues to assist families and new staff in a program for children with autism (Hamblin, Buckholdt, Ferritor, Kozloff, & Blackwell, 1971; Kozloff, 1983). The mentoring relationship had the following phases:

1. The trainee and mentor discuss introductory written materials on learning and teaching.
2. The trainee spends a week or so watching an experienced teacher or parent working with a child in class. Observations are usually from behind a one-way mirror. The mentor helps the trainee use correct terms to describe what is going on. For instance, "Notice how Ms. Blake waits until Jerry is looking at her for a little longer before she reinforces him. That is an example of *shaping* the duration of a behavior." When the trainee is skillful at using correct terms, he or she takes data on several variables (e.g., the number of correct responses and the number of reinforcements).
3. The mentor and trainee write a program plan that the trainee is to follow when working in the classroom with the child who was observed. At first, the trainee is to reinforce certain desirable behaviors. Later, he or she provides cues (e.g., models to imitate) and reinforcement. Then, the trainee learns to prompt, shape, and chain behavior.

Initially, the trainee is assisted by the mentor or teacher who is sitting nearby. Gradually, the mentor fades out of the room and coaches the trainee, who is wearing a small earphone, through a walkie-talkie from behind a one-way mirror.

4. In the case of families, the mentor-coach and family then develop program plans for the home. The mentor makes frequent home visits to help enact the plans.

5. In time, a mentor helps both family members and new staff to plan, evaluate, and revise programs on their own. Periodically, the mentor provides instruction and on-site coaching on new teaching methods.

6. Former trainees may begin to provide the same training to new staff and families.

Teaming

The work of special education staff (teachers, aides, and therapists) is specialized. Usually, each works alone with children or families using skills not shared by other staff (Drotar, 1989). The common result for children is fragmented instruction. The common result for staff is isolation and shrinking skill in relation to the body of skill defining special education (Rosenholtz, 1984). Teaming, in contrast, involves collaborative assessment, planning, instruction, and program evaluation by a relatively constant group. *Each level or class in a program might have its own team,* consisting of the classroom teacher, aide, a child's parents and other family members, staff therapists, perhaps a teacher from the next level in the curriculum, an administrator, and others with a continuing or temporary interest (e.g., pediatrician, audiologist, orthopedist, cafeteria worker).

Teaming can have many desirable effects:

1. It makes available the important contributions of persons who are generally not included.
2. Group discussions and observations of one another's work increase members' competencies (Griffin, 1991). This strengthens job security because multiskilled persons are hard to replace.
3. Sharing expertise can yield truly innovative practices and ideas.
4. Members provide performance evaluation, coaching, and social support to one another.
5. Teaming increases the quality of a program and job satisfaction and reduces staff turnover (Merkel & Pollard, 1987).

This author is not suggesting the kind of teaming in which members act alone and meet later to summarize information and plan programs. Instead, this author advocates *joint* operations (e.g., a teacher and communication therapist conduct an assessment together) (Campbell, 1987). Furthermore, through workshops, discussion of publications, live and videotape demonstrations, and on-site coaching, *members share specialized competence.* Finally, chairing and scheduling team meetings, organizing tasks, and synthesizing discussions into plans might be the job of one member—the *educational synthesizer* (Bricker, 1976). Of course, the role of synthesizer can be rotated. Examples of teaming are presented below.

Team Assessment   In a team approach, families provide information on their child's medical history and psychosocial development; their child's participation in the family round of daily life; the effectiveness of different cues, prompts, and reinforcers; opportunities in the home and other places where their child might contribute, generalize, and/or adapt skills; and family challenges, resources, and needs (Audet & Hummel, 1990). The classroom teacher and various therapists also visit the home to identify prompts and obstacles in the physical environment, obtain an additional look at certain of the child's behaviors, and assess parents' teaching competence and parent–child exchanges. In addition to home data, team therapists conduct assessments of the child (if possible, while other members observe). Likewise, therapists and parents observe in class to assess the child's behavior in relation to classroom exchanges, instructional practices, and the physical environment.

In sum, team assessment involves each member sharing his or her special knowledge and skill, supplementing and cross-checking the others' observations. This yields a more representative picture of a child's functional behavioral repertoire and of the child's environments. It also decreases misunderstandings and communication delays.

Team Program Planning Assessment information is used to improve congruence between a child's functional behavioral repertoire and the child's present and possibly future life environments. Two sorts of program plans are prepared: 1) a long-term plan for achieving goals regarding educational, living, recreational, and working circumstances; and 2) short-term plans, suggested by the long-term plan, for improving child–caregiver exchanges; altering instruction to suit a child's needs; helping a child acquire, use, generalize, and adapt skills; increasing social support and assistance to the family; providing coaching to the classroom teacher; and altering other relevant features of the child's environments.

Plans are a synthesis of members' contributions. For instance, the occupational therapist identifies strong and weak links in a child's dressing skills, as revealed through task analyses. The teacher and parents point out the cues, prompts, and reinforcers that are generally effective with the child. The physical therapist suggests how to adapt the task, provide manual prompts, and increase the child's strength and flexibility. Finally, parents identify tasks and incidental opportunities in the home for extra practice on weak links.

Team Instruction A team approach to instruction has three features. First, members *share* specialized methods. The communication therapist, for instance, teaches others how to elicit and shape speech acts, and parents show others the prompts that help their child walk. Second, instruction is *coordinated*. For instance, some competencies (e.g., bed making) are only taught in the home, perhaps with on-site coaching from another team member. Other competencies (e.g., reading) are taught in class only, while parents observe. Once a child is well into the acquisition phase, parents generalize reading to the home and other places, perhaps with assistance from a reading specialist. Widely used skills (e.g., talking, cooperating, dressing) are simultaneously taught at home, school, and other community environments. Third, *instruction is ecologically sound.* Speech and play therapy, for instance, are not done in clinics and private offices. Rather, *therapy is done where improvement will do the most good.*

Ongoing Program Evaluation As described in Chapter 4, this volume, and in *Guidelines and Protocols,* team members record how plans are enacted and the effects. Plans are upgraded or revised accordingly. For example, task analyses may show that Indra is making faster progress learning to dress at home than in school. Observations reveal that the family uses more extensive manual prompting than Indra's teacher. Thus, the team decides to try the family's method in school. However, home observations may show that a family is not properly following the written plan for improving exchanges. They still reinforce problem behaviors and fail to reinforce many desirable behaviors. During a team meeting, or with a coach during home visits, parents note that the plan, which they helped prepare, requires too much at once. Thus, the plan is revised so exchanges are improved in smaller steps. The transition from a specialized division of labor to teaming is discussed later in this chapter.

Group Training Programs

Group training is another method of sharing skills, coordinating activities, and creating a sense of community. Group training can be organized in several ways:

1. There can be separate programs for families, staff, volunteers, or all participants at once.
2. Training can address a few topics (e.g., productive exchanges) or a range of topics (e.g., parenting children with disabilities).
3. Training can be for a few meetings, 3 or 4 months, or an ongoing (e.g., biweekly) feature of a school.
4. Programs can be run by administrators, teachers, therapists, parents (e.g., helping new families), or outside consultants.

5. Groups of up to approximately 20 participants work well. More participants than that makes discussion difficult. However, a large group could divide into smaller groups for discussion after the major topic of a meeting is covered.
6. Groups in which children's disabilities are somewhat different may help participants generalize and adapt principles of assessment, planning, and teaching. However, when disabilities are quite different, materials relevant for some trainees may be irrelevant for others. In this case, there should be either separate training programs, or, after the material for a meeting is presented, caregivers of children with similar disabilities should meet as subgroups to plan how to use the material in their own environments.

Variations of the training programs described in this chapter have been conducted by this author and his colleagues since 1968. Training covers a range of topics and lasts 3 or 4 months. However, it could be extended indefinitely. The programs have been used for families alone, staff alone, and for families and staff together (Kaufman, 1976; Kozloff, 1979, 1983; Kozloff et al., 1988). The programs have three stages: pre-program, program, and maintenance.

Pre-Program Stage   There are five tasks in the pre-program stage: 1) contacting prospective participants, 2) assessing and strengthening readiness to participate, 3) determining goals and formalizing a working relationship, 4) assessing needs and strengths, and 5) organizing assessment information and planning change programs. Below, each task is described as it might be accomplished with families. However, the same methods are used with teachers, therapists, and volunteers.

Task One: Making Contact   Families usually have little experience working with school staff. Thus, organizers may have to inform them of an upcoming program and arouse their interest. There are several ways to make contact, including the following:

1. Personal letters or phone calls to families
2. Brochures or flyers on bulletin boards in schools, libraries, and grocery stores
3. Presentations during open meetings for families
4. Discussions with families when children are being enrolled, or during parent–teacher interaction at any time

During initial contacts, it is important to cite likely benefits of participation. These often include increased self-confidence, greater influence on children's education and life chances, greater skill at effecting beneficial change, children becoming easier to live with and teach, and children making faster progress (Baker, Landen, & Kashima, 1991). If possible, *tangible evidence of benefits* should be provided through videotape, films, vignettes, and testimonials.

In this author's opinion, it is unwise to require families to participate in training as a condition of children's enrollment. Coerced involvement is not the sort of involvement desired. Furthermore, if a school program is effective and supportive, most families eventually will want some form of training. Therefore, after an initial contact in which a training program is described and families are invited to participate, it should be up to them to take the next step. The families can contact organizers for more information or to indicate a desire to join. In this way, families make an initial commitment. Responses can be facilitated by a "tear off and mail" slip at the bottom of brochures, or by having a "sign up for more information" sheet at the end of meetings describing upcoming training.

Task Two: Assessing and Strengthening Readiness   The success of teaming, training programs, and peer/mentor coaching depends on caregivers' readiness to: 1) participate in a collaborative relationship, 2) conduct educational programs with a developmental-functional orientation (chaps. 3–6, this volume), and 3) improve their skills and other features of environments in which they operate. The *Family and School Assessment and Programming Guide* (*FSAPG*), located in the companion to this book, *Guidelines and Protocols for Practice,* helps to evaluate caregivers' readiness. The *FSAPG* defines 38 features of successful special education programs; the first 9 items concern readiness (e.g., a recognition of the need to conduct education programs in the family and community; expectation of success).

When caregivers are weak on the nine readiness items, they are unlikely to join or perform well in teaming, coaching, and training. Therefore, it is important for members of a school program to strengthen and sustain their own and their partners' readiness. This can be done during team meetings, peer or mentor coaching, periodic interviews with administrators, and/or interviews that are part of the assessment process. Methods for assessing, strengthening, and sustaining readiness are described in Chapter 9, this volume.

If caregivers—perhaps partly as a result of successful interviews—are strong on the nine readiness items, trainers or interviewers can encourage full participation in a training program. If readiness is weak (e.g., a prospective trainee has many reservations about the developmental-functional approach), then full participation is not a good idea. Instead, trainers or interviewers might suggest other options, such as the following:

1. Sustaining contact with teachers by telephone and/or logs going back and forth from home and school. Families and teachers inform one another of children's progress and ask for or get advice on how to teach certain behaviors.
2. Visiting classrooms and/or having periodic home visits for support and coaching.
3. Attending some meetings of their child's team.
4. Participating in a workshop on topics of interest (e.g., handling problem behaviors).

After taking some of these steps, many families become motivated to participate in more lengthy training programs. In addition, if child-sitting assistance is available through a help network, these families may be able to attend.

Task Three: Formalizing a Working Relationship Formalizing a working relationship helps establish participants' responsibilities to one another. Formalizing a working relationship has three steps.

1. Determine the collaborative relationship a family is interested in and ready for.
2. Specify terms of the working relationship. In a comprehensive training program, for instance, families receive weekly or biweekly home visits, access to a hotline, written materials, weekly or biweekly group training meetings lasting 2 hours, protection of privacy, and information on how to educate their children. At the same time, families are responsible for attending group meetings, taking data, conducting instructional programs in the home, and being available for agreed upon home visits.
3. Put the agreement in writing.

Task Four: Assessing Needs and Strengths It is important to assess participants' needs and strengths prior to and during the early stages of training. This makes it possible to plan the content of the program and evaluate its effectiveness. In a comprehensive program for families and/or staff, assessment focuses on many topics. These include children's competence and involvement; child–caregiver exchanges; caregiver teaching skills; social support and assistance needed and received by caregivers; and caregivers' assessments of themselves, children, and the family or class. Assessment methods include interviews, questionnaires, and direct observations.

Task Five: Organizing Assessment Information and Planning Change Programs Assessment information is shared with trainees. It is then used to plan *with* them a tentative educational program for their children and programs for improving their own teaching skills, child–caregiver exchanges, and on-site assistance. In the case of families of infants and toddlers, the assessment is used to prepare individualized family service plans (IFSPs), as required by PL 99-457. The assessments and plans for individual trainees are also used to plan the training curriculum for the group.

The companion volume to this book, *Guidelines and Protocols for Practice,* describes assessment and program planning in detail.

Program Stage   Major features of a training program include coaching, group meetings, curriculum, and evaluation.

Coaching   Each trainee (e.g., family, teacher, therapist) has a coach who helps plan change programs, offers help by telephone, reads logs or other data, and provides on-site evaluation and assistance. Coaches can be staff trainers, team members, and other families.

Group Meetings   The format of group meetings is as follows:

1. Each trainee, team, or family briefly describes and evaluates its work since the last meeting (e.g., increasing mutual reward exchanges with children). During group discussion, members help each other solve problems and plan further changes in home or school programs. Members are encouraged to make positive comments instead of pessimistic ones, and to comment and ask questions of a prescriptive rather than passive nature (e.g., "How do I stop myself from reacting when she whines?", rather than "Why do I react when she whines?").
2. The leader reviews ideas from the last meeting (e.g., types of exchanges and their effects). Then the current topic is presented (e.g., how to replace counterproductive exchanges). Videotape, film, role-playing, and group discussion are used.
3. The leader suggests uses of the presented material and helps individuals and the group develop an assignment for the next week (e.g., productive ways to respond to undesirable behavior).
4. Trainees and coaches plan individualized programs for the coming week(s). Plans specify, for instance, changes in instruction for the child, improvements in team or family interaction, data to take, and the date and time of the coach's on-site visit. One copy of the plan is kept by the trainee or family and another by the coach.

Curriculum   The training curriculum is divided into units, some requiring several meetings. Because ideas in early units are closely connected and participants generally need more support early in training, the first six meetings are weekly. After that, they are biweekly. Between-meeting contacts with coaches consist of telephone calls, logs, and on-site visits. The following is the sequence of units that this author and his colleagues have used in more than 20 programs.

1. Review objectives, activities, and ground rules for communication. Present fundamentals of the developmental-functional approach; that is, common human needs discussed in Chapter 1, this volume, models of the functional behavioral repertoire and psychosocial development, and implications of these for practices.
2. Examine families' and teachers' past experiences (i.e., difficulties, successes). This provides an opportunity to reinforce past efforts and successes, introduce social learning and exchange concepts, strengthen an internal locus of control, and build ésprit de corps.
3. Examine how learning occurs during exchanges. Analyze exchanges in trainees' homes and classrooms, some of which might be on videotape if permission was granted. Discuss how to institute productive exchanges and replace counterproductive exchanges. Each trainee or family writes a program for changing a few exchanges.
4. Discuss how to conduct a comprehensive home or school program to improve exchanges, strengthen children's attentiveness and participation (involvement), begin to replace problem behaviors, and increase caregivers' competence and confidence. Such a program is described in Chapter 5, this volume.
5. Trainees use methods described in *Guidelines and Protocols* to make additional assessments of children and family or school. Next, they use guidelines, also found in *Guidelines and Protocols,* for planning long-term and short-term goals.
6. Trainees learn basic methods such as reinforcing, prompting, chaining, and shaping. They also learn when to teach during special sessions, incidental opportunities, or routine tasks. Trainees

fill out a teaching program plan (program plan forms can be found in the companion to this volume, *Guidelines and Protocols for Practice*). In coming week(s) they conduct their first teaching programs to strengthen specific competencies of the child.

7. Trainees learn to identify and remedy difficulties in teaching programs (e.g., lack of reinforcer effectiveness). Teaching program plans are revised or upgraded.

8. Remaining units address such topics as: 1) conducting teaching programs in all competency areas (described in chap. 6, this volume); 2) replacing problem behaviors; 3) increasing family (or team) cooperation and integration; 4) increasing social-emotional support; 5) reducing personal (emotional) difficulties using relaxation, scheduled breaks, and cognitive-behavioral techniques; 6) obtaining needed services; 7) improving household or classroom organization; and 8) anticipating and learning to handle problems such as a decrease in motivation or in a child's progress.

Evaluation   Methods described in *Guidelines and Protocols* are used to evaluate children's and trainees' progress and to upgrade or revise teaching programs for children and training programs. For example, trainees and coaches conduct informal interviews and direct observations to see whether plans are being implemented properly and beneficial changes are occurring. If so, new objectives are selected and new plans are prepared. If not, possible difficulties are identified, and plans and methods are revised.

Maintenance Stage   Group meetings are held at least monthly. During these maintenance meetings, trainees learn to conduct advanced teaching programs with their children (e.g., on harder skills) and to solve new problems.

PROGRAM DEVELOPMENT

Program development should follow four guidelines: 1) envisioning a program with a developmental-functional orientation, 2) focusing on tasks relevant to the mission, 3) allowing a vision to be flexible, and 4) making changes gradually.

Envisioning a Program with a Developmental-Functional Orientation

Short-term responses to crises, windfalls, and bright ideas have little chance of producing an excellent program. *A long-range plan based on a vision of what the program can become is necessary.*

First, a program has several levels of special and/or regular education classrooms and associated home and community activities. Each focuses on children's competent participation in more complex forms of social organization. In addition, each class has entry and exit criteria, a set of competencies to teach, and instructional methods to use. Educational practices in any class are guided by a model of the functional behavioral repertoire, a model of children's psychosocial development, an understanding of productive and conflictual exchanges, and the five phases of learning.

Second, caregivers in each level or class conduct assessments, plan programs, provide instruction, and evaluate children's progress and their own practices as a team. Furthermore, they provide each other with social support and peer or mentor coaching.

Finally, communication and empowerment within the program are facilitated by newsletters, a library that includes program materials, increased responsibility and authority of staff and families, positive involvement of administrators, and group training. At the same time, the school sustains connections to persons and organizations in the larger community that provide funds, materials, services, and volunteers.

Creating a shared vision might involve the following steps over the course of several months.

1. Guided by a mission to foster psychosocial development, administrators, staff, and interested families *critically evaluate* the existing program and *suggest changes*. The format includes

position papers, interviews, and group discussions. Important recommendations for improving the program are received from reviews of current literature on effective practices, visits to other programs, group discussion, and presentations by outside speakers.

2. Task forces are formed, each focusing on a specific innovation (e.g., teaming, training programs, assessment practices, accessing community resources, levels of the curriculum, instructional practices). Each task force prepares and distributes a tentative plan.

3. A committee on program development is formed, consisting of representatives from task forces, the director of special education, building principals, and perhaps a planning consultant. The committee reviews task force plans and suggests revisions. Task forces may revise their tentative plans.

4. Based on revised task force plans, the committee on program development circulates a document describing the entire envisioned program. The document is discussed at a meeting for all participants.

It is important that the vision becomes part of the culture of the organization. This can be done by: 1) circulating the document describing the currently agreed upon vision; 2) creating pictorial representations of the envisioned program (e.g., depicting levels of the curriculum, teams, connections to the community); 3) summarizing the vision in a newsletter; 4) putting up signs that stress important features of the vision (e.g., "Are exchanges with children reciprocal or conflictual?"); and 5) identifying and reinforcing conduct consistent with the vision.

Focusing on Tasks Relevant to the Mission

Special education programs are commonly organized around job titles, such as classroom aide, teacher of children with moderate disabilities, and physical therapist. It is unlikely that a good program can be created merely by shuffling the same jobs. Instead, the organization should be looked at anew.

Organizational development can be planned in a way similar to behavioral development. Before teaching a child to dress, for instance, one analyzes dressing into component tasks and analyzes each task into component actions. Next, one assesses the child's performance of each task, noting strong and weak action links. Finally, one teaches the child to perform the right actions and tasks at the right spots in the dressing sequence.

The same task analytic approach can help organize a program so that it accomplishes its mission (Belohlav, 1990). First, one identifies organizational tasks that must be done to further psychosocial development. These include: 1) helping children acquire, become more fluent at, generalize, adapt, and maintain functional skills; 2) helping children participate in daily life; and 3) helping others see children as persons with a right to respectful treatment and a place in the social order. Second, one identifies tasks that are and are not done well enough in the current program. Third, when necessary, one reorganizes participants' activities so that mission-relevant tasks are accomplished.

The third point implies that *some jobs based on tradition or credentials must evolve*. Physical therapists, for example, are skilled at increasing strength and flexibility. However, if their future contributions are constrained by the historical fact that therapists usually work alone with children in separate rooms, then physical therapists will contribute little to the mission-relevant task of helping children generalize, adapt, and maintain competent performances in daily life. In sum, the job of physical (and other) therapists must evolve so that they can work in classrooms and homes as team members. Similarly, the job of classroom aide may have to evolve to include coaching families in the home, training volunteers, and helping to put out newsletters.

As with other features of a program, current and future job descriptions should be evaluated by participants themselves, guided by the program vision. It will take much discussion and several years of experimenting with job revision before a new set of jobs or roles is institutionalized.

Flexibility, Not a Fixed Vision

A vision should not be treated as if carved in stone. It should be used as a *horizon* that tells people where they want to go. Future publications and members' experiences will make some planned innovations obsolete. Other innovations will prove too costly or less effective than expected. For example, large training programs for families may be less effective than small ones conducted by each team. In sum, the vision must be revised over time.

Gradual Changes

One is tempted to turn visions into master plans. The temptation should be resisted. The deductive, rational, master plan approach has serious drawbacks. First, participants may feel the plan and the process of program development are no longer in their control; this produces resistance. Second, even if the vision is shared by everyone, which is unlikely, some participants will develop reservations. Ignoring or trying to suppress reservations is likely to produce conflict. Thus, program development ought to be open enough to hear and incorporate future reservations and suggestions.

Third, the deductive approach treats each innovation as if it were one more brick put in place. However, programs are dynamic—one part affects another. Thus, some innovations will facilitate other features of a program and some innovations will have potentially negative side effects. For instance, teaming increases communication and coordination *within* teams, but may weaken communication and increase competition *between* teams. Thus, a more humble empirical strategy is often better than a deductive strategy. "If change is to be permanent, it must be gradual" (Bennis, 1989, p. 149).

A gradual strategy might operate as follows. Guided by the vision, participants decide to work on *one or two innovations at a time*—fewer rather than more (Wright, 1990). Wise choices are innovations likely to yield greater productivity, sharing, and a capacity for more innovation with the least effort and time.

After an innovation is selected, those instituting it evaluate the benefits, effort and time involved, and the capacity for more innovations resulting from it. Evaluative data help decide whether to modify the new practice, scrap it, or build on it. Teaming, hotlines, and student volunteers are examples of starting points and subsequent changes.

Transition to Teaming One innovation is to replace a specialized division of labor with teaming. This transition might have the following steps:

1. Administrators circulate position papers and journal articles (e.g., Campbell, 1987) that describe teaming and show how it supports the mission.
2. Administrators host a meeting for staff and families. Presentations are made by schools where teaming is successful. The future of teaming in the program is discussed.
3. Administrators meet separately with classroom teachers, physical therapists, communication therapists, and interested families. Administrators stress that teaming is not a threat to jobs or professional status. Instead, it increases each member's skills and value.
4. Each group of stakeholders develops its position on teaming. Administrators have more meetings with each group to discuss team assessment, program planning, instruction, program evaluation, and training. Administrators address reservations and work out ways to facilitate members' participation. For instance, classroom teachers and therapists may need extra assistants and flexible schedules to work with families.
5. Nearly final plans are discussed at a meeting. A committee develops and circulates a written description of the school's new teaming practices and written forms to be used (e.g., forms for educational program plans). Workshops teach members how to collaboratively assess, plan, teach, evaluate, and provide peer coaching.
6. Team assessment of children is then instituted. Teams record how it works. They find that

teaming increases communication, sharing of skills, job satisfaction, and the adequacy of assessment information.

7. Team assessment leads to a team approach to program planning, instruction, and peer coaching.
8. Anticipating that teams may become insulated from one another, teams give presentations to each other and observe each other's practices.
9. Sharing produces information that is incorporated in a handbook of program operation.

Hotlines   A hotline for families can be created. Families can use it to obtain information, advice on handling problem behaviors, emotional support, and assistance in the home. The hotline's availability and effectiveness decrease vulnerability and increase interest in participating in children's educations. An open meeting should be held and the importance of family participation discussed. The meeting will lead to a written form families can fill out to indicate what help they need. This is followed by workshops on identified topics, which lead to more families participating in their children's teams.

Student Volunteers   Presentations to junior and senior high school students can result in recruiting help in classrooms. This can lead to the development of a "special friends" program (Cole et al., 1988), in which, for instance, students without disabilities join students with disabilities in a variety of community environments after school and on weekends. This leads to the development of a curriculum for community instruction and to contacts with businesses as sites for instruction and employment. Finally, after-school, weekend, and summer programs can be created, which are staffed primarily by junior and senior high school students (Hamre-Nietupski et al., 1992).

SUMMARY

This chapter presents features of organizations that can increase commitment, communication, job satisfaction, and ultimately children's psychosocial development. These features include the development of a shared program mission, positive administration, connections to the community and families, libraries and program documents, teaming, peer or mentor coaching, and training programs. The chapter also suggests a strategy for program development that is vision-guided, gradual, and focuses on mission-relevant tasks rather than traditional job titles.

REFERENCES

Audet, L.R., & Hummel, L.J. (1990). A framework for assessment and treatment of language-learning disabled children with psychiatric disorders. *Topics in Language Disorders, 10*(4), 57–74.

Baker, B.L., Landen, S.J., & Kashima, K.J. (1991). Effects of parent training on families of children with mental retardation: Increased burden or generalized benefit? *American Journal on Mental Retardation, 96*(2), 127–136.

Belohlav, J.A. (1990). *Championship management: An action model for high performance.* Cambridge, MA: Productivity Press.

Bennis, W. (1989). *Why leaders can't lead.* San Francisco: Jossey-Bass.

Bricker, D. (1976). Educational synthesizer. In M. Thomas (Ed.), *Hey, don't forget about me!* (pp. 84–97). Reston, VA: Council for Exceptional Children.

California Research Institute. (1991). Strategies on the integration of students with severe disabilities. *TASH Newsletter, 16*(2), 7–10.

Campbell, P.H. (1987). The integrated programming team: An approach for coordinating professionals of various disciplines in programs for students with multiple handicaps. *Journal of The Association for Persons with Severe Handicaps, 12*(2), 107–116.

Cole, D.A., Vandercook, T., & Rynders, J. (1988). Comparison of 2 peer interaction programs: Children with and without severe disabilities. *American Educational Research Journal, 25*(3), 415–439.

Demchak, M., Kontos, S., & Neisworth, J.T. (1992). Using a pyramid model to teach behavior management procedures to childcare providers. *Topics in Early Childhood Special Education, 12*(4), 458–477.

Drotar, D. (1989). Psychological research in pediatric settings: Lessons from the field. *Journal of Pediatric Psychology, 14,* 63–74.

Early Intervention Program for Infants and Toddlers with Handicaps: Final Regulations. (1989). *Federal Register, 54,* 26306–26348.

Eicher, D.M., & Thompson, J.L.P. (1986, February). Alienation, occupational self-direction and worker consciousness: An exploration. *Work and Occupations, 13,* 47–65.

Fitzgerald, M.T., & Fischer, R.M. (1987). A family involvement model for hearing-impaired infants. *Topics in Language Disorders, 7*(3), 1–18.

Fitzgerald, M.T., & Karnes, D.E. (1987). A parent-implemented language model for at-risk and developmentally delayed preschool children. *Topics in Language Disorders, 7*(3), 31–46.

Forester, J. (1982). Planning in the face of power. *Journal of the American Planning Association, 48,* 67–80.

Gardner, S.L. (1992). Key issues in developing school-linked, integrated services. *The Future of Children, 2*(1), 85–94.

Gibson, J.L., Ivancevich, J.M., & Donnelly, J.H., Jr. (1985). *Organizations: Behavior, structure, processes* (5th ed.). Plano, TX: Business Publications Incorporated.

Griffin, G.A. (1991). Interactive staff development: Using what we know. In A. Lieberman & L. Miller (Eds.), *Staff development for education in the '90s: New demands, new realities, new perspectives* (pp. 243–258). New York: Teachers College Press.

Hamblin, R.L., Buckholdt, D., Ferritor, D., Kozloff, M., & Blackwell, L. (1971). *The humanization processes.* New York: John Wiley & Sons.

Hamre-Nietupski, S., Krajewski, L., Riehle, R., Sensor, K., Nietupski, J., Moravec, J., McDonald, J., & Cantine-Stull, P. (1992). Enhancing integration during the summer: Combined education and community recreation options for students with severe disabilities. *Education and Training in Mental Retardation, 27,* 68–74.

Haring, T.G., & Breen, C.G. (1992). A peer-mediated social network intervention to enhance the social integration of persons with moderate and severe handicaps. *Journal of Applied Behavior Analysis, 25,* 319–333.

Home and School Institute. (1985). *Senior corps handbook.* Washington, DC: Home and School Institute.

Hundert, J., & Hopkins, B. (1992). Training supervisors in a collaborative team approach to promote peer interaction of children with disabilities in integrated preschools. *Journal of Applied Behavior Analysis, 25*(2), 385–400.

Kaufman, K.F. (1976). Teaching parents to teach their children: The behavior modification approach. In B. Feingold & C. Bank (Eds.), *Developmental disabilities of early childhood* (pp. 96–120). Springfield, IL: Charles C Thomas.

Kozloff, M.A. (1979). *A program for families of children with learning and behavior problems.* New York: John Wiley & Sons.

Kozloff, M.A. (1983). *Reaching the autistic child.* Cambridge, MA: Brookline Books. (Originally published by Research Press, 1973.)

Kozloff, M.A., Helm, D.T., Cutler, B.C., Douglas-Steele, D., Wells, A., & Scampini, L. (1988). Training programs for families of children with autism or other handicaps. In R.D. Peters & R.J. McMahon (Eds.), *Social learning and systems approaches to marriage and the family* (pp. 217–250). New York: Brunner/Mazel.

Kram, K.E. (1985). *Mentoring at work.* Glenview, IL: Scott, Foresman.

McClure, R.M. (1991). Individual growth and institutional renewal. In A. Lieberman & L. Miller (Eds.), *Staff development for education in the '90s: New demands, new realities, new perspectives* (pp. 221–241). New York: Teachers College Press.

McLaughlin, M.W. (1991). Enabling professional development: What have we learned? In A. Lieberman & L. Miller (Eds.), *Staff development for education in the '90s: New demands, new realities, new perspectives* (pp. 61–82). New York: Teachers College Press.

Meisels, S.J. (1989). Meeting the mandate of Public Law 99-457: Early childhood intervention in the nineties. *American Journal of Orthopsychiatry, 59*(3), 451–460.

Merkel, W.T., & Pollard, C.A. (1987). Applying modern management principles to clinical administration of a behaviorally oriented inpatient unit. *Hospital and Community Psychiatry, 38,* 152–159.

Morril, W.A. (1992). Overview of service delivery to children. *The Future of Children, 2*(1), 32–43.

Nietupski, J., Hamre-Nietupski, S., Houselog, M., Donder, D.J., & Anderson, R.J. (1988, June). Proactive administrative strategies for implementing community-based programs for students with moderate/severe handicaps. *Education and Training in Mental Retardation, 23,* 138–146.

Oja, S.N. (1991). Adult development: Insights on staff development. In A. Lieberman & L. Miller (Eds.), *Staff development for education in the '90s: New demands, new realities, new perspectives* (pp. 37–61). New York: Teachers College Press.

Pavalko, R.M. (1988). *Sociology of occupations and professions* (2nd ed.). Itaska, IL: F.E. Peacock Publishers.

Platt, J.M., & Platt, J.S. (1980). Volunteers for special education: A mainstreaming support system. *Teaching Exceptional Children, 13,* 31–34.

PL 99-457, Education of the Handicapped Act Amendments of 1986. (22 September 1986). *Congressional Record, 132*(125), H 7893–7912.

Rosenholtz, S. (1989). *Teachers' workplace: The social organization of schools.* New York: Longman.

Rosenholtz, S.J. (1984). *Myths: Political myths about reforming teaching.* Denver: Education Commission of the States.

Schein, E.H. (1985). *Organizational culture and leadership.* San Francisco: Jossey-Bass.

Schleien, S.J., Heyne, L.A., & Breihan Berken, S. (1988). Integrating physical education to teach appropriate play skills to learners with autism: A pilot study. *Adapted Physical Activity Quarterly, 5,* 182–192.

Schleien, S.J., Rynders, J.E., & Mustonen, T. (1988). Art and integration: What can we create? *Therapeutic Recreation Journal, 22*(4), 18–29.

Smylie, M.A. (1988). The enhancement function of staff development: Organizational and psychological antecedents to individual teacher change. *American Education Research Journal, 25*(1), 1–30.

Timm, M.A., & Rule, S. (1981). RIP: A cost effective parent-implemented program for young handicapped children. *Early Development and Care, 7,* 147–163.

Willerman, M., McNeely, S.L., & Koffman, E.C. (1991). *Teachers helping teachers: Peer observation and assistance.* New York: Praeger.

Wright, R.O. (1990). *A little bit at a time: Secrets of productive quality.* Berkeley: Ten Speed Press.

CHAPTER 9

INTERVIEWING

INTERVIEWS HAVE TWO SPECIFIC PURPOSES IN SPECIAL EDUCATION. THEY CAN BE USED AS AN ENVIRONment for strengthening caregivers' readiness to participate in school programs, or they can be used to collect assessment information. This chapter examines the two uses of interviews, provides guidelines for conducting interviews, and shows how to transform interview data into assessment information that will be useful for planning programs.

TWO PURPOSES OF INTERVIEWING

One purpose of interviewing is to help caregivers to provide *information* that will be useful in planning or revising education programs for children and assistance for caregivers. Methods for collecting and using interview information are found throughout this chapter.

Interviews are also used to strengthen and sustain caregivers' *readiness.* This author and his colleagues identified 38 features of successful education programs. Nine items concern caregivers' readiness to participate in school programs. Caregivers who reveal strength on the nine readiness items are likely to participate effectively in transdisciplinary teams, training programs, and curricula with a developmental-functional orientation. Those who are weak on the nine items, however, will have difficulty participating. Thus, it is important to assess caregiver readiness.

The nine readiness items, as well as 29 other features of successful programs, are described in the *Family and School Assessment and Programming Guide* (*FSAPG*), which can be found in the companion to this book, *Guidelines and Protocols for Practice.* Items are usually defined in terms of caregiver behaviors. For example, the following is Item 1 of the *FSAPG.*

1. **A caregiver trusts his or her consultant (trainer, mentor, assessment interviewer, team partner).**

    A caregiver believes that the consultant respects his or her abilities, needs, and intentions; keeps personal information confidential; and shares his or her interests in meeting a child's needs. For example, the caregiver:
    a. Smiles and nods frequently at the consultant.
    b. Is at ease—smiles, jokes, makes eye contact, addresses consultant by name.
    c. Discusses topics and shares information that might otherwise make a person feel vulnerable (e.g., personal troubles).
    d. Indicates trust by stating, for example, "You are different from others we have gone to for help," or "You are so easy to talk to."

Challenges: Lack of trust may be indicated by the following. A caregiver:

a. Does not seem at ease—rarely smiles or nods, has a serious expression, addresses consultant by title.
b. Presents little information of a potentially threatening nature.
c. Makes statements such as "Some people are more interested in research than in helping families" or "How do I know you won't let others see videotapes of my teaching?"

[Sources include a caregiver's comments and demeanor during interviews and observations; *CLI* questions 5–8; *CIQ* questions 162–182.]

Caregivers can use the *FSAPG* to assess and keep track of their own and each other's readiness. Mr. Eaton, for instance, teaches a sixth grade class in the school where Juan is enrolling. While interviewing Juan's adoptive parents, the Silvas, Mr. Eaton is alert to behaviors of the Silvas that are relevant to the nine readiness items. He uses his impressions of their readiness (e.g., trust and expectations of success) to guide how he asks questions and responds to the Silvas' answers. This helps to strengthen or sustain their readiness.

Readiness can be strengthened in several interview situations. For example: 1) parents enrolling their child in school, 2) administrators interviewing prospective staff and volunteers, 3) administrators helping staff specify personal goals and identify what they need from the organization, 4) peer and mentor coaches helping partners identify goals and evaluate performance, 5) trainers interviewing prospective trainees, and 6) caregivers being interviewed as part of the assessment of children's psychosocial development.

Techniques for strengthening readiness include arranging a comfortable environment; expressing empathy; helping interviewees create a success story; demonstrating competence; describing the benefits of teaming, training, and involvement in children's educations; and handling reservations about participation. These techniques are discussed in detail later in this chapter.

GUIDELINES FOR INTERVIEWING

Interviewing is complex. Mishler (1986) points out that the interview

> is a form of discourse . . . [that is] shaped and organized by asking and answering questions. An interview is a joint product of *what* interviewees and interviewers talk about together and *how* they talk with each other. The record of an interview . . . is a representation of that talk." (emphasis added) (Mishler, p. vii)

Interviewers do not just ask questions and receive rich, relevant answers. What interviewers receive (e.g., openness) is a function of what they give (e.g., empathetic listening). Interviewing is complex because it is emotionally charged. It may raise issues of trust, honesty, power, self-worth, and the remembrance or disclosure of painful events. An interviewer's success at handling such issues and strengthening interviewees' readiness is affected by three occurrences: 1) understanding an interviewee's perspective, 2) understanding interviews as storytelling, and 3) arranging a comfortable environment.

Interviewee's Perspective

Many parents experience sadness because of their child's disability, wonder if they are in any way to blame, and worry about the future. In addition, family resources may be taxed and parents may be angry with relatives and professionals for not providing adequate help. Many families are bewildered by children's needs and feel personally responsible for insufficient progress. They may, in addition, feel isolated, stigmatized, misunderstood, and vulnerable. School staff may have similar experiences. (See chap. 2, this volume.)

As a result of their experiences, caregivers may be sensitive to an interviewer's demeanor and questions (even when the interviewer is a peer coach or team member). Specifically, caregivers may be sensitive to an interviewer's possible: 1) lack of real interest in or empathy for the caregiver's experience; 2) concern only for quick answers; 3) lack of appreciation for the caregiver's effort, expertise, and successes; 4) belief that the caregiver is not doing enough; 5) lack of honesty about the interview (to help children or to find shortcomings?); and 6) lower competence than the role of interviewer implies. Thus, interviewers must monitor their behavior and be responsive to interviewees' sensitivities. In this way, interviewers will be better able to express interest, empathy, appreciation, honesty, and competence, thereby strengthening caregivers' readiness and increasing the amount of useful assessment information.

Storytelling and Empowerment

The Hardys participated in an assessment interview a few years ago when they enrolled Jerry in school for the first time. They were asked questions from an interview schedule (e.g., "How old was Jerry when you realized something was wrong with his development?") and felt constrained to give brief answers ("Jerry was 2 years old."). Although the interview took 2 hours, it yielded superficial information. Neither the interviewer nor the Hardys learned *how* the Hardys had come to believe Jerry had a disability, how family members handled feelings, or how the perception of Jerry as having "something wrong" affected exchanges with him. Yet, the interviewer and the Hardys needed this information to develop plans to increase family resources and further Jerry's psychosocial development.

In addition, the Hardys were dissatisfied by the interview. It felt so disempowering. After all, the interviewer chose the questions, said little about himself, controlled the time the Hardys had to answer, decided when the interview was over, and did not give the Hardys a chance to comment on the interviewer's behavior, their feelings about the interview, or the interviewer's analysis of their own demeanor and answers. That is one reason why the Hardys never took part in the school's parent training; they feared it would be unenlightening and disempowering.

Much social interaction involves telling stories—about childhood, jobs, hopes, and plans. Creating and telling stories is one way people make sense of and direct their lives. An interview can be an environment where interviewees develop and tell their stories (Mishler, 1986). The interviewer can assist the interviewee to: 1) remember and reveal charged events; 2) put feelings, thoughts, and happenings into words; 3) discover patterns (meanings, themes, morals); 4) change old stories (e.g., sad tales) by reinterpreting events and trends; 5) realize a story's implications; and 6) act on the realization.

Interviews can empower interviewees to "find and speak in their own 'voices'" (Mishler, 1986, p. 118) and to "apply the understanding arrived at to action in accord with [their] own interests" (p. 119). For instance, when Mr. Eaton helps the Silvas realize how much they have done for Juan's development, even though the Silvas have had few outside resources, they will become energized to get what they need to be even more effective.

Arranging a Comfortable Interview Environment

Scheduling, physical environment, creating a partnership, and closing are all features of an environment that help to put interviewees at ease.

Scheduling Interviews should be scheduled when convenient for interviewees. Indicate how long interviews may last and try to adhere to the time frame. When interviewing families, suggest, if applicable, that both parents attend. If that is not possible, or if the child is from a single-parent family, ask that another person come along who may assist in the child's education or assist the family. The interview should be in a convenient and comfortable place for interviewees. This might be a family's home or a teacher's classroom. This author and his colleagues have even interviewed caregivers in restaurants and cars (e.g., while a parent was running errands).

Physical Environment   The interview partners should sit at a comfortable conversational distance and face each other. The interviewer should not sit at a desk or in a larger chair, as this suggests hierarchy. Lighting should be soft and wall decorations should be relaxing or signify common interests (e.g., pictures of children playing). The room should be quiet and private and the interviewee should have easy access to tissues, paper and pencil, refreshments, and toilet facilities (Gorden, 1992). The interviewer should dress in a way that balances formality and informality. Wearing a grey suit when visiting a family is as much of a turnoff as jeans and a tee shirt.

Creating a Partnership   To create a partnership during an interview, it is best to explain the interview in a way that begins to instill trust and confidence (two features of readiness). The following excerpt is from the start of the first interview with the Silvas while they were enrolling Juan in school. The interviewer, Mr. Eaton, has two tasks: describe the school program and strengthen the Silvas' readiness to participate in Juan's education.

Mr. Eaton:	Hello Mr. and Ms. Silva (uses family name to signify respect). I'm Bill Eaton (uses his first name, rather than Mr.). I teach our sixth grade class. I want to introduce our school to you—to describe what we try to do for our students and with their families, and how we run classrooms, parents' groups, and the telephone hotline. I'll try to answer any questions you might have.
Ms. Silva:	Well, we are glad to meet you, Bill. Is "Bill" okay?
Mr. Eaton:	Yes, please.
Ms. Silva:	Then please call me Selena.
Mr. Silva:	And I'm Bob.
Mr. Eaton:	Hi. I see from this information sheet that you adopted Juan (uses active voice, rather than "Juan was adopted") about 4 months ago. He was at the Pinebrook Center for most of his life, wasn't he?
Ms. Silva:	Yes.
Mr. Eaton:	In a very real way, you two have given him a life.
Mr. Silva:	Well, I don't know (blushes).
Mr. Eaton:	I don't mean to embarrass you, but I've been to Pinebrook many times. No matter how many new carpets they put down, it's still not a home. (Creates a context for the Silvas to talk about the home they are giving Juan.)
Ms. Silva:	I guess that's what we want for Juan—a home.
Mr. Eaton:	Well, I won't embarrass you any more by saying that Juan is a lucky fellow, but I will say that I believe we're on the same side. We, too, want to assist Juan to live enjoyably in society. I guess that's what I hear you saying you want, too. (Suggests that they have similar goals. Sets stage for Silvas to elaborate.)
Mr. Silva:	Yes. But, you know, it is not so easy. He's a great kid. He has a lot of smarts and heart. But . . . (pauses).
Mr. Eaton:	(Does not interrupt Mr. Silva's silence.)
Mr. Silva:	I'm trying to say that we don't know how to help him talk better, play sports, and do a lot of other things. And we worry about his future. Will he ever ride a bus, go shopping, have a job?
Mr. Eaton:	(Leans forward) Yes. It isn't easy (expresses empathy). But maybe ("maybe" indicates cautious optimism and honesty) together we can figure out what will assist you to help Juan. If *you think* you *want* it, we can show you how to teach Juan a lot of skills (asserts that the Silvas have control), and we can make plans for his future and work together to achieve one goal after another. (Mr. Eaton indicates that he, the school, and the Silvas can be partners. He stresses empowerment of the Silvas by

assisting them to learn what they might want to know, rather than what he thinks they should know.)

The above vignette shows how Mr. Eaton explains the purpose of the interview, indicates that his and the school's goals may be similar to the Silvas' goals, and stresses the Silvas' empowerment. To increase the sense of partnership, an interviewer might also discuss the following issues:

1. Protection of *privacy* (e.g., written documents and tape recordings will be in locked drawers in locked rooms, and written permission must be obtained from interviewees before information is given to anyone not on a list approved by interviewees).
2. Interviewees' right to be identified if they wish (e.g., having innovative ideas cited in group meetings or newsletters).
3. Interviewees are not objects of study, but reporters (persons on the scene) and informants (people in the know).
4. Interviewees can take notes just as the interviewer does.
5. The record of an interview (e.g., interviewer's notes and later analyses) are joint property that interviewees have a right to review and amend (Mishler, 1986).

With regard to any sort of tape recording, one should obtain permission ahead of time, keep recorders in plain sight, and discuss the protection of privacy.

Closing the Interview   It is wise to take a break in the middle of a long interview and to end on time or when attention weakens. If needed, another interview can be scheduled. It is important to express appreciation for interviewees' time and willingness to share information. Interviewees can be asked if they have questions or wish to add or change anything said earlier (Sommer & Sommer, 1986). The interviewer can even suggest that interviewees go home and think about the interview. During subsequent interviews, they can bring up anything they thought about.

ASKING QUESTIONS

Important considerations when asking questions during an interview are strategies, phrasing, and pacing.

Strategies

There are two strategies for developing and asking questions during an interview: deductive and inductive. Deduction is useful when topics have specific features relevant to most interviewees. A family's experiences trying to receive assistance is one such topic. This author and his colleagues used the deductive strategy for developing questions for the *Caregiver Life Interview* (*CLI*), which can be found in *Guidelines and Protocols for Practice*.

First, the topic was *conceptualized*. What is meant by "experiences trying to receive assistance"? After much discussion, it was agreed that the topic involved the following: the kinds of help a family sought, the sequence of persons or places contacted, the help received, and parents' evaluations. Next, questions were developed for each of the *specific* experiences. Below are questions 5–8 of the *CLI*.

5. Please tell me where you have gone over the years for assistance with (child). Start with the first person or place you went to. (Caregivers then list names or places, dates, specialties, and help sought.)
6. I would like to know what *kind* of help you received from each place or person. (Caregivers describe and evaluate the help from each place or person.)
7. Please tell me what schools or programs (child) has attended. (Caregivers indicate dates, educational or treatment methods used, results, home-school coordination, and their evaluations.)

8. Please tell me about other kinds of help, such as training for yourself in how to teach (child) or how to obtain services, counseling for yourself or for the family, baby-sitting or home child care, homemaker services, respite care, after-school and summer programs. (Caregivers then describe whether they received any such services, and, if so, the timeliness and benefits of the services.)

The inductive strategy, in contrast, is useful when a topic does *not* imply specific experiences, or even similar experiences for different people. Questions about such topics would be general and open-ended. They would invite an interviewee to develop his or her own story. The topic of societal reaction is an example.

Societal reaction involves distancing reactions (e.g., stares) that children and caregivers receive from an "audience." In this author's opinion, the deductive strategy (e.g., asking about specific distancing reactions received from specific persons in specific places) would not be useful. The reason is that societal reaction is often deeply felt by caregivers and may have wide-reaching effects on how they see themselves and participate in the community. Thus, caregivers should explore societal reaction in *their own way*—not be constrained by preformed questions that assume that the interviewer already knows what is relevant. Moreover, a few preformed questions would not yield a rich picture of the experience of societal reaction.

Using an inductive strategy, the *CLI* asks open-ended questions about societal reaction. The interviewer then probes for clarification and elaboration. Below are questions 9–11, concerning societal reaction, from the *CLI*. Brackets suggest probes.

9. Please tell me what stands out in your memory when you think about how other people react to (child). [Strangers, other teachers, friends, family, and neighbors; caregivers' feelings about other people's reactions.] (Note that the question does not bias the answer toward negative experiences.)
10. What stands out in your memory when you think about how other people have reacted to you as a parent [or teacher] of a child with special needs?
11. Please tell me all about being with (child) in public. [Homes of neighbors and relatives, stores, movies, restaurants.] (Interviewer probes for where the caregiver takes the child, how often, the child's behavior in these places, and the caregiver's response to the situation.)

Question 9 invites interviewees to talk about any aspect of societal reaction they wish. The interviewer then helps the interviewee build a bigger picture. Juan's parents, for instance, began answering question 9 in the following way:

Mr. Silva: We were at the Twin Creeks Mall, buying Juan new clothes. There were some kids hanging around smoking. They saw Juan coming. You know how he walks kind of awkward? Well, I could see them staring and talking about Juan.

Mr. Eaton: Mm hmm.

Ms. Silva: It hurt. Pretty bad. Made me mad, too.

Mr. Silva: We decided, well, we're not going to let anybody make Juan feel ashamed. We wouldn't go there anymore.

Ms. Silva: But we knew that keeping Juan away from public places would only make *us* feel better. It wouldn't do Juan any good. In fact, it would be just like before for him. You know—walled in.

Mr. Eaton wants to know more. He probes by asking, "So, how do you feel about taking Juan to public places *now*?" The Silvas say they receive more accepting reactions than distancing ones, and so they feel good about going places with Juan. Mr. Eaton asks more probe questions about *where* the family goes and how Juan *participates*.

In sum, the inductive combination of open-ended general questions followed by probes for details helps interviewees tell their own stories—connecting one event to another, connecting events and feelings, relating one family member's experiences to another's experiences, and tracing events through time.

General to Specific Many topics require several questions. Whether a deductive or inductive strategy is used, it is well to move from general to specific questions. Answers to the first (general) questions help interviewees remember details asked about later. For instance, the *CLI* explores a family's round of daily life and the child's participation. Note the progression in questions 27–32 (abbreviated versions) on the *CLI*. Probes are in brackets.

27. Please give me a brief picture of daily life in your family [or school] from getting up in the morning through the night. [In the case of teachers, start with arriving at school.] What are the major portions of each day, the activities in each major portion, and the tasks in each activity?

28. For each task and activity that you mentioned, please tell me more about (child's) involvement or what (child) is doing. [Ask about the child's: 1) *proximity* (e.g., where the child is when breakfast is being made or a group lesson is taking place); 2) *awareness* of what is going on; and 3) *participation*.]

29. During each task and activity, is anyone with (child)? What, if anything, do you (and/or others) do to get (child) to be present, interested in, attentive to, and participating in what is going on? How successful do you believe your efforts are?

30. Also, during each task and activity, how much would you say that (child) needs to be *supervised;* that is helped, looked after, or watched? Would you say none (1), a little (2), some or a moderate amount (3), a lot (4), or almost complete or constant (5)? (The interviewee translates the answer to a score on a five-point scale.)

31. Now, please rate each task and activity that we just talked about on how easy or difficult it is for you. Very easy (1), moderately difficult (3), and quite hard (5).

32. Are there any differences in your round of daily life—the major portions, activities, or tasks—from day to day or from weekdays to weekend days? If so, what are the differences?

As can be seen, question 27 asks for a general description of daily life. Subsequent questions fill in the details.

Phrasing Questions

The following guidelines may increase an interviewee's trust in the interviewer, his or her understanding of questions, and his or her memory of relevant experiences.

First, when starting a new topic, ask questions that *"stir up associations* and stimulate the respondent's memory and help him or her to relive the original experience" (Gorden, 1992, p. 26). In Chapter 8, this volume, for example, Ms. Reed told her mentor, Ms. Wright, that she was unhappy with her handling of children's problem behaviors. Before Ms. Wright can offer much help, however, she needs details. Which problem behaviors? What methods of handling them? To jog Ms. Reed's memory, Ms. Wright asks, "Tell me about the worst day and the best day you have ever had interacting with students." Undoubtedly, Ms. Reed will vividly recall extreme days. After Ms. Reed describes exchanges with children during the best and worst days, Ms. Wright asks what differences there are between the extreme days and now.

Second, ask questions that suggest an interviewee's *unique qualifications*. This increases the incentive to give accurate, detailed information (Gorden, 1992). For instance, during an assessment interview with the Silvas a week after Juan was enrolled, Mr. Eaton wanted to find out the effective cues, prompts, and reinforcers for Juan. He prefaced specific questions by saying, "Now, you have seen Juan learning and doing all kinds of behavior over the past 4 months—coming into the kitchen for supper, getting dressed, cooperating with requests, and so forth. At this point, you probably know a good deal about how he learns. Let's take things that are rewards or reinforcers for him . . . ."

By suggesting that the Silvas have special knowledge, Mr. Eaton indicates that they have important contributions to make. His recognition also gives them incentive to support the claim that they are knowledgeable by remembering Juan's behavior and rewarding events.

Third, the interviewer should maximize the message that he or she is *sensitive and empathetic* (Gorden, 1992; Kozloff, 1979). Thus, the *CLI* suggests prefacing interviews in the following way:

> I know that this is not news to you. Being the parent (or other relative) of a child with disabilities is not easy. There is the plain fact that the child is not the child whom the family expected. Then there is the money that has to be spent on tests and doctors, the difficulty of satisfying a child's needs, and the reactions of other people. I would like us to start by talking about what your family life has been like from the time you found out that (child) has a disability.

Similarly, before asking about marital or co-worker interaction, the *CLI* says:

> Trying to live with, cope with, and teach children with special needs makes special demands on parents [or teachers]. So, I would like to ask you a few questions about the ways that you work together as a family [or team].

Such prefatory comments suggest the interviewer's appreciation for interviewees' feelings.

Fourth, *provide definitions.* For instance, one topic on the *CLI* is alienation versus authenticity. If an interviewer asks Mrs. Hardy, "Do you ever feel alienated from your children, spouse, or yourself?", Mrs. Hardy would say "no" because to her "alienation" means anger at something. However, on the *CLI* "alienation" means detachment and a sense of unreality. Although Mrs. Hardy sometimes feels detached from her family (by definition alienation), her "no" answer is erroneously taken by the interviewer to indicate no alienation. Thus, before asking caregivers about alienation, question 40 on the *CLI* defines it, as shown below:

> 40.   When tasks, a line of work, or even our roles in life seem forced on us, or when we feel we are not successful at what we have to do, we may get the feeling that what we are doing is no longer part of us, is strange, is not quite real anymore . . . . We can almost hear ourselves say things such as, "Where am I?" or "Who am I?" . . . Such feelings and thoughts, called "alienation," are understandable. Can you tell me if the feelings I have just described seem familiar to you?

With the definition of alienation in mind, Mrs. Hardy is more likely to say, "Yes. I guess I do feel that way sometimes. Alienated."

Fifth, *provide a time perspective* (Gorden, 1992). For instance, caregivers' views of a child's development are important. The *CLI* helps caregivers describe a child's development during a specific time period by phrasing question 43 as follows:

> 43.   During the past 6 months, what changes would you say have taken place in (child) that stand out in your mind—either desirable or undesirable changes?

Without a time frame, Mrs. Hardy might cite improvements in Jerry's manual dexterity that occurred years ago, which an interviewer may assume are recent improvements.

Sixth, *use words that are clearly understood.* Also use *concrete terms.* For instance, it is unwise to say, "Tell me about Juan's knowledge of time and space." What counts for knowledge? What are time and space? Instead, ask, "Does Juan *do* anything that leads you to believe that he knows *where* things go, where things happen, *when* things are going to happen, or when things did happen? If so, what does he do?" In addition, ask if interviewees understand the terms; provide definitions if needed.

Seventh, *avoid loaded questions*. One load is emotional. For example, the question, "Do you ever feel like spanking your child?" will evoke anxiety in some people. Thus, they may say "no" even though they have occasionally spanked their child. Similarly, the question, "How do you get along with one another?" may result in spouses saying, "Oh, fine," even though they argue. To avoid emotional loading, the *CLI* phrases question 26, about marital interaction, in a neutral way:

> 26. In general, tell me if or how living with [or teaching] (child) has affected your relationship with one another—not only ways your relationship may have been strained, but ways it might have become stronger, too.

Bias is a second load. The question, "How have services been inadequate over the years?" leads people to think of and report negative experiences, even if they have had positive experiences. Thus, the *CLI* phrases question 5 in a way that invites interviewees to express their own view.

> 5. Please tell me where you have gone over the years for assistance with (child). Start with the first person or place you went to. (The interviewer then asks the interviewee to evaluate each.)

Note, too, how the earlier question about marital interaction invited an interviewee to cite both positive and negative experiences. Similarly, the question about alienation implied that it is normal under stressful conditions. Such phrasing increases the chances that interviewees will give accurate and rich answers.

Pacing

There are three guidelines for pacing. First, allow time to answer. The point is to assist in the creation of a story. Thus, the interviewer should avoid looking at his or her watch; fidgeting; nodding rapidly (as though to say, "Get on with it."); or saying, "Well, now to the next question." Second, do not interrupt, as it breaks the flow of the narrative. It also may give the impression that the interviewee is boring, saying too much, or saying things that are irrelevant. Third, gently help an interviewee to stay near the topic. The difference between weaving a bigger picture (to be encouraged) and straying farther away usually becomes clear. In the latter case, one might say, "I think we may be getting a bit too far away from what we were talking about. You were telling me about how you handle Jerry's tantrums?"

EVALUATING AND INTERPRETING RESPONSES

Interviewers must evaluate and properly respond to interviewees' behaviors throughout the interview. There are two kinds of interviewee behavior to consider: 1) vocal and nonvocal messages about perceptions and feelings, and 2) answers to questions (which may be supplemented by nonvocal messages, such as facial expressions).

Evaluating Messages About Perceptions and Feelings

Interviewees express perceptions and feelings about many things: the interview, the interviewer, a school's programs, themselves, their children, and their family or co-workers. Some messages are direct. For instance, Mr. Silva smiles and says, "Bill, I feel that I can trust you." Often, messages are indirect. For instance, in response to the question, "Would you say that you get enough support from your relatives?", Ms. Silva's face reddens, she smirks, and says, "Oh, yeah, right!"

Whether a message is direct or indirect, understanding its meaning involves interpreting (often guessing). As such, interpretations may be checked out by more questions. For example, Mr.

Eaton hears Ms. Silva's above response as expressing an assumption that families should support their members, confusion about why her relatives provide little support, and pain and anger. Mr. Eaton checks his interpretation by asking follow-up questions such as: 1) "You don't get much help from relatives?"; 2) "You expected more, did you?"; 3) "Were any relatives more helpful than others?"; and 4) "Do I hear you right? You are pretty bitter, angry, maybe hurt?"

It is often essential to be familiar with interviewees' backgrounds. How interviewees express feelings and understand questions is affected by sex, social class, and culture. For instance, persons of Asian descent may smile when unhappy. American women may express sadness through tears and direct commentary, whereas American men may remain physically tense and silent (Lynch & Hanson, 1992; Tannen, 1990).

Below are examples of this author's interpretations of messages about feelings and perceptions. Note, again, that interpretations depend on an interviewer's familiarity with an interviewee's personal and cultural background.

1. Direct eye contact, nods, smiles, relaxed postures, and comments, such as "You certainly are different from others we have seen for help over the years" or "You are so easy to talk to" may indicate trust. Less trust is perhaps implied by arms folded across the chest, avoidance of eye contact, tight lips, frowns, questions such as "How can I be sure that what we say stays in this room?", and comments such as "Not many people know what it's like to be a teacher."

2. Confidence in the interviewer and/or in the interviewer's school may be indicated by smiles and nods in response to the interviewer's suggestions, as well as by comments such as "I feel that you can help us" or "At last someone understands." Less confidence is perhaps shown by looking away when the interviewer is talking and remarks such as "You know, we had Billy in a program like this before" or "I don't think that method will work."

3. Optimism might be heard in comments such as "Well, we've never given up and we're not going to start now"; "If other parents can do it, so can we"; or "It might take awhile, but Indra is going to walk." Comments such as these that are said with steady eye contact and a forceful voice indicate optimism. Less optimism is suggested by comments such as "We've tried everything and nothing has worked" or "Maybe it will work" said with a soft voice.

4. High energy may be heard in forceful comments, such as "I may be tired, but I'll give it my best shot." Low energy may be signified by a low rate of speaking and remarks, such as "You know, I'm not as strong as I used to be."

Note that messages about perceptions and feelings (e.g., energy, optimism, trust) may be relevant to a caregiver's readiness to participate in a collaborative relationship.

Evaluating Answers to Questions

Answers can be evaluated with respect to relevance, completeness, and validity (Gorden, 1992). Consider question 20 from the *CLI*.

20. We have been talking about behaviors that you do not like. Now, let us talk about the behaviors or skills you would like to see (child) do better, more often, or in more places; in other words, desirable behaviors. At this time, do you try to teach or direct (child) to do certain desirable behaviors, such as cooperating, communicating, playing, or doing chores? If so, please give me examples of what you do, how you teach (child), and how well it seems to work. In other words, how does (child) respond to your teaching efforts, and does (child's) behavior improve?

Gorden (1992) offers the following six guidelines for evaluating the relevance of caregivers' answers. First, does the answer fit major concepts in the question? If an interviewee talks about efforts to teach a child desirable behaviors, it is relevant information. However, if an interviewee says, "Yes, my husband and I *talked* about teaching Sally to choose her own clothes for school," the information (though useful) is not relevant to the topic of *actual* teaching efforts. The interviewer must ask follow-up questions, such as "Great! And have you begun to teach her to choose clothing?"

Second, "is the information about the right object, person or event" (p. 123)? Information about teaching siblings may not be relevant to the question of teaching the child with a disability.

Third, "is the information about the relevant time period" (p. 124)? If the question asked begins with, "At this time, do you try to teach . . . ?" and the interviewee talks about teaching when the child was younger, or about plans for the future, the information, though important, is irrelevant to the question. The interviewer should follow up with questions about the present.

Fourth, "is the information about the relevant place" (p. 125)? Describing how a child behaves at a neighbor's house would be irrelevant if the question asked is about restaurants and parks.

Fifth, does the response cover the how and why of the events asked about? For example, a caregiver might answer the question about teaching desirable behaviors by stressing how much he or she *wants* desirable behaviors to improve, and how *hard* he or she tries. Yet, if the caregiver does not describe *what* he or she does, then the information, though important, is somewhat irrelevant to the question.

Sixth, is the information at the correct level of abstraction? The above question asks about specific behaviors, teaching, and outcomes. If the interviewee talks about "rewarding good behavior," or says "Yes, she's better now," such information, though meaningful to the interviewee, is too general. The interviewer must ask for elaboration.

In addition to relevance, Gorden advises evaluating *completeness*. Of course, there are no complete answers. At issue is whether information is sufficiently detailed for practical purposes (e.g., program planning). The discussion below has several points that beg for elaboration.

Mr. Eaton: Could you describe Juan's participation during the evening meal—cooking, eating, and clean up?

Mr. Silva: Oh, he participates *pretty much*. He's there *watching* us cook. He helps out *some,* too. During the meal, he *dishes* himself food, passes *what* you ask him, and eats pretty *neatly*. Afterward, he'll *stay* and *help* clean up if you *ask* him.

Mr. Silva's information is relevant. He talks about the present and focuses on behaviors that fit a definition of "participation." However, more information is needed (indicated by words in italics). Thus, Mr. Eaton asks probe questions. For example:

Mr. Eaton: Very nice! I'm glad to hear that Juan is so involved. That must feel pretty good.

Mr. Silva: It does.

Mr. Eaton: Fill me in on a few things, okay? You said that Juan is there watching you cook. Is he close to the action or on the other side of the room? Is he paying a lot of attention, or just occasionally noticing what you are doing? And how long does he watch? (Mr. Eaton might give Mr. Silva the chance to answer each question separately.)

After Mr. Silva answers the first probe, Mr. Eaton requests more detail. For instance: "Is Juan interested in some cooking tasks more than others?", "How does he help?", "What cues start him helping?" Such information can be used to plan teaching programs for home and school.

Finally, Gorden (1992) suggests evaluating the *validity* of information. Clues to validity include the following:

1. Consistency between words and nonvocal behavior. For instance, Ms. Silva smiles, looks at Mr. Silva, and has a relaxed posture while saying that Mr. Silva helps her a lot.
2. Consistency between several pieces of information supplied by the interviewee. Late in the

interview, for example, Mr. Silva says, "Yes, Juan is a cooperative kid." Earlier, he had given examples of Juan's cooperation.

3. Consistency between interviewees. For instance, Mr. and Ms. Silva both assert that Juan hears well.
4. Consistency between what interviewees say and what the interviewer already believes to be the case based on other information.

RESPONDING

There are six ways to respond to messages and answers so as to sustain partnership, strengthen readiness, and enable interviewees to build their story. These include expressing empathy, building understanding, probing for clarification and elaboration, creating a success story, suggesting action, and addressing reservations.

Empathy

Some interviewer responses communicate that the interviewer understands, and under similar conditions would share, an interviewee's feelings. For instance, when a caregiver describes a difficult situation, the interviewer can lean forward, nod his or her head, and say "Mm hmm," "I think I understand," or "That must have been tough." When a caregiver relates uplifting events, the interviewer displays empathy through smiles, nodding, and comments such as "Yes, it sounds like that made you happy."

Building Understanding

There are two benefits of teaching concepts and principles. First, it helps empower interviewees by enabling them to describe and analyze events. This also increases expectations of success. Second, it demonstrates an interviewer's competence, thus increasing interviewees' confidence. The following excerpt shows an interviewer providing concepts that *label* events.

Ms. Reed: (Describes worst day.) During the reading lesson, Tim whined and whined. I stared at him. Then I told him to stop. Finally, I went and sat with him. Then he was quiet and did his reading. This happened day after day.

Ms. Wright: Sounds tiring.

Ms. Reed: But I knew that going over and sitting with Tim positively reinforced all of the whining.

Ms. Wright: Good observation!

Ms. Reed: Yet, I kept on reinforcing the whining—against my better judgment! I don't understand why!

Ms. Wright: It bothers you that you reacted in a way that you knew was not productive. (Interpretation)

Ms. Reed: Yes. Like I was out of control!

Ms. Wright: Well, I can imagine how frustrating that would be. We've all been there. Look, one reason you kept reinforcing Tim's whining was that you had not found an easy enough alternative response. The other reason is that Tim *always reinforced you* for reinforcing him!

Ms. Reed: Reinforced me? How?

Ms. Wright: By stopping his whining as soon as you sat with him. That's *negative* reinforcement. Sitting with him resulted in speedy *removal* of a painful event. (Ms. Wright then helps Ms. Reed to identify other examples of negative reinforcement.)

The next vignette with Ms. Tyler, Jerry's teacher, and Mrs. Hardy, Jerry's mother, illustrates *post-dicting* (predicting past events) in a way that increases the interviewee's understanding and appreciation of the interviewer's competence.

Ms. Tyler:	So, Jerry keeps you on the run all day by making messes and getting into things. That sounds very tiring.
Mrs. Hardy:	And he's hard to take at night. In and out of bed, getting a drink, yelling from his room, knocking on our door.
Ms. Tyler:	That must strain the nerves! (Empathizes.)
Mrs. Hardy:	I'll say!
Ms. Tyler:	So how do you handle Jerry's nighttime behavior? (Sets occasion to help Mrs. Hardy analyze exchanges and demonstrate Ms. Tyler's competence.)
Mrs. Hardy:	Well, we tried ignoring it, but it didn't work.
Ms. Tyler:	I bet when you stopped responding to his yelling and roaming around, his behavior went through the roof! He talked louder and longer—maybe even pounded on your door—to get you to respond. (Ms. Tyler post-dicts a past event.)
Mrs. Hardy:	Exactly! He yelled "Mommy!" a trillion times!
Ms. Tyler:	What happened was an "extinction burst." It's very common. When a behavior stops paying off, we try harder to get the rewards back. Like banging on a soda machine that won't deliver.
Mrs. Hardy:	Yeah! So, the extinction burst explains why I get upset and try harder whenever Jerry stops doing good behaviors that I'm used to him doing.

If employed several times during an interview, post-dicting can be a convincing demonstration of competence. After all, the interviewer must know something if he or she can predict what happens when he or she is not even there.

Clarification and Elaboration

When an answer seems incomplete, ambiguous, irrelevant to the question, or inconsistent with other information, the interviewer probes for clarification and elaboration. The following probes are offered by Gorden (1992); Kozloff (1979); and Willerman, McNeely, and Koffman (1991).

1. The interviewer offers *encouragement*, such as "Go on," "Mm hmm," "I see, and . . . ," and "Yeah!"
2. The interviewer uses *silence*, as shown below.

Mr. Silva:	When I try to teach Juan to play catch, he just drops the ball like his hands are made of rubber. I feel like . . . Oh, I don't know.
Mr. Eaton:	(Keeps looking in Mr. Silva's direction, but says nothing.)
Mr. Silva:	. . . like he'll never learn. (Mr. Eaton will follow up on this response.)

3. The interviewer offers an *interpretation or paraphrases* what the interviewee said. For example: "Are you saying that you feel pretty confident?"; "I hear you saying that you need more emotional support"; "I could be wrong, but it sounds like you were trying to get some peace and quiet." Below is Mr. Eaton's response to Mr. Silva's last statement.

Mr. Silva:	. . . like he'll never learn.
Mr. Eaton:	You thought maybe he would never learn? And then you felt what—afraid? (Paraphrase plus interpretation.)
Mr. Silva:	Afraid. I guess so. Yes.

4. The interviewer asks for *more information*. For instance: "Wow! Could you give me more details?", "And so (pause)", "Do you have another example of that?" Mr. Eaton asks Mr. Silva for clarification in the following way.

Mr. Silva:	Afraid. I guess so. Yes.
Mr. Eaton:	I think I understand. (Expresses empathy.) You are in the yard teaching Juan to play like other kids do, but he keeps dropping the ball no matter how gently you

	toss it to him. (Recreates memories to stir up feelings.) Then you get scared that he'll never learn. Tell me what you mean when you say "never learn." (Asks for more.) You mean, never learn to play catch? (Interpretation.)
Mr. Silva:	No. More than not playing catch.
Mr. Eaton:	It's more than not playing catch. (Paraphrase.)
Mr. Silva:	Yeah. If I can't teach him something as simple as playing catch, then (pause) . . .
Mr. Eaton:	Yes? (As though to say, "Please continue.")
Mr. Silva:	Then I can't teach him *anything!*
Mr. Eaton:	Can't teach him anything! (Empathizes by reflecting message.) That's a scary thing to think. It would keep a father up at night. (Empathizes.)

Creating a Success Story

A caregiver's interpretations of negative events may be overgeneralized. This can yield stories that are disempowering, which will weaken readiness to participate. For instance, caregivers may overlook and underestimate children's progress and their own competencies and personal strengths. They may overestimate the frequency and impact of their mistakes and children's problem behaviors. They may believe that the course of events has been and will continue to be a sad story or an exercise in futility. Thus, they may have little incentive to participate in training programs, peer coaching, and teaming (see chap. 7, this volume).

Yet, an interviewer should not invalidate an interviewee's evaluations by suggesting that negative events have not happened, or that the interviewee should view events differently. Such remarks may breed resentment. Instead, an interviewer can help an interviewee to identify praiseworthy and beneficial events and reframe negative ones. For example, during a recent assessment interview, Ms. Tyler inserted the following positive comments in response to Mrs. Hardy's comments:

1. "You have an intuitive grasp of learning principles."
2. "You showed a lot of persistence in obtaining services."
3. "I appreciate your willingness to relate events as painful as that."
4. "You and Mr. Hardy reinforce each other a lot, don't you?"
5. "That was great how you prompted before Jerry made errors."
6. "Your descriptions are full of interesting details."
7. "It sounds like Jerry is talking in longer sentences. Your teaching seems to be working."
8. "It sounds like you have really helpful friends."
9. "It's nice to hear you describe your strengths and successes."

The Silva interview, above, is another example of when an interviewer can help a caregiver identify positive events and reframe negative ones. Mr. Silva is creating a story in which Juan dropping the ball is evidence of Juan not learning to play catch. To Mr. Silva, this indicates his own incompetence not only at teaching Juan to play catch, but (overgeneralizing) incompetence at teaching more important behaviors. Given his desire to provide a good home, Mr. Silva may conclude that he is failing Juan. Yet, Mr. Eaton can help Mr. Silva reframe events and rewrite the story.

First, Mr. Eaton can show how playing catch involves more than grabbing the ball out of the air. In other words, *learning a skill is not an all or nothing event.* Has there been any improvement in the way Juan holds the baseball glove, watches the ball, or throws the ball? If so, then perhaps Mr. Silva will agree that Juan's playing has improved in several ways. Using Mr. Silva's logic, Mr. Silva must be effective at teaching some things. Then Mr. Eaton might suggest how Mr. Silva can teach Juan the action of catching. Perhaps Mr. Silva could use a bigger ball or stand closer. Framing the situation as *solving problems rather than documenting incompetence* gives Mr. Silva evidence of success and practical next steps.

Second, Mr. Eaton can suggest that Juan may not be ready to benefit much from instruction on playing catch. Perhaps he is not skillful at component movements, such as flexing and extending fingers. Thus, Mr. Silva need not conclude that he cannot teach or that Juan cannot learn. Instead, Mr. Silva might strengthen the weak links in Juan's catching, or select a different sport entirely.

Third, Mr. Eaton can direct Mr. Silva's attention to the past 4 months. Has Juan learned anything? If Mr. Silva answers "yes," Mr. Eaton can help him compile an impressive list of behavior changes across the five phases of learning (e.g., new behaviors learned, old behaviors that are more fluent and generalized). Then Mr. Eaton can help Mr. Silva describe what he and Ms. Silva did to foster the changes, even if it was without planning (e.g., providing opportunities, prompts, reinforcement). In this way, Mr. Silva creates a record of his effective teaching that he can project into the future.

Suggestions for Action

Interviewers also can help interviewees see the action implications of stories. For example:

1. Having examined Jerry's nighttime behaviors with Mrs. Hardy, Ms. Tyler suggests several new ways to respond.
2. Having learned what the Silvas want, Mr. Eaton suggests how they can get assistance from the school's family network.
3. Having identified improvements in Juan's competence and participation, Mr. Eaton suggests instructional objectives that are within Juan's and his parents' reach.
4. Ms. Tyler and Mr. Eaton point out benefits of the Hardys and Silvas joining a parent training program.

Addressing Reservations

Interviewers can address caregivers' reservations about the developmental-functional approach or about participation in school programs. Below are common reservations and ways to handle them.

First, some caregivers may believe that reinforcement is bribery. This can be addressed by pointing out how common reinforcement is. Caregivers can be asked how long they would work at a hard job if they never received praise or money for it. One can also reframe reinforcement as informational feedback on the corrrectness of behavior, which everyone needs in order to learn. Lastly, one can stress that unusual reinforcement (e.g., continuous schedules) is faded out as children become more skillful.

Second, caregivers may believe that "bad" behavior should be punished. If they defend punishment because they fear that without it they will lose control over a child's problem behaviors, one can give examples of how properly using cues, prompts, and reinforcement enables caregivers to replace problem behaviors without punishment. Also, one can show that punishment is a poor tool because it is nearly impossible to use properly (i.e., immediately, every time, and severe enough to stop the behavior in its tracks) and may have negative side effects.

Third, some caregivers may not see how their behavior affects children's behavior. Thus, they may have little incentive to change their own behavior. In this case, one can identify ways that a caregiver has been effective in improving a child's behavior. Next, one can point out that each person has something like an equation—a set of conditions that the person needs in order to learn. If there have been times when the caregiver was unable to teach some behavior, it is not because he or she is basically incompetent, but that he or she does not know (and can never know) all of a child's needs. By working as a team, the child's needs may be identified and the caregiver will be more effective.

Fourth, a caregiver may be pessimistic about a child's development. In this case, express appreciation for the caregiver's hard work and empathize with the caregiver's frustration and fear. To boost optimism, help the caregiver identify beneficial changes over the years. Show how, without much assistance, the caregiver fostered many of those changes. Using current best practices, there is every reason to believe that the child will change even more.

Fifth, caregivers who are overly stressed may feel too tired to participate in training or teaming. The interviewer can help them relive the process by which they became overly stressed and determine what assistance would have sustained optimism and energy. If feasible, the interviewer can point out how such assistance is offered in the school program (e.g., on-site coaching, helping networks). Then the interviewer can suggest small steps to make the caregiver's life easier (e.g., rearranging some tasks in the home or class, attending a workshop on replacing problem behaviors).

Sixth, some families may assert that assessment, program planning, and teaching are not their job. They may be unaware of the benefits of family involvement. Or, it may be a way to protect themselves from more perceived failure. In either case, an interviewer can identify the benefits of family involvement (better assessment information and, therefore, better instruction; increased ability to teach the child; social support from team members). The interviewer should empathize with families who are overly stressed, but also suggest how school programs will provide what others have not.

COLLECTING ASSESSMENT INFORMATION THROUGH INTERVIEWS

Assessment Interviews

Interviewing plays a major role in both comprehensive and specific assessments. Assessment interviews with families are either part of a comprehensive assessment of children and family life, or a part of a training program for families. The practices described on the following pages can easily be used in assessment interviews with other caregivers as well.

Comprehensive Assessments   Children should receive a comprehensive assessment soon after they are enrolled in school, perhaps each year thereafter, and whenever there are major questions about progress or placement. A comprehensive assessment of a child requires information on two sets of variables: 1) variables that describe psychosocial development (e.g., medical condition, competencies, participation); and 2) variables that describe the child's environments (e.g., child–caregiver exchanges, the organization of the round of daily life). Several methods are used to collect information on each set. These include direct observation (the subject of chap. 10, this volume), questionnaires, caregivers' data, and interviews. (Comprehensive assessment is described in detail in *Guidelines and Protocols.*)

Specific Assessments   Some assessments examine fewer variables and require only one or two methods of data collection (e.g., trainers assessing trainees' strengths and needs when planning curricula, peer and mentor coaches assessing their partners' teaching performance, and administrators helping teams to assess practices and identify needed resources).

Caregiver Life Interview

This author used his understanding of families to develop the *Caregiver Life Interview*. The *CLI* contains 48 questions that help families recall and recount important events from the birth of their child to the present. The *CLI* covers the following topics:

1. How the child's developmental disability was recognized and how members reacted (questions 1–4)
2. History of experiences trying to find assistance (questions 5–8)
3. Experience of societal reaction versus acceptance, and effects on participation in the community (questions 9–13)
4. History of family's efforts to teach their child, exchanges with their child, and child's desirable and undesirable behaviors (questions 14–23)

5. Marital relations (questions 24–26)
6. The organization of tasks and activities in the family's round of daily life (questions 27–34)
7. Family members' reactions to problems (question 35)
8. Family members' assumptions about personal responsibility for the child's development and future life (question 36)
9. Family members' emotional difficulties (questions 37–38)
10. Family members' perceptions of locus of control (question 39)
11. Family members' experiences of authenticity versus alienation (question 40)
12. Obstacles to beneficial change (question 41)
13. Family members' perceptions of desirable and undesirable changes in the family from the time the child was born (question 42)
14. Family members' perceptions of desirable and undesirable changes in the child during the past 6 months, and the factors that have facilitated or hindered beneficial changes (questions 43–47)
15. Family's current needs (question 48)

Using the *CLI* along with interview techniques described in this chapter, interviewers can help families create their story, strengthen readiness, and gather information needed to plan educational programs for children and to help families obtain empowering resources (e.g., on-site assistance, training). Note that the *CLI* can be used for interviewing teachers, therapists, and other caregivers.

Note Taking During Interviews

An easy way to organize note taking is to write each question from the *CLI*, or the interview schedule being used, at the top of separate sheets of paper. The interviewer takes some notes on the sheets while interviewees are talking. Notes might consist of *lists* (e.g., people a family can count on for help) and *key phrases* (e.g., "We really need someone to watch us interact with Jerry."). As soon as possible after an interview, the interviewer should *add to the notes* from memory. Of course, tape recording is a valuable way to gather and save interview data. Still, the interviewer should take notes during recorded interviews and indicate footage to listen to later.

An interviewer's notes can also help score a caregiver's *Family and School Assessment and Programming Guide (FSAPG)* found in *Guidelines and Protocols*. For instance, Mr. Eaton heard Mr. and Ms. Silva's answers to many interview questions. He now has a good idea of how much external social-emotional support the Silvas receive and from whom. He can transfer the information to item 36 on the Silvas' *FSAPG*. By contributing interview information to other *FSAPG* items, Mr. Eaton and the Silvas get an overall view of the family's strengths and needs.

Follow-up interviews may be scheduled at least several days after the first assessment interview. Follow-up interviews give interviewers and interviewees the chance to ask more questions (e.g., probe for clarification), comment on the interview, amend prior answers, and summarize what appear to be the child's and interviewee's strengths and needs.

Notes are valuable only when they are turned into information on three areas: 1) caregivers' readiness (used to guide efforts to strengthen readiness); 2) children's psychosocial development (used to plan educational programs); and 3) caregivers' strengths and needs (used to plan participation and assistance, such as teaming, social support, coaching, respite care, and training). Even when one knows what information is sought, notes do not automatically provide it. Rather, notes must be compiled, summarized, and shaped into forms that say something. Such forms may be lists, stories, and rating scales.

Lists   Question 43 on the *CLI* asks:

43. During the past 6 months, what changes would you say have taken place in (child) that stand out in your mind—either desirable or undesirable changes?

An interviewer's notes can readily be turned into a list with two columns—one for desirable and the other for undesirable changes cited by the caregiver. Such a list could have several practical implications. For instance, if the list has many undesirable and few desirable changes, the interviewer can:

1. Assume that the caregiver is stressed (which can be checked by probes or by other questions on the *CLI*). Thus, the interviewer knows that he or she must empathize and build cautious optimism about the chances of improvement.
2. Expect that the caregiver needs help (perhaps on-site coaching) with child–caregiver exchanges. The caregiver also might benefit from respite care and other assistance.
3. Expect that the child needs to learn a lot of simple desirable alternative ways to affect his or her environment.
4. Suggest that caregivers may have developed a somewhat inaccurate perception of the child. A high rate of undesirable behavior, for example, may make it hard to notice desirable behaviors. Thus, caregivers may need help re-examining perceptions of the child.

Caregivers' answers to question 48 on the *CLI*—concerning types of assistance needed—are another example of raw data that can be turned into useful lists.

Stories: Themes, Vignettes, and Evaluations   Interviewees' answers and comments can express themes, vignettes, and evaluations that are part of a life story. Mrs. Hardy's responses to *CLI* questions 5–8, regarding finding help, reveal several *themes*. Superficially, Mrs. Hardy cites a series of unsuccessful efforts. For instance, a pediatrician said they should wait another year ("By then it was too late!"). A neurologist gave no diagnosis ("Maybe it's autism, maybe it's not.") Jerry's first school was worthless ("He ran around all day."). Yet, throughout her narration, Mrs. Hardy's words and gestures express themes, such as never give up ("So, we went down the hall to see another doctor!"); loving Jerry despite the difficulties; and eternal, but cautious optimism ("Every now and then you do something and it works. He learns!"). These themes suggest that the Hardys are ready to participate in Jerry's program and that they might be great role models for others (e.g., in a family network or training program).

The Silvas' description of societal reaction at the mall is an example of a *vignette*—a slice of life. If the Silvas related episodes of societal reaction that resulted in no longer taking their child to public places, then the interviewer could assume that the family might benefit from discussions with other families and teachers having similar experiences. In addition, the family might benefit from training in how to handle stares and whispers.

Caregivers' responses to many questions on the *CLI* reveal *evaluations* about themselves, their children, their spouse, the family, and the future. For instance, a caregiver might make frequent comments suggesting that personal resources are taxed, external resources are lacking, and the caregiver believes he or she can do little to improve matters. One implication is providing immediate, load-lifting assistance (e.g., help handling the child). In addition, the caregiver may benefit from social support, perhaps from other families. At some point, too, the family division of labor may have to be equalized.

Rating Scales   Some questions on the *CLI* are set up as rating scales. For example, question 30 asks caregivers to rate a child's need for supervision during routine tasks. The ratings are: 1 (none), 2 (a little), 3 (some or a moderate amount), 4 (a lot), and 5 (almost complete or constant). Question 31 asks caregivers to rate the difficulty (e.g., hassle, effort) each task poses for him or her given the child's need for supervision. The ratings are 1 (very easy), 3 (moderately difficult), and 5 (quite hard).

Such estimates provide too little detail for planning programs, but they do direct attention to features of tasks that might be improved. Moreover, by comparing ratings across tasks, one can identify which tasks to work on. For example, if a caregiver rates cooking as most difficult because a child requires a lot of supervision, it suggests that others in the family ought to help supervise the child at this time. Finally, questions about supervision and difficulty can be asked several times over the course of a caregiver's training and/or a child's education to see if there are any perceived changes.

SUMMARY

This chapter presents guidelines for arranging the interview environment, asking questions, evaluating or interpreting interviewees' behaviors, and responding to interviewees' behaviors. It also describes how to use interviews to strengthen caregivers' readiness to participate and to collect assessment information.

REFERENCES

Gorden, R. (1992). *Basic interviewing skills.* Itaska, IL: F.E. Peacock Publishers, Inc.

Kozloff, M.A. (1979). *A program for families of children with learning and behavior problems.* New York: John Wiley & Sons.

Lynch, E.W., & Hanson, M.J. (Eds.). (1992). *Developing cross-cultural competence: A guide for working with young children and their families.* Baltimore: Paul H. Brookes Publishing Co.

Mishler, E.G. (1986). *Research interviewing: Context and narrative.* Cambridge, MA: Harvard University Press.

Sommer, R., & Sommer, B.B. (1986). *A practical guide to behavioral research* (2nd ed.). New York: Oxford University Press.

Tannen, D. (1990). *You just don't understand.* New York: Morrow.

Willerman, M., McNeely, S.L., & Koffman, E. (1991). *Teachers helping teachers: Peer observation and assistance.* New York: Praeger.

DIRECT OBSERVATION

PEOPLE USUALLY HAVE ONE OF THREE VIEWS ABOUT TAKING DATA. AT ONE EXTREME ARE THOSE WHO say it competes with teaching and reduces children to objects. At the other are those who love counting and graphing so much that sometimes these seem more important than what children are learning. The majority, however, are willing to observe and record, but do not know how. This chapter helps the reader become a more proficient observer while avoiding the extremes. It examines direct observation as a way of gathering information during initial assessment and program evaluation and offers suggestions on how to observe effectively and efficiently. It discusses the methods of narrative recording, descriptive analysis, task analysis, event recording, and functional analysis. It also shows how to increase proficiency by creating sound definitions, checking observer reliability, and correcting problems of inaccuracy.

GUIDELINES

This section discusses the selection of events to observe, levels of measurement, how much to record at once, and ways to create a comfortable observation environment.

Benefits of Direct Observation

Direct observation provides the detail needed to adequately understand a child's behavior. For example, Mr. Eaton needs more than a general impression of Juan's performance before he can let Juan cross the street on his own. Mr. Eaton needs to know if Juan looks both ways, crosses only if oncoming vehicles are far off, and walks quickly to the other side. Direct observation can provide such detail.

Direct observation also contributes to the accuracy of knowledge by offering another source of information. For instance, Jerry's teachers describe his climbing and running as clumsy. Likewise, the physical therapist reports that Jerry cannot walk a balance beam. Observations at home confirm the judgment of awkward running; however, Jerry skillfully climbs kitchen counters to get cookies and walks along the back of a couch. These behaviors are invariably followed by someone yelling at him to get down. The common finding of awkward running may point to a real deficit; climbing on counters and walking on couches at home, however, suggest that Jerry's coordination is influenced by familiarity with the environment, incentives, and reinforcement.

Finally, observation provides distance. It is easier for Ms. Tyler to tolerate tantrums when she describes them and thinks of how to respond. Furthermore, observing helps her sustain the attention needed to follow plans.

Degree and Precision of Recording

Observing many behaviors at once and recording with a high degree of precision leads to fatigue and inaccuracy. A general rule is to limit observation and the exactness of measurement to what is needed for decision making.

Exactness   Team members record Jerry's disruptive behavior (e.g., whining, yelling, throwing things) during school lessons. The least exact, although still accurate, measurement would be to keep a *list* of disruptive behaviors observed: "There was whining and yelling, but no throwing." This is measurement at the *nominal* level. Other examples include recording that Luke's speech during play involved one-word and two-word utterances, and that Robin and her mother engaged in three *kinds* of exchanges in the afternoon (mutual reward, nagging, and rewarded coercion). Nominal level measurement states which classes of events happen, but gives no details on what Luke said or how skillfully Robin's mother reinforced desirable behavior.

More exact measurement of disruptive behaviors would involve *rating features* of the behaviors, for example, with four-point scales. For instance, whining occurred: 1) most of the time, 2) about half the time, 3) occasionally, 4) rarely or never. This is measurement at the *ordinal* level. It involves dividing dimensions of an event (e.g., frequency, duration, intensity, skillfulness, dangerousness) into fairly large degrees of more and less. Thus, it gives more information than nominal measures. The following are other examples of ordinal level measurements.

1. Generally, how intense (loud, effortful) were Jerry's disruptive behaviors? 1) highly intense, 2) moderately intense, 3) moderately mild, 4) very mild.
2. How skillfully did Juan change the sheets on his bed? 1) very skillfully, no prompts needed; 2) fairly skillfully, needed prompts on a few components; 3) fairly unskillfully, needed prompts on about half the components; 4) unskillfully, needed prompts on most of the components.

Ordinal level measurement lets an observer *summarize* impressions. For example, Ms. Silva saw and mentally noted every step of Juan's bed making, but waited until the end of the session to make her rating. Although it provides more information than nominal measurement, ordinal measurement is not sensitive to and does not let a rater express smaller differences. Thus, it may not give details needed for planning or revising programs.

More precisely still, one can count and record how many times Jerry performed each kind of disruptive behavior and how long each episode lasted. This is measurement at the *ratio* level. Other examples include counting how many one-word and two-word utterances Luke produced, and how many times Robin and her mother enacted mutual reward, rewarded coercion, and nagging exchanges. Ratio level measurement requires looking closely at the stream of events so that one notices and can record instances of targeted behaviors. In return, it gives information other levels do not. When is so much precision needed? It depends on questions to be answered and decisions to be made.

Questions and Decisions   Jerry's team wants to know if Jerry's disruptive behavior inhibits his participation in lessons so much that it should be reduced immediately. Answering the question and making the decision do *not* require counting every instance of disruptive behavior. A *consistent* ordinal rating at the *end* of many lessons (e.g., "Disruptive behavior happened often and usually inhibited participation.") would be precise enough. A related question is, "Are Jerry's disruptive behaviors reinforced more than rarely—so often that caregivers need coaching?" Although an observer could count every disruptive behavior and every reinforcement, the decision to advise coaching only requires an ordinal level summary, such as: "Disruptive behavior was reinforced about 25% of the time. This is too often." In other words, the decision does not hinge on whether disruptions are reinforced 25% or 35% of the time. Anything more than 1% or 2% is what the team wants to know.

In contrast, Chuck's team just started a program to reduce self-injurious behavior. The evaluation question is whether the program is working so well it can be continued or must be revised immediately before Chuck hurts himself anymore. An ordinal rating—self-injurious behavior has decreased a lot this week—is too inexact. The team has to know *how many* self-injurious behaviors occur each hour (or minute), how long episodes last, and how long intervals between episodes last, before it can decide whether to continue the program or determine how to improve it.

In sum, if the question is whether a behavior is problematic, a skill needs strengthening, or some aspect of an environment (e.g., noise level) should be improved, then ordinal ratings will probably suffice because the exact behavior rates or the exact decibel levels of noise do not matter. However, if one were deciding which behaviors to address ("Should we reduce whining, throwing things, yelling, or all three?"), then one needs more exact information—the rate of each behavior. Likewise, to learn if a program to increase Luke's rate of two-word and three-word utterances is having any effect, and how much of an effect, exact measures, such as the rate of Luke's two- and three-word utterances, are needed. Finally, to decide how reliable a child's dressing skill is from day to day, and to determine which steps are weak and need extra practice, a *precise* description of each step is needed.

How Much To Observe and Record at Once   As part of the assessment of Luke's communication competence, Ms. Reed asks him either to pick up and use or to hand her named foods and utensils during their preparation of a snack. It would be interesting to know the exact number of correct, approximately correct, and incorrect responses Luke makes to each object; how many minutes he pays attention; how many times and for how many minutes he engages in problem behavior; and how often Ms. Reed effectively prompts and reinforces Luke's desirable behavior. Yet, an observer could not accurately record all these events at once. Even if counting were done by viewing portions of videotape again and again, 20 minutes of tape takes hours to score. This much information is not needed.

Only two questions must be answered for purposes of program planning: Which objects did Luke get right, and which did he get wrong? Is there anything about his behavior, Ms. Reed's teaching, or the situation that inhibits Luke? For now, only Luke's responses to each object require ratio level measurement (i.e., need to be described and counted). This is because an adequate teaching program plan must list the objects on which Luke needs instruction, and only ratio measurement can provide that list. For example, Luke made correct responses to spoons, cups, forks, plates, butter, bread, can opener, and can of soup more than 75% of the time. He made wrong or trial-and-error responses to bowls, knives, drinking glass, cutting board, and onion more than 25% of the time.

However, to prepare an adequate program plan does not require measurement of how many times Ms. Reed reinforced and prompted properly, or how many minutes Luke paid attention. The team only needs to know *if* these should be improved and *how problematic* these are. Information could be obtained from ordinal level ratings made at the end of the session. If ratings suggest problems ("Ms. Reed *occasionally* reinforces Luke for picking up the wrong utensil."), then additional observations could be made with more exact measures.

Making it Easier To Record

In most cases, recordings can be made with pencil, paper, and wristwatch. If pencil and paper are too cumbersome, golf counters and grocery price accumulators will also work. If observations are recorded with pencil and paper, it is often best for someone else to observe while caregivers are involved in teaching or assessment. After a session, however, caregivers can make ordinal ratings of the session. In-class observers can include teachers, aides, specialists, parents, and volunteers. At-home observers can include spouses, neighbors, team members, and a child's older sibling.

Recordings can also be made from audio- or videotape. Tape is especially useful in helping caregivers learn to observe and record. A proficient observer and a new observer might watch portions of a tape together; the mentor can help the new observer identify important events (e.g., cues, prompts, reinforcers, differences between skillful and less skillful performances). They continue watching, identifying, and discussing until the new observer sees things about the same way as the mentor. Tape can also be used to assess observers' reliability. Finally, tape preserves important happenings that require more exact measurement. For example, live observation does not reveal just what difficulties Indra has using her hands. Such information might be obtained by examining and re-examining videotapes of several tasks.

Arranging a Comfortable Observation Environment

As with interviewing, direct observation should be a collaboration between observers and those being observed (observees). Observees should be treated as partners and informants, not subjects. Questions to answer and events to observe should be discussed during team meetings ahead of time, and items of special importance to observees should be included in the observation schedule.

Observations should be scheduled when convenient for observees, and last only as long as comfortable. In addition, especially in the case of families, the possibility of tape recordings must be discussed well in advance, as well as the protection of privacy (e.g., keeping tapes in locked cabinets, only letting those on a select list see tapes). Permission to observe and tape record should be in writing. Caregivers should not be pressured into being videotaped. Their reluctance is best understood as lack of trust that may be strengthened through empathic communication about experiences that have fostered mistrust.

Observation should be understood and presented as a way to collect information that serves observees' interests. Instead of merely documenting weakness, observation should reveal how caregivers are, for instance, able to manage problem behaviors and teach desirable behaviors. Such information is useful for program planning.

It is important to familiarize caregivers and children with being observed. Small talk before sessions helps. Also, observers and caregivers should review what is to be observed, how long the session will last, and how each can expect the other to act. For instance, if the caregiver asks what he or she should do, the observer may respond as follows:

> During everyday tasks and activities, such as a meal, just try to do what you usually do. Naturally, you will be aware that I am watching. So, you may be a bit tense. Don't try to make yourself act natural, you'll only feel more awkward. In a little while, I'm sure you'll loosen up. I'll keep out of the way. Is it okay if I stand near the doorway?
>
> Now, as we discussed during the team meeting, before an instructional session, such as on imitation, we will review the models you can try to get Juan to imitate. Just try to follow the written instructions, and don't worry if you forget to ask him something. After all, this is not an experiment.
>
> Any time you want to talk about what is going on or ask a question, feel free. If the phone rings and you want to get it, go ahead. Any time you want to stop, that's fine too. In other words, this is daily life; no one is wearing a white coat.

It is a good idea to accustom observees to one's presence and to recording equipment. For instance, parents can be taught how to use video recorders before taping begins. In addition, before starting pencil and paper or electronic recordings, the observer should spend time just watching while caregivers go about their business. When they no longer seem as self-conscious, recording can begin.

The observer should try to stay out of the way (e.g., at the other end of a room) unless he or she will be coaching as well. While available to speak to caregivers, it is best not to strike up lengthy conversations with a child's siblings in the home or with other children in class. Such conversations can take place between observation sessions.

During and after observations, caregivers should be praised for their efforts. In addition, observers and caregivers should discuss their impressions, as shown below. Later, the observer makes notes on the discussions.

Ms. Silva: He can do a lot better than that (commenting on Juan's recent performance on setting the table).

Observer: How so?

Ms. Silva: Well, he dawdled between each plate and cup. Usually, he moves from one to the other real quick.

Observer: So, he knows how, but just wasn't interested in doing it?

Ms. Silva: Yeah. He didn't make any errors. He just took too long between steps.

Observer: Good observation. So his fluency was off. How often do you usually reinforce Juan during this task?

Ms. Silva: I praise him right after every step. I guess I didn't do that this time, did I?

Preliminary to later program planning, Ms. Silva and the observer discuss how Juan is usually reinforced for each step. Because he was not reinforced this time, perhaps he was waiting or was confused. A possible suggestion for program plans (written later) would be to gradually thin reinforcement schedules, teach Juan to notice and comment on step completions, and eventually delay reinforcement until he is done. For now, however, the observer and Ms. Silva decide to observe additional tasks—some in which Juan is reinforced nearly continuously and some in which reinforcement is ordinarily less frequent—to determine the possible effects of reinforcement schedules on attention and fluency. If video recordings are made, these too can be reviewed, perhaps soon after recording.

Extended Record Keeping

Information collected through direct observation can be summarized in several ways. At the end of a day, for instance, an observer might have a list of the new words Indra used, a list of steps she skillfully performed in several tasks, the percentage of word models she correctly imitated, and the amount of time she paid attention during lessons. *These figures should be put on a form that covers a week or more.* This enables one to keep track of the behaviors from day to day. (Chap. 4 in *Guidelines and Protocols* discusses extended record keeping in more detail.)

METHODS OF DIRECT OBSERVATION

Widely used methods of direct observation include narrative recording, descriptive analysis, task analysis, counting, and functional analysis.

Narrative Recording

Narrative recording is used when it is important to: 1) shift attention from one kind of event to another, 2) capture the flow of events, 3) adjust focus back and forth between the level of movements or actions and the level of tasks or activities, 4) describe how (not just how often) behaviors and social interactions are performed, and 5) write as much as may be important.

Narrative recording is especially useful at the start of an assessment. For example, when beginning the assessment of child–caregiver exchanges, it is premature to count how often different exchanges happen because one does not yet know *what* kinds may happen. Instead, one begins with narrative recording to describe *how* people initiate and reciprocate interaction (Ainsworth, Blehar, Waters, & Wall, 1978). After analyzing the narrative record and identifying *types* of exchanges, one might begin to count exchanges. Narrative recording is also useful in program evaluation. Because it does not confine observations to predetermined categories, it may, for instance, help to identify events that hinder a child's progress, as well as identify improvement.

Narrative recording can be done with pencil and paper, leaving wide margins for making notes to oneself. Narrative recordings can also be made from videotape. As much as possible, the observer describes action and other concrete events; that is, the observer avoids summarizing what happened or making inferences about what people are thinking or trying to do. When inferences are made, they should be in brackets, as shown below.

> Mrs. Hardy walks out of den. Jerry looks up from television, turns, and visually tracks her. Raises his right arm and says "Momma, Momma!" [He seems to be trying to get her attention and call her back.} Mrs. Hardy turns, looks at him, and says, "I'll be right back, honey." Jerry smiles. [Mrs. Hardy's response seems consistent with Jerry's communicative intent. What other communicative intentions does he express?]

During narrative recording, one often adjusts the level of focus (Barker, 1963, 1968). For instance, Mr. Hawkins is accurate when he writes, "Indra stapled five booklets in 24 minutes." Because Indra has a neuromuscular disorder affecting her performance at the level of movements, however, Mr. Hawkins' global statement is not much help in planning instruction to improve Indra's fluency. Thus, shifting to the microscopic level, he also writes: "Indra steadies pages with her left elbow. The heel of her right hand rests along the length of the stapler arm. She leans forward, pressing the stapler arm down with the weight of her upper body."

In the narrative record, descriptive sentences should be short, use everyday language, include only one event, and describe events in sequence. Thus, it is easy to analyze an entry that reads: "Juan smacks the pocket of his baseball glove. Mr. Silva says, 'Ready?' Juan nods and raises his glove chest high, pocket facing up. Mr. Silva pitches underhand. Juan steps forward. The ball lands in the pocket." It will be much harder to analyze an entry that reads, "Having smacked the pocket of his glove and heard Mr. Silva say 'Ready?', Juan nods and holds his glove up." Finally, a narrative should include features of the environment, such as time of day, location, materials involved, and background sounds and activities.

There are three kinds of narrative recording. *Running records* capture the flow of events. *Specimen descriptions* record specific recurring events. And at all times, *field notes* should be made on events and comments that reveal the cultural side of families and schools.

Running Records   Mitchell's team faces the following broad questions: 1) What does Mitchell do when he is on his own? 2) What does Mitchell's mother mean when she says that late afternoons are mayhem? 3) What happens during lessons that Ms. Gonzales evaluates Mitchell's participation as improved? Addressing the latter question of Mitchell's classroom participation, the team does not restrict itself to counting a few predetermined behaviors before it even has a record of the *flow* of events in lessons.

Figure 10.1 is part of a running record of Mitchell's behavior. The narrative reads as a sportscaster's play-by-play description. The page is divided into three columns—possible cues for a child's behavior, the child's behavior, and a caregiver's responses. Sometimes, a caregiver's response can also be heard as a cue for the child to make a next response. Examining the running record in Figure 10.1 reveals a pattern: In contrast to exchanges with Mitchell in past months, Ms. Gonzales no longer accidentally reinforces undesirable behaviors. Instead, she immediately reinforces small amounts of productive participation. Having thus identified several *kinds of events* (exchanges in this case) in the running record, the team decides to use the next kind of narrative recording—specimen description—to obtain more details on exchanges.

Specimen Descriptions   Specimen descriptions are used to record specified recurring events. Examples include episodes of problem behavior; child–caregiver exchanges (e.g., mutual reward vs. nagging); routine tasks and activities (e.g., meals); and a child's methods of locomotion. The work of Barker and Wright (1966) and Pettit and Bates (1990) provides useful examples of specimen description.

Specimen description has three steps. First, instead of continuously recording the flow of events, as in a running record, the observer *waits for occurrences of targeted items* (e.g., Indra's efforts at locomotion). Each episode is described as thoroughly as possible. In step two, right after observations, the observer reviews the recording and *adds details* (e.g., on prompts in the physical

Child: Mitchell B.	**Teacher/Parent:** Ms. Gonzales	**Date:** 9/6/93
Location: Classroom	**Observer:** Ms. Wright	
Time start: 10:35 A.M.	**Time end:** 10:55 A.M.	**Total time:** 20 minutes
Purpose of observation: Evaluation of participation in lessons		

Possible cues:	**Child's behavior:**	**Caregiver's responses:**
Ms. G.: "Okay. Play time is over, kids. Get your cushions and come to the board."	Mitchell puts down toy car; walks straight to pile of cushions in the corner. Looks at Ms. G. Quickly picks up cushion and carries it to area in front of blackboard and sits behind Sam, 2 feet to Robin's right.	"Thank you, Mitchell. That was so fast!"
	Smiles	
Ms. G.: "Now, I'm going to read you a story about two friends: a cat and a dog." Begins reading.	Looks rather intently at Ms. G. as she reads. Thirty seconds into story, starts making loud breathing noises, looking at Ms. G.	Ms. G. does not look at Mitchell. Gets up and walks among the children, still reading.
	Continues noises; increases loudness. Looks at Ms. G.	Strokes Robin's head.
	Watches Ms. G. stroke Robin's head. Still making noises.	
		Pats Sam's shoulder while reading.
	Stops noises and looks at picture of dog and cat from the story on blackboard.	Leans forward and strokes Mitchell's cheek.
	Smiles.	
Walks slightly behind Mitchell and to his left; keeps reading.	Continues looking at pictures on board.	Silently comes back and rubs Mitchell's head.

Figure 10.1. Running record of Mitchell's behavior.

environment). The narrative is then *divided into codable units*. This might involve circling entries on a page. In Indra's case, codable units include: 1) short and discrete episodes of locomotion (e.g., getting on the couch, getting from one end of the couch to the other, getting off the couch, standing up); and 2) short episodes arranged into sequences that constitute a task or activity (e.g., getting from the couch to the kitchen). In step three, the observer actually *codes* or *names the events or units* (e.g., locomotion by crawling, climbing, scooting sideways, scooting forward, walking with support, walking without support).

From a set of specimen descriptions it is possible to calculate the *rates* and *durations* of events. In Indra's case, the observer counted the number of times per hour that Indra moved from one place to another; calculated the percentage of successful and unsuccessful locomotions; calculated the percentage of episodes involving crawling on the floor, scooting on the floor, walking with support, and walking without support; and determined the duration of locomotion events (e.g., how long it took to get from the couch to the kitchen). Note that repeated (e.g., weekly) specimen descriptions could be used in program evaluation. An increase in the percentage of episodes involving walking (over crawling and scooting), and a decrease in the time it takes to get from one place to another, suggest that Indra's instruction is effective.

Field Notes and Cultural Situations   Social situations have an objective and intersubjective (cultural) side. Objective means that members of families and schools coordinate behavior into durable script-like social patterns, such as exchanges, tasks and activities, schedules, divisions of labor, roles, role relationships, and hierarchies of power and authority. These are objective in the sense that they can be observed as if they were objects. For instance, in describing the objective side of snack time in class, one would include cues that bring children to the table, seating patterns, who says what, the order in which foods are eaten, how food is served, how children hold utensils, and what happens if a child throws food or leaves the table. Yet, an important question is: How is the coordination of individual behavior into social patterns done, and what keeps patterns going? The answer is that people develop common ways to see and hear; shared conceptions of time, space, people, objects, and activities; and typical ways to make sense of—explain, justify, and legitimize—what is going on. This is the cultural or intersubjective side of social life (Berger & Luckmann, 1967).

There are two main implications of the fact that social life is both objectively real and intersubjectively real. First, an outside observer's understanding of objective happenings in a group (family, school) is probably different from group members' understanding. Second, group members' shared understandings constitute reality for them. Thus, some people will feel threatened by and may reject comments that challenge their view of situations. It is, therefore, important to foster a partnership with observees. It is also wise to present impressions in a way that is not insulting. It is better to say, "It may be that Luke needs more chances to ask for things," than "Luke isn't getting enough chances to ask for things." It is also important to plan programs with caregivers that are *congruent* with their conceptions. One may even have to help caregivers alter certain conceptions (e.g., that reinforcement is bribery) so they can make changes. Below are examples of the cultural side of families and schools, and what to look and listen for during observations.

Time   The clock says 4:30 P.M., but Mitchell's mother calls it "late afternoon mayhem." Her husband knows what she means—noise from the television, Mitchell's hyperactive behavior, siblings running around, and Mitchell's mother with too much to do. In other words, intersubjective time in a family or school is rarely the same as clock time. In order to better understand family members' moods, energy, and interpersonal exchanges, it is important to understand how they divide time into units. Are there, for instance, easy times and hard times; too-much-to-do times and relaxing times; my time, family time, and a child's time; typical days and unusual days; bad days and good days; serious time and casual time; mealtime, playtime, and work time (Brotherson & Goldstein, 1992)?

Also, how do group members' conceptions of time affect objective patterns of family and school life? For instance, is Mitchell's hyperactive behavior more aversive during "mayhem" time; and is this when "hyper" behavior is more likely to be reinforced? If so, one may have to help the family decrease extraneous noise and activity before they can interact productively with Mitchell, and perhaps even before Mitchell slows down.

Space   An observer sees spaces carved out by walls, floors, furniture, and halls. Group members can of course see these, but they also see areas and routes—spaces where family- and school-relevant events happen. Thus, it is important to learn and see the areas caregivers and children operate in as they see them. Are there areas for quiet versus noisy activity, private places and social places, clean versus messy places, places for teaching, places that are dangerous and places that are safe? Are there certain routes children are expected to learn? Observers should also note how group members' conceptions of places and routes affect exchanges, instruction, and a child's membership. For example, is instruction inconsistent because members give a lot of opportunities, prompts, and reinforcement only in "teaching areas," allowing a child to engage in bizarre and aimless behavior in other places? Is a child tacitly confined to certain areas because other areas are considered dangerous, private, or sacred?

Objects Objects may be seen as having tangible features such as weight, color, and shape. Schools and families have additional intersubjective categories; for example, there may be dangerous and safe objects, personal property and public property, objects that stay in one area and objects that can be moved, objects to keep out of your mouth, objects that can be used as toys, objects to eat with, and objects that can be used as prompts. It is important to understand how object categories affect interaction and instruction. Does a child get punished for handling objects in certain categories? Is a child denied the opportunity to learn about many things because they are in restricted categories, such as "things we eat with," or "things that do not belong to you"? Do caregivers see that many objects could be used as prompts (e.g., a strap to help a child pull a door open)?

Persons Cultures have membership categories (Sacks, 1991)—members in good standing, children, adults, good providers, and so forth. People use rules to assign others to categories. For instance, if a child seems constantly in motion and inattentive, the child may satisfy the criteria and be assigned to the category of children with attention deficit hyperactivity disorders. It is important to discover the categories, rules, and criteria for membership in schools and families. What competencies does a child need, and at what age, to be seen as a member, an increasingly competent member, or a very competent member? Also, what are the practices by which categorization is done? For example, what clothing does a child wear, how do people respond to a child's errors, and how do people talk about the child (Helm, 1981)? Answers help explain how a child plays certain roles and how caregivers' perceptions of a child may have to be improved before they are comfortable making many changes.

Interaction Sometimes when Jerry teases his parents (e.g., runs away when called), they get angry and chase him. Other times (e.g., when he slowly walks away when called), they laugh and ignore it. Sometimes when Jerry whines and cries, it yields cuddling. Other times his parents threaten to punish him if he does not stop. An observer judges Jerry's teasing, crying, and whining to be aversive to the parents. Why, then, do they sometimes reinforce these behaviors (the rewarded coercion exchange) and sometimes not? Are Mr. and Mrs. Hardy simply inconsistent?

The Hardys' behavior is *reasonable to them*; they use different categories than the observer does for understanding interaction and Jerry's behavior. For them, there is playful teasing, which they ignore, and malicious teasing, which they inadvertently reinforce by getting angry. There is interaction in which they comfort Jerry when he seems to be in pain; and interaction in which they fight with him because they believe he is trying to control them (e.g., to let him stay awake longer). Suggesting that the Hardys ignore all whining, crying, and teasing will not work. They are not going to ignore Jerry when they believe he is in pain. Nor will they ignore whining and crying that they see aimed at controlling them; that would be letting him do whatever he wants. Thus, the observer/consultant must understand how the Hardys make sense of exchanges and *tailor comments and suggestions to their categories*. For example:

Ms. Tyler (Observer):	Now, the exchange where you say Jerry is trying to control you—to make you let him stay up later, or give him dessert even though he didn't eat his dinner . . .
Mr. Hardy:	Yes?
Ms. Tyler:	Well, it seems you feel strongly about not letting him win, right? You keep telling him to stop and warning him he better stop it.
Mrs. Hardy:	Right!
Ms. Tyler:	So, what happens when you threaten or don't give in right away?
Mr. Hardy:	He yells louder and whines longer. You know, tries harder.

Ms. Tyler:	Am I wrong or did you give in a few times after Jerry really worked himself up?
Mr. Hardy:	Yes, you saw right. Sometimes he wears us down.
Ms. Tyler:	I can imagine! Who can tolerate that? Still, you know that Jerry *learns* something when you give in *after* he has escalated.
Mrs. Hardy:	Sure. He learns to escalate!
Ms. Tyler:	Right. So it looks like your effort to keep Jerry from controlling you may have the opposite effect. He learns how to get you to give in.
Mr. Hardy:	Well, that explains why our efforts haven't worked!
Ms. Tyler:	I'm afraid so. Maybe we can think of something else to do that will give you more control *before* his behavior gets so nasty you can't take it.
Mrs. Hardy:	Well, let's start thinking.

In the above vignette, Ms. Tyler empathizes with the strain Jerry's tantrums have on the Hardys—almost saying she would react the same way. Also, Ms. Tyler does not invalidate the Hardys' view of the exchange—as involving control. Instead, Ms. Tyler suggests that there may be some additional things in the Hardys' interests to consider; namely, what Jerry and his parents are learning. Ms. Tyler then helps the Hardys determine how they can experience some control over the situation while teaching desirable behavior.

Evidence of Family and School Members' Conceptions   Evidence of the intersubjective side of families and schools can be obtained by asking questions and listening to comments family and school members direct to the observer, child, or others during and after activities. *The observer records such comments whenever they occur.* Below are several of the hundreds of things said during a few hours of observation in Mitchell's class. The observer's tentative interpretations are in brackets along with possible questions to check interpretations and build a bigger picture.

12:45 P.M.   "Mitchell. Please get out of the closet. You know you're not supposed to go in there." [The closet is restricted? What other places do you want Mitchell to stay out of? What is it about these places or about Mitchell that makes these restricted?]

12:50 P.M.   "Put your lunch box where it belongs, please." [Lunch boxes have a place? A competent member knows this? Are children supposed to learn that things have a special place? What are the special places that you want Mitchell to learn about? How would you see Mitchell if he did, or did not, learn where things go?]

1:04 P.M.   "It's time to be quiet. Let's settle down." [There is a time to run around and a time to sit down? A child should learn to control his or her energy? Are there times when it is okay for Mitchell to run around? When are these times? How does his running around at the wrong time make you feel?]

1:22 P.M.   "Give that back to Johnny. It belongs to him." [Some objects are private property? A competent child knows this? A law abiding child lives by it? Are you teaching Mitchell that different things belong to different people? What sorts of things belong to Mitchell? How do you teach him this?]

1:24 P.M.   "Be careful with that. You could get cut." [Some objects are dangerous? What kinds of things are dangerous? Do you think Mitchell could learn to handle the less dangerous items safely?]

1:30 P.M.   "If you want to play, play over there. This is where we eat." [A competent child knows where to engage in different behaviors? What other areas are there in class? Which behaviors are supposed to go with which areas?]

1:40 P.M.   "Andrew is in a bad mood. That's why he is not paying attention." [Performance is accounted for by transitory internal states? Does his mood affect other behaviors? How often is he in bad and good moods? What are the signs of his mood? Do you try to improve his moods?]

2:10 P.M.   "Do you believe it? (said to observer) There is so much to do and they (teacher aides) just leave me to do it." [Divisions of labor should be more balanced? Co-workers should be more sensitive? "You sound irritated. How often would you say you are left with all this work? Can the division of labor be negotiated? When you are stuck with all this work, how does it affect your teaching?"]

In addition to following up on caregivers' comments, the observer asks questions about what he or she sees and hears. For example:

Observer: You praised Mitchell with enthusiasm when he brought materials back to the shelf.
Ms. Gonzales: You bet. He's finally catching on.
Observer: To what?
Ms. Gonzales: That materials have a certain place. He used to have no idea.
Observer: So that is real progress. He seems like a different child to you?
Ms. Gonzales: Yes. More alert to where he is. It is as if he knows there are scripts for doing things.
Observer: That's great! What other areas are there here and what other scripts does a competent child learn to follow?
Ms. Gonzales: Well, there is where we eat, where we play, where we keep coats and hats, where we do group lessons, and where we do individual desk work. Oh yes, then there's my place, at the desk.
Observer: What is the script for desk work? I mean, how is a child supposed to do desk work? Is there a sequence of steps; are there rules? [The observer might ask to observe desk work to see how well Mitchell follows the script, whether the script may be too rigid or too loose, and how Ms. Gonzales teaches the script.]

In addition to notes on caregivers' comments and answers to questions, the observer sketches areas and routes conceived and used by members. Later, *notes and sketches are organized into categories,* such as family or school times, places, scripts, rules of respect, conceptions of competence, and so forth. More observations may provide more details of how family and school members' conceptions guide and make sense of the objective patterns. Useful resources on qualitative observation and informal interviewing include: Buckholdt and Gubrium (1979); Cohen, Stern, and Balaban (1983); Fetterman (1989); Fine and Sandstrom (1988); Henry (1971); Lofland and Lofland (1984); Mehan (1979); Patton (1990); and Spradley (1980).

Descriptive Analysis

Descriptive analysis is inductive. First, one observes specific events, perhaps using narrative recording. Having identified commonalities among some events, categories are then created (e.g., kinds of exchanges). Additional observation may suggest sequences and patterns of influence among categories of events. Finally, generalizations are tested by more observation. One of the first and finest presentations of descriptive analysis is the article by Bijou, Peterson, and Ault (1968). Below is an example of descriptive analysis.

Mr. Steele, the physical therapist on Indra's team, is collecting specimen descriptions of Indra's locomotion at home and school. He finds that Indra is likely to go from one part of the house or classroom to another if activities in other places are quite audible. Also, Indra is much more likely to crawl or scoot on the floor in the presence of her father and Mr. Hawkins, her teacher, than in the presence of her mother. Further observation reveals an interesting pattern: Mr. Hawkins and Indra's father either coax Indra to stand up if she is on the floor, or coax and manually prompt her to walk if she is already standing up (her response being to slump back to the floor). In contrast, Indra's mother merely states Grandma's Law—"Well, honey, as soon as you get to the kitchen we'll make chocolate pudding"—and walks away. Indra then gets up and walks.

This descriptive analysis suggests connections between some of Indra's behaviors and certain features of the environment (e.g., reinforcement for crawling and scooting keeps Indra crawling and scooting). Using this finding, Indra's team (which includes Mr. Hawkins and Indra's father) decides that the two men will try Indra's mother's method.

Findings from descriptive analyses are not always solid enough to warrant using them to plan programs, however. This is especially true if being wrong (e.g., about what controls self-injurious behavior) leads to ineffective and harmful plans. In this case, one would conduct more rigorous *functional analyses* of suspected relationships, as discussed later in this chapter.

Task Analysis

Task analysis is a useful way to assess behavior sequences that have a definite objective. Examples include washing, dressing, crossing a street, opening a package, and sweeping a floor. This section shows how task analysis can be accomplished using both narrative recording and already-structured forms.

Task Analysis with Narrative Recording   Indra's skill at brushing her teeth is assessed from a running, narrative record of her performance. The focus is on movements and actions. Written notes or videotape are analyzed as follows.

First, Indra's performance is described as a series of steps, each of which accomplishes a necessary part of the overall work. This will probably reveal gaps where her performance deteriorates or even stops.

Second, at each identified step, one describes: 1) Indra's skill (i.e., use of effective movements at the right spots, the degree to which actions were independent of prompting); 2) fluency of movements and actions (e.g., speed, smooth linking into sequences, expending necessary energy, staying with a step until completed); 3) strong and weak components of a step; and 4) any cues, prompts, and reinforcement provided by a caregiver. Also described are successful and unsuccessful transitions from one step to the next.

Third, Indra's performance is summarized by listing strong and weak steps, and strong and weak movement and/or action components within steps. Also, suggestions are made regarding cues, prompts, and reinforcers the child may need and instruction to improve weak links. Figure 10.2 depicts part of a task analysis based on a running narrative record.

Task Analysis with Forms   Many assessment instruments and curriculum guides contain prepared task analysis forms. Tasks are broken into steps and the observer assesses performance of each step. The *Child Assessment and Programming Guide (CAPG)*, located in *Guidelines and Protocols*, has many such task analyses. Below is item D22.

D22. The child builds structures using repeated series of actions (e.g., the child puts together Tinker Toys, Lincoln Logs, or Lego sets).

    a. The child performs and coordinates the component movements of: (For each of the following components, choose the number representing the most accurate answer and write it on the line next to the component.)

                1 = Perfectly or nearly perfectly   3 = Gross approximation
                2 = Good approximation   4 = Poor or no performance

      _____ Reaching for, grasping, and picking up the object that is to be fitted (e.g., a Tinker Toy rod) (D1, 3 or 8, 10)

_____ Reaching for, grasping, and picking up the object (e.g., Tinker Toy spool) into which the other (e.g., Tinker Toy rod) is to be fitted (D1, 3 or 8, 10)

_____ Positioning and steadying the objects that are to be fitted (e.g., moving the Tinker Toy rod and spool so that the rod is aimed at the hole) (D21)

_____ Precisely positioning or fitting the object to be fitted (e.g., pushing rod into hole) (C1–7; D19)

_____ Repeating the cycle

b. Do the child's actions of putting pieces together have some sort of aim (e.g., building a house, or putting them all together)?

_____

_____

_____

_____

_____

c. How attentive is the child during this task? (circle one)

Very attentive   Fairly attentive   Rather inattentive   Very inattentive

d. What are the strong and weak links in the above sequence?

_____

_____

_____

_____

_____

e. What kinds of cues and/or prompts does the child seem to need or might the child's performance benefit from? (circle one or more)

Repeated starting request   Model or demonstration
   (e.g., "Let's make a house.")

Verbal instruction (e.g., "Hold   Manual or move child
   the spool in your other hand.")

Gesture (e.g., pointing)   Device, tool, or alternative method (e.g.,
                                          puts all of the same kind in place first)

f. How might the child use and generalize this behavior (e.g., as play activity)?

_____

_____

_____

_____

_____

g. What problem behaviors, if any, interfere with this behavior?

_____

_____

_____

_____

_____

Child: Indra   **Observer:** Mr. Hawkins   **Date:** 9/13/93
Time start: 12:20 P.M.   **Time end:** 12:36 P.M.   **Total time:** 16 minutes
Task: Brushing teeth   **Materials:** Regular brush; tube paste
Location: Classroom bathroom
Purpose: Initial assessment; comparison with assessment at home.

Action sequence	Description
1. Unscrews toothpaste cap	Already done by Mr. Hawkins. Too frustrating otherwise.
2. Loads brush with paste	Holds brush in left hand, palmar grip. Toothpaste tube laying on sink, near right-hand faucet. Lowers brush to paste, lines up with nozzle, and rests it on sink. Presses tube with heel of right hand. Prompt/reinforcement: "Okay. Good. That's enough." Stops squeezing.
3. Inserts brush in mouth	Picks up brush with right hand; raises arm at shoulder and elbow. Rotates wrist inward while bending head toward brush and opening mouth. Inserts brush. Closes lips around handle. Quickly opens mouth, rotates wrist upward, and begins brushing front teeth. Reinforcement: "Very nice."
4. Brushes teeth	Spastic movements of head, wrist, and forearm, but clearly knows script for up and down and for going from one tooth to another. Brushes left side. Does not reinsert brush or turn it around to do right side. Prompt: Manual (at wrist) to remove and reinsert brush; instruction: "Now let's do the other side." Manual prompt removed when she begins to brush.
5. Removes brush from mouth. Stops. Prompt: "Now rinse your mouth."	
6. Rinses mouth. Stops. Prompt: "Now rinse the brush." (Points to brush.)	
7. Rinses brush. Stops. Prompt: Points to running water.	
8. Turns off faucet	
9. Replaces brush and paste	

Comments: Knows scripts within steps. Needs to learn cues for steps 6–8. Reinforcement, prompts, and prompting strategy (graduated guidance) seem effective. Suggest brush with larger handle and support for right wrist. Attention strong. Cooperated with cues and prompts. Seemed to enjoy task.

Figure 10.2. Task analysis based on narrative recording.

The overall sequence and each step in it can be assessed in several ways.

1.   Using ordinal scales, the observer *rates* how well the child performs each step. For example: 1) perfectly or nearly perfectly, 2) good approximation, 3) gross approximation, 4) poor or no performance.

2. Attentiveness, effort, enjoyment, cooperation, and problem behaviors are also rated ordinally: a) predominant, b) occurred a lot, c) occurred some, d) occurred rarely or not at all. Or, these are described in more detail.
3. Strong and weak links are identified.
4. Cues, prompts, or reinforcements at any step are identified. Also cues, prompts, and reinforcement that might improve performance are suggested.

Repeated analyses of the same and other tasks will reveal regularities, such as weak and strong links and preferences for certain reinforcers. They will also show variations, such as alternative ways a child accomplishes the same steps and the effects of different materials, locations, and teaching styles. Thus, repeated task analyses can be used to evaluate progress.

Creating Task Analysis Forms   Preparing task analysis forms can increase skill at observing and teaching. There are several ways to prepare forms: inductive or empirical method and deductive or rational method. It is best to become skilled at both.

Inductive or Empirical   Forms can be created by first observing a number of more skillful children performing the same task. It is best if children vary in skill and if the task is completed under somewhat diverse conditions. Then, either from videotape or live observations, the following are identified, as in the work of Connolly and Dalgleish (1989):

1. Common sequences of steps
2. Effective alternative sequences; for instance, some children may put on the left sock and left shoe and then the right sock and right shoe
3. Common actions by which children accomplish each step, as well as effective alternatives; for instance, some children pull off the sleeves of a sweater by grasping the cuffs with the opposite hand; other children effectively pull on the cuffs with their teeth
4. Cues that start each step and consequences informing children that a step is done

The above information is then used to create a form, such as the one shown in Table 4.2, Chapter 4, this volume.

Deductive or Rational   Forms also can be created deductively—imagining how a task is completed. One begins at the end and works backwards, or begins with the first step and works forward. At each step, one imagines (perhaps tries or observes) alternative ways of accomplishing the same function.

Counting

Narrative recording and task analysis describe the flow of behavior. However, when interest is in *how often and how long* recurring behaviors are performed, continuous event recording and intermittent recording are used.

Continuous Event Recording   Counting episodes is sometimes called continuous event recording. In addition to recording that an event happened, one can measure its duration. Some events, especially those with a low rate, might be recorded whenever they happen throughout the day. Examples include proper toileting versus accidents, self-initiated chores, or self-initiated play (perhaps along with the duration of each episode). Other events can be continuously recorded during specific relevant periods. For example, during routine tasks and activities one could record a child's communicative acts (comments, questions, answers, requests); attention (recording the duration of each episode); correct responses and action sequences (e.g., identifying named objects, drying dishes); and disruptive behavior.

Forms for continuous event recording can be as simple as those shown in Figure 10.3. Summary measures include the *total* number and/or duration of events, overall *rates* and local rates, and *percentages*.

Example 1

Toileting (all day)
Self-initiated toileting: 9:05 A.M., 12:04 P.M., 6:30 P.M.
Toileting accidents: 7:00 A.M., 2:40 P.M., 8:50 P.M.
Summary: 6 episodes—3 self-initiated and 3 accidents, or 50% self-initiated.

Example 2

Drying dishes after evening meal (14 minutes) (Two different event recording methods could be used.)
1. Hash marks for each dried dish:
    𝟞𝟞𝟞𝟞𝟞𝟞𝟞𝟞 / (11)
2. Recording and naming dishes in the order dried:
    plate, cup, cup, glass, plate, plate, cup, bowl, bowl, cup, bowl (11)
Summary: 11 dishes in 14 minutes or .79 dishes per minute (rather slow). Method 2 provides more information than method 1; it tells how many dishes were dried and in which order.

Example 3

Motor imitation during 20-minute session
C = correct imitation   A = approximately correct imitation
I = incorrect imitation   O = no response
Two different methods of event recording could be used:
1. Recording each model and the child's response in order:
    Open mouth (C), raise arm (C), clap hands (C), pat table (C), stack one block on another (A), stack ring on dowel (I), stick out tongue (C), raise arm (O)
    (This method shows if and how a child's performance changes within models and through the session.)
2. Listing models and the child's response to each in order:
    Open mouth: C C C   (100% correct)
    Raise arm: C O C   (67% correct)
    Clap hands: C A C   (67% correct)
    Pat table: C O C   (67% correct)
    Stack block: A C C   (67% correct)
    Stack ring: I A C   (33% correct)
    Stick out tongue: C O O   (33% correct)
    (This method preserves the order of presentation within each model and may show changes in response to each model.)

Example 4

Episodes of attention/inattention during 20-minute story
on = attending   off = not attending. Thus, 2 on = 2 minutes attending.
1 on, 2 off, 1 on, 3 off, 1 on, 2 off, 3 on, 1 off, 2 on, 2 off, 2 on
Summary:
1. Attention = 10 minutes during a 20-minute period, or attention for 50% of the time and inattention for 50% of the time
2. Shifts in attention = 10
3. Average duration of attention episodes = 10 minutes during 6 episodes, or 1.67 minutes of attention per episode
4. Average duration of inattention episodes = 10 minutes during 5 episodes, or 2 minutes of inattention per episode. (Child sustains attention for less time than inattention.)

Figure 10.3. Examples of simple continuous event recording forms.

At the end of an observation period one will know the total number of times targeted events occurred (assuming the counts were accurate), and perhaps the total duration of certain events. These totals can be useful. Indra, for example, made progress if she walked the length of her classroom 4 times on day 1 and 8 times on day 5 of a new teaching program.

Another summary is the *rate* of behavior. Rate is calculated as the number of events divided by the amount of time. During a 2-hour home observation, for instance, Luke emitted 60 spontaneous one-word utterances (e.g., "Mine") and 20 two-word utterances (e.g., "My truck"). The combined rate is 80 utterances/120 minutes, or .67 utterances per minute; the rate of one-word utterances is 60/120, or .5 utterances per minute; and the rate of two-word utterances is 20/120, or .17 per minute.

Rates are especially important when observation periods are not the same length. If one session is 120 minutes and the next is 90 minutes, comparing the total number of utterances may give a false impression of how much Luke talks. During the second session, 90 minutes long, Luke spoke a total of 70 one-word and two-word utterances. This is 10 less than during the first session, but the rate is higher: .77 utterances per minute compared to .67 per minute. Thus, when observation periods are of unequal length, it is wise to calculate rates.

While it is important to know the overall rate of a behavior (i.e., the rate for a whole observation period), this figure can obscure rates during shorter intervals in the period. During a 20-minute play session with Ms. Tyler, for instance, Jerry performed 30 communicative acts. This is an overall rate of 1.5 communicative acts per minute. However, 20 of Jerry's 30 communicative acts were in the first 5 minutes of play, and the other 10 acts were spread over the remaining 15 minutes. The overall rate (1.5 acts per minute) now seems less important than the fact that Jerry emitted 4 communicative acts per minute in the first 5 minutes (20/5), and only .67 communicative acts per minute during the remaining 15 minutes (10/15). This information is significant. It could mean that after 5 minutes Jerry became bored with the toys or ran out of things to say, that Ms. Tyler provided less stimulus for talk, or all three. Thus, it is often important to calculate *local rates* (rates during shorter portions of a period), which can be examined by dividing an observation period into segments, recording events in each segment, and calculating the overall rate and the rates in each segment. This indicates if local rates change.

Figure 10.4 presents minute-by-minute event recording of Jerry's 20-minute collaborative play session. Note that the *types* of communicative acts (e.g., offers, protests) were recorded. This is more informative than a mere hash mark (/) indicating that *some* communicative act occurred. Even better, though, would be recording *exactly* what Jerry says or does (e.g., "Holds up object to Ms. Tyler"). Later, each utterance and gesture would be coded as one or another type of act. In this way, one learns how many ways (forms) Jerry communicates the same intention or function. One can also assess the quality of Jerry's speech. By recording events in the environment (e.g., reinforcement), one may learn if or how a child's behavior varies with those events.

Table 10.1 is a bit different from Figure 10.4. It depicts several of Mitchell's behaviors over a longer (7 hour) home observation recorded by Ms. Gonzales, his teacher. Reinforcement is scored whenever Mitchell's mother or father praises, acknowledges, hugs, or pats Mitchell after he has started playing.

Intermittent Recording   It is not feasible to count every instance of a behavior using pencil and paper if the rate is high or if more than several behaviors are recorded at once. In addition, if the interest is in what proportion of time a child engages in a behavior, it is not necessary to count each instance. In these cases, intermittent recording, sometimes called *interval recording* or *time sampling,* can be used. There are many variations of intermittent recording. All involve dividing an observation period into relatively short (often consecutive) intervals, and then recording *what* a child did during each interval. The following is an example of intermittent recording.

Sampling Hyperactive versus Calm Behavior   Barney is diagnosed with attention deficit hyperactivity disorder. Continuous event recording shows that he alternates between hyperactive and calm behavior in episodes lasting about 30 seconds. Before agreeing to use medication, the team wants to differentially reinforce slightly longer episodes of Barney's attention and calm sitting or standing to see what effect this has. Although differential reinforcement is done all day, measurement is made only during two lessons at school and two routine tasks at home each day for 2 weeks.

It is impossible (and unnecessary) to continuously record every instance of Barney's attention versus inattention, fidgeting versus calm sitting or standing. Thus, sampled lessons and tasks are divided into consecutive 30-second intervals. A recording sheet is divided into rows of small boxes, one for each interval. The observer records a "C" for calm sitting or standing and an "A" for paying attention to the task, if either of these are happening *at the moment a 30-second interval ends*. This is called *momentary time sampling* (Saudargas & Zanolli, 1990). An alternative is to

Consecutive minutes	Jerry's communicative acts	Reinforcement by Ms. Tyler
1	Offer, comment, comment, offer, question	ℋℋ (5)
2	Question, offer, show object, show object	//// (4)
3	Question, question, offer, offer, offer	/ (1)
4	Question, express preference, answer question	// (2)
5	Answer question, answer question, affirmation	/ (1)
6	Offer	0
7	Question	/ (1)
8	Protest	0
9		
10	Question	0
11	Answer question	/ (1)
12	Express preference	0
13		
14	Offer	0
15		
16	Affirmation	/ (1)
17		
18	Protest	0
19		
20	Protest	/ (1)

Summary:
1. Thirty communicative acts in 20 minutes = 1.5 per minute
2. Locate rate for first 5 minutes = 20/5, or 4 acts/minute; local rate for last 5 minutes = 3/5, or .6 acts/minute
3. Eight kinds of communicative acts: offers object (8, or 27% of total); asks question (7, or 23%); answers question about objects or actions (4, or 13%); protests (3, or 10%); comments on object or action (2, or 6%); shows object (2, or 6%); expresses preference (2, or 6%); affirms, agrees, or indicates "Yes" (2, or 6%)
4. Seventeen reinforcements/30 communicative acts = 57% acts reinforced, with local rate of reinforcement falling from continuous reinforcement during first 2 minutes. [Note decrease in overall rate of communicative acts but increase in protest acts.]

Figure 10.4. Continuous event recording that reveals local rates.

Table 10.1. Event recording of self-initiated play, mess making, and cooperation

Self-initiated play	Reinforcement	Mess making	Cooperation with requests for chores
			9:05 A.M. Cooperative with request to put away dishes
9:45–9:52 A.M.	// (2)		
		10:10 A.M.: Drawer spilled out	
10:20–10:32 A.M.	//// (4)		
			10:35 A.M.: Noncooperative with request to help sweep floor
			11:15 A.M.: Noncooperative with request to help clear table
11:46–12:00 P.M.	Ⅼⅼⅼ-/// (8)		
1:15–1:20 P.M.	0		
		1:22 P.M.: Sink water	
2:10–2:20 P.M.	/// (3)		
			2:30 P.M.: Noncooperative with request to put groceries away
2:40–2:46 P.M.	0		
		2:50 P.M.: Strips beds and couch	
3:05–3:20 P.M.	Ⅼⅼⅼ-/// (8)		
			3:25 P.M.: Cooperative with request to dry dishes
3:30–3:46 P.M.	Ⅼⅼⅼ-// (7)		
		4:14 P.M.: Sink water	
		4:32 P.M.: Kicks toys around	
			4:40 P.M.: Noncooperative with request to pick up toys
		4:50 P.M.: Tears story books	

Summary:
1. Total episodes of play = 8
2. Episodes of play per hour = 8 episodes/7 hours, or 1.1/hour
3. Total duration of play = 85 minutes
4. Average duration of play = 85 minutes/8 episodes, or 10.6 minutes per episode
5. Local duration of play is similar from hour to hour
6. Six episodes of mess making, with rate increasing near 4 P.M.
7. Cooperated with two out of six requests to help with chores, or 33%
8. Thirty-two reinforcements during play; rate of reinforcement = 32 reinforcements/85 minutes of play, or .38 reinforcements per minute (1 reinforcement about every 3 minutes)

write a "C" or an "A" in the box if calm sitting or standing or attending occurred *at any time during the interval*. Either way, the observer only marks whether the behaviors occurred, *not how many times*. In other words, the most a behavior can be recorded is once per interval.

Why are intervals 30 seconds long? A 30-second interval is short enough that Barney is not likely to switch between calm and fidgety or attentive and inattentive behavior more than once during an interval. Also, because each day's four sampled lessons and tasks will involve about 90 minutes in all, Barney's behavior will be sampled 180 times. This is a fairly large sample and may yield findings that are representative of Barney's behavior *throughout* the day. (Consider the unrepresentative picture of hyperactive vs. calm behavior if only 9 intervals 10 minutes, each were scored. By chance, Barney could be observed again and again during a hyperactive state.) Also, 180 samples allows one to track change in Barney's behavior during sessions.

One summary is the percentage of intervals in which targeted behaviors happened. For instance, Barney paid attention in 26 (65%) of the 40 intervals in a lesson. He was calm in 12 (30%) of the intervals and he paid attention and was calm in 8 (20%) of the intervals.

A second way to summarize time samples is to describe *local changes* in behavior across the observation session. Below is how Barney was scored, using momentary time sampling, during the first 25 30-second intervals of a routine task. "X" means he was neither attentive nor calm at the moment the interval ended. "R" means a caregiver praised, acknowledged, or gave Barney a turn while he was attending or calm.

```
 1 2 3 4 5 6 7 8 9 10 11 12 13 14 15 16 17 18 19 20 21 22 23 24 25
 X X X X X A A A A A AC AC AC AC AC AC AC AC AC   X   A   A   A   X   X   X   X
       RR  RR        R        R              R                  R
```

Notice that Barney's behavior improved beginning at the sixth interval. However, the calm and attentive behavior lasted only about 4 minutes. The record also shows that Barney often paid attention while fidgeting (i.e., some intervals have an "A," but not a "C"). Thus, perhaps the team does not need to be too concerned with fidgeting. Finally, note that the teacher reinforced Barney in only about 50% of the intervals in which Barney was attentive and/or calm, and that the rate of reinforcement fell as the lesson progressed. This may account for Barney's decreasing attention and calm behavior.

Functional Analysis

Descriptive analysis, discussed earlier in this chapter, is inductive; it moves from the specific (events) to the general (relationships among classes of events). Functional analysis differs from descriptive analysis in several ways. First, it is *deductive*. It begins with hypothesized relationships (e.g., that Jerry's probability of cooperating is affected by the immediacy of reinforcement). Second, it tests whether alleged relationships are functional and/or causal versus merely coincidental. It does this by engineering variations in an environment to see if behavior changes in the expected way, rather than discovering naturally occurring covariation as in descriptive analysis. Third, functional analysis tries to hold *constant* other possibly influential factors from one observation to another so that any effects of the hypothesized "causal" events will be obvious. In sum, functional analysis is experimental analysis.

Descriptive and functional analyses have strong and weak points. Many believe functional analyses convincingly demonstrate functional relationships (Hamblin, Buckholdt, Ferritor, Kozloff, & Blackwell, 1971; Iwata, Vollmer, & Zarcone, 1990; O'Neill, Horner, Albin, Storey, & Sprague, 1990; Sidman, 1960). If Jerry's probability of cooperating is higher on days when reinforcement is immediate, and lower on days when it is delayed, and if this association holds true day after day, then the immediacy of reinforcement probably affects Jerry's cooperation. Possible disadvantages, however, include the following: 1) the time and rigor of an experimental analysis may not be possible in typical educational environments (Durand & Crimmins, 1988); 2) the relationships demonstrated in a controlled environment may not apply once the controls are removed; and 3) changing from one experimental condition to another (e.g., alternating between immediate and delayed reinforcement) may have unpredictable effects.

A major strength of descriptive analysis is that the environment is not manipulated. Thus, discovered relationships are not likely to have been produced by experimental arrangements. Moreover, the descriptive analyst's observations are not bound by a list of variables and their definitions. However, the demonstration of relationships may not be as powerful as in functional analysis. Basically, a descriptive analyst can say that, over time, the less Indra's father and Mr. Hawkins nag Indra to walk, and the more they use Grandma's Law to encourage walking, the more Indra walks; or, Indra walks more often when she hears what is going on in another room. However, many other events in Indra's environment could account for improvements and variations in her walking. Indeed, descriptive analysis cannot easily rule out the possibility that Indra began walking more often before Mr. Hawkins and her father began nagging less often.

The decision to use functional analysis may be assisted by the following rule: If an instructional program is based on the belief that a child's behavior is influenced by certain events and not others, and if being wrong may harm the child, then functional analysis, in addition to descriptive analysis, is called for. The following example shows how functional analysis might be used.

Five-year-old Mike recently began hitting his face rapidly, but not hard enough to do any damage. Realizing that short-run, crisis-managing efforts to stop the behavior will not make it go away, and may make it worse, Mike's team adopted a proactive, preventive stance. They must determine what events are "controlling" Mike's behavior so they can prepare a sensible long-term program plan. The team recognizes time constraints; they do not have months to assess Mike's behavior. At the same time, they do not want to be too far off in their assessment. In sum, the team needs a strategy for collecting solid information in a relatively short time.

To begin with, during interviews with other team members, Mike's parents and teachers assert that hitting is fairly predictable. Sometimes Mike does it when he has been alone for a while and is bored. Other times he does it when he is asked to do certain tasks or is having difficulty with tasks. This is useful information; it suggests that hitting has several functions: self-reinforcement (reducing boredom), positive reinforcement when people comfort him (or even "punish" him) to stop the behavior, and negative reinforcement when it gets him out of tasks. Although useful, the information is not sufficient to plan a program. Direct observation is needed.

Guided by interview information, descriptive analysis is used next. Mike is observed both when he is alone and when he participates in collaborative tasks to see if any events can be discovered that seem to predispose him to hitting, that initiate or cue the behavior, and that reinforce it. Observers also note desirable behaviors Mike can be taught to use instead of hitting.

Several days of descriptive analysis at school and home yield the following findings. First, when alone, Mike plays creatively with a toy for a few minutes. Then play becomes repetitive and he switches to another toy. Having exhausted the toys, he whimpers and begins to hit himself. About 50% of the time, someone comes in and comforts or plays with him. If no one comes, he stops hitting himself in a few minutes and leaves. Second, Mike's hitting increases when it is noisy or when he receives a lot of questions, comments, and requests from others. Third, when tasks, such as dressing, are difficult, he becomes fussy. If he is made to continue the task and it does not become easier, he starts hitting himself. The result is caregivers trying to soothe him with words and touch or letting him escape from the task. The same situation occurs during school lessons if Mike is not called on for more than a few minutes—he becomes fussy and then hits himself. About 50% of the time this produces interaction with a teacher or aide. Fourth, in addition to hitting, Mike engages in whining and uncooperative behavior at a high rate. The latter two are reinforced about as often as hitting. In sum, descriptive analysis suggests several functional relationships and possible instructional methods, as follows:

1. When Mike's environment has low hedonic value, any behavior, such as hitting and whining, that brings social contact and/or removes demands is strongly reinforced. Thus, it may help to reduce noise; increase social contact (e.g., during play and lessons); reduce unnecessary comments, questions, and requests; reduce errors by using graduated guidance (or time delay); and use materials that are easier for Mike to manipulate (e.g., velcro tabs instead of buttons).
2. Hitting, whining, and noncooperation seem to be both positively reinforced by social contact and negatively reinforced by escape from aversive situations. Thus, it may help to reinforce short intervals in which neither hitting nor whining occur, and to reinforce cooperation with requests during tasks and lessons. Also, tasks and lessons might be ended before they become aversive.
3. Mike's play repertoire could be increased so he does not use hitting to decrease boredom and/or receive social contact.
4. Mike could be taught alternative ways to protest and to request contact.

The team's last step is to use functional analysis in the context of a tentative instructional program to determine whether the suspected relationships found by descriptive analysis are more than coincidental (Belfiore, Browder, & Lin, 1993; Sasso et al., 1992). Functional analysis is an experiment and, as with other experiments, there are experimental periods in which different events are manipulated and the apparent effects observed. Several experimental designs, ABAB or reversal, multiple baseline, and multiple treatment, are discussed on the following pages.

ABAB or Reversal Design   The ABAB design is quite common and it can be used with individuals or groups. It is the design involved when people with, for example, arthritis, are observed for a time to obtain a baseline measure of the amount of their joint fluid (the A period). Next, they take a new drug for a period of time and the amount of fluid is again recorded (the B period). Then they stop using the drug *for a short time* to see if fluid builds up (return to A period—the reversal). Finally, they go back on the drug (return to the B period). If fluid decreases with the drug and increases without it, and if nothing else in the participants' lives (e.g., diet) is systematically changing along with the experimental periods, then the ABAB design gives powerful evidence of the drug's effect. Note that the ABAB design may be permitted in the case of arthritis, but would be outrageous if used to test an anti-cancer drug because the effect of the drug is partly demonstrated by the return of cancer when the drug is temporarily discontinued in the reversal phase (A2).

If Mike's team were to use an ABAB design, it would mean that in the first experimental period, the baseline phase (A1), which might last several days, caregivers would respond to Mike's hitting as usual (i.e., they would try to stop him). Continuous or intermittent event recording of hitting and caregivers' reactions to hitting would be done during several tasks, lessons, and play periods each day. In a few days, when the rate of hitting is stable, the second experimental period, the intervention phase (B1), begins. Now, as planned, caregivers no longer try to stop Mike's hitting. Instead, they try to reinforce almost any other desirable behavior.

If after several days in the B1 period, Mike's hitting decreases significantly, it is a *fairly* convincing demonstration of a functional relationship; that is, caregivers' reactions appear to reinforce hitting, whereas no longer reacting appears to extinguish hitting. However, the demonstration may not be convincing enough. It may be that the reduction in hitting was the result of something besides the removal of caregivers' reactions. Thus, during the third experimental period (A2), the reversal, caregivers return to their usual (apparently reinforcing) reactions to hitting. It is found that indeed *hitting accelerates.* Finally, during the fourth period, B2, caregivers return to reinforcing desirable behaviors and not reacting to hitting. Hitting then decreases as it did during B1.

In this author's opinion, the ABAB design in this circumstance is unnecessary. Interviews and descriptive analyses already point to a connection between caregivers' reactions and the rate of

Mike's hitting. Also, the A1, B1 portion of the experiment lends more support. The added confirmation gained by the reversal is paid for by Mike hitting himself for several more days. In other words, one must weigh the value of any potential additional confirmation gained from using the ABAB design against the potential or actual harm.

This comment is not meant to discourage the use of the ABAB design, as it is appropriate in many circumstances. For instance, it could be used to test which prompting strategy yields fewer errors and is preferred by a student: A1 (graduated guidance), B1 (time delay), A2 (return to graduated guidance), and B2 (return to time delay). Also, it could be used to determine which caregiver style elicits more speech: A1 (caregiver is highly directive when playing with child), B1 (caregiver allows child to lead play), A2 (return to highly directive style), and B2 (return to child's leading).

Multiple Baseline and Multiple Treatment Designs   Mike's team did not use an ABAB design. Instead, they used a design that combines features of the *multiple baseline* (Cooper et al., 1992; Schloss & Wood, 1990) and *multiple treatment* designs (Oke & Schreibman, 1990). In a multiple baseline design, Mike's hitting, whining, and noncooperation are measured at the same time throughout the experiment. However, instruction is applied to each behavior *one at a time*. If observation shows that a behavior changes only when instruction is applied to it, evidence is gained on the effect of the instruction. In a multiple treatment design, the same behavior is given *different "treatments" one after another*. Each next treatment is added to the former ones, or each next treatment replaces the former one. Following is a description of how Mike's team designed the analysis.

The A, or baseline, period lasted 3 days. Three behaviors (hitting, whining, and noncooperation) were measured during several lessons, everyday tasks, and when Mike was alone. (Naturally, cooperation could not be measured when Mike was alone.) Caregivers responded to the three behaviors as they usually did—trying to soothe him or letting him out of tasks—about 50% of the time.

In the B period, caregivers continued to respond as usual to the three behaviors, but tested how much increasing the hedonic value of Mike's environment would reduce hitting. They decreased noise, comments, questions, the length of tasks, and the difficulty of materials, and increased the number of hugs and smiles Mike received during the day. Within 3 days, hitting began to decrease a little. However, noncooperation and whining continued at their usual high rates.

The C period lasted 1 week. In addition to sustaining the hedonic value of Mike's environment, caregivers provided more toys and instruction on playing (e.g., how to operate electronic games). There was a further decrease in the rate of hitting. Whining decreased a little, but noncooperation remained high.

In the D period, another "treatment" was added to the others. Mike was no longer reinforced for hitting, whining, and noncooperation, but he was frequently reinforced during intervals when he was not hitting (e.g., was playing or performing tasks). During the course of 1 week, hitting continued to decrease.

The E period also lasted 1 week. Instruction on communicating without whining was added. Whenever Mike made requests or protests without whining, he was reinforced. If he did whine, caregivers waited until he stopped and prompted him to ask in another manner (Sprague & Horner, 1992). During this period, whining and hitting decreased even more.

Finally, the F period lasted 1 week and focused on cooperation. Caregivers made simple requests of Mike, did not badger him if he was uncooperative, and enthusiastically reinforced cooperation on a continuous schedule. All of the prior conditions were continued. The data showed that hitting and whining continued to decrease, play and proper forms of asking and protesting increased, and for the first time cooperation increased.

One weakness of the multiple baseline and multiple treatment designs is that one cannot tell if the results during a certain period depend on what happened in earlier periods. It may be that Mike's hitting decreased in the C period only because the team had increased the hedonic value of the environment during the B period. Aside from using experimental groups that receive the different "treatments" in different orders, there is not much that can be done to determine which instructional method works best at which time. Even so, information from a group experiment may not apply to an individual who was not in the experiment. This did not worry Mike's team, however, because practically speaking: 1) the different "treatments" represent sound practice, and 2) it was feasible to continue the multiple "treatments" even if some were not really as important as they appeared. Thus, the whole set of conditions existing during the F period became part of Mike's educational plan.

PROFICIENCY

Part of a team's work is to increase proficiency at observing and recording. Item 12 of the *Family and School Assessment and Programming Guide (FSAPG),* in *Guidelines and Protocols,* can be used to describe caregivers' proficiency. Two important aspects of proficient observing and recording are definitions of items (events, variables) to observe and observer reliability.

Definitions of Items To Observe

To observe and accurately record such things as "self-initiated play," "communicative acts," or "mutual reward exchanges," observers need definitions. There are no right or true definitions; there are only better and worse definitions. What makes a good definition? A good definition directs observers' attention so that relevant events are recorded and irrelevant ones are not. More importantly, decisions based on the recordings (the data) have beneficial consequences. For example, if observers are guided by a definition of cooperation that is too narrow, they will miss recording and reinforcing many instances of behavior that ought to be considered cooperation (e.g., cooperation that is merely too slow). Similarly, if definitions are vague, observations and teaching will be unreliable.

It is important for caregivers to become skillful at examining and improving definitions in existing assessment instruments. Also, because no published assessment protocol covers everything of importance to each child, teams should create some of their own definitions and recording instruments. Below are guidelines for evaluating and creating definitions.

1. Words used in definitions should as much as possible refer to observable events. The definition of *skillful performance,* for instance, should be based on what children actually do. What observers believe a child "really knows inside" should not be part of the definition and scoring of skill. Thus, if a child makes many errors or is quite disfluent when dressing, observers should not be able to rate the performance "skillful" because they believe the child really knows how to do the task, but does not want to. It may be true that the child does not want to dress and is protesting, but this is a different behavior and it should be scored separately from the skillfulness of the performance.

2. The main part of a definition should be stated positively. A poor definition of cooperation would be: "Score cooperation if a child does not walk away, yell, run, stamp his or her feet, or say 'No' in response to a request." After all, the number of things children might not do is endless. A better definition is: "Score cooperation if a child's next course of action is, within a reasonable time, consistent with a caregiver's request."

3. If a definition is so broad that it includes events that really ought to be in a different category, narrow the definition and create new definitions for the excluded events. For instance, if play is defined so broadly that bizarre self-stimulatory behavior is included as play, either the definition of play should be revised to state that bizarre self-stimulation is excluded, or play should be divided into "normative play" and "bizarre self-stimulatory play."

4. Words in definitions should be clear and simple so the definition is likely to mean (point to) the same events for different observers. If a definition has vague or ambiguous words, observers

may not know what they are looking at and may not agree on what they see. Thus, the terms must be sharpened. For example, the phrase "within a reasonable time" in number 2 above is ambiguous. It results in one observer scoring a child who dawdles as cooperative and another scoring the same child as uncooperative. Therefore, "reasonable" needs clarification. Also, cooperation might be divided into two parts: immediate and delayed cooperation. This may be a useful distinction.

5. Definitions should include both abstract features of the concept defined and concrete examples. If, for instance, play is defined only by examples (stacking blocks, puzzles, make believe), observers may not record a child's banging pots and pans or rolling phonograph records around the room as play. Providing abstract features of the play concept enables observers to judge whether unspecified events fit the definition. Thus, a better definition of play is: "Enacting familiar actions and routines, or modifying familiar actions and routines, for purposes of self-amusement. This includes pretending (e.g., to eat, talk on the telephone, prepare food); building structures (e.g., out of blocks, boxes); making sounds (e.g., with pots, pans, toy cars); making objects move (e.g., rolling toy cars); and so forth."

Observer Reliability

Before beginning the assessment process, before assessing specific behaviors, and periodically thereafter, team members should examine the reliability of observing and recording. For instance, *Guidelines and Protocols* shows how to assess children's involvement and task competence and caregivers' involvement and teaching competence during instructional sessions. Before conducting an assessment of these behaviors, it is a good idea for team members to first discuss and practice using the definitions provided. For instance, the definition of "child's involvement" may be unclear to certain members, or they may be unsure of how to use the scoring codes for rating "caregiver's teaching competence." If so, the team can practice observing and recording live and/or from videotapes representing instructional sessions to be assessed. While observing, members help one another identify relevant events. If necessary, they improve the definitions and scoring codes. When members are able to identify relevant events live or from tape, and feel comfortable recording, it is time to check and improve reliability in a more rigorous way.

There are two kinds of reliability: intra-observer and inter-observer. *Intra-observer reliability* is the degree to which an observer scores the same thing the same way at different times. It can be assessed by having team members score a videotape and then rescore it several days later. Thus, Mr. Eaton watches a videotape of Luke during a play session and he counts (or writes) all one-word and two-word utterances (continuous event recording). Three days later he repeats the process with the same tape. The first time, he recorded a total of 50 utterances. The second time he recorded 45. A simple *index* of his reliability is 45/50, or 90% agreement.

Note that the figure 45/50 does *not* mean that on day 2 Mr. Eaton simply missed 5 of the utterances that he scored on day 1. It is possible that Luke actually produced 70 utterances, and that Mr. Eaton recorded 50 of them the first day and many different ones the second day. In fact, it is possible for an observer to count 25 of Luke's utterances one day and 25 different utterances the next day. In other words, the reliability index would be 100% even though the observer's recordings were completely different.

A more informative way to assess reliability is to divide a videotaped observation into shorter segments and compare each day's scorings segment by segment. In this way, Mr. Eaton can identify which utterances he caught in each segment, which he missed, and perhaps why he missed them (e.g., he was not listening, Luke said several things at once, or Mr. Eaton was tired). In this method, the reliability index is calculated by first determining the number of intervals in the two separate scorings in which Mr. Eaton's recordings were in agreement. For instance, the tape of Luke's play session had 30 1-minute intervals. For interval 5, Mr. Eaton recorded 3 utterances on day 1 and 3 utterances on day 2. This is one agreement. For interval 6, he recorded 0 utterances on day 1 and 0 on day 2. This is another agreement. For interval 10, he recorded 3 utterances on day 1 and 2 utterances on day 2. This is a disagreement. Reliability, therefore, is the number of intervals in which there is agreement divided by the number of agreements plus disagreements. Mr. Eaton's two separate recordings agreed 28 times and disagreed 2 times, which is 28/30, or 93% agreement.

Inter-observer reliability is the second type of observer reliability. It refers to the amount of agreement between two observers scoring the same thing. For instance, Ms. Tyler and Mrs. Hardy score the same activity live or from tape. If they use continuous event recording, their reliability is calculated as with Mr. Eaton—either overall or segment by segment.

When using time sampling or interval recording, however, one calculates reliability exactly as in Mr. Eaton's segment-by-segment method. For example, Ms. Tyler and Mrs. Hardy scored three children's play during consecutive 30-second intervals. They assessed inter-observer reliability by comparing how they had recorded each child interval by interval. It is counted as an agreement if they both recorded that a child was alone, in parallel play, or in group play during an interval (Smith & Connolly, 1980). The index of inter-observer reliability is the number of intervals in which recordings agree divided by the number of agreements plus disagreements. Note that they can calculate the reliability of both their recording of each child's play and all three children's play. In the latter case, it would be an agreement only if they agreed on the scoring of the three children in an interval.

When reliability is low—perhaps less than 90%–95%—observers review tapes and/or live activity, noting whether they are using different definitions, the recording method is cumbersome, or they are affected by fatigue.

SUMMARY

This chapter presents guidelines for selecting events to measure, deciding how much precision is called for, and creating a comfortable observation environment. It also describes methods of observation and analysis including narrative recording, continuous event recording, time sampling, task analysis, descriptive analysis, and functional analysis. It ends by suggesting how to increase proficiency by examining the quality of definitions that guide observation and the reliability of recording.

REFERENCES

Ainsworth, M.D.S., Blehar, M.D., Waters, E., & Wall, S. (1978). *Patterns of attachment*. Hillsdale, NJ: Lawrence Erlbaum Associates.

Barker, R.G. (1963). *The stream of behavior*. New York: Appleton-Century-Crofts.

Barker, R.G. (1968). *Ecological psychology*. Stanford, CA: Stanford University Press.

Barker, R.G., & Wright, H.F. (1966). *One boy's day: A specimen record of behavior*. Hamden, CT: Archon Books.

Belfiore, P.J., Browder, D.M., & Lin, C. (1993). Using descriptive and experimental analyses for the treatment of self-injurious behavior. *Education and Training in Mental Retardation 28*(1), 57–65.

Berger, P., & Luckmann, T. (1967). *The social construction of reality*. Garden City, NJ: Doubleday.

Bijou, S.W., Peterson, R.F., & Ault, M.H. (1968). A method to integrate descriptive and experimental field studies at the level of data and empirical concepts. *Journal of Applied Behavior Analysis, 1*, 175–191.

Brotherson, M.J., & Goldstein, B.L. (1992). Time as a resource and constraint for parents of young children with disabilities: Implications for early intervention services. *Topics in Early Childhood Special Education, 12*(4), 508–527.

Buckholdt, D.R., & Gubrium, J.F. (1979). *Caretakers: Treating emotionally disturbed children*. Beverly Hills: Sage Publications.

Cohen, D.H., Stern, V., & Balaban, N. (1983). *Observing and recording the behavior of young children* (3rd ed.). New York: Teachers College Press.

Connolly, K., & Dalgleish, M. (1989). The emergence of tool-using skill in infancy. *Developmental Psychology, 25*(6), 894–912.

Cooper, L.J., Wacker, D.P., Thursby, D., Plagmann, L.A., Harding, J., Millard, T., & Derby, M. (1992). Analysis of the effects of task preferences, task demands, and adult attention on child behavior in outpatient and classroom settings. *Journal of Applied Behavior Analysis, 25*(4), 823–840.

Durand, V.M., & Crimmins, D.B. (1988). Identifying the variables maintaining self-injurious behavior. *Journal of Autism and Developmental Disorders, 18*, 99–117.

Fetterman, D. (1989). *Ethnography step by step*. Beverly Hills: Sage Publications.

Fine, G.A., & Sandstrom, K.L. (1988). *Knowing children: Participant observation with minors*. Beverly Hills: Sage Publications.

Hamblin, R.L., Buckholdt, D., Ferritor, D., Kozloff, M., & Blackwell, L. (1971). *The huamization processes*. New York: John Wiley & Sons.

Helm, D.T. (1981). *Conferring membership: Interacting with "incompetents."* Unpublished doctoral dissertation, Department of Sociology, Boston University, Boston.

Henry, J. (1971). *Pathways to madness*. New York: Random House.

Iwata, B.A., Vollmer, T.R., & Zarcone, J.R. (1990). The experimental (functional) analysis of behavior disorders: Methodology, applications, and limitations. In A.C. Repp & N.N. Singh (Eds.), *Perspectives on the use of nonaversive and aversive interventions for persons with developmental disabilities* (pp. 301–330). Sycamore, IL: Sycamore Publishing Company.

Lofland, J., & Lofland, L.H. (1984). *Analyzing social settings* (2nd ed.). Belmont, CA: Wadsworth.

Mehan, H. (1979). *Learning lessons*. Cambridge, MA: Harvard University Press.

Oke, N.J., & Schreibman, L. (1990). Training social interactions to a high-functioning autistic child: Assessment of collateral behavior change and generalization in a case study. *Journal of Autism and Developmental Disorders, 20*(4), 479–497.

O'Neill, R.E., Horner, R.H., Albin, R.W., Storey, K., & Sprague, J.R. (1990). *A functional analysis of problem behavior: A practical assessment guide*. Sycamore, IL: Sycamore Publishing Company.

Patton, M.Q. (1990). *Qualitative evaluation and research methods* (2nd ed.). Beverly Hills: Sage Publications.

Pettit, G.S., & Bates, J.E. (1990). Describing family interaction patterns in early childhood: A social systems perspective. *Journal of Applied Developmental Psychology, 11*, 395–418.

Sacks, H. (1991). On the analyzability of stories by children. In F.C. Waksler (Ed.), *Studying the social worlds of children* (pp. 195–214). New York: The Falmer Press.

Sasso, G.M., Reimers, T.M., Cooper, L.J., Wacker, D., Berg, W., Steege, M., Kelly, L., & Allaire, A. (1992). Use of descriptive and experimental analyses to identify the functional properties of aberrant behavior in school settings. *Journal of Applied Behavior Analysis, 25*(4), 809–821.

Saudargas, R.A., & Zanolli, K. (1990). Momentary time sampling as an estimate of percentage of time: A field validation. *Journal of Applied Behavior Analysis, 23*, 533–537.

Schloss, P.J., & Wood, C.E. (1990). Effects of self-monitoring on maintenance and generalization of conversational skills of persons with mental retardation. *Mental Retardation, 28*(2), 105–113.

Sidman, M. (1960). *Tactics of scientific research*. New York: Basic Books.

Smith, P.K., & Connolly, K.J. (1980). *The ecology of preschool behavior*. Cambridge, England: Cambridge University Press.

Spradley, J.P. (1980). *Participant observation*. New York: Holt, Rinehart & Winston.

Sprague, J.R., & Horner, R.H. (1992). Covariation within functional response classes: Implications for treatment of severe problem behavior. *Journal of Applied Behavior Analysis, 25*(3), 735–745.

CONCLUSION

MANY PERSONS, INCLUDING THIS AUTHOR, BELIEVE THAT EDUCATION FOR CHILDREN WITH DISABILITIES cannot continue as it is currently organized. Despite so much hard work, education often has the following outcomes.

1. Many children spend years learning nonfunctional, age-inappropriate behaviors.
2. Interaction between children and caregivers frequently crystallizes into patterns that relentlessly worsen children's problem behaviors and drain caregivers of energy and patience.
3. Children judged "impossible to manage" are often moved to restrictive and expensive placements.
4. Innovative ideas of teachers and families are seen as unfeasible ("Sorry. It can't be done.") or as threats to existing practices and job descriptions.
5. Scarce time and money are squandered in family–school conflicts that stem from discrepancies between what is and what could be.

People often respond to problems with "solutions" that worsen the problems (Watzlawick, Weakland, & Fisch, 1974). Instead of searching for areas of agreement, for example, each person in an argument tries to invalidate the other's perception. Similarly, instead of recognizing how children and caregivers are ill-served by overspecialization and isolation, and then devising ways to integrate everyone's complementary skills into classroom-home-community curricula, educators "solve" the problem of children's lack of progress by creating more specialties (a recent one being the "generalist") or by running a workshop on teaching methods.

What is needed is a different way of looking at the situation. That is what this book provides. Building on thinking and research in many fields, this volume suggests fundamental and feasible ways to rethink psychosocial development and reorganize education for children with disabilities. Below are some of the more important ideas, along with implications for practice.

THE FUNCTIONAL BEHAVIORAL
REPERTOIRE AND PSYCHOSOCIAL DEVELOPMENT

The models of the functional behavioral repertoire and psychosocial development, presented in Chapters 3–6, show that the human repertoire is gradually organized on a number of levels as children interact with corresponding levels of the environment. Respondent reflexes (e.g., attention and feelings) develop within respondent conditioning trials, whereas operant actions (e.g., skills) develop within contingencies of reinforcement. Social competencies (and many problem behaviors) are fostered in exchanges with caregivers. A child's competence (or incompetence) at tasks and activities is produced by the organization of tasks and activities in the child's daily life and by opportunities for participation. Roles and identities, finally, are fashioned within a personalization process that assigns a child to a more (or less) valued membership category.

The first major implication of the above is as follows: Instead of identifying how children with disabilities deviate from an image of the "standard" child, assessment focuses on the extent to which a child competently participates in his or her environments and on the extent to which environments provide cues, prompts, reinforcement, and opportunities that are congruent with the child's needs, competencies, capacities, and preferences. The purpose of education is to foster psychosocial development by increasing the congruence.

Second, creating a foundation of productive child–caregiver exchanges is a top priority. Caregivers' teaching skills have virtually no effect if pervasive exchange patterns turn children and caregivers into adversaries. In this author's opinion, teacher certification should require demonstrated competence at observing and identifying exchanges and responding productively to desirable and undesirable behavior. Similarly, as soon as possible, families should be assisted in creating and sustaining productive exchanges.

Third, behaviors can change in at least five main ways. These include acquisition of skill, fluency, generalization, adaptation, and maintenance. Assessment determines which phases different behaviors are "in"; plans and instructional practices are geared to fostering all of the phases.

Fourth, psychosocial development is not understood as the addition of one after another behavior to a list of what a child can do. Instead, the concern is: 1) how simpler behaviors (reaching, visually tracking, grasping) can be linked into advanced sequences (e.g., self-feeding), and 2) how skill at one behavior (e.g., eating with a fork) can increase skill at others (e.g., serving food, brushing teeth).

Fifth, the conditions fostering psychosocial development at one time may not do so as children become older and more competent. Thus, caregivers examine ongoing congruence between a child's behavioral repertoire and environment. How can increasing capacities be used? How might competencies be generalized and adapted? Can more normative cues, prompts, and reinforcers be introduced? Can a child play more advanced roles?

CAREGIVERS

Psychosocial development progresses when the environment is congruent with children's needs and strengths. Likewise, caregivers provide such environments when their own strengths are utilized and needs are met. Chapters 4, 6, and 7 stress the importance of family in all educational practices, from assessment through ongoing evaluation. Chapter 7 also examines challenges families contend with and suggests issues to consider (e.g., need for social support and hands-on assistance) when creating collaborative relationships with families.

Chapter 2 critically examines the organization of typical school programs. It asserts that specialization, isolation, multiple and conflicting functions, lack of leadership, and staff's general lack of power result in fragmentation of "services," alienation, staff turnover, and short-run crisis management rather than program development. Chapter 8 suggests ways to provide support and assistance, coordinate complementary skills, empower stakeholders, and create programs with a developmental-functional orientation through leadership, transdisciplinary teaming, peer or mentoring relationships, utilization of community resources, training programs, help networks, program libraries, newsletters, and operations manuals. These not only cost less than lawyers, therapies, and residential programs now used to "solve" problems, but will eliminate many problems.

TOOLS

To help caregivers improve assessment, planning, and program evaluation practices, Chapters 9 and 10 discuss a variety of methods for collecting and analyzing information. Chapter 9 shows how to create a comfortable interview setting, strengthen interviewees' readiness to participate in a developmental-functional program, help interviewees tell their story, and extract information useful for planning programs.

Chapter 10 focuses on direct observation. In particular, it discusses levels of measurement precision, narrative recording, continuous and intermittent event recording, task analysis, and rating scales. It also shows how to discover relationships through descriptive (naturalistic, inductive) analysis and functional (experimental, deductive) analysis.

GUIDELINES AND PROTOCOLS FOR PRACTICE

Although much is covered, this book does not provide all of the ideas and methods needed. The companion volume, *Guidelines and Protocols for Practice,* continues where this one ends. It contains guidelines for planning assessments, assessing a child's functional behavioral repertoire in relation to the child's environments, identifying caregivers' needs, and planning programs. In addition, the companion volume contains 17 instruments that can be copied and used. These include the following: 1) instruments for collecting qualitative information from caregivers, 2) instruments for collecting information through direct observation, 3) instruments for summarizing children's and caregivers' strengths and needs (the *Family and School Assessment and Programming Guide* and the *Child Assessment and Programming Guide*), and 4) instruments for planning programs.

REFERENCE

Watzlawick, P., Weakland, J., & Fisch, R. (1974). *Change: Principles of problem formation and problem resolution.* New York: W.W. Norton.

INDEX

Page numbers followed by t *and* f *denote tables and figures, respectively.*